DATA SCIENCE FOR MARKETING ANALYTICS
SECOND EDITION

A practical guide to forming a killer marketing
strategy through data analysis with Python

Mirza Rahim Baig, Gururajan Govindan, and Vishwesh Ravi Shrimali

DATA SCIENCE FOR MARKETING ANALYTICS
SECOND EDITION

Authors: Mirza Rahim Baig, Gururajan Govindan, and Vishwesh Ravi Shrimali

Reviewers: Cara Davies and Subhranil Roy

Managing Editors: Prachi Jain and Abhishek Rane

Acquisitions Editors: Royluis Rodrigues, Kunal Sawant, and Sneha Shinde

Production Editor: Salma Patel

Editorial Board: Megan Carlisle, Mahesh Dhyani, Heather Gopsill, Manasa Kumar, Alex Mazonowicz, Monesh Mirpuri, Bridget Neale, Abhishek Rane, Brendan Rodrigues, Ankita Thakur, Nitesh Thakur, and Jonathan Wray

First published: March 2019

First edition authors: Tommy Blanchard, Debasish Behera, and Pranshu Bhatnagar

Second edition: September 2021

Production reference: 1060921

ISBN: 978-1-80056-047-5
Published by Packt Publishing Ltd.
Livery Place, 35 Livery Street
Birmingham B3 2PB, UK

Table of Contents

Chapter 2: Data Exploration and Visualization 57

Chapter 3: Unsupervised Learning and Customer Segmentation 113

Chapter 7: Supervised Learning: Predicting Customer Churn

Chapter 8: Fine-Tuning Classification Algorithms   369

PREFACE

ABOUT THE BOOK

Unleash the power of data to reach your marketing goals with this practical guide to data science for business.

This book will help you get started on your journey to becoming a master of marketing analytics with Python. You'll work with relevant datasets and build your practical skills by tackling engaging exercises and activities that simulate real-world market analysis projects.

You'll learn to think like a data scientist, build your problem-solving skills, and discover how to look at data in new ways to deliver business insights and make intelligent data-driven decisions.

As well as learning how to clean, explore, and visualize data, you'll implement machine learning algorithms and build models to make predictions. As you work through the book, you'll use Python tools to analyze sales, visualize advertising data, predict revenue, address customer churn, and implement customer segmentation to understand behavior.

This second edition has been updated to include new case studies that bring a more application-oriented approach to your marketing analytics journey. The code has also been updated to support the latest versions of Python and the popular data science libraries that have been used in the book. The practical exercises and activities have been revamped to prepare you for the real-world problems that marketing analysts need to solve. This will show you how to create a measurable impact on businesses large and small.

By the end of this book, you'll have the knowledge, skills, and confidence to implement data science and machine learning techniques to better understand your marketing data and improve your decision-making.

ABOUT THE AUTHORS

Mirza Rahim Baig is an avid problem solver who uses deep learning and artificial intelligence to solve complex business problems. He has more than a decade of experience in creating value from data, harnessing the power of the latest in machine learning and AI with proficiency in using unstructured and structured data across areas like marketing, customer experience, catalog, supply chain, and other e-commerce sub-domains. Rahim is also a teacher - designing, creating, teaching data science for various learning platforms. He loves making the complex easy to understand. He is also an author of *The Deep Learning Workshop*, a hands-on guide to start your deep learning journey and build your own next-generation deep learning models.

Gururajan Govindan is a data scientist, intrapreneur, and trainer with more than seven years of experience working across domains such as finance and insurance. He is also an author of *The Data Analysis Workshop*, a book focusing on data analytics. He is well known for his expertise in data-driven decision making and machine learning with Python.

Vishwesh Ravi Shrimali graduated from BITS Pilani, where he studied mechanical engineering. He has a keen interest in programming and AI and has applied that interest in mechanical engineering projects. He has also written multiple blogs on OpenCV, deep learning, and computer vision. When he is not writing blogs or working on projects, he likes to go on long walks or play his acoustic guitar. He is also an author of *The Computer Vision Workshop*, a book focusing on OpenCV and its applications in real-world scenarios; as well as, *Machine Learning for OpenCV (2nd Edition)* - which introduces how to use OpenCV for machine learning applications.

WHO THIS BOOK IS FOR

This marketing book is for anyone who wants to learn how to use Python for cutting-edge marketing analytics. Whether you're a developer who wants to move into marketing, or a marketing analyst who wants to learn more sophisticated tools and techniques, this book will get you on the right path. Basic prior knowledge of Python is required to work through the exercises and activities provided in this book.

ABOUT THE CHAPTERS

Chapter 1, Data Preparation and Cleaning, teaches you skills related to data cleaning along with various data preprocessing techniques using real-world examples.

Chapter 2, Data Exploration and Visualization, teaches you how to explore and analyze data with the help of various aggregation techniques and visualizations using Matplotlib and Seaborn.

Chapter 3, Unsupervised Learning and Customer Segmentation, teaches you customer segmentation, one of the most important skills for a data science professional in marketing. You will learn how to use machine learning to perform customer segmentation with the help of scikit-learn. You will also learn to evaluate segments from a business perspective.

Chapter 4, Evaluating and Choosing the Best Segmentation Approach, expands your repertoire to various advanced clustering techniques and teaches principled numerical methods of evaluating clustering performance.

Chapter 5, Predicting Customer Revenue using Linear Regression, gets you started on predictive modeling of quantities by introducing you to regression and teaching simple linear regression in a hands-on manner using scikit-learn.

Chapter 6, More Tools and Techniques for Evaluating Regression Models, goes into more details of regression techniques, along with different regularization methods available to prevent overfitting. You will also discover the various evaluation metrics available to identify model performance.

Chapter 7, Supervised Learning: Predicting Customer Churn, uses a churn prediction problem as the central problem statement throughout the chapter to cover different classification algorithms and their implementation using scikit-learn.

Chapter 8, Fine-Tuning Classification Algorithms, introduces support vector machines and tree-based classifiers along with the evaluation metrics for classification algorithms. You will also learn about the process of hyperparameter tuning which will help you obtain better results using these algorithms.

Chapter 9, Multiclass Classification Algorithms, introduces a multiclass classification problem statement and the classifiers that can be used to solve such problems. You will learn about imbalanced datasets and their treatment in detail. You will also discover the micro- and macro-evaluation metrics available in scikit-learn for these classifiers.

CONVENTIONS

Code words in text, database table names, folder names, filenames, file extensions, pathnames, dummy URLs, and, user input are shown as follows:

"**df.head(n)** will return the first **n** rows of the DataFrame. If no **n** is passed, the function considers **n** to be **5** by default."

Words that you see on the screen, for example, in menus or dialog boxes, also appear in the same format.

A block of code is set as follows:

```
sales = pd.read_csv("sales.csv")
sales.head()
```

New important words are shown like this: "a **box plot** is used to depict the distribution of numerical data and is primarily used for comparisons".

Key parts of code snippets are emboldened as follows:

```
df1 = pd.read_csv("timeSpent.csv")
```

CODE PRESENTATION

Lines of code that span multiple lines are split using a backslash (\). When the code is executed, Python will ignore the backslash, and treat the code on the next line as a direct continuation of the current line.

For example,

```
df = pd.DataFrame({'Currency': pd.Series(['USD','EUR','GBP']),\
                   'ValueInINR': pd.Series([70, 89, 99])})

df = pd.DataFrame.from_dict({'Currency': ['USD','EUR','GBP'],\
                             'ValueInINR':[70, 89, 99]})
df.head()
```

Comments are added into code to help explain specific bits of logic. Single-line comments are denoted using the **#** symbol, as follows:

```
# Importing the matplotlib library
import matplotlib.pyplot as plt


#Declaring the color of the plot as gray
plt.bar(sales['Product line'], sales['Revenue'], color='gray')
```

Multi-line comments are used as follows:

```
"""
Importing classification report and confusion matrix from
sklearn metrics
"""
from sklearn.metrics import classification_report
from sklearn.metrics import precision_recall_fscore_support
```

MINIMUM HARDWARE REQUIREMENTS

For an optimal experience, we recommend the following hardware configuration:

- Processor: Dual Core or better

- Memory: 4 GB RAM

- Storage: 10 GB available space

DOWNLOADING THE CODE BUNDLE

Download the code files from GitHub at https://packt.link/59F3X. Refer to these code files for the complete code bundle. The files here contain the exercises, activities, and some intermediate code for each chapter. This can be a useful reference when you become stuck.

On the GitHub repo's page, you can click the green **Code** button and then click the **Download ZIP** option to download the complete code as a ZIP file to your disk (refer to *Figure 0.1*). You can then extract these code files to a folder of your choice, for example, **C:\Code**.

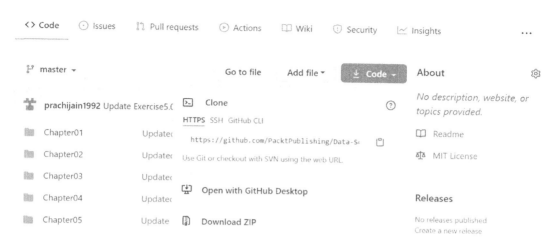

Figure 0.1: Download ZIP option on GitHub

On your system, the extracted ZIP file should contain all the files present in the GitHub repository:

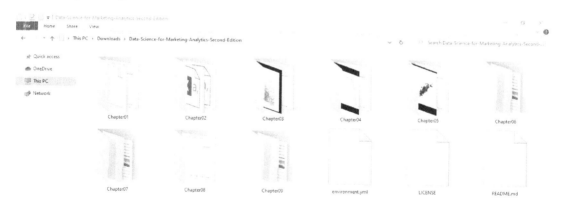

Figure 0.2: GitHub code directory structure (Windows Explorer)

SETTING UP YOUR ENVIRONMENT

Before you explore the book in detail, you need to set up specific software and tools. In the following section, you shall see how to do that.

INSTALLING ANACONDA ON YOUR SYSTEM

The code for all the exercises and activities in this book can be executed using Jupyter Notebooks. You'll first need to install the Anaconda Navigator, which is an interface through which you can access your Jupyter Notebooks. Anaconda Navigator will be installed as a part of Anaconda Individual Edition, which is an open-source Python distribution platform available for Windows, macOS, and Linux. Installing Anaconda will also install Python. Head to https://www.anaconda.com/distribution/.

1. From the page that opens, click the **Download** button (annotated by *1*). Make sure you are downloading the **Individual Edition**.

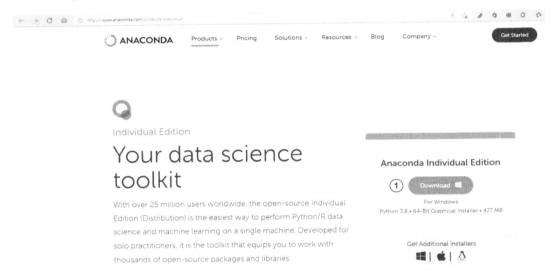

Figure 0.3: Anaconda homepage

2. The installer should start downloading immediately. The website will, by default, choose an installer based on your system configuration. If you prefer downloading Anaconda for a different operating system (Windows, macOS, or Linux) and system configuration (32- or 64-bit), click the **Get Additional Installers** link at the bottom of the box (refer to *Figure 0.3*). The page should scroll down to a section (refer to *Figure 0.4*) that lets you choose from various options based on the operating system and configuration you desire. For this book, it is recommended that you use the latest version of Python (3.8 or higher).

Anaconda Installers

Windows ⊞

Python 3.8

64-Bit Graphical Installer (477 MB)

32-Bit Graphical Installer (409 MB)

MacOS

Python 3.8

64-Bit Graphical Installer (440 MB)

64-Bit Command Line Installer (433 MB)

Linux

Python 3.8

64-Bit (x86) Installer (544 MB)

64-Bit (Power8 and Power9) Installer (285 MB)

64-Bit (AWS Graviton2 / ARM64) Installer (413 M)

64-bit (Linux on IBM Z & LinuxONE) Installer (292 M)

Figure 0.4: Downloading Anaconda Installers based on the OS

3. Follow the installation steps presented on the screen.

Figure 0.5: Anaconda setup

4. On Windows, if you've never installed Python on your system before, you can select the checkbox that prompts you to add Anaconda to your **PATH**. This will let you run Anaconda-specific commands (like **conda**) from the default command prompt. If you have Python installed or had installed an earlier version of Anaconda in the past, it is recommended that you leave it unchecked (you may run Anaconda commands from the Anaconda Prompt application instead). The installation may take a while depending on your system configuration.

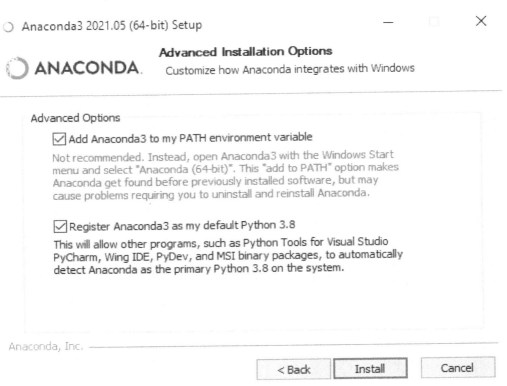

Figure 0.6: Anaconda installation steps

For more detailed instructions, you may refer to the official documentation for Linux by clicking this link (https://docs.anaconda.com/anaconda/install/linux/), macOS using this link (https://docs.anaconda.com/anaconda/install/mac-os/), and Windows using this link (https://docs.anaconda.com/anaconda/install/windows/).

5. To check if Anaconda Navigator is correctly installed, look for **Anaconda Navigator** in your applications. Look for an application that has the following icon. Depending on your operating system, the icon's aesthetics may vary slightly.

Anaconda Navigator (Anaconda3)

App

Figure 0.7: Anaconda Navigator icon

You can also search for the application using your operating system's search functionality. For example, on Windows 10, you can use the *Windows Key + S* combination and type in **Anaconda Navigator**. On macOS, you can use Spotlight search. On Linux, you can open the terminal and type the **anaconda-navigator** command and press the *return* key.

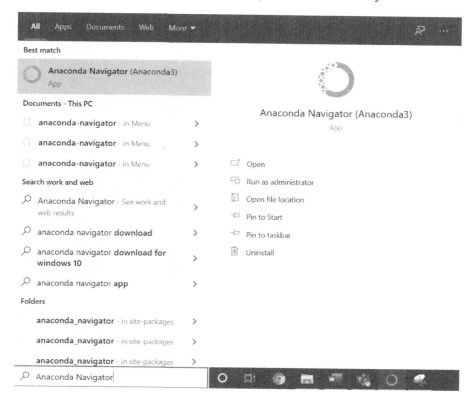

Figure 0.8: Searching for Anaconda Navigator on Windows 10

For detailed steps on how to verify if Anaconda Navigator is installed, refer to the following link: https://docs.anaconda.com/anaconda/install/verify-install/.

6. Click the icon to open Anaconda Navigator. It may take a while to load for the first time, but upon successful installation, you should see a similar screen:

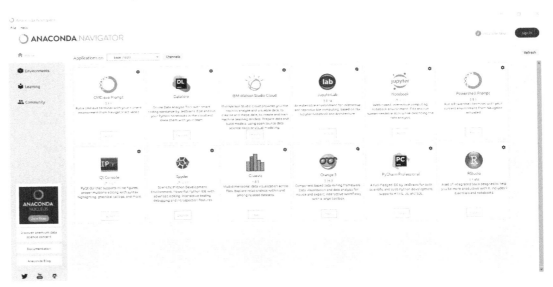

Figure 0.9: Anaconda Navigator screen

If you have more questions about the installation process, you may refer to the list of frequently asked questions from the Anaconda documentation: https://docs.anaconda.com/anaconda/user-guide/faq/.

LAUNCHING JUPYTER NOTEBOOK

Once the Anaconda Navigator is open, you can launch the Jupyter Notebook interface from this screen. The following steps will show you how to do that:

1. Open Anaconda Navigator. You should see the following screen:

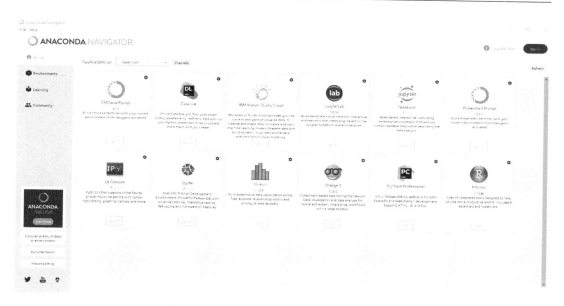

Figure 0.10: Anaconda Navigator screen

2. Now, click **Launch** under the **Jupyter Notebook** panel to start the notebook interface on your local system.

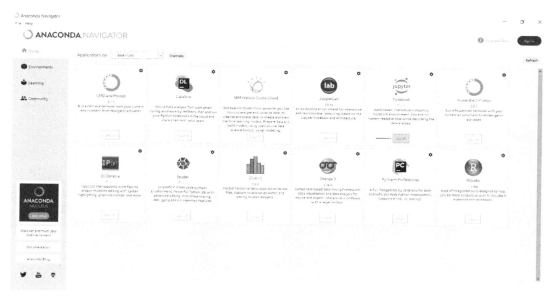

Figure 0.11: Jupyter notebook launch option

3. On clicking the **Launch** button, you'll notice that even though nothing changes in the window shown in the preceding screenshot, a new tab opens up in your default browser. This is known as the **Notebook Dashboard**. It will, by default, open to your root folder. For Windows users, this path would be something similar to `C:\Users\<username>`. On macOS and Linux, it will be `/home/<username>/`.

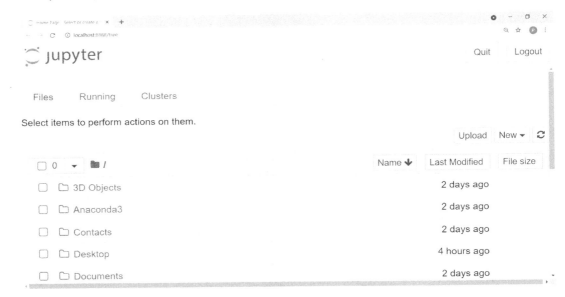

Figure 0.12: Notebook dashboard

Note that you can also open a Jupyter Notebook by simply running the command **jupyter notebook** in the terminal or command prompt. Or you can search for Jupyter Notebook in your applications just like you did in *Figure 0.8*.

4. You can use this Dashboard as a file explorer to navigate to the directory where you have downloaded or stored the code files for the book (refer to the *Downloading the Code Bundle* section on how to download the files from GitHub). Once you have navigated to your desired directory, you can start by creating a new Notebook. Alternatively, if you've downloaded the code from our repository, you can open an existing Notebook as well (Notebook files will have a `.inpyb` extension). The menus here are quite simple to use:

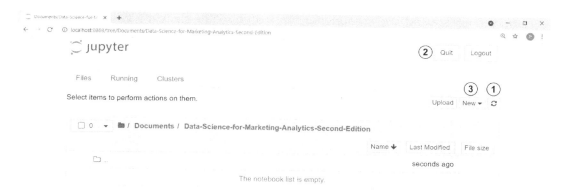

Figure 0.13: Jupyter notebook navigator menu options walkthrough

If you make any changes to the directory using your operating system's file explorer and the changed file isn't showing up in the Jupyter Notebook Navigator, click the **Refresh Notebook List** button (annotated as *1*). To quit, click the **Quit button** (annotated as *2*). To create a new file (a new Jupyter Notebook), you can click the **New** button (annotated as *3*).

5. Clicking the **New** button will open a dropdown menu as follows:

Figure 0.14: Creating a new Jupyter notebook

> **NOTE**
>
> A detailed tutorial on the interface and the keyboard shortcuts for Jupyter Notebooks can be found here:
> https://jupyter-notebook.readthedocs.io/en/stable/notebook.html.

You can get started and create your first notebook by selecting **Python 3**; however, it is recommended that you also set up the virtual environment we've provided. Installing the environment will also install all the packages required for running the code in this book. The following section will show you how to do that.

INSTALLING THE DS-MARKETING VIRTUAL ENVIRONMENT

As you run the code for the exercises and activities, you'll notice that even after installing Anaconda, there are certain libraries like **kmodes** which you'll need to install separately as you progress in the book. Then again, you may already have these libraries installed, but their versions may be different from the ones we've used, which may lead to varying results. That's why we've provided an **environment.yml** file with this book that will:

1. Install all the packages and libraries required for this book at once.

2. Make sure that the version numbers of your libraries match the ones we've used to write the code for this book.

3. Make sure that the code you write based on this book remains separate from any other coding environment you may have.

You can download the **environment.yml** file by clicking the following link: http://packt.link/dBv1k.

Save this file, ideally in the same folder where you'll be running the code for this book. If you've downloaded the code from GitHub as detailed in the *Downloading the Code Bundle* section, this file should already be present in the parent directory, and you won't need to download it separately.

To set up the environment, follow these steps:

1. On macOS, open Terminal from the Launchpad (you can find more information about Terminal here: https://support.apple.com/en-in/guide/terminal/apd5265185d-f365-44cb-8b09-71a064a42125/mac). On Linux, open the Terminal application that's native to your distribution. On Windows, you can open the Anaconda Prompt instead by simply searching for the application. You can do this by opening the Start menu and searching for *Anaconda Prompt*.

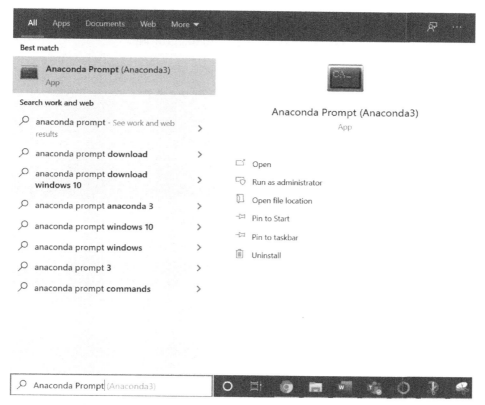

Figure 0.15: Searching for Anaconda Prompt on Windows

A new terminal like the following should open. By default, it will start in your home directory:

Figure 0.16: Anaconda terminal prompt

In the case of Linux, it would look like the following:

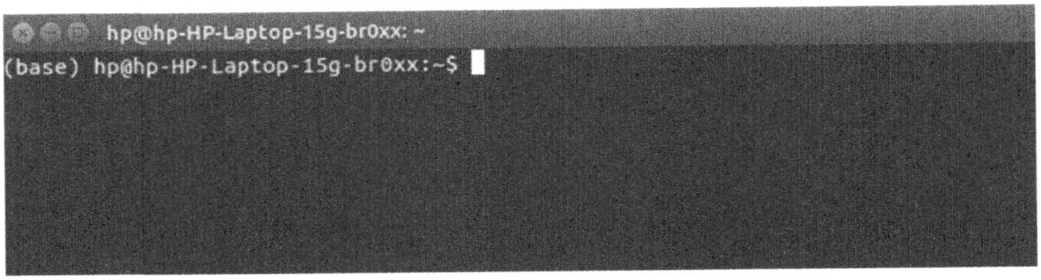

Figure 0.17: Terminal in Linux

2. In the terminal, navigate to the directory where you've saved the **environment.yml** file on your computer using the **cd** command. Say you've saved the file in **Documents\Data-Science-for-Marketing-Analytics-Second-Edition**. In that case, you'll type the following command in the prompt and press *Enter*:

```
cd Documents\Data-Science-for-Marketing-Analytics-Second-Edition
```

Note that the command may vary slightly based on your directory structure and your operating system.

3. Now that you've navigated to the correct folder, create a new **conda** environment by typing or pasting the following command in the terminal. Press *Enter* to run the command.

```
conda env create -f environment.yml
```

This will install the **ds-marketing** virtual environment along with the libraries that are required to run the code in this book. In case you see a prompt asking you to confirm before proceeding, type *y* and press *Enter* to continue creating the environment. Depending on your system configuration, it may take a while for the process to complete.

> **NOTE**
>
> For a complete list of **conda** commands, visit the following link: https://conda.io/projects/conda/en/latest/index.html. For a detailed guide on how to manage **conda** environments, please visit the following link: https://conda.io/projects/conda/en/latest/user-guide/tasks/manage-environments.html.

4. Once complete, type or paste the following command in the shell to activate the newly installed environment, **ds-marketing**.

```
conda activate ds-marketing
```

If the installation is successful, you'll see the environment name in brackets change from **base** to **ds-marketing**:

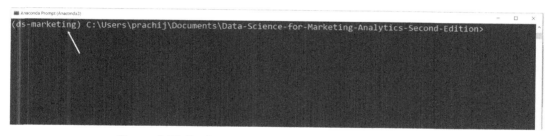

Figure 0.18: Environment name showing up in the shell

5. Run the following command to install **ipykernel** in the newly activated **conda** environment:

```
pip install ipykernel
```

> **NOTE**
>
> On macOS and Linux, you'll need to specify **pip3** instead of **pip**.

6. In the same environment, run the following command to add **ipykernel** as a Jupyter kernel:

```
python -m ipykernel install --user --name=ds-marketing
```

7. **Windows only:** If you're on Windows, type or paste the following command. Otherwise, you may skip this step and exit the terminal.

```
conda install pywin32
```

8. Select the created kernel **ds-marketing** when you start your Jupyter notebook.

Figure 0.19: Selecting the ds-marketing kernel

A new tab will open with a fresh untitled Jupyter notebook where you can start writing your code:

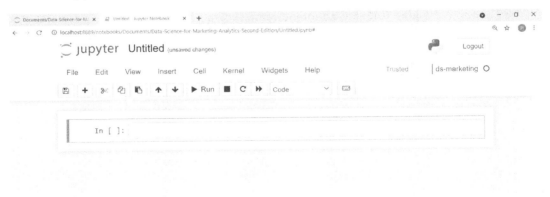

Figure 0.20: A new Jupyter notebook

RUNNING THE CODE ONLINE USING BINDER

You can also try running the code files for this book in a completely online environment through an interactive Jupyter Notebook interface called Binder. Along with the individual code files that can be downloaded locally, we have provided a link that will help you quickly access the Binder version of the GitHub repository for the book. Using this link, you can run any of the `.inpyb` code files for this book in a cloud-based online interactive environment. Click the following link to open the online Binder version of the book's repository to give it a try: https://packt.link/GdQOp. It is recommended that you save the link in your browser bookmarks for future reference (you may also use the `launch binder` link provided in the **README** section of the book's GitHub page).

Depending on your internet connection, it may take a while to load, but once loaded, you'll get the same interface as you would when running the code in a local Jupyter Notebook (all your shortcuts should work as well):

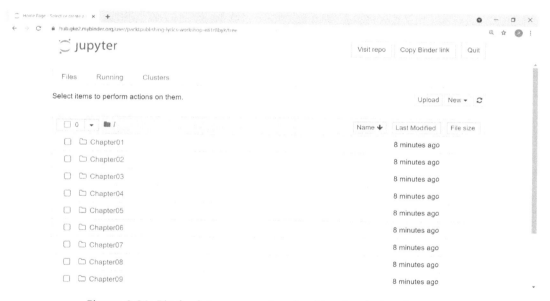

Figure 0.21: Binder lets you run Jupyter Notebooks in a browser

Binder is an online service that helps you read and execute Jupyter Notebook files (`.inpyb`) present in any public GitHub repository in a cloud-based environment. However, please note that there are certain memory constraints associated with Binder. This means that running multiple Jupyter Notebooks instances at the same time or running processes that consume a lot of memory (like model training) can result in a kernel crash or kernel reset. Moreover, any changes you make in these online Notebooks would not be stored, and the Notebooks will reset to the latest version present in the repository whenever you close and re-open the Binder link. A stable internet connection is required to use Binder. You can find out more about the Binder Project here: https://jupyter.org/binder.

This is a recommended option for readers who want to have a quick look at the code and experiment with it without downloading the entire repository on their local machine.

GET IN TOUCH

Feedback from our readers is always welcome.

General feedback: If you have any questions about this book, please mention the book title in the subject of your message and email us at `customercare@packtpub.com`.

Errata: Although we have taken every care to ensure the accuracy of our content, mistakes do happen. If you have found a mistake in this book, we would be grateful if you could report this to us. Please visit www.packtpub.com/support/errata and complete the form.

Piracy: If you come across any illegal copies of our works in any form on the Internet, we would be grateful if you could provide us with the location address or website name. Please contact us at `copyright@packt.com` with a link to the material.

If you are interested in becoming an author: If there is a topic that you have expertise in and you are interested in either writing or contributing to a book, please visit https://authors.packtpub.com/.

PLEASE LEAVE A REVIEW

Let us know what you think by leaving a detailed, impartial review on Amazon. We appreciate all feedback – it helps us continue to make great products and help aspiring developers build their skills. Please spare a few minutes to give your thoughts – it makes a big difference to us. You can leave a review by clicking the following link: https://packt.link/r/1800560478.

To Azra, Aiza, Duha and Aidama - you inspire courage, strength, and grace.

- Mirza Rahim Baig

To Appa, Amma, Vindhya, Madhu, and Ishan - The Five Pillars of my life.

- Gururajan Govindan

To Nanaji, Dadaji, and Appa - for their wisdom, inspiration, and unconditional love.

- Vishwesh Ravi Shrimali

1

DATA PREPARATION AND CLEANING

OVERVIEW

In this chapter, you'll learn the skills required to process and clean data to effectively ready it for further analysis. Using the **pandas** library in Python, you will learn how to read and import data from various file formats, including JSON and CSV, into a DataFrame. You'll then learn how to perform slicing, aggregation, and filtering on DataFrames. By the end of the chapter, you will consolidate your data cleaning skills by learning how to join DataFrames, handle missing values, and even combine data from various sources.

INTRODUCTION

"*Since you liked this artist, you'll also like their new album,*" "*Customers who bought bread also bought butter,*" and "*1,000 people near you have also ordered this item.*" Every day, recommendations like these influence customers' shopping decisions, helping them discover new products. Such recommendations are possible thanks to data science techniques that leverage data to create complex models, perform sophisticated tasks, and derive valuable customer insights with great precision. While the use of data science principles in marketing analytics is a proven, cost-effective, and efficient strategy, many companies are still not using these techniques to their full potential. There is a wide gap between the possible and actual usage of these techniques.

This book is designed to teach you skills that will help you contribute toward bridging that gap. It covers a wide range of useful techniques that will allow you to leverage everything data science can do in terms of strategies and decision-making in the marketing domain. By the end of the book, you should be able to successfully create and manage an end-to-end marketing analytics solution in Python, segment customers based on the data provided, predict their lifetime value, and model their decision-making behavior using data science techniques.

You will start your journey by first learning how to clean and prepare data. Raw data from external sources cannot be used directly; it needs to be analyzed, structured, and filtered before it can be used any further. In this chapter, you will learn how to manipulate rows and columns and apply transformations to data to ensure you have the right data with the right attributes. This is an essential skill in a data analyst's arsenal because, otherwise, the outcome of your analysis will be based on incorrect data, thereby making it a classic example of garbage in, garbage out. But before you start working with the data, it is important to understand its nature - in other words, the different types of data you'll be working with.

DATA MODELS AND STRUCTURED DATA

When you build an analytical solution, the first thing that you need to do is to build a data model. A data model is an overview of the data sources that you will be using, their relationships with other data sources, where exactly the data from a specific source is going to be fetched, and in what form (such as an Excel file, a database, or a JSON from an internet source).

> **NOTE**
>
> Keep in mind that the data model evolves as data sources and processes change.

A data model can contain data of the following three types:

- **Structured Data**: Also known as completely structured or well-structured data, this is the simplest way to manage information. The data is arranged in a flat tabular form with the correct value corresponding to the correct attribute. There is a unique column, known as an **index**, for easy and quick access to the data, and there are no duplicate columns. For example, in *Figure 1.1*, `employee_id` is the unique column. Using the data in this column, you can run SQL queries and quickly access data at a specific row and column in the dataset easily. Furthermore, there are no empty rows, missing entries, or duplicate columns, thereby making this dataset quite easy to work with. What makes structured data most ubiquitous and easy to analyze is that it is stored in a standardized tabular format that makes adding, updating, deleting, and updating entries easy and programmable. With structured data, you may not have to put in much effort during the data preparation and cleaning stage.

Data stored in relational databases such as MySQL, Amazon Redshift, and more are examples of structured data:

employee_id	first_name	last_name	hire_date	confirmation_date	employee_level
FTE_1782	John	Doe	31-03-2016	29-07-2016	EE
FTE_1783	Patrick	Forrester	24-05-2013	21-09-2013	MGR
FTE_1784	Pierre	Blanchet	25-08-2007	23-12-2007	TL
FTE_1785	Prachi	Jain	28-03-2011	26-07-2011	AM
FTE_1786	Sally	Pressfield	01-01-2012	30-04-2012	SR_MGR
FTE_1787	Sean	Lobo	15-10-2020	12-02-2021	VP
FTE_1788	Abhishek	Rane	19-02-2012	18-06-2012	EE
FTE_1789	George	Allen	01-01-2016	30-04-2016	TL
FTE_1790	Jacob	Shapiro	22-07-2006	19-11-2006	MGR
FTE_1791	Jane	Doe	29-07-2016	26-11-2016	SR_MGR
FTE_1792	Isabella	Lopez	14-06-2015	12-10-2015	EE
FTE_1793	Joseph	Tennenbaum	13-03-2007	11-07-2007	EE
FTE_1794	Karl	Weber	12-01-2002	12-05-2002	MGR
FTE_1795	Valentina	Garcia	22-03-2014	20-07-2014	TL
FTE_1796	Hans	Schmidt	30-04-2020	28-08-2020	SR_MGR
FTE_1797	Scott	James	27-03-2017	25-07-2017	MGR
FTE_1798	Sonali	Dsouza	02-02-2001	02-06-2001	TL
FTE_1799	Shubham	Gupta	19-08-2013	17-12-2013	EE
FTE_1800	Vincent	Cosentino	22-06-2012	20-10-2012	MGR

Figure 1.1: Data in a MySQL table

- **Semi-structured data**: You will not find semi-structured data to be stored in a strict, tabular hierarchy as you saw in *Figure 1.1*. However, it will still have its own hierarchies that group its elements and establish a relationship between them. For example, metadata of a song may include information about the cover art, the artist, song length, and even the lyrics. You can search for the artist's name and find the song you want. Such data does not have a fixed hierarchy mapping the unique column with rows in an expected format, and yet you can find the information you need.

  Another example of semi-structured data is a JSON file. JSON files are self-describing and can be understood easily. In *Figure 1.2*, you can see a JSON file that contains personally identifiable information of Jack Jones.

  Semi-structured data can be stored accurately in NoSQL databases.

```
[
    {
        "id": "E101"
        "name": "Jack Jones"
        "email": "jackjones123@example.com"
        "age": 35
        "address": "31, Chivas Place"
        "city": "San Diego"
        "state": "California"
    }
]
```

Figure 1.2: Data in a JSON file

- **Unstructured data**: Unstructured data may not be tabular, and even if it is tabular, the number of attributes or columns per observation may be completely arbitrary. The same data could be represented in different ways, and the attributes might not match each other, with values leaking into other parts.

  For example, think of reviews of various products stored in rows of an Excel sheet or a dump of the latest tweets of a company's Twitter profile. We can only search for specific keywords in that data, but we cannot store it in a relational database, nor will we be able to establish a concrete hierarchy between different elements or rows. Unstructured data can be stored as text files, CSV files, Excel files, images, and audio clips.

Marketing data, traditionally, comprises all three aforementioned data types. Initially, most data points originate from different data sources. This results in different implications, such as the values of a field could be of different lengths, the value for one field would not match that of other fields because of different field names, and some rows might have missing values for some of the fields.

You'll soon learn how to effectively tackle such problems with your data using Python. The following diagram illustrates what a data model for marketing analytics looks like. The data model comprises all kinds of data: structured data such as databases (top), semi-structured data such as JSON (middle), and unstructured data such as Excel files (bottom):

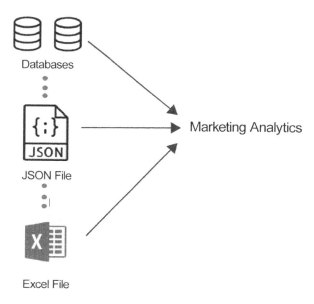

Figure 1.3: Data model for marketing analytics

As the data model becomes complex, the probability of having bad data increases. For example, a marketing analyst working with the demographic details of a customer can mistakenly read the age of the customer as a text string instead of a number (`integer`). In such situations, the analysis would go haywire as the analyst cannot perform any aggregation functions, such as finding the average age of a customer. These types of situations can be overcome by having a proper data quality check to ensure that the data chosen for further analysis is of the correct data type.

This is where programming languages such as Python come into play. Python is an all-purpose general programming language that integrates with almost every platform and helps automate data production and analysis.

Apart from understanding patterns and giving at least a basic structure to data, Python forces the data model to accept the right value for the attribute. The following diagram illustrates how most marketing analytics today structure different kinds of data by passing it through scripts to make it at least semi-structured:

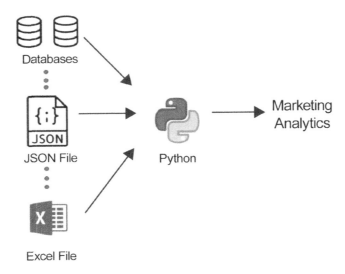

Figure 1.4: Data model of most marketing analytics that use Python

By making use of such structure-enforcing scripts, you will have a data model of semi-structured data coming in with expected values in the right fields; however, the data is not yet in the best possible format to perform analytics. If you can completely structure your data (that is, arrange it in flat tables, with the right value pointing to the right attribute with no nesting), it will be easy to see how every data point individually compares to other points with the help of common fields. You can easily get a feel of the data—that is, see in what range most values lie, identify the clear outliers, and so on—by simply scrolling through it.

While there are a lot of tools that can be used to convert data from an unstructured/semi-structured format to a fully structured format (for example, Spark, STATA, and SAS), the tool that is most widely used for data science, and which can be integrated with practically any framework, has rich functionalities, minimal costs, and is easy to use in our use case, is **pandas**.

PANDAS

pandas is a software library written in Python and is the basic building block for data manipulation and analysis. It offers a collection of high-performance, easy-to-use, and intuitive data structures and analysis tools that are of great use to marketing analysts and data scientists alike. The library comes as a default package when you install **Anaconda** (refer to the *Preface* for detailed instructions).

> **NOTE**
>
> Before you run the code in this book, it is recommended that you install and set up the virtual environment using the **environment.yml** file we have provided in the GitHub repository of this book.
>
> You can find the **environment.yml** file at the following link: https://packt.link/dBv1k.
>
> It will install all the required libraries and ensure that the version numbers of the libraries on your system match with ours. Refer to the *Preface* for more instructions on how to set this up.

However, if you're using any other distribution where pandas is not pre-installed, you can run the following command in your terminal app or command prompt to install the library:

```
pip install pandas
```

> **NOTE**
>
> On macOS or Linux, you will need to modify the preceding command to use **pip3** instead of **pip**.

The following diagram illustrates how different kinds of data are converted to a structured format with the help of pandas:

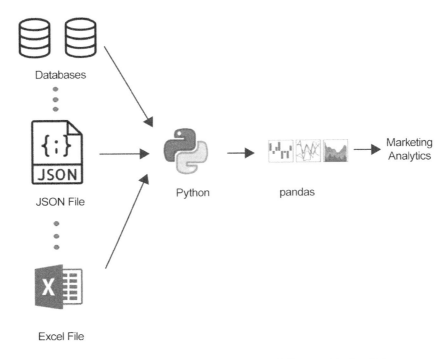

Figure 1.5: Data model to structure the different kinds of data

When working with pandas, you'll be dealing with its two primary object types: **DataFrames** and **Series**. What follows is a brief explanation of what those object types are. Don't worry if you are not able to understand things such as their structure and how they work; you'll be learning more about these in detail later in the chapter.

- **DataFrame**: This is the fundamental tabular structure that stores data in rows and columns (like a spreadsheet). When performing data analysis, you can directly apply functions and operations to DataFrames.

- **Series**: This refers to a single column of the DataFrame. Series adds up to form a DataFrame. The values can be accessed through its index, which is assigned automatically while defining a DataFrame.

In the following diagram, the **users** column annotated by *2* is a series, and the **viewers**, **views**, **users**, and **cost** columns, along with the index, form a DataFrame (annotated by *1*):

Figure 1.6: A sample pandas DataFrame and series

Now that you have a brief understanding of what pandas objects are, let's take a look at some of the functions you can use to import and export data in pandas.

IMPORTING AND EXPORTING DATA WITH PANDAS DATAFRAMES

Every team in a marketing group can have its own preferred data source for its specific use case. Teams that handle a lot of customer data, such as demographic details and purchase history, would prefer a database such as MySQL or Oracle, whereas teams that handle a lot of text might prefer JSON, CSV, or XML. Due to the use of multiple data sources, we end up having a wide variety of files. In such cases, the pandas library comes to our rescue as it provides a variety of **APIs (Application Program Interfaces)** that can be used to read multiple different types of data into a pandas DataFrame. Some of the most commonly used APIs are shown here:

Data Source Type	Read Function	Write Function	Format Type
CSV	read_csv	to_csv	Text
JSON	read_json	read_json	Text
HTML	read_html	to_html	Text
XML	read_xml	to_xml	Text
Excel	read_excel	to_excel	Binary
Stata	read_stata	to_stata	Binary
SAS	read_sas	to_sas	Binary
Clipboard	read_clipboard	to_clipboard	Text
Python Pickle File Format	read_pickle	to_pickle	Binary

Figure 1.7: Ways to import and export different types of data with pandas DataFrames

So, let's say you wanted to read a CSV file. You'll first need to import the **pandas** library as follows:

```
import pandas as pd
```

Then, you will run the following code to store the CSV file in a DataFrame named **df** (**df** is a variable):

```
df = pd.read_csv("sales.csv")
```

In the preceding line, we have **sales.csv**, which is the file to be imported. This command should work if your Jupyter notebook (or Python process) is run from the same directory where the file is stored. If the file was stored in any other path, you'll have to specify the exact path. On Windows, for example, you'll specify the path as follows:

```
df = pd.read_csv(r"C:\Users\abhis\Documents\sales.csv")
```

Note that we've added **r** before the path to take care of any special characters in the path. As you work with and import various data files in the exercises and activities in this book, we'll often remind you to pay attention to the path of the CSV file.

When loading data, pandas also provides additional parameters that you can pass to the **read** function, so that you can load the data the way you want. Some of these parameters are provided here. Please note that most of these parameters are optional. Also worth noting is the fact that the default value of the index in a DataFrame starts with **0**:

- **skiprows = k**: This parameter skips the first **k** rows.

- **nrows = k**: This parameter parses only the first **k** rows.

- **names = [col1, col2...]**: This parameter lists the column names to be used in the parsed DataFrame.

- **header = k**: This parameter applies the column names corresponding to the **k**th row as the header for the DataFrame. **k** can also be **None**.

- **index_col = col**: This parameter sets **col** as the index of the DataFrame being used.

  index_col can also be a list of column names (used to create a **MultiIndex**) or it can be **None**. A MultiIndex DataFrame uses more than one column of the DataFrame as the index.

- **`usecols = [11, 12...]`**: This provides either integer positional indices in the document columns or strings that correspond to column names in the DataFrame to be read; for example, **`[0, 1, 2]`** or **`['foo', 'bar', 'baz']`**.

For example, if you want to import a CSV file into a DataFrame, **df**, with the following conditions:

- The first row of the file must be the header.

- You need to import only the first 100 rows into the file.

- You need to import only the first 3 columns.

The code corresponding to the preceding conditions would be as follows:

```
df= pd.read_csv("sales.csv",header=1,nrows=100,usecols=[0,1,2])
```

> **NOTE**
>
> There are similar specific parameters for almost every inbuilt function in pandas. You can find details about them with the documentation for pandas available at the following link: https://pandas.pydata.org/pandas-docs/stable/.

Once the data is imported, you need to verify whether it has been imported correctly. Let's understand how to do that in the following section.

VIEWING AND INSPECTING DATA IN DATAFRAMES

Once you've successfully read a DataFrame using the pandas library, you need to inspect the data to check whether the right attribute has received the right value. You can use several built-in pandas functions to do that.

The most commonly used way to inspect loaded data is using the **head()** command. By default, this command will display the first **five** rows of the DataFrame. Here's an example of the command used on a DataFrame called **df**:

```
df.head()
```

The output should be as follows:

	Year	Product	line	Product.1	type	Product.2	Order
0	2004	Camping	Equipment	Cooking	Gear	TrailChef	Water
1	2004	Camping	Equipment	Cooking	Gear	TrailChef	Water
2	2004	Camping	Equipment	Cooking	Gear	TrailChef	Water
3	2004	Camping	Equipment	Cooking	Gear	TrailChef	Water
4	2004	Camping	Equipment	Cooking	Gear	TrailChef	Water

Figure 1.8: Output of the df.head() command

Similarly, to display the last **five** rows, you can use the **df.tail()** command. Instead of the default **five** rows, you can even specify the number of rows you want to be displayed. For example, the **df.head(11)** command will display the first **11** rows.

Here's the complete usage of these two commands, along with a few other commands that be useful while examining data. Again, it is assumed that you have stored the DataFrame in a variable called **df**:

- **df.head(n)** will return the first **n** rows of the DataFrame. If no **n** is passed, the function considers **n** to be **5** by default.

- **df.tail(n)** will return the last **n** rows of the DataFrame. If no **n** is passed, the function considers **n** to be **5** by default.

- **df.shape** will return the dimensions of a DataFrame (number of rows and number of columns).

- **df.dtypes** will return the type of data in each column of the pandas DataFrame (such as **float**, **object**, **int64**, and so on).

- **df.info()** will summarize the DataFrame and print its size, type of values, and the count of non-null values.

So far, you've learned about the different functions that can be used on DataFrames. In the first exercise, you will practice using these functions to import a JSON file into a DataFrame and later, to inspect the data.

EXERCISE 1.01: LOADING DATA STORED IN A JSON FILE

The tech team in your company has been testing a web version of its flagship shopping app. A few loyal users who volunteered to test the website were asked to submit their details via an online form. The form captured some useful details (such as age, income, and more) along with some not-so-useful ones (such as eye color). The tech team then tested their new profile page module, using which a few additional details were captured. All this data was stored in a JSON file called `user_info.json`, which the tech team sent to you for validation.

> **NOTE**
>
> You can find the `user_info.json` file at the following link: https://packt.link/Gi2O7.

Your goal is to import this JSON file into pandas and let the tech team know the answers to the following questions so that they can add more modules to the website:

- Is the data loading correctly?

- Are there any missing values in any of the columns?

- What are the data types of all the columns?

- How many rows and columns are present in the dataset?

> **NOTE**
>
> All the exercises and activities in this chapter can be performed in both the Jupyter notebook and Python shell. While you can do them in the shell for now, it is highly recommended to use the Jupyter notebook. To learn how to install Jupyter and set up the Jupyter notebook, refer to the *Preface*. It will be assumed that you are using a Jupyter notebook from this point on.

1. If you installed Anaconda as described in the *Preface*, a shortcut for Jupyter Notebook must have appeared on your system. Click it to launch *Jupyter Notebook*.

2. The **Notebook Dashboard** should appear in a new browser window (it opens in your default system browser) as follows:

Figure 1.9: Notebook Dashboard

3. Using the **Notebook Dashboard**, navigate to the directory where you want to create your first Jupyter notebook. Click **New**. You'll see **Python 3** along with several other options (as shown in *Figure 1.10*). If you've installed the virtual environment, you'll see **ds-marketing** as an option as well. Click **ds-marketing** if you're planning to use the virtual environment; otherwise, click **Python 3**. Either of these actions will open a new Jupyter notebook in a separate browser tab:

Figure 1.10: Loading the YML environment

> **NOTE**
>
> To ensure that the version numbers of libraries we've used while writing this book match yours, make sure you install and use the **ds-marketing** virtual environment we have provided. Please refer to the *Preface* for detailed instructions.

4. Click the space that says **Untitled** in the header and rename the file as **Exercise1.01**. A **.ipnyb** extension will be added automatically:

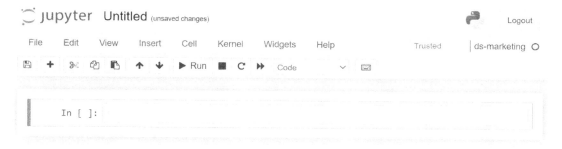

Figure 1.11: Renaming a file

5. In a new code cell, type in or paste the following command to import the **pandas** library. Use the *Shift + Enter* keyboard combination to execute the code:

```
import pandas as pd
```

> **NOTE**
>
> You can find more information on what code cells are, what keyboard shortcuts to use, and what the structure of a notebook is, by visiting this guide in the official documentation: https://jupyter-notebook.readthedocs.io/en/stable/.

6. Create a new DataFrame called **user_info** and read the **user_info.json** file into it using the following command:

```
user_info = pd.read_json("user_info.json")
```

> **NOTE**
>
> **user_info.json** should be stored in the same directory from which you are running **Exercise1.01.ipnyb**. Alternatively, you'll have to provide the exact path to the file as shown in the earlier *Importing and Exporting Data with pandas DataFrames* section.

7. Now, examine whether your data is properly loaded by checking the first five values in the DataFrame. Do this using the **head()** command:

```
user_info.head()
```

You should see the following output:

	_id	index	guid	isActive	balance	picture	age
0	5c0a28d7a647437fd3d3a6aa	0	832f1af4-fb18-4ba8-b032-f4cbf343dbe9	False	$3,806.93	http://placehold.it/32x32	20
1	5c0a28d780f6278b11586ab1	1	4306cb37-9506-48c2-8ccf-e69a063589ee	True	$3,330.01	http://placehold.it/32x32	22
2	5c0a28d722e2e29d9bce2b64	2	5019e436-7cc4-48ee-a384-3483131f8ee1	True	$1,619.46	http://placehold.it/32x32	40

Figure 1.12: Viewing the first few rows of user_info.json

> **NOTE**
>
> The preceding image does not contain all the columns of the DataFrame. It is used for demonstration purposes only.

As you can see from the preceding screenshot, the data is successfully loaded into a pandas DataFrame. Therefore, you can now answer the first question with *yes*.

8. Now, to answer the second question, you'll need to use the **info()** command:

```
user_info.info()
```

You should get the following output:

```
<class 'pandas.core.frame.DataFrame'>
RangeIndex: 6 entries, 0 to 5
Data columns (total 22 columns):
 #   Column        Non-Null Count  Dtype
---  ------        --------------  -----
 0   _id           6 non-null      object
 1   index         6 non-null      int64
 2   guid          6 non-null      object
 3   isActive      6 non-null      bool
 4   balance       6 non-null      object
 5   picture       6 non-null      object
 6   age           6 non-null      int64
 7   eyeColor      6 non-null      object
 8   name          6 non-null      object
 9   gender        6 non-null      object
 10  company       6 non-null      object
 11  email         6 non-null      object
 12  phone         6 non-null      object
 13  address       6 non-null      object
 14  about         6 non-null      object
 15  registered    6 non-null      object
 16  latitude      6 non-null      float64
 17  longitude     6 non-null      float64
 18  tags          6 non-null      object
 19  friends       6 non-null      object
 20  greeting      6 non-null      object
 21  favoriteFruit 6 non-null      object
dtypes: bool(1), float64(2), int64(2), object(17)
memory usage: 1.1+ KB
```

Figure 1.13: Information about the data in user_info

> **NOTE**
>
> The **64** displayed with the type above is an indicator of precision and varies on different platforms.

From the preceding output, you can see that there are a total of **22** columns and **6** rows present in the JSON file. You may notice that the **isActive** column is a Boolean, the **age** and **index** columns are integers, and the **latitude** and **longitude** columns are floats. The rest of the columns are Python objects. Also, the number of observations in each column is the same (**6**), which implies that there are no missing values in the DataFrame. The preceding command not only gave us the answer to the second question, but it helped us answer the third and fourth questions as well. However, there is another quick way in which you can check the number of rows and columns in the DataFrame, and that is by using the **shape** attribute of the DataFrame.

9. Run the following command to check the number of rows and columns in the **user_info** DataFrame:

```
user_info.shape
```

This will give you **(6, 22)** as the output, indicating that the DataFrame created by the JSON has **6** rows and **22** columns.

In this exercise, you loaded the data, checked whether it had been loaded correctly, and gathered some more information about the entries contained therein. All this was done by loading data stored in a single source, which was the JSON file. As a marketing analyst, you will come across situations where you'll need to load and process data from different sources. Let's practice that in the exercise that follows.

EXERCISE 1.02: LOADING DATA FROM MULTIPLE SOURCES

You work for a company that uses Facebook for its marketing campaigns. The **data.csv** file contains the views and likes of 100 different posts on Facebook used for a marketing campaign. The team also uses historical sales data to derive insights. The **sales.csv** file contains some historical sales data recorded in a CSV file relating to different customer purchases in stores in the past few years.

Your goal is to read the files into pandas DataFrames and check the following:

- Whether either of the datasets contains null or missing values

- Whether the data is stored in the correct columns and the corresponding column names make sense (in other words, the names of the columns correctly convey what type of information is stored in the rows)

NOTE

You can find the **data.csv** file at https://packt.link/NmBJT, and the **sales.csv** file at https://packt.link/ER7fz.

Let's first work with the **data.csv** file:

1. Start a new Jupyter notebook. You can name it **Exercise 1.02**. Then, import **pandas** by running the following command in a new Jupyter notebook cell. Use the *Shift + Enter* keyboard combination to run the code:

```
import pandas as pd
```

2. Create a new DataFrame called **campaign_data**. Use the **read_csv** method to read the contents of the **data.csv** file into it:

```
campaign_data = pd.read_csv("data.csv")
```

NOTE

Again, make sure that you're running the Jupyter notebook from the same directory where the **data.csv** file is stored. Otherwise, change the path (emboldened) as shown earlier in the *Importing and Exporting Data with pandas DataFrames* section.

3. Examine the first five rows of the DataFrame using the **head()** function:

```
campaign_data.head()
```

Your output should look as follows:

	Campaign Data
views	likes
90006	402
101141	389
97297	403
117182	397

Figure 1.14: Viewing raw campaign data

From the preceding output, you can observe that **views** and **likes** appear as rows. Instead, they should be appearing as column names.

4. To read the column names, you will now read the data into **campaign_data** again (which is running the code in *Step 2* once more), but this time you'll need to use the **header** parameter to make sure that the entries in the first row are read as column names. The **header** = **1** parameter reads the first row as the header:

```
campaign_data = pd.read_csv("data.csv", header = 1)
```

Run the **head** command again:

```
campaign_data.head()
```

You should get the following output:

	views	likes
0	90006	402
1	101141	389
2	97297	403
3	117182	397
4	99637	404

Figure 1.15: Output of the head command

You will observe that **views** and **likes** are now displayed as column names.

5. Now, examine the last five rows using the **tail()** function:

```
campaign_data.tail()
```

You should get the following output:

	views	likes
95	100464	391
96	96382	387
97	94971	389
98	103070	410
99	110387	411

Figure 1.16: The last few rows of campaign_data

There doesn't seem to be any misalignment of data or missing values toward the end of the DataFrame.

6. Although we have seen the last few rows, we still cannot be sure that all values in the middle (hidden) part of the DataFrame are devoid of any null values. Check the data types of the DataFrame to be sure using the following command:

```
campaign_data.info()
```

You should get the following output:

```
<class 'pandas.core.frame.DataFrame'>
RangeIndex: 100 entries, 0 to 99
Data columns (total 2 columns):
 #   Column  Non-Null Count  Dtype
---  ------  --------------  -----
 0   views   100 non-null    int64
 1   likes   100 non-null    int64
dtypes: int64(2)
memory usage: 1.7 KB
```

Figure 1.17: info() of campaign_data

As you can see from the preceding output, the DataFrame has two columns with **100** rows and has no null values.

7. Now, analyze the **sales.csv** file. Create a new DataFrame called **sales**. Use the **read_csv()** method to read the contents of the **sales.csv** file into it:

```
sales = pd.read_csv("sales.csv")
```

> **NOTE**
>
> Make sure you change the path (emboldened) to the CSV file based on its location on your system. If you're running the Jupyter notebook from the same directory where the CSV file is stored, you can run the preceding code without any modification.

8. Look at the first five rows of the **sales** DataFrame using the following command:

```
sales.head()
```

Your output should look as follows:

	Year	Product	line	Product.1	type	Product.2	Order	method	type.1	Retailer	country	Revenue
0	2004	Camping	Equipment	Cooking	Gear	TrailChef	Water	Bag	Telephone	United	States	315044.33
1	2004	Camping	Equipment	Cooking	Gear	TrailChef	Water	Bag	Telephone	Canada	NaN	14313.48
2	2004	Camping	Equipment	Cooking	Gear	TrailChef	Water	Bag	Telephone	Mexico	NaN	156644.47
3	2004	Camping	Equipment	Cooking	Gear	TrailChef	Water	Bag	Telephone	Brazil	NaN	59191.72
4	2004	Camping	Equipment	Cooking	Gear	TrailChef	Water	Bag	Telephone	Japan	NaN	7029.33

Figure 1.18: First few rows of sales.csv

From the preceding screenshot, the **Year** column appears to have correct values, but the entries in the **line** column do not make sense. Upon closer examination, it's clear that the data that should have been loaded under a single column called **Product line** is split into two columns (**Product** and **line**). Thus, the first few products under this column should have read as **Camping Equipment**. The **Product.1** and **type** columns suffer from a similar problem. Furthermore, the **Order** and **method** columns don't make much sense. In fact, the values of the **Order** and **method** columns being **Water** and **Bag** in one of the rows fail to convey any information regarding the data.

9. To check for null values and examine the data types of the columns, run the following command:

```
sales.info()
```

Your output should look as follows:

```
<class 'pandas.core.frame.DataFrame'>
RangeIndex: 100 entries, 0 to 99
Data columns (total 12 columns):
 #   Column     Non-Null Count  Dtype
---  ------     --------------  -----
 0   Year       100 non-null    int64
 1   Product    100 non-null    object
 2   line       100 non-null    object
 3   Product.1  100 non-null    object
 4   type       100 non-null    object
 5   Product.2  100 non-null    object
 6   Order      100 non-null    object
 7   method     100 non-null    object
 8   type.1     100 non-null    object
 9   Retailer   100 non-null    object
 10  country    9 non-null      object
 11  Revenue    100 non-null    float64
dtypes: float64(1), int64(1), object(10)
memory usage: 9.5+ KB
```

Figure 1.19: Output of sales.info()

From the preceding output, you can see that the **country** column has missing values (since all the other columns have 100 entries). You'll need to dig deeper and find out the exact cause of this problem. By the end of this chapter, you'll learn how to address such problems effectively.

Now that you have loaded the data and looked at the result, you can observe that the data collected by the marketing campaigns team (**data.csv**) looks good and it has no missing values. The data collected by the sales team, on the other hand (stored in **sales.csv**), has quite a few missing values and incorrect column names.

Based on what you've learned about pandas so far, you won't be able to standardize the data. Before you learn how to do that, you'll first have to dive deep into the internal structure of pandas objects and understand how data is stored in pandas.

STRUCTURE OF A PANDAS DATAFRAME AND SERIES

You are undecided as to which data structure to use to store some of the information that comes in from different marketing teams. From your experience, you know that a few elements in your data will have missing values. You are also expecting two different teams to collect the same data but categorize it differently. That is, instead of numerical indices (**0-10**), they might use custom labels to access specific values. pandas provides data structures that help store and work with such data. One such data structure is called a **pandas series**.

A pandas series is nothing more than an indexed NumPy array. To create a pandas series, all you need to do is create an array and give it an index. If you create a series without an index, it will create a default numeric index that starts from **0** and goes on for the length of the series, as shown in the following diagram:

Index ➝	0	1	2	3	4	5	6	7	8	9
Array ➝	'one'	'five'	'seven'	'fourteen'	'Six'	'ninety'	'eight'	'twelve'	'fourteen'	'ten'

Figure 1.20: Sample pandas series

> **NOTE**
>
> As a series is still a NumPy array, all functions that work on a NumPy array work the same way on a pandas series, too. To learn more about the functions, please refer to the following link:
> https://pandas.pydata.org/pandas-docs/stable/reference/series.html.

As your campaign grows, so does the number of series. With that, new requirements arise. Now, you want to be able to perform operations such as concatenation on specific entries in several series at once. However, to access the values, these different series must share the same index. And that's exactly where DataFrames come into the picture. A pandas DataFrame is just a dictionary with the column names as keys and values as different pandas series, joined together by the index.

A DataFrame is created when different columns (which are nothing but series) such as these are joined together by the index:

	age			balance
0	20		0	$3,806.93
1	22		1	$3,330.01
2	40	....	2	$1,619.46
3	29		3	$3,334.12
4	33		4	$1,368.48

⇨

	_id	about	address	age	balance	company
0	5c0a28d7a647437fd3d3a6aa	Nostrud consectetur elit occaecat dolore incid...	698 Kansas Place, Bethpage, Louisiana, 7695	20	$3,806.93	RODEMCO
1	5c0a28d780f6278b11586ab1	Sunt id ipsum velit voluptate. Ullamco non non...	309 Kingsway Place, Kilbourne, New York, 3771	22	$3,330.01	VIAGRAND
2	5c0a28d722e2e29d9bce2b64	Laborum ad excepteur amet sunt aliqua veniam c...	347 Seeley Street, Witmer, Kansas, 9369	40	$1,619.46	EQUITOX
3	5c0a28d76b5e8859a754cb4f	Eu amet aliqua magna ipsum quis et ut reprehen...	178 Stewart Street, Ferney, Wyoming, 9118	29	$3,334.12	ANARCO
4	5c0a28d7ebb99c08e2288c76	Sunt amet exercitation aliqua cillum commodo o...	189 Rogers Avenue, Lindisfarne, Mississippi, 1961	33	$1,368.48	MEGALL

Figure 1.21: Series joined together by the same index create a pandas DataFrame

In the preceding screenshot, you'll see numbers **0-4** to the left of the **age** column. These are the indices. The **age**, **balance**, **_id**, **about**, and **address** columns, along with others, are series, and together they form a DataFrame.

This way of storing data makes it very easy to perform the operations you need on the data you want. You can easily choose the series you want to modify by picking a column and directly slicing off indices based on the value in that column. You can also group indices with similar values in one column together and see how the values change in other columns.

pandas also allows operations to be applied to both rows and columns of a DataFrame. You can choose which one to apply by specifying the axis, **0** referring to rows, and **1** referring to columns.

For example, if you wanted to apply the **sum** function to all the rows in the **balance** column of the DataFrame, you would use the following code:

```
df['balance'].sum(axis=0)
```

In the following screenshot, by specifying **axis=0**, you can apply a function (such as **sum**) on all the rows in a particular column:

	_id	about	address	age	balance	company	email	eyeColor	favoriteFruit	friends	
0	5c0a28d7a647437fd3d3a6aa	Nostrud consectetur elit occaecat dolore incid...	698 Kansas Place, Bethpage, Louisiana, 7695	20	$3,806.93	RODEMCO	graceberry@rodemco.com	green	strawberry	[{'id': 0, 'name': 'Small Pena'}, {'id': 1, 'n...	832f1af4-fb18-4ba8-b032-f4cbf343dbe9
1	5c0a28d780f6278b11586ab1	Sunt id ipsum velit voluptate. Ullamco non non...	309 Kingsway Place, Kilbourne, New York, 3771	22	$3,330.01	VIAGRAND	hilarysellers@viagrand.com	brown	apple	[{'id': 0, 'name': 'Spears Smith'}, {'id': 1, ...	4306cb37-9506-48c2-8ccf-e69a063589ee
2	5c0a28d722e2e29d9bce2b64	Laborum ad excepteur amet sunt aliqua veniam c...	347 Seeley Street, Witmer, Kansas, 9369	40	$1,619.46	EQUITOX	sherrigilbert@equitox.com	green	apple	[{'id': 0, 'name': 'Sexton Watts'}, {'id': 1, ...	5019e436-7cc4-48ee-a384-3483131f8ee1
3	5c0a28d76b5e8859a754cb4f	Eu amet aliqua magna ipsum quis et ut reprehen...	178 Stewart Street, Ferney, Wyoming, 9118	29	$3,334.12	ANARCO	caldwellpatterson@anarco.com	blue	strawberry	[{'id': 0, 'name': 'Anne Holcomb'}, {'id': 1, ...	d2c4b1eb-2974-463a-b288-d1dae5dec187
4	5c0a28d7ebb99c08e2288c76	Sunt amet exercitation aliqua cillum commodo o...	189 Rogers Avenue, Lindisfarne, Mississippi, 1961	33	$1,368.48	MEGALL	headmcconnell@megall.com	brown	strawberry	[{'id': 0, 'name': 'Elnora Peck'}, {'id': 1, '...	df0b59ed-2e81-43f1-9ae0-16f138e738be

axis = 1 or axis = 'columns' / *axis = 0 or axis = 'index'*

Figure 1.22: Understanding axis = 0 and axis = 1 in pandas

By specifying **axis=1**, you can apply a function on a row that spans across all the columns. In the next section, you will learn how to use pandas to manipulate raw data to gather useful insights from it.

DATA MANIPULATION

Now that we have deconstructed the structure of the pandas DataFrame down to its basics, the remainder of the wrangling tasks, that is, creating new DataFrames, selecting or slicing a DataFrame into its parts, filtering DataFrames for some values, joining different DataFrames, and so on, will become very intuitive. Let's start by selecting and filtering in the following section.

> **NOTE**
>
> Jupyter notebooks for the code examples listed in this chapter can be found at the following links: https://packt.link/xTvR2 and https://packt.link/PGIzK.

SELECTING AND FILTERING IN PANDAS

If you wanted to access a particular cell in a spreadsheet, you would do so by addressing that cell in the familiar format of (*column name, row name*). For example, when you call cell *A63*, *A* refers to the column and *63* refers to the row. Data is stored similarly in pandas, but as (*row name, column name*) and we can use the same convention to access cells in a DataFrame.

For example, look at the following DataFrame. The `viewers` column is the index of the DataFrame:

	viewers	views	users	cost	Gender
0	Sushmita	31.20	Sushmita	2.000000	F
1	Adam	17.90	Adam	20.000000	M
2	Benny	265.23	Benny	15.000000	M
3	Anurag	42.47	Anurag	12.333333	F

Figure 1.23: Sample DataFrame

To find the cost of acquisition of Adam and Anurag along with their views, we can use the following code. Here, **Adam** and **Anurag** are the rows, and **cost**, along with **views**, are the columns:

```
df.loc[['Adam','Anurag'],['cost','views']]
```

Running the preceding command will generate the following output:

	cost	views
viewers		
Adam	20.000000	17.90
Anurag	12.333333	42.47

Figure 1.24: Use of the loc function

If you need to access more than a single cell, such as a subset of some rows and columns from the DataFrame, or change the order of display of some columns on the DataFrame, you can make use of the syntax listed in the following table:

Operation	Syntax	Result
Select a column	df [col]	Series
Select multiple columns	df [[coli, col2..]]	DataFrame
Select a row by label	df.loc[label]	Series
Select a row by integer location	df.iloc[loc]	Series
Slice rows	af [start_idx: end_idx]	DataFrame
Select multiple rows by Boolean vector	df[bool_vec)	DataFrame

Figure 1.25: A table listing the syntax used for different operations on a pandas DataFrame

In the next section, you'll learn how to create DataFrames in Python.

CREATING DATAFRAMES IN PYTHON

Let's say you've loaded campaign data into a DataFrame. In the **revenue** column, you see that the figures are not in their desired currencies. To convert the revenue numbers to various other currencies, you may need to create a *test DataFrame*, containing exchange rates that will remain constant throughout your revenue calculation.

There are two ways of creating such test DataFrames—by creating completely new DataFrames, or by duplicating or taking a slice of a previously existing DataFrame:

- **Creating new DataFrames**: You typically use the **DataFrame** function to create a completely new DataFrame. The function directly converts a Python object into a pandas DataFrame. The **DataFrame** function in general works with any iterable collection of data, such as **dict** and **list**. You can also pass an empty collection or a singleton collection to it.

   For example, you will get the same DataFrame through either of the following lines of code:

```
df=pd.DataFrame({'Currency': pd.Series(['USD','EUR','GBP']),\
                 'ValueInINR': pd.Series([70, 89, 99])})

df=pd.DataFrame.from_dict({'Currency': ['USD','EUR','GBP'],\
                 'ValueInINR':[70, 89, 99]})
df.head()
```

Running the command in either of these two ways will generate the following output:

	Currency	ValueInINR
0	USD	70
1	EUR	89
2	GBP	99

Figure 1.26: Output generated by two different ways to create a DataFrame

- **Duplicating or slicing a previously existing DataFrame**: The second way to create a DataFrame is by copying a previously existing DataFrame. Your first intuition would be to do something like **obj1 = obj2**. However, since both the objects share a reference to the same object in memory, changing **obj2** will also change **obj1**, and vice versa.

  You can tackle this with a standard library function called **deepcopy**. The **deepcopy** function allows the user to recursively go through the objects being pointed to by the references and create entirely new objects.

  So, when you want to copy a previously existing DataFrame and don't want the previous DataFrame to be affected by modifications in the new DataFrame, you need to use the **deepcopy** function. You can also slice the previously existing DataFrame and pass it to the function, and it will be considered a new DataFrame.

  For example, the following code snippet will recursively copy everything in **df** (refer *Figure 1.26)* to **df1**. Now, any changes you make to **df1** won't have an impact on **df**:

```
import pandas
import copy
df1 = df.copy(deep=True)
```

  The contents of **df1** will be the same as what we see in *Figure 1.26*.

In the next section, you will look at functions that can help you to add or remove attributes in a pandas DataFrame.

ADDING AND REMOVING ATTRIBUTES AND OBSERVATIONS

pandas provides the following functions to add and delete rows (observations) and columns (attributes):

- **df['col'] = s**: This adds a new column, **col**, to the DataFrame, **df**, creating a new column that has values from the series, **s**.

- **df.assign(c1 = s1, c2 = s2...)**: This method adds new columns, **c1**, **c2**, and so on, with series, **s1**, **s2**, and so on, to the **df** DataFrame in one go.

- **df.append(df2)**: This method adds values from the **df2** DataFrame to the bottom of the **df** DataFrame wherever the columns of **df2** match those of **df**.

- **df.drop(labels, axis)**: This method removes the rows or columns specified by the labels and corresponding axis, or those specified by the index or column names directly.

    For example, in the DataFrame created in *Figure 1.26*, if we wanted to drop the **Currency** column, the corresponding code would be as follows:

    ```
    df=df.drop(['Currency'],axis=1)
    ```

    The output should be as follows:

	ValueInINR
0	70
1	89
2	99

Figure 1.27: Output when the Currency column is dropped from the df DataFrame

- **df.dropna(axis, how)**: Depending on the parameter passed to **how**, this method decides whether to drop rows (or columns if **axis = 1**) with missing values in any of the fields or in all of the fields. If no parameter is passed, the default value of **how** is **any**, and the default value of the **axis** is 0.

- **df.drop_duplicates(keep)**: This method removes rows with duplicate values in the DataFrame, and keeps the first (**keep = 'first'**), last (**keep = 'last'**), or no occurrence (**keep = False**) in the data.

DataFrames can also be sequentially combined with the **concat** function:

- **pd.concat([df1,df2..])**: This method creates a new DataFrame with **df1**, **df2**, and all other DataFrames combined sequentially. It will automatically combine columns having the same names in the combined DataFrames.

In the next section, you will learn how to combine data from different DataFrames into a single DataFrame.

COMBINING DATA

Let's say the product team sends you details about the prices of the popular products your company makes. The data is stored in a DataFrame called **df_products** and contains the following information:

	CampaignYear	ProductPrice	ProductVersion
0	2015	199	v1
1	2016	199	v1
2	2017	199	v1
3	2018	299	v2
4	2019	299	v2
5	2020	349	v2
6	2021	349	v3

Figure 1.28: Contents of the df_products DataFrame

The finance team has also sent you details regarding the revenue for these products, stored in a DataFrame called **df_revenue**. It contains the following details:

	CampaignYear	Revenue
0	2016	9473
1	2017	8422
2	2018	9987
3	2019	7994
4	2020	9530
5	2021	9444

Figure 1.29: Contents of the df_revenue DataFrame

Notice that in both these DataFrames, the **CampaignYear** column is common; however, since the finance team didn't have details of the 2015 campaign, that entry is missing in the **df_revenue** DataFrame. Now, let's say you wanted to combine data from both these DataFrames into a single DataFrame. The easiest way you'd go about this is to use the **pd.merge** function:

```
df_combined = pd.merge(df_products, df_revenue)
```

> **NOTE**
>
> In the preceding code, **df_products** is considered the left DataFrame, while **df_revenue** is considered the right DataFrame.

The contents of the combined DataFrame should look as follows:

	CampaignYear	ProductPrice	ProductVersion	Revenue
0	2016	199	v1	9473
1	2017	199	v1	8422
2	2018	299	v2	9987
3	2019	299	v2	7994
4	2020	349	v2	9530
5	2021	349	v3	9444

Figure 1.30: Contents of the merged DataFrame

As you can see from the output in *Figure 1.30*, the DataFrames are merged on the common column (which is **CampaignYear**). One thing you'll notice is that the data for **CampaignYear 2015** is missing. To make sense of this phenomenon, let's understand what is happening behind the scenes.

When we ran the **merge ()** command, pandas merged **df_products** and **df_revenue** based on a common column in the two datasets – this was **CampaignYear**. If there were multiple shared columns in the two datasets, we'd have to specify the exact column we want to merge on as follows:

```
df_combined = pd.merge(df_products, df_revenue, \
                       on = "CampaignYear")
```

Now, since the **CampaignYear** column is the only column shared between the two DataFrames and the entry for 2015 is missing in one of the DataFrames (and hence not a shared value), it is excluded in the combined dataset.

What if we still wanted to examine the price and version of the product for 2015 and have revenue as blank for that year? We can fine-tune the merging of DataFrames by using the **how** parameter.

With the help of the **how** parameter, you can merge DataFrames in four different ways:

How to Join	Syntax	Description
Inner Join	pd.merge(df, dfi, how = "inner")	Joins the rows that have the key(s) present in both the DataFrames.
Outer Join	pd.merge(df, dfi, how = 'outer')	Joins the rows that have the key(s) present in any of the DataFrames
Left Join	pd.merge(df, dfi, how = 'left')	Joins the rows that have the key(s) present in the first DataFrame.
Right Join	pd. merge(df, df1, how = 'right')	Joins the rows that have the key(s) present in the second DataFrame.

Figure 1.31: Table describing different joins

The following diagram shows two sample DataFrames, **df1** and **df2**, and the results of the various joins performed on these DataFrames:

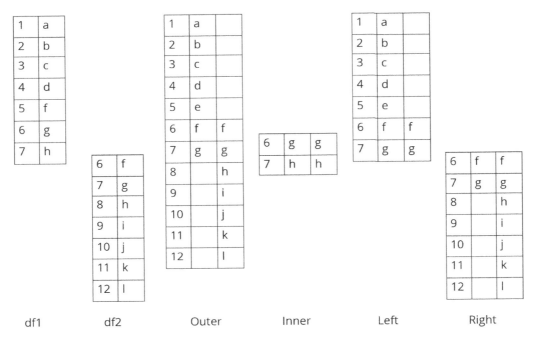

Figure 1.32: Table showing two DataFrames and the outcomes of different joins on them

In the preceding diagram, **outer join** returns all the records in **df1** and **df2** irrespective of a match (any missing values are filled with **NaN** entries). For example, if we wanted to do an outer join with the products and revenue DataFrames, we would have to run the following command:

```
df_combined_outer = pd.merge(df_products, df_revenue, \
                             how = 'outer')
```

The output should be as follows:

	CampaignYear	ProductPrice	ProductVersion	Revenue
0	2015	199	v1	NaN
1	2016	199	v1	9473.0
2	2017	199	v1	8422.0
3	2018	299	v2	9987.0
4	2019	299	v2	7994.0
5	2020	349	v2	9530.0
6	2021	349	v3	9444.0

Figure 1.33: Outer join

You can see that with **outer join**, even the row that did not match (**2015**) is included.

Inner join returns records with matching values in **df1** and **df2**. From *Figure 1.32*, you can see that those are **6** and **7**. If you merged the products and revenue DataFrames using an inner join, you'd have the same output that you see in *Figure 1.33*. By default, pandas uses an inner join.

Left join returns all the records in the left DataFrame and the matched records in the right DataFrame. If any values are missing, it will fill those entries with **NaN** values. In the products and revenue DataFrames, a left join on the **CampaignYear** column would return even the row representing **2015**, except that the entry for revenue would be **NaN**.

Right join works similar to left join, except that it returns all the records from the right DataFrame along with just the matching records from the left DataFrame.

So far, you have seen how to merge DataFrames with the same column names. But what if you tried to merge DataFrames containing common data but with differently named columns? In such cases, you will have to specify the column names of the left and the right DataFrame as follows:

```
df_combined_specific = pd.merge(df_products, df_revenue, \
                                left_on="CampaignYear", \
                                right_on="CampaignYear2")
```

In the preceding code block, **left_on** specifies the column name of the left DataFrame (**df_products**), while **right_on** specifies the column name of the right DataFrame (**df_revenue**).

You have seen how to join DataFrames in this section. In the next section, you will be looking at how to handle missing values.

HANDLING MISSING DATA

As a marketing analyst, you will encounter data with missing values quite a lot. For example, let's say you join a **Product category** table with an **Ad viewership** table. Upon merging these two, you may find that not all product categories will have a corresponding value in the **Ad Viewership** table. For example, if a company ran no ads for winter clothes in tropical countries, values for those products in the **Ad Viewership** table would be missing. Such instances are quite common when dealing with real-world data.

Here's another example of missing data where the **category** column in the DataFrame has a missing value (demarcated by **NaN**):

	cities	adult_viewers	aged_viewers	young_viewers
0	[Delhi, Mumbai]	2500000	2300000	2000000
1	[Lucknow, Bhopal]	3500000	2800000	3000000
2	[Chennai, Bangalore]	1600000	2000000	1500000
3	[Kolkata, Hyderabad]	2000000	2000000	1500000

Figure 1.34: Sample DataFrame

While the way you can treat missing values varies based on the position of the missing values and the particular business use case, here are some general strategies that you can employ:

- You can get rid of missing values completely using **df.dropna**, as explained in the *Adding and Removing Attributes and Observations* section previously.

- You can also replace all the missing values simultaneously using **df.fillna()**.

When using **fillna()**, the value you want to fill in will depend heavily on the context and the use case for the data. For example, you can replace all missing values with the mean of the column where the missing value is present:

```
df.fillna(df.mean())
```

You should then get the following output:

	category	cities	adult_viewers	aged_viewers	young_viewers
0	1.0	[Delhi, Mumbai]	2500000	2300000	2000000
1	2.0	[Lucknow, Bhopal]	3500000	2800000	3000000
2	3.0	[Chennai, Bangalore]	1600000	2000000	1500000
3	2.0	[Kolkata, Hyderabad]	2000000	2000000	1500000

Figure 1.35: Output of the df.fillna(df.mean()) command

Or the median of the data, as in this example:

```
df.fillna(df.median())
```

You should then get the following output:

	category	cities	adult_viewers	aged_viewers	young_viewers
0	1.0	[Delhi, Mumbai]	2500000	2300000	2000000
1	2.0	[Lucknow, Bhopal]	3500000	2800000	3000000
2	3.0	[Chennai, Bangalore]	1600000	2000000	1500000
3	2.0	[Kolkata, Hyderabad]	2000000	2000000	1500000

Figure 1.36: Output of the df.fillna(df.median()) command

Or, with some values, such as **−1** (or any number of your choice) if you want the record to stand apart during your analysis:

```
df.fillna(-1)
```

You should then get the following output:

	category	cities	adult_viewers	aged_viewers	young_viewers
0	1.0	[Delhi, Mumbai]	2500000	2300000	2000000
1	2.0	[Lucknow, Bhopal]	3500000	2800000	3000000
2	3.0	[Chennai, Bangalore]	1600000	2000000	1500000
3	-1.0	[Kolkata, Hyderabad]	2000000	2000000	1500000

Figure 1.37: Using the df.fillna function

To help deal with missing values better, there are some other built-in functions you can use. These will help you quickly check whether your DataFrame contains any missing values.

You can check for slices containing missing values using the **isnull()** function:

```
df.isnull()
```

This command will return output like the following:

	category	cities	adult_viewers	aged_viewers	young_viewers
0	False	False	False	False	False
1	False	False	False	False	False
2	False	False	False	False	False
3	True	False	False	False	False

Figure 1.38: Using the .isnull function

The entries where there are null values will show up as **True**. If not, they'll show up as **False**.

Similarly, you can check whether individual elements are **NA** using the **isna** function. Here, we are using the **isna** function with the **category** column:

```
df[['category']].isna
```

The command will provide you with a Boolean output. **True** means that the element is null, and **False** means it is not:

	category
0	False
1	False
2	False
3	True

Figure 1.39: Using the isna function used on a column

In the next exercise, you will be combing different DataFrames and taking care of the missing values.

EXERCISE 1.03: COMBINING DATAFRAMES AND HANDLING MISSING VALUES

As part of its forthcoming holiday campaign, the business wanted to understand the cost of acquisition of customers for an e-commerce website specializing in kids' toys. As a marketing analyst, you now have to dig through the historical records of the previous campaign and suggest the marketing budget for the current campaign.

In this exercise, you will be importing two CSV files, **timeSpent.csv** and **cost.csv**, into the DataFrames **df1** and **df2**. The **df1** DataFrame has the details of the users, along with the time spent on the website. The **df2** DataFrame consists of the cost of acquisition of a user.

You will combine the DataFrame containing the time spent by the users with the other DataFrame containing the cost of acquisition of the user. You will merge both these DataFrames to get an idea of user behavior.

Perform the following steps to achieve the aim of this exercise:

1. Import the **pandas** modules that you will be using in this exercise:

    ```
    import pandas as pd
    ```

2. Load the CSV files into the DataFrames **df1** and **df2**:

    ```
    df1 =pd.read_csv("timeSpent.csv")
    df2 =pd.read_csv("cost.csv")
    ```

    > **NOTE**
    >
    > You can find the **timeSpent.csv** file at https://packt.link/bpfVk and the **cost.csv** file at https://packt.link/pmpkK.
    >
    > Also, do make sure that you modify the path (emboldened) based on where these files are saved on your system.

3. Examine the first few rows of the first DataFrame using the **head()** function:

    ```
    df1.head()
    ```

    You should get the following output:

	users	timeSpent
0	Sushmita	31.266056
1	Adam	17.900529
2	Benny	265.236086
3	Anurag	42.470696

    Figure 1.40: Contents of df1

    You can see that the DataFrame, **df1**, has two columns – **users** and **timeSpent**.

4. Next, look at the first few rows of the second dataset:

    ```
    df2.head()
    ```

You should get the following output:

	users	cost
0	Adam	20.0
1	Anurag	NaN
2	Benny	15.0
3	Sushmita	2.0
4	Apoorva	7.0

Figure 1.41: Contents of df2

As you can see, DataFrame **df2** has two columns – **users** and **cost**. In the cost column, there is a **NaN** value.

5. Do a left join of **df1** with **df2** and store the output in a DataFrame, **df**. Use a left join as we are only interested in users who are spending time on the website. Specify the joining key as **"users"**:

```
df = df1.merge(df2, on="users", how="left")
df.head()
```

Your output should now look as follows:

	users	timeSpent	cost
0	Sushmita	31.266056	2.0
1	Adam	17.900529	20.0
2	Benny	265.236086	15.0
3	Anurag	42.470696	NaN

Figure 1.42: Using the merge and fillna functions

6. You'll observe some missing values (**NaN**) in the preceding output. These types of scenarios are very common as you may fail to capture some details pertaining to the users. This can be attributed to the fact that some users visited the website organically and hence, the cost of acquisition is zero.

    These missing values can be replaced with the value **0**. Use the following code:

    ```
    df=df.fillna(0)
    df.head()
    ```

    Your output should now look as follows:

	users	timeSpent	cost
0	Sushmita	31.266056	2.0
1	Adam	17.900529	20.0
2	Benny	265.236086	15.0
3	Anurag	42.470696	0.0

    Figure 1.43: Imputing missing values with the fillna function

    Now, the DataFrame has no missing values and you can compute the average cost of acquisition along with the average time spent. To compute the average value, you will be using the built-in function **describe**, which gives the statistics of the numerical columns in the DataFrame. Run the following command:

    ```
    df.describe()
    ```

You should then get the following result:

	timeSpent	cost
count	4.000000	4.000000
mean	89.218342	9.250000
std	117.774200	9.776673
min	17.900529	0.000000
25%	27.924674	1.500000
50%	36.868376	8.500000
75%	98.162044	16.250000
max	265.236086	20.000000

Figure 1.44: Mean value of the columns

From the preceding screenshot, you can infer that the average cost of acquisition of a user is $9.25 and, on average, a user spends around 89 seconds on the website. Based on the traffic you want to attract for the forthcoming holiday season, you can now compute the marketing budget using the following formula:

```
Marketing Budget = Number of users * Cost of Acquisition
```

In this exercise, you have successfully dealt with missing values in your data. Do keep in mind that handling missing values is more of an art than science and each scenario might be different. In the next section, you will learn how to apply functions and operations on a DataFrame.

APPLYING FUNCTIONS AND OPERATIONS ON DATAFRAMES

By default, operations on all pandas objects are element-wise and return the same type of pandas objects. For instance, look at the following code:

```
df['viewers'] = df['adult_viewers']\
                +df['aged_viewers']+df['young_viewers']
```

The preceding code will add a **viewers** column to the DataFrame, with the value for each observation equaling the sum of the values in the **adult_viewers**, **aged_viewers**, and **young_viewers** columns.

Similarly, the following code will multiply every numerical value in the **viewers** column of the DataFrame by **0.03** or whatever value you want to keep as your target **CTR** (**click-through rate**):

```
df['expected clicks'] = 0.03*df['viewers']
```

Hence, your DataFrame will look as follows once these operations have been performed:

	category	cities	adult_viewers	aged_viewers	young_viewers	viewers	expected clicks
0	1.0	[Delhi, Mumbai]	2500000	2300000	2000000	6800000	204000.0
1	2.0	[Lucknow, Bhopal]	3500000	2800000	3000000	9300000	279000.0
2	3.0	[Chennai, Bangalore]	1600000	2000000	1500000	5100000	153000.0
3	NaN	[Kolkata, Hyderabad]	2000000	2000000	1500000	5500000	165000.0

Figure 1.45: Operations on pandas DataFrames

pandas also supports several built-in functions on pandas objects:

Function Name	Description
sum	Compute sum of elements
prod	Compute product of elements
mean	Compute mean of elements
std	Compute standard deviation
var	Compute variance
min	Find minimum value
max	Find maximum value
median	Compute median of elements
any	Evaluate whether any elements passed to the collection are true
all	Evaluate whether all elements passed to the collection are true

Figure 1.46: Built-in functions used in pandas

> **NOTE**
>
> Remember that pandas objects are Python objects, too. Therefore, you can write your custom functions to perform specific tasks on them.

To apply built-in or custom functions to pandas, you can make use of the **map** and **apply** functions. You can pass any built-in, NumPy, or custom functions as parameters to these functions and they will be applied to all elements in the column:

- **map**: **map** executes a function on each value present in the column. For example, look at the following DataFrame:

	viewers	views	users	cost	Gender
0	Sushmita	31.266056	Sushmita	2.000000	Female
1	Adam	17.900529	Adam	20.000000	Male
2	Benny	265.236086	Benny	15.000000	Male
3	Anurag	42.470696	Anurag	12.333333	Female

Figure 1.47: A sample DataFrame

Now, suppose you want to change the values of the **Gender** column to denote **Female** as **F** and **Male** as **M**. This can be achieved with the help of the **map** function. You'll need to pass values to the **map** function in the form of a dictionary:

```
df['Gender']=df['Gender'].map({"Female":"F","Male":"M"})
```

You should get the following result:

	viewers	views	users	cost	Gender
0	Sushmita	31.266056	Sushmita	2.000000	F
1	Adam	17.900529	Adam	20.000000	M
2	Benny	265.236086	Benny	15.000000	M
3	Anurag	42.470696	Anurag	12.333333	F

Figure 1.48: Using the map function

In the preceding screenshot, you can see that the values in the **Gender** column are now displayed as **M** and **F**.

- **apply**: This applies the function to the object passed and returns a DataFrame. It can easily take multiple columns as input. It also accepts the **axis** parameter, depending on how the function is to be applied. For example, let's say in the following DataFrame you wanted to sum all the purchases made by the user across the different categories and store the sum in a new column:

	viewers	views	users	electronics	food	furniture
0	Sushmita	31.266056	Sushmita	42.470696	14.177886	77.557639
1	Adam	17.900529	Adam	31.266056	209.896774	107.488676
2	Benny	265.236086	Benny	265.236086	0.658621	112.095155
3	Anurag	42.470696	Anurag	17.900529	192.594603	152.935554

Figure 1.49: Sample DataFrame

You can achieve this with the help of the **apply** function as follows:

```
df1['purchase']=df1[['electronics','food','furniture']]\
            .apply(np.sum,axis=1)
df1
```

> **NOTE**
>
> In the preceding code, since you're using NumPy, you will need to import the **numpy** library before trying out the code. You can do so by using **import numpy as np**.

You should then get the following result:

	viewers	views	users	electronics	food	furniture	purchase
0	Sushmita	31.266056	Sushmita	42.470696	14.177886	77.557639	134.206221
1	Adam	17.900529	Adam	31.266056	209.896774	107.488676	348.651506
2	Benny	265.236086	Benny	265.236086	0.658621	112.095155	377.989862
3	Anurag	42.470696	Anurag	17.900529	192.594603	152.935554	363.430686

Figure 1.50: Using the apply function

In the preceding screenshot, you can see that a new column, **purchase**, is created, which is the sum of the **electronics**, **food**, and **furniture** columns.

In this section, you have learned how to apply functions and operations to columns and rows of a DataFrame. In the next section, you will look at how to group data.

GROUPING DATA

Let's suppose, based on certain conditions, that you wanted to apply a function to multiple rows of a DataFrame. For example, you may need to do so when you want to calculate the sum of product prices separately for each currency. The pythonic way to solve this problem is to slice the DataFrame on the key(s) you want to aggregate on and then apply your function to that group, store the values, and move on to the next group. pandas provides a better way to do this, using the **groupby** function.

Let's look at the following DataFrame:

	viewers	views	users	cost	Gender
0	Sushmita	31.266056	Sushmita	2.000000	F
1	Adam	17.900529	Adam	20.000000	M
2	Benny	265.236086	Benny	15.000000	M
3	Anurag	42.470696	Anurag	12.333333	F

Figure 1.51: Sample DataFrame

If you want to find out the total cost of acquisition based on gender, you can use the following code:

```
df.groupby('Gender')['cost'].sum()
```

You should then get the following output:

```
Gender
F     14.333333
M     35.000000
Name: cost, dtype: float64
```

Figure 1.52: Using the groupby function

In the preceding screenshot, you can see that the male users have a higher cost of acquisition than female users. In the next exercise, you will implement some of the operations you have learned so far.

EXERCISE 1.04: APPLYING DATA TRANSFORMATIONS

In *Exercise 1.01, Loading Data Stored in a JSON File*, you worked with a JSON file that contained the details of the users of a shopping app. There, your task was to validate whether the data was loaded correctly and to provide some answers about the information contained in it. Since you confirmed that the data was loading correctly, you'll be working with the same dataset once again, but this time, you'll be analyzing the underlying data. Also, this time, you'll be answering some interesting questions that the marketing team has come up with:

- What is the average age of the users?

- Which is the favorite fruit of the users?

- Do you have more female customers?

- How many of the users are active?

This exercise aims to get you used to performing regular and **groupby** operations on DataFrames and applying functions to them. You will use the **user_info.json** file on GitHub.

> **NOTE**
>
> You can find the **user_info.json** file at the following link:
> https://packt.link/Gi2Q7.

1. Import the **pandas** module using the following command:

```
import pandas as pd
```

2. Read the **user_info.json** file into a pandas DataFrame, **user_info**, using the following command:

```
user_info = pd.read_json('user_info.json')
```

> **NOTE**
>
> Make sure you change the path (emboldened) to the JSON file based on its location on your system. If you're running the Jupyter notebook from the same directory where the JSON file is stored, you can run the preceding code without any modification.

3. Now, examine whether your data is properly loaded by checking the first few values in the DataFrame. Do this using the **head()** command:

```
user_info.head()
```

You should get the following output:

	_id	index	guid	isActive	balance	picture	age
0	5c0a28d7a647437fd3d3a6aa	0	832f1af4-fb18-4ba8-b032-f4cbf343dbe9	False	$3,806.93	http://placehold.it/32x32	20
1	5c0a28d780f6278b11586ab1	1	4306cb37-9506-48c2-8ccf-e69a063589ee	True	$3,330.01	http://placehold.it/32x32	22

Figure 1.53: Output of the head function on user_info

> **NOTE**
>
> Not all columns and rows are shown in the preceding output.

The data consists of session information of the customers, along with their demographic details, contact information, and other details.

4. Now, look at the attributes and the data inside them using the following command:

```
user_info.info()
```

You should get the following output:

```
<class 'pandas.core.frame.DataFrame'>
RangeIndex: 6 entries, 0 to 5
Data columns (total 22 columns):
 #    Column          Non-Null Count   Dtype
---   ------          --------------   -----
 0    _id             6 non-null       object
 1    index           6 non-null       int64
 2    guid            6 non-null       object
 3    isActive        6 non-null       bool
 4    balance         6 non-null       object
 5    picture         6 non-null       object
 6    age             6 non-null       int64
 7    eyeColor        6 non-null       object
 8    name            6 non-null       object
 9    gender          6 non-null       object
 10   company         6 non-null       object
 11   email           6 non-null       object
 12   phone           6 non-null       object
 13   address         6 non-null       object
 14   about           6 non-null       object
 15   registered      6 non-null       object
 16   latitude        6 non-null       float64
 17   longitude       6 non-null       float64
 18   tags            6 non-null       object
 19   friends         6 non-null       object
 20   greeting        6 non-null       object
 21   favoriteFruit   6 non-null       object
dtypes: bool(1), float64(2), int64(2), object(17)
memory usage: 1.1+ KB
```

Figure 1.54: Output of the info function on user_info

5.   Now, let's start answering the questions:

What is the average age of the users? To find the average age, use the following code:

```
user_info['age'].mean()
```

You will get the output as **27.83**, which means that the average age of the users is 27.83.

Which is the favorite fruit among the users? To answer this question, you can use the **groupby** function on the **favoriteFruit** column and get a count of users with the following code:

```
user_info.groupby('favoriteFruit')['_id'].count()
```

You should get the following output:

```
favoriteFruit
apple          3
strawberry     3
Name: _id, dtype: int64
```

Figure 1.55: Output of the count function

From the preceding screenshot, you can see that there is no clear winner as both **apple** and **strawberry** have the same count of **3**.

Do you have more female customers? To answer this question, you need to count the number of male and female users. You can find this count with the help of the **groupby** function. Use the following code:

```
user_info.groupby('gender')['_id'].count()
```

You should get the following output:

```
gender
female     3
male       3
Name: _id, dtype: int64
```

Figure 1.56: Output of the count function

From the preceding screenshot, you can infer that you have an equal split of customers concerning gender. Now, let's move on to our last question.

How many of the users are active? Similar to the preceding questions, you can use the **groupby** function on the **isActive** column to find out the answer.

Use the following code:

```
user_info.groupby('isActive')['_id'].count()
```

You should get the following output:

```
isActive
False    3
True     3
Name: _id, dtype: int64
```

Figure 1.57: Output of the count function

From the preceding screenshot, you see that three customers are active while the other three are inactive.

This exercise acts as a short introduction to applying data transformations, functions, and getting an overview of aggregation, which can come in handy during the exploratory phase of a project.

Now that you have learned the different aspects of data preparation and cleaning, let's test your skills with the help of the following activity.

ACTIVITY 1.01: ADDRESSING DATA SPILLING

The data we receive in most cases is not clean. There will be issues such as missing values, incorrect data types, data not loaded properly in the columns, and more. As a marketing analyst, you will have to clean this data and render it in a usable format so that you can analyze it further to mine useful information.

In this activity, you will now solve the problem that you encountered in *Exercise 1.02, Loading Data from Multiple Sources*. You will start by loading **sales.csv**, which contains some historical sales data about different customer purchases in stores in the past few years. As you may recall, the data loaded in the DataFrame was not correct as the values of some columns were getting populated wrongly in other columns. The goal of this activity is to clean the DataFrame and make it into a usable form.

You need to read the files into pandas DataFrames and prepare the output so that it can be used for further analysis. Follow the steps given here:

1. Open a new Jupyter notebook and import the **pandas** module.

2. Load the data from **sales.csv** into a separate DataFrame, named **sales**, and look at the first few rows of the generated DataFrame.

> **NOTE**
>
> You can find the **sales.csv** file at https://packt.link/IDGB4.

You should get the following output:

	Year	Product	line	Product.1	type	Product.2	Order	method	type.1	Retailer	country	Revenue
0	2004	Camping	Equipment	Cooking	Gear	TrailChef	Water	Bag	Telephone	United	States	315044.33
1	2004	Camping	Equipment	Cooking	Gear	TrailChef	Water	Bag	Telephone	Canada	NaN	14313.48
2	2004	Camping	Equipment	Cooking	Gear	TrailChef	Water	Bag	Telephone	Mexico	NaN	156644.47
3	2004	Camping	Equipment	Cooking	Gear	TrailChef	Water	Bag	Telephone	Brazil	NaN	59191.72
4	2004	Camping	Equipment	Cooking	Gear	TrailChef	Water	Bag	Telephone	Japan	NaN	7029.33

Figure 1.58: Output of the head function on sales.csv

3. Analyze the data type of the fields.

4. Look at the first column. If the value in the column matches the expected values, move on to the next column or otherwise fix it with the correct value.

5. Once you have fixed the first column, examine the other columns one by one and try to ascertain whether the values are right.

> **HINT**
>
> As per the information from the product team, the file contains information about their product line, which is camping equipment, along with information about their flagship product.

Once you have cleaned the DataFrame, your final output should appear as follows:

	Year	Order method	Revenue	Product line	Product type	Product	Retailer country
0	2004	Telephone	315044.33	Camping Equipment	Cooking Gear	TrailChef Water Bag	United States
1	2004	Telephone	14313.48	Camping Equipment	Cooking Gear	TrailChef Water Bag	Canada
2	2004	Telephone	156644.47	Camping Equipment	Cooking Gear	TrailChef Water Bag	Mexico
3	2004	Telephone	59191.72	Camping Equipment	Cooking Gear	TrailChef Water Bag	Brazil
4	2004	Telephone	7029.33	Camping Equipment	Cooking Gear	TrailChef Water Bag	Japan

Figure 1.59: First few rows of the structured DataFrame

NOTE

The solution for this activity can be found on page 474.

SUMMARY

In this chapter, you have learned how to structure datasets by arranging them in a tabular format. Then, you learned how to combine data from multiple sources. You also learned how to get rid of duplicates and needless columns. Along with that, you discovered how to effectively address missing values in your data. By learning how to perform these steps, you now have the skills to make your data ready for further analysis.

Data processing and wrangling are the most important steps in marketing analytics. Around 60% of the efforts in any project are spent on data processing and exploration. Data processing when done right can unravel a lot of value and insights. As a marketing analyst, you will be working with a wide variety of data sources, and so the skills you have acquired in this chapter will help you to perform common data cleaning and wrangling tasks on data obtained in a variety of formats.

In the next chapter, you will enhance your understanding of pandas and learn about reshaping and analyzing DataFrames to visualize and summarize data better. You will also see how to directly solve generic business-critical problems efficiently.

2

DATA EXPLORATION AND VISUALIZATION

OBJECTIVES

In this chapter, you will learn to explore, analyze, and reshape your data so that you can shed light on the attributes of your data that are important to the business – a key skill in a marketing analyst's repertoire. You will discover functions that will help you derive summary and descriptive statistics from your data. You will build pivot tables and perform comparative tests and analyses to discover hidden relationships between various data points. Later, you will create impactful visualizations by using two of the most popular Python packages, Matplotlib and seaborn.

INTRODUCTION

"How does this data make sense to the business?" It's a critical question you'll need to ask every time you start working with a new, raw dataset. Even after you clean and prepare raw data, you won't be able to derive actionable insights from it just by scanning through thousands of rows and columns. To be able to present the data in a way that it provides value to the business, you may need group similar rows, re-arrange the columns, generate detailed charts, and more. Manipulating and visualizing the data to uncover insights that stakeholders can easily understand and implement is a key skill in a marketing analyst's toolbox. This chapter is all about learning that skill.

In the last chapter, you learned how you can transform raw data with the help of pandas. You saw how to clean the data and handle the missing values after which the data can be structured into a tabular form. The structured data can be further analyzed so that meaningful information can be extracted from it.

In this chapter, you'll discover the functions and libraries that help you explore and visualize your data in greater detail. You will go through techniques to explore and analyze data through solving some problems critical for businesses, such as identifying attributes useful for marketing, analyzing key performance indicators, performing comparative analyses, and generating insights and visualizations. You will use the pandas, Matplotlib, and seaborn libraries in Python to solve these problems.

Let us begin by first understanding how we can identify the attributes that will help us derive insights from our data.

IDENTIFYING AND FOCUSING ON THE RIGHT ATTRIBUTES

Whether you're trying to meet your marketing goals or solve problems in an existing marketing campaign, a structured dataset may comprise numerous rows and columns. In such cases, deriving actionable insights by studying each attribute might prove challenging and time-consuming. The better your data analysis skills are, the more valuable the insights you'll be able to generate in a shorter amount of time. A prudent marketing analyst would use their experience to determine the attributes that are not needed for the study; then, using their data analysis skills, they'd remove such attributes from the dataset. It is these data analysis skills that you'll be building in this chapter.

Learning to identify the right attributes is one aspect of the problem, though. Marketing goals and campaigns often involve target metrics. These metrics may depend on domain knowledge and business acumen and are known as **key performance indicators** (**KPIs**). As a marketing analyst, you'll need to be able to analyze the relationships between the attributes of your data to quantify your data in line with these metrics. For example, you may be asked to derive any of the following commonly used KPIs from a dataset comprising 30 odd columns:

- **Revenue**: What are the total sales the company is generating in a given time frame?

- **Profit**: What is the money a company makes from its total sales after deducting its expenses?

- **Customer Life Cycle Value**: What is the metric that indicates the total revenue the company can expect from a customer throughout his association?

- **Customer Acquisition cost**: What is the amount of money a company spends to convert a prospective lead to a customer?

- **Conversion rate**: How many of all the people you have targeted for a marketing campaign have actually bought the product or used the company's services?

- **Churn**: How many customers have stopped using the company's services or have stopped buying the product?

> **NOTE**
>
> These are only the commonly used KPIs. You'll find that there are numerous more in the marketing domain.

You will of course have to get rid of columns that are not needed, and then use your data analysis tools to calculate the needed metrics. pandas, the library we encountered in the previous chapter, provides quite a lot of such tools in the form of functions and collections that help generate insights and summaries. One such useful function is `groupby`.

THE GROUPBY( ) FUNCTION

Take a look at the following data stored in an Excel sheet:

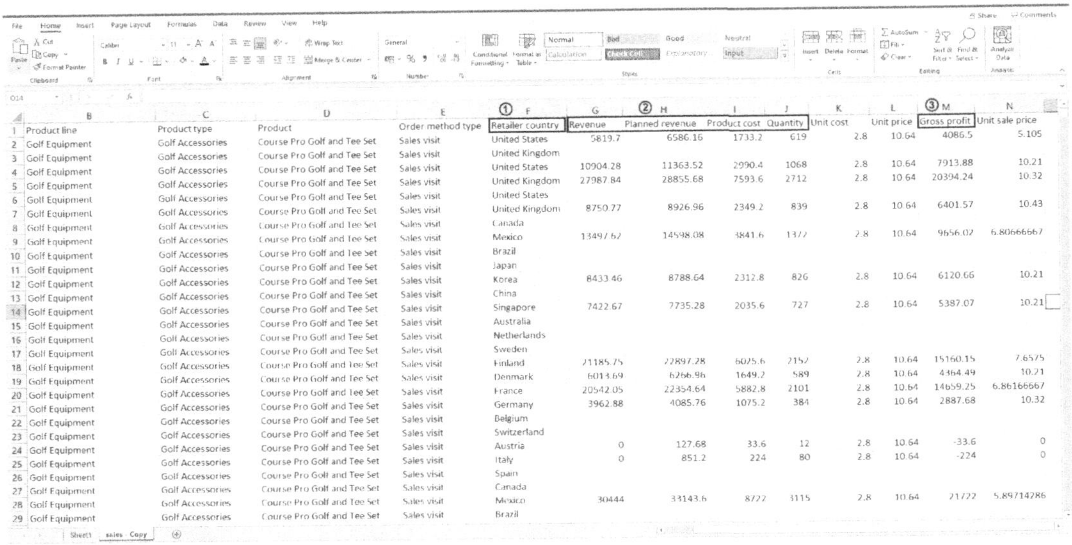

	B	C	D	E	① F	G	② H	I	J	K	L	③ M	N
1	Product line	Product type	Product	Order method type	Retailer country	Revenue	Planned revenue	Product cost	Quantity	Unit cost	Unit price	Gross profit	Unit sale price
2	Golf Equipment	Golf Accessories	Course Pro Golf and Tee Set	Sales visit	United States	5819.7	6586.16	1733.2	619	2.8	10.64	4086.5	5.105
3	Golf Equipment	Golf Accessories	Course Pro Golf and Tee Set	Sales visit	United Kingdom								
4	Golf Equipment	Golf Accessories	Course Pro Golf and Tee Set	Sales visit	United States	10904.28	11363.52	2990.4	1068	2.8	10.64	7913.88	10.21
5	Golf Equipment	Golf Accessories	Course Pro Golf and Tee Set	Sales visit	United Kingdom	27987.84	28855.68	7593.6	2712	2.8	10.64	20394.24	10.32
6	Golf Equipment	Golf Accessories	Course Pro Golf and Tee Set	Sales visit	United States								
7	Golf Equipment	Golf Accessories	Course Pro Golf and Tee Set	Sales visit	United Kingdom	8750.77	8926.96	2349.2	839	2.8	10.64	6401.57	10.43
8	Golf Equipment	Golf Accessories	Course Pro Golf and Tee Set	Sales visit	Canada								
9	Golf Equipment	Golf Accessories	Course Pro Golf and Tee Set	Sales visit	Mexico	13497.62	14598.08	3841.6	1372	2.8	10.64	9656.02	6.80666667
10	Golf Equipment	Golf Accessories	Course Pro Golf and Tee Set	Sales visit	Brazil								
11	Golf Equipment	Golf Accessories	Course Pro Golf and Tee Set	Sales visit	Japan								
12	Golf Equipment	Golf Accessories	Course Pro Golf and Tee Set	Sales visit	Korea	8433.46	8788.64	2312.8	826	2.8	10.64	6120.66	10.21
13	Golf Equipment	Golf Accessories	Course Pro Golf and Tee Set	Sales visit	China								
14	Golf Equipment	Golf Accessories	Course Pro Golf and Tee Set	Sales visit	Singapore	7422.67	7735.28	2035.6	727	2.8	10.64	5387.07	10.21
15	Golf Equipment	Golf Accessories	Course Pro Golf and Tee Set	Sales visit	Australia								
16	Golf Equipment	Golf Accessories	Course Pro Golf and Tee Set	Sales visit	Netherlands								
17	Golf Equipment	Golf Accessories	Course Pro Golf and Tee Set	Sales visit	Sweden								
18	Golf Equipment	Golf Accessories	Course Pro Golf and Tee Set	Sales visit	Finland	21185.75	22897.28	6025.6	2152	2.8	10.64	15160.15	7.6575
19	Golf Equipment	Golf Accessories	Course Pro Golf and Tee Set	Sales visit	Denmark	6013.69	6266.96	1649.2	589	2.8	10.64	4364.49	10.21
20	Golf Equipment	Golf Accessories	Course Pro Golf and Tee Set	Sales visit	France	20542.05	22354.64	5882.8	2101	2.8	10.64	14659.25	6.86166667
21	Golf Equipment	Golf Accessories	Course Pro Golf and Tee Set	Sales visit	Germany	3962.88	4085.76	1075.2	384	2.8	10.64	2887.68	10.32
22	Golf Equipment	Golf Accessories	Course Pro Golf and Tee Set	Sales visit	Belgium								
23	Golf Equipment	Golf Accessories	Course Pro Golf and Tee Set	Sales visit	Switzerland								
24	Golf Equipment	Golf Accessories	Course Pro Golf and Tee Set	Sales visit	Austria	0	127.68	33.6	12	2.8	10.64	-33.6	0
25	Golf Equipment	Golf Accessories	Course Pro Golf and Tee Set	Sales visit	Italy	0	851.2	224	80	2.8	10.64	-224	0
26	Golf Equipment	Golf Accessories	Course Pro Golf and Tee Set	Sales visit	Spain								
27	Golf Equipment	Golf Accessories	Course Pro Golf and Tee Set	Sales visit	Canada								
28	Golf Equipment	Golf Accessories	Course Pro Golf and Tee Set	Sales visit	Mexico	30444	33143.6	8722	3115	2.8	10.64	21722	5.89714286
29	Golf Equipment	Golf Accessories	Course Pro Golf and Tee Set	Sales visit	Brazil								

Figure 2.1: Sample sales data in an Excel sheet

You don't need to study all the attributes of the data as you'll be working with it later on. But suppose, using this dataset, you wanted to individually calculate the sums of values stored in the following columns: **`Revenue`**, **`Planned Revenue`**, **`Product Cost`**, **`Quantity`** (all four columns annotated by *2*), and **`Gross profit`** (annotated by *3*). Then, you wanted to segregate the sums of values for each column by the countries listed in column **`Retailer_country`** (annotated by *1*). Before making any changes to it, your first task would be to visually analyze the data and find patterns in it.

Looking at the data, you can see that country names are repeated quite a lot. Now instead of calculating how many uniquely occurring countries there are, you can simply *group* these rows together using pivot tables as follows:

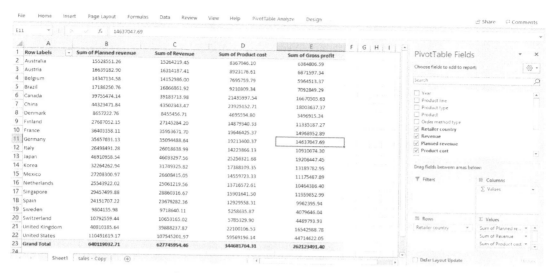

Figure 2.2: Pivot of sales data in Excel

In the preceding figure, not only is the data grouped by various countries, the values for **Planned Revenue**, **Revenue**, **Product cost**, and **Gross profit** are summed as well. That solves our problem. But what if this data was stored in a DataFrame?

This is where the **groupby** function comes in handy.

```
groupby(col)[cols].agg_func
```

This function groups rows with similar values in a column denoted by **col** and applies the aggregator function **agg_func** to the column of the DataFrame denoted by **cols**.

For example, think of the sample sales data as a DataFrame **df**. Now, you want to find out the total planned revenue by country. For that, you will need to group the countries and focusing on the **Planned revenue** column, sum all the values that correspond to the grouped countries. In the following command, we are grouping the values present in the **Retailer country** column and adding the corresponding values of the **Planned revenue** column.

```
df.groupby('Retailer country')['Planned revenue'].sum()
```

You'd get an output similar to the following:

```
Retailer country
Australia     15528551.26
Austria       16639182.90
Belgium       14347134.58
Brazil        17186250.76
Canada        39755474.14
China         44323471.84
Denmark        8657222.76
Finland       27687052.15
France        36403358.11
Germany       35657691.13
Name: Planned revenue, dtype: float64
```

Figure 2.3: Calculating total Planned Revenue Using groupby()

The preceding output shows the sum of planned revenue grouped by country. To help us better compare the results we got here with the results of our pivot data in *Figure 2.2*, we can also chain another command as follows:

```
df.groupby('Retailer country')['Planned revenue'].sum().round()
```

You should get the following output:

```
Retailer country
Australia     15528551.0
Austria       16639183.0
Belgium       14347135.0
Brazil        17186251.0
Canada        39755474.0
China         44323472.0
Denmark        8657223.0
Finland       27687052.0
France        36403358.0
Germany       35657691.0
Name: Planned revenue, dtype: float64
```

Figure 2.4: Chaining multiple functions to groupby

If we compare the preceding output to what we got in *Figure 2.2*, we can see that we have achieved the same results as the pivot functionality in Excel but using a built-in pandas function.

Some of the most common aggregator functions that can be used alongside **groupby** function are as follows:

- **count()**: This function returns the total number of values present in the column.

- **min()**: This function returns the minimum value present in the column.

- **max()**: This function returns the maximum value present in the column.

- **mean()**: This function returns the mean of all values in the column.

- **median()**: This function returns the median value in the column.

- **mode()**: This function returns the most frequently occurring value in the column.

Next, let us look into another pandas function that can help us derive useful insights.

THE UNIQUE( ) FUNCTION

While you know how to group data based on certain attributes, there are times when you don't know which attribute to choose to group the data by (or even make other analyses). For example, suppose you wanted to focus on *customer life cycle* value to design targeted marketing campaigns. Your dataset has attributes such as *recency*, *frequency*, and *monetary values*. Just looking at the dataset, you won't be able to understand how the attributes in each column vary. For example, one column might comprise lots of rows with numerous unique values, making it difficult to use the **groupby()** function on it. The other might be replete with duplicate values and have just two unique values. Thus, examining how much your values vary in a column is essential before doing further analysis. pandas provides a very handy function for doing that, and it's called **unique()**.

For example, let's say you have a dataset called **customerdetails** that contains the names of customers, their IDs, and their countries. The data is stored in a DataFrame **df** and you would like to see a list of all the countries you have customers in.

	Customer ID	Customer Name	Country
0	101	Tom	Australia
1	102	Fred	Canada
2	103	Amy	Spain
3	104	Sergio	Spain
4	105	Amy	India
5	106	Dominic	Austria
6	107	Xi	China
7	108	Hector	Japan
8	109	Annie	Switzerland

Figure 2.5: DataFrame df

Just by looking at the data, you see that there are a lot of countries in the column titled **Country**. Some country names are repeated multiple times. To know where your customers are located around the globe, you'll have to *filter out* all the unique values in this column. To do that, you can use the unique function as follows:

```
df['Country'].unique()
```

You should get the following output:

```
array(['Australia', 'Canada', 'Spain', 'India', 'Austria', 'China',
       'Japan', 'Switzerland', 'UK', 'New Zealand', 'USA'], dtype=object)
```

Figure 2.6: Different country names

You can see from the preceding output that the customers are from the following countries – Australia, Canada, Spain, India, Austria, China, Japan, Switzerland, the UK, New Zealand, and the USA.

Now that you know which countries your customers belong to, you may also want to know how many customers are present in each of these countries. This can be taken care of by the **value_counts()** function provided by pandas.

THE VALUE_COUNTS( ) FUNCTION

Sometimes, apart from just seeing what the unique values in a column are, you also want to know the count of each unique value in that column. For example, if, after running the **unique()** function, you find out that **Product 1**, **Product 2**, and **Product 3** are the only three values that are repeated in a column comprising 1,000 rows; you may want to know how many entries of each product there are in the column. In such cases, you can use the **value_counts()** function. This function displays the unique values of the categories along with their counts.

Let's revisit the **customerdetails** dataset we encountered in the previous section. To find out the number of customers present in each country, we can use the **value_counts()** function as follows:

```
df['Country'].value_counts()
```

You will get output similar to the following:

```
UK                 2
Australia          2
Spain              2
USA                2
Austria            2
Canada             2
New Zealand        2
India              2
Japan              2
Switzerland        1
China              1
Name: Country, dtype: int64
```

Figure 2.7: Output of value_counts function

From the preceding output, you can see that the count of each country is provided against the country name. Now that you have gotten a hang of these methods, let us implement them to derive some insights from sales data.

EXERCISE 2.01: EXPLORING THE ATTRIBUTES IN SALES DATA

You and your team are creating a marketing campaign for a client. All they've handed you is a file called **sales.csv**, which as they explained, contains the company's historical sales records. Apart from that, you know nothing about this dataset.

Using this data, you'll need to derive insights that will be used to create a comprehensive marketing campaign. Not all insights may be useful to the business, but since you will be presenting your findings to various teams first, an insight that's useful for one team may not matter much for the other team. So, your approach would be to gather as many actionable insights as possible and present those to the stakeholders.

You neither know the time period of these historical sales nor do you know which products the company sells. Download the file **sales.csv** from GitHub and create as many actionable insights as possible.

> **NOTE**
>
> You can find **sales.csv** at the following link: https://packt.link/Z2gRS.

1. Open a new Jupyter Notebook to implement this exercise. Save the file as **Exercise2-01.ipnyb**. In a new Jupyter Notebook cell, import the **pandas** library as follows

```
import pandas as pd
```

2. Create a new pandas DataFrame named **sales** and read the **sales.csv** file into it. Examine if your data is properly loaded by checking the first few values in the DataFrame by using the **head()** command:

```
sales = pd.read_csv('sales.csv')
sales.head()
```

NOTE

Make sure you change the path (highlighted) to the CSV file based on its location on your system. If you're running the Jupyter Notebook from the same directory where the CSV file is stored, you can run the preceding code without any modification.

Your output should look as follows:

	Year	Product line	Product type	Product	Order method type	Retailer country	Revenue	Planned revenue	Product cost	Quantity	Unit cost	Unit price	Gross profit	Unit sale price
0	2004	Golf Equipment	Golf Accessories	Course Pro Golf and Tee Set	Sales visit	United States	5819.70	6586.16	1733.2	619.0	2.8	10.64	4086.50	5.105
1	2004	Golf Equipment	Golf Accessories	Course Pro Golf and Tee Set	Sales visit	United Kingdom	NaN	NaN	NaN	NaN	NaN	NaN	NaN	NaN
2	2005	Golf Equipment	Golf Accessories	Course Pro Golf and Tee Set	Sales visit	United States	10904.28	11363.52	2990.4	1068.0	2.8	10.64	7913.88	10.210
3	2005	Golf Equipment	Golf Accessories	Course Pro Golf and Tee Set	Sales visit	United Kingdom	27987.84	28855.68	7593.6	2712.0	2.8	10.64	20394.24	10.320
4	2006	Golf Equipment	Golf Accessories	Course Pro Golf and Tee Set	Sales visit	United States	NaN	NaN	NaN	NaN	NaN	NaN	NaN	NaN

Figure 2.8: The first five rows of sales.csv

3. Examine the columns of the DataFrame using the following code:

```
sales.columns
```

This produces the following output:

```
Index(['Year', 'Product line', 'Product type', 'Product', 'Order method type',
       'Retailer country', 'Revenue', 'Planned revenue', 'Product cost',
       'Quantity', 'Unit cost', 'Unit price', 'Gross profit',
       'Unit sale price'],
      dtype='object')
```

Figure 2.9: The columns in sales.csv

4. Use the **info** function to print the datatypes of columns of **sales** DataFrame using the following code:

```
sales.info()
```

This should give you the following output:

```
<class 'pandas.core.frame.DataFrame'>
RangeIndex: 17823 entries, 0 to 17822
Data columns (total 14 columns):
 #   Column             Non-Null Count  Dtype
---  ------             --------------  -----
 0   Year               17823 non-null  int64
 1   Product line       17823 non-null  object
 2   Product type       17823 non-null  object
 3   Product            17823 non-null  object
 4   Order method type  17823 non-null  object
 5   Retailer country   17823 non-null  object
 6   Revenue            6045 non-null   float64
 7   Planned revenue    6045 non-null   float64
 8   Product cost       6045 non-null   float64
 9   Quantity           5860 non-null   float64
 10  Unit cost          6045 non-null   float64
 11  Unit price         6045 non-null   float64
 12  Gross profit       6045 non-null   float64
 13  Unit sale price    6045 non-null   float64
dtypes: float64(8), int64(1), object(5)
memory usage: 1.9+ MB
```

Figure 2.10: Information about the sales DataFrame

From the preceding output, you can see that **Year** is of **int** data type and columns such as **Product line**, **Product type**, etc. are of the **object** types.

5. To check the time frame of the data, use the **unique** function on the **Year** column:

```
sales['Year'].unique()
```

You will get the following output:

```
array([2004, 2005, 2006, 2007], dtype=int64)
```

Figure 2.11: The number of years the data is spread over

You can see that we have the data for the years **2004 – 2007**.

6. Use the **unique** function again to find out the types of products that the company is selling:

```
sales['Product line'].unique()
```

You should get the following output:

```
array(['Golf Equipment', 'Camping Equipment', 'Outdoor Protection',
        'Mountaineering Equipment'], dtype=object)
```

Figure 2.12: The different product lines the data covers

You can see that company is selling four different types of products.

7. Now, check the **Product type** column:

```
sales['Product type'].unique()
```

You will get the following output:

```
array(['Golf Accessories', 'Sleeping Bags', 'Cooking Gear', 'First Aid',
        'Insect Repellents', 'Climbing Accessories'], dtype=object)
```

Figure 2.13: The different types of products the data covers

From the above output, you can see that you have six different product types namely **Golf Accessories**, **Sleeping Bags**, **Cooking Gear**, **First Aid**, **Insect Repellents**, and **Climbing Accessories**.

8. Check the **Product** column to find the unique categories present in it:

```
sales['Product'].unique()
```

You will get the following output:

```
array(['Course Pro Golf and Tee Set', 'Hibernator Self - Inflating Mat',
        'TrailChef Deluxe Cook Set', 'Deluxe Family Relief Kit',
        'Course Pro Golf Bag', 'TrailChef Water Bag',
        'TrailChef Kitchen Kit', 'TrailChef Cook Set',
        'TrailChef Single Flame', 'TrailChef Double Flame',
        'Hibernator Camp Cot', 'BugShield Lotion Lite',
        'Compact Relief Kit', 'Insect Bite Relief', 'Course Pro Umbrella',
        'Course Pro Gloves', 'Firefly Climbing Lamp',
        'Firefly Rechargeable Battery', 'Granite Chalk Bag',
        'TrailChef Canteen', 'TrailChef Cup', 'TrailChef Kettle',
        'TrailChef Utensils', 'Hibernator Lite', 'Hibernator Extreme',
        'Hibernator Pad', 'Hibernator Pillow', 'BugShield Natural',
        'BugShield Spray', 'BugShield Lotion', 'BugShield Extreme',
        'Calamine Relief', 'Aloe Relief', 'Granite Carabiner',
        'Granite Belay', 'Granite Pulley', 'Firefly Charger', 'Hibernator'],
       dtype=object)
```

Figure 2.14: Different products covered in the dataset

The above output shows the different products that are sold.

9. Now, check the **Order method type** column to find out the ways through which the customer can place an order:

```
sales['Order method type'].unique()
```

You will get the following output:

```
array(['Sales visit', 'Telephone', 'Web', 'Special', 'Mail', 'E-mail',
       'Fax'], dtype=object)
```

Figure 2.15: Different ways in which people making purchases have ordered

As you can see from the preceding figure, there are seven different order methods through which a customer can place an order.

10. Use the same function again on the **Retailer country** column to find out the countries where the client has a presence:

```
sales['Retailer country'].unique()
```

You will get the following output:

```
array(['United States', 'United Kingdom', 'Canada', 'Mexico', 'Brazil',
       'Japan', 'Korea', 'China', 'Singapore', 'Australia', 'Netherlands',
       'Sweden', 'Finland', 'Denmark', 'France', 'Germany', 'Belgium',
       'Switzerland', 'Austria', 'Italy', 'Spain'], dtype=object)
```

Figure 2.16: The countries in which products have been sold

The preceding output shows the geographical presence of the company.

11. Now that you have analyzed the categorical values, get a quick summary of the numerical fields using the **describe** function:

```
sales.describe()
```

This gives the following output:

	Year	Revenue	Planned revenue	Product cost	Quantity	Unit cost	Unit price	Gross profit	Unit sale price
count	17823.000000	6.045000e+03	6.045000e+03	6.045000e+03	5860.000000	6045.000000	6045.000000	6.045000e+03	6045.000000
mean	2005.164955	1.038455e+05	1.058923e+05	5.701932e+04	4691.273549	58.882618	48.900855	4.336203e+04	44.795072
std	0.956260	1.836042e+05	1.881274e+05	1.117846e+05	8950.955313	348.369401	62.814500	7.185831e+04	58.399255
min	2004.000000	0.000000e+00	0.000000e+00	3.360000e+01	5.000000	0.850000	3.660000	-1.336560e+04	0.000000
25%	2004.000000	1.364924e+04	1.383736e+04	5.759760e+03	625.000000	2.760000	7.000000	7.009650e+03	6.580000
50%	2005.000000	4.154119e+04	4.189571e+04	1.906720e+04	1695.000000	9.000000	18.000000	1.894653e+04	17.650000
75%	2006.000000	1.120026e+05	1.144758e+05	5.796000e+04	4858.000000	34.970000	66.770000	5.002308e+04	62.760000
max	2007.000000	3.644349e+06	3.477910e+06	2.061750e+06	164142.000000	7833.000000	265.140000	1.416160e+06	265.140000

Figure 2.17: Description of the numerical columns in sales.csv

You can observe that the mean revenue the company is earning is around **$103,846**. The **describe** function is used to give us an overall idea about the range of the data present in the DataFrame.

12. Analyze the spread of the categorical columns in the data using the **value_counts()** function. This would shed light on how the data is distributed. Start with the **Year** column:

```
sales['Year'].value_counts()
```

This gives the following output:

```
2004    5451
2005    5451
2006    5451
2007    1470
Name: Year, dtype: int64
```

Figure 2.18: Frequency table of the Year column

From the above result, you can see that you have around **5451** records in the years **2004**, **2005**, and **2006** and the number of records in the year **2007** is **1470**.

13. Use the same function on the **Product line** column:

```
sales['Product line'].value_counts()
```

This gives the following output:

```
Camping Equipment          8562
Outdoor Protection         4410
Mountaineering Equipment   3087
Golf Equipment             1764
Name: Product line, dtype: int64
```

Figure 2.19: Frequency table of the Product line column

As you can see from the preceding output, **Camping Equipment** has the highest number of observations in the dataset followed by **Outdoor Protection**.

14. Now, check for the **Product type** column:

```
sales['Product type'].value_counts()
```

This gives the following output:

```
Cooking Gear              5880
Climbing Accessories      3087
Sleeping Bags             2682
First Aid                 2205
Insect Repellents         2205
Golf Accessories          1764
Name: Product type, dtype: int64
```

Figure 2.20: Frequency table of the Product line column

Cooking gear followed by **climbing accessories** has the highest number of observations in the dataset which means that these product types are quite popular among the customers.

15. Now, find out the most popular order method using the following code:

```
sales['Order method type'].value_counts()
```

This gives the following output:

```
Mail           2547
Web            2547
Telephone      2547
Special        2547
Fax            2547
E-mail         2547
Sales visit    2541
Name: Order method type, dtype: int64
```

Figure 2.21: Frequency table of the Product line column

Almost all the order methods are equally represented in the dataset which means customers have an equal probability of ordering through any of these methods.

16. Finally, check for the **Retailer country** column along with their respective counts:

```
sales['Retailer country'].value_counts()
```

You should get the following output:

```
United Kingdom    865
United States     865
Switzerland       847
Netherlands       847
Japan             847
Singapore         847
China             847
France            847
Spain             847
Korea             847
Denmark           847
Austria           847
Sweden            847
Australia         847
Italy             847
Canada            847
Belgium           847
Germany           847
Finland           847
Brazil            847
Mexico            847
Name: Retailer country, dtype: int64
```

Figure 2.22: Frequency table of the Product line column

The preceding result shows that data points are evenly distributed among all the countries showing no bias.

17. Get insights into country-wide statistics now. Group attributes such as **Revenue, Planned revenue, Product cost, Quantity**, and **Gross profit** by their countries, and sum their corresponding values. Use the following code:

```
sales.groupby('Retailer country')[['Revenue',\
                        'Planned revenue',\
                        'Product cost',\
                        'Quantity',\
                        'Gross profit']].sum()
```

You should get the following output:

Retailer country	Revenue	Planned revenue	Product cost	Quantity	Gross profit
Australia	1.526422e+07	1.552855e+07	8367046.10	649467.0	6384806.59
Austria	1.631419e+07	1.663918e+07	8923176.61	719084.0	6871597.34
Belgium	1.415299e+07	1.434713e+07	7695759.79	622150.0	5964513.37
Brazil	1.686686e+07	1.718625e+07	9210809.34	744353.0	7092849.29
Canada	3.918371e+07	3.975547e+07	21435997.54	1701123.0	16670505.63
China	4.350234e+07	4.432347e+07	23925152.71	1935454.0	18003637.37
Denmark	8.455457e+06	8.657223e+06	4695594.80	368479.0	3496915.24
Finland	2.714528e+07	2.768705e+07	14879340.33	1207265.0	11335187.27
France	3.595367e+07	3.640336e+07	19646425.37	1620252.0	14968952.89
Germany	3.509449e+07	3.565769e+07	19213400.37	1576459.0	14637047.69
Italy	2.601864e+07	2.649849e+07	14223866.13	1142868.0	10910074.30
Japan	4.603330e+07	4.691096e+07	25256321.68	2047615.0	19208447.45
Korea	3.174933e+07	3.226426e+07	17388109.35	1432122.0	13189782.95
Mexico	2.660842e+07	2.720830e+07	14559723.33	1173878.0	11175487.89
Netherlands	2.506122e+07	2.554392e+07	13716572.61	1121981.0	10464386.40
Singapore	2.886032e+07	2.945750e+07	15901641.50	1270886.0	11959852.99
Spain	2.367628e+07	2.415171e+07	12929558.31	1052358.0	9962395.94
Sweden	9.718640e+06	9.804136e+06	5258635.87	432962.0	4079646.04
Switzerland	1.065317e+07	1.079256e+07	5785329.90	465683.0	4489793.93
United Kingdom	3.988824e+07	4.081019e+07	22100106.53	1656837.0	16542988.78
United States	1.075452e+08	1.104916e+08	59569196.14	4549587.0	44714622.05

Figure 2.23: Total revenue, cost, quantities sold, and profit in each country
in the past four years

From the preceding figure, you can infer that Denmark had the least revenue
and the US had the highest revenue in the past four years. Most countries
generated revenue of around **20,000,000** USD and almost reached their
revenue targets.

18. Now find out the country whose product performance was affected the worst when sales dipped. Use the following code to group data by **Retailer country**:

```
sales.dropna().groupby('Retailer country')\
                [['Revenue',\
                  'Planned revenue',\
                  'Product cost',\
                  'Quantity',\
                  'Unit cost',\
                  'Unit price',\
                  'Gross profit',\
                  'Unit sale price']].min()
```

You should get the following output:

Retailer country	Revenue	Planned revenue	Product cost	Quantity	Unit cost	Unit price	Gross profit	Unit sale price
Australia	0.0	294.00	120.78	49.0	0.85	3.66	-558.00	0.000000
Austria	0.0	0.00	33.60	5.0	0.85	3.66	-360.00	0.000000
Belgium	0.0	0.00	70.18	6.0	0.85	3.66	-280.72	0.000000
Brazil	966.0	966.00	455.63	138.0	0.85	3.66	510.37	3.192857
Canada	198.0	198.00	93.39	33.0	0.85	3.66	53.40	2.875000
China	0.0	618.00	291.49	103.0	0.85	3.66	-840.00	0.000000
Denmark	0.0	738.00	312.96	40.0	0.85	3.66	-2561.74	0.000000
Finland	486.0	486.00	223.56	81.0	0.85	3.66	262.44	3.141429
France	0.0	230.12	90.24	43.0	0.85	3.66	-190.40	0.000000
Germany	234.0	0.00	110.37	32.0	0.85	3.66	-1119.04	0.000000
Italy	0.0	330.00	154.56	55.0	0.85	3.66	-224.00	0.000000
Japan	0.0	0.00	67.20	22.0	0.85	3.66	-1225.18	0.000000
Korea	276.0	276.00	130.18	46.0	0.85	3.66	-3831.84	3.137143
Mexico	432.0	432.00	203.76	51.0	0.85	3.66	-542.00	2.615000
Netherlands	0.0	308.57	113.28	40.0	0.85	3.66	-13365.60	0.000000
Singapore	576.0	576.00	271.68	32.0	0.85	3.66	1.28	3.142857
Spain	348.0	348.00	160.08	40.0	0.85	3.66	103.68	2.200000
Sweden	0.0	0.00	67.76	23.0	0.85	3.66	-1438.56	0.000000
Switzerland	0.0	162.00	74.52	27.0	0.85	3.66	-2790.00	0.000000
United Kingdom	0.0	264.00	124.52	44.0	0.85	3.66	-4009.68	0.000000
United States	0.0	156.90	57.60	24.0	0.85	3.66	-186.00	0.000000

Figure 2.24: The lowest price, quantity, cost prices, and so on for each country

Since most of the values in the gross profit column are negative, you can infer that almost every product has at some point made a loss in the target markets. Brazil, Spain, Finland, and Canada are some exceptions.

19. Similarly, generate statistics for other categorical variables, such as **Year**, **Product line**, **Product type**, and **Product**. Use the following code for the **Year** variable:

```
sales.groupby('Year')[['Revenue',\
                       'Planned revenue',\
                       'Product cost',\
                       'Quantity',\
                       'Unit cost',\
                       'Unit price',\
                       'Gross profit',\
                       'Unit sale price']].sum()
```

This gives the following output:

Year	Revenue	Planned revenue	Product cost	Quantity	Unit cost	Unit price	Gross profit	Unit sale price
2004	1.528977e+08	1.567331e+08	8.538058e+07	7318558.0	97750.174438	92781.46	62482134.57	84841.786496
2005	1.908502e+08	1.947044e+08	1.029861e+08	8453776.0	113381.098628	103147.42	81126260.32	93071.003707
2006	2.228721e+08	2.270020e+08	1.209524e+08	8786835.0	134772.241249	82126.84	95563977.64	76786.074337
2007	6.112591e+07	6.167953e+07	3.536268e+07	2931694.0	10041.912620	17549.95	22951118.87	16087.343791

Figure 2.25: Total revenue, cost, quantities, and so on sold every year

From the above figure, it appears that revenue, profits, and quantities have dipped in the year **2007**.

20. Use the following code for the **Product line** variable:

```
sales.groupby('Product line')[['Revenue',\
                               'Planned revenue',\
                               'Product cost',\
                               'Quantity',\
                               'Unit cost',\
                               'Unit price',\
                               'Gross profit',\
                               'Unit sale price']].sum()
```

You should get the following output:

Product line	Revenue	Planned revenue	Product cost	Quantity	Unit cost	Unit price	Gross profit	Unit sale price
Camping Equipment	4.860065e+08	4.966410e+08	2.862390e+08	15200145.0	323199.354903	214876.61	1.825174e+08	195361.436414
Golf Equipment	4.205702e+07	4.235803e+07	1.525444e+07	2367637.0	14195.740000	39488.03	2.483757e+07	36115.529168
Mountaineering Equipment	5.254793e+07	5.293751e+07	2.522232e+07	3672582.0	11540.322032	24108.88	2.639106e+07	23103.209617
Outdoor Protection	4.713449e+07	4.818252e+07	1.796598e+07	6250499.0	7010.010000	17132.15	2.837751e+07	16206.033132

Figure 2.26: Total revenue, cost, quantities, and so on, generated by each product division

The preceding figure indicates that the sale of **Camping Equipment** contributes the highest to the overall revenue of the company.

21. Now, find out which order method contributes to the maximum revenue:

```
sales.groupby('Order method type')[['Revenue',\
                                     'Planned revenue',\
                                     'Product cost',\
                                     'Quantity',\
                                     'Gross profit']].sum()
```

You should get the following output:

Order method type	Revenue	Planned revenue	Product cost	Quantity	Gross profit
E-mail	3.238293e+07	3.301196e+07	1.768881e+07	1503654.0	1.352462e+07
Fax	1.376507e+07	1.399805e+07	7.399451e+06	653190.0	5.993243e+06
Mail	9.749679e+06	9.942812e+06	5.211545e+06	483151.0	4.175907e+06
Sales visit	6.946909e+07	7.141927e+07	3.870416e+07	3084491.0	2.890578e+07
Special	6.642340e+06	6.618693e+06	3.550795e+06	324760.0	2.824776e+06
Telephone	7.056328e+07	7.230265e+07	3.889483e+07	3200421.0	2.907046e+07
Web	4.251736e+08	4.328256e+08	2.332322e+08	18241196.0	1.776287e+08

Figure 2.27: Average revenue, cost, quantities, and so on generated by each method of ordering

Observe that the highest sales were generated through the internet (more than all the other sources combined).

Now that you've generated the insights, it's time to select the most useful ones, summarize them, and present them to the business as follows:

Metric	Observation
Product with maximum revenue contribution	Camping Equipment
Order method with the highest sales	Internet
Markets with positive gross profit	Brazil, Canada, Finland, Spain, and Singapore
The country with the least revenue in the last four years	Denmark
The country with the highest revenue in the last four years	USA

Figure 2.28: Summary of the derived insights

In this exercise, you have successfully explored the attributes in a dataset. In the next section, you will learn how to generate targeted insights from the prepared data.

> **NOTE**
>
> You'll be working with the **sales.csv** data in the upcoming section as well. It's recommended that you keep the Jupyter Notebook open and continue there.

FINE TUNING GENERATED INSIGHTS

Now that you've generated a few insights, it's important to fine-tune your results to cater to the business. This can involve small changes like renaming columns or relatively big ones like turning a set of rows into columns. pandas provides ample tools that help you fine-tune your data so that you can extract insights from it that are more comprehensible and valuable to the business. Let's examine a few of them in the section that follows.

SELECTING AND RENAMING ATTRIBUTES

At times, you might notice variances in certain attributes of your dataset. You may want to isolate those attributes so that you can examine them in greater detail. The following functions come in handy for performing such tasks:

- **loc[label]**: This method selects rows and columns by a **label** or by a boolean condition.

- **loc[row_labels, cols]**: This method selects rows present in **row_labels** and their values in the **cols** columns.

- `iloc[location]`: This method selects rows by integer location. It can be used to pass a list of row indices, slices, and so on.

In the **sales** DataFrame you can use the loc method to select, based on a certain condition, the values of **Revenue**, **Quantity**, and **Gross Profit** columns:

```
sales.loc[sales['Retailer country']=='United States', \
          ['Revenue', 'Quantity', 'Gross profit']].head()
```

This code selects values from the **Revenue**, **Quantity**, and **Gross profit** columns only if the Retailer country is the United States. The output of the first five rows should be:

	Revenue	Quantity	Gross profit
0	5819.70	619.0	4086.50
2	10904.28	1068.0	7913.88
4	NaN	NaN	NaN
63	159492.97	16137.0	114309.37
65	159040.72	15773.0	114876.32

Figure 2.29: Sub-selecting observations and attributes in pandas

Let's also learn about `iloc`. Even though you won't be using it predominantly in your analysis, it is good to know how it works. For example, in the **sales** DataFrame, you can select the first two rows (**0,1**) and the first 3 columns (**0,1,2**) using the **iloc** method as follows.

```
sales.iloc[[0,1],[0,1,2]]
```

This should give you the following output:

	Year	Product line	Product type
0	2004	Golf Equipment	Golf Accessories
1	2004	Golf Equipment	Golf Accessories

Figure 2.30: Sub-selecting observations using iloc

At times, you may find that the attributes of your interest might not have meaningful names, or, in some cases, they might be incorrectly named as well. For example, Profit may be named as P&L, making it harder to interpret. To address such issues, you can use the **rename** function in pandas to rename columns as well as the indexes.

The **rename** function takes a dictionary as an input, which contains the current column name as a key and the desired renamed attribute name as value. It also takes the axis as a parameter, which denotes whether the index or the column should be renamed.

The syntax of the function is as follows.

```
df.rename({'old column name':'new column name'},axis=1)
```

The preceding code will change the **'old column name'** to **'new column name'**. Here, **axis=1** is used to rename across columns. The following code renames the **Revenue** column to **Earnings**:

```
sales=sales.rename({'Revenue':'Earnings'}, axis = 1)
sales.head()
```

Since we're using the parameter **axis=1**, we are renaming across columns. The resulting DataFrame will now be:

	Year	Product line	Product type	Product	Order method type	Retailer country	Earnings	Planned revenue	Product cost	Quantity
0	2004	Golf Equipment	Golf Accessories	Course Pro Golf and Tee Set	Sales visit	United States	5819.70	6586.16	1733.2	619.0
1	2004	Golf Equipment	Golf Accessories	Course Pro Golf and Tee Set	Sales visit	United Kingdom	NaN	NaN	NaN	NaN
2	2005	Golf Equipment	Golf Accessories	Course Pro Golf and Tee Set	Sales visit	United States	10904.28	11363.52	2990.4	1068.0

Figure 2.31: Output after using the rename function on sales

NOTE

The preceding image does not show all the rows of the output.

From the preceding output, you can observe that the **Revenue** column is now represented as **Earnings**. In the next section, we will understand how to transform values numerical values into categorical ones and vice versa.

Up until this chapter, we've been using the **sales.csv** dataset and deriving insights from it. Now, in the upcoming section and exercise, we will be working on another dataset (we will revisit **sales.csv** in *Exercise 2.03, Visualizing Data with pandas*).

In the next section, we will be looking at how to reshape data as well as its implementation.

RESHAPING THE DATA

Sometimes, changing how certain attributes and observations are arranged can help understand the data better, focus on the relevant parts, and extract more information.

Let's consider the data present in **CTA_comparison.csv**. The dataset consists of Click to Action data of various variants of ads for a mobile phone along with the corresponding views and sales. **Click to Action** (**CTA**) is a marketing terminology that prompts the user for some kind of response.

> **NOTE**
>
> You can find the **CTA_comparison.csv** file here: https://packt.link/RHxDI.

Let's store the data in a DataFrame named **cta** as follows:

```
cta = pd.read_csv('CTA_comparison.csv')
cta
```

> **NOTE**
>
> Make sure you change the path (highlighted) to the CSV file based on its location on your system. If you're running the Jupyter Notebook from the same directory where the CSV file is stored, you can run the preceding code without any modification.

You should get the following DataFrame:

	time	CTA Variant	views	sales
0	12:30:00	A	500	100
1	13:30:00	B	800	50
2	14:30:00	C	300	14
3	15:30:00	A	700	94
4	16:30:00	C	300	20
5	17:30:00	B	800	45
6	18:30:00	B	800	56

Figure 2.32: Snapshot of the data in CTA_comparison.csv

NOTES

The outputs in *Figure 2.32*, *Figure 2.33*, and *Figure 2.34* are truncated.
These are for demonstration purposes only.

The DataFrame consists of CTA data for various variants of the ad along with the corresponding timestamps.

But, since we need to analyze the variants in detail, the **CTA Variant** column should be the index of the DataFrame and not **time**. For that, we'll need to reshape the data frame so that **CTA Variant** becomes the index. This can be done in pandas using the **set_index** function.

You can set the index of the **cta** DataFrame to **CTA Variant** using the following code:

```
cta.set_index('CTA Variant')
```

The DataFrame will now appear as follows:

CTA Variant	time	views	sales
A	12:30:00	500	100
B	13:30:00	800	50
C	14:30:00	300	14
A	15:30:00	700	94
C	16:30:00	300	20
B	17:30:00	800	45
B	18:30:00	800	56
C	19:30:00	250	18

Figure 2.33: Changing the index with the help of set_index

You can also reshape data by creating multiple indexes. This can be done by passing multiple columns to the **set_index** function. For instance, you can set the **CTA Variant** and **views** as the indexes of the DataFrame as follows:

```
cta.set_index(['CTA Variant', 'views'])
```

The DataFrame will now appear as follows:

CTA Variant	views	time	sales
A	500	12:30:00	100
B	800	13:30:00	50
C	300	14:30:00	14
A	700	15:30:00	94
C	300	16:30:00	20
B	800	17:30:00	45
B	800	18:30:00	56
C	250	19:30:00	18

Figure 2.34: Hierarchical Data in pandas through set_index

In the preceding figure, you can see that **CTA Variant** and **views** are set as indexes. The same hierarchy can also be created, by passing multiple columns to the **groupby** function:

```
cta_views = cta.groupby(['CTA Variant', 'views']).count()
cta_views
```

This gives the following output:

CTA Variant	views		
A	500	2	2
	700	1	1
B	800	3	3
C	250	1	1
	300	2	2

Figure 2.35: Grouping by multiple columns to generate hierarchies

Using this hierarchy, you can see that **CTA Variant** B with **800** views is present thrice in the data.

Sometimes, switching the indices from rows to columns and vice versa can reveal greater insights into the data. This reshape transformation is achieved in pandas by using the **unstack** and **stack** functions:

- **unstack(level)**: This function moves the row index with the name or integral location level to the innermost column index. By default, it moves the innermost row:

```
h1 = cta_views.unstack(level = 'CTA Variant')
h1
```

This gives the following output:

CTA Variant	time			sales		
views	A	B	C	A	B	C
250	NaN	NaN	1.0	NaN	NaN	1.0
300	NaN	NaN	2.0	NaN	NaN	2.0
500	2.0	NaN	NaN	2.0	NaN	NaN
700	1.0	NaN	NaN	1.0	NaN	NaN
800	NaN	3.0	NaN	NaN	3.0	NaN

Figure 2.36: Example of unstacking DataFrames

You can see that the row index has changed to only **views** while the column has got the additional **CTA Variant** attribute as an index along with the existing **time** and **sales** columns.

- **stack(level)**: This function moves the column index with the name or integral location level to the innermost row index. By default, it moves the innermost column:

```
h1.stack(0)
```

This gives the following output:

views	CTA Variant	A	B	C
250	sales	NaN	NaN	1.0
	time	NaN	NaN	1.0
300	sales	NaN	NaN	2.0
	time	NaN	NaN	2.0
500	sales	2.0	NaN	NaN
	time	2.0	NaN	NaN
700	sales	1.0	NaN	NaN
	time	1.0	NaN	NaN
800	sales	NaN	3.0	NaN
	time	NaN	3.0	NaN

Figure 2.37: Example of stacking a DataFrame

Now the stack function has taken the other **sales** and **time** column values to the row index and only the **CTA Variant** feature has become the column index.

In the next exercise, you will implement stacking and unstacking with the help of a dataset.

EXERCISE 2.02: CALCULATING CONVERSION RATIOS FOR WEBSITE ADS.

You are the owner of a website that randomly shows advertisements **A** or **B** to users each time a page is loaded. The performance of these advertisements is captured in a simple file called **conversion_rates.csv**. The file contains two columns: **converted** and **group**. If an advertisement succeeds in getting a user to click on it, the **converted** field gets the value **1**, otherwise, it gets **0** by default; the **group** field denotes which ad was clicked – **A** or **B**.

As you can see, comparing the performance of these two ads is not that easy when the data is stored in this format. Use the skills you've learned so far, store this data in a data frame and modify it to show, in one table, information about:

1. The number of views ads in each group got.

2. The number of ads converted in each group.

3. The conversion ratio for each group.

> **NOTE**
>
> You can find the **conversion_rates.csv** file here: https://packt.link/JyEic.

1. Open a new Jupyter Notebook to implement this exercise. Save the file as **Exercise2-02.ipnyb**. Import the **pandas** library using the **import** command, as follows:

```
import pandas as pd
```

2. Create a new pandas DataFrame named **data** and read the **conversion_rates.csv** file into it. Examine if your data is properly loaded by checking the first few values in the DataFrame by using the **head()** command:

```
data = pd.read_csv('conversion_rates.csv')
data.head()
```

NOTE

Make sure you change the path (highlighted) to the CSV file based on its location on your system. If you're running the Jupyter Notebook from the same directory where the CSV file is stored, you can run the preceding code without any modification.

You should get the following output:

	converted	group
0	0	B
1	0	B
2	0	A
3	0	B
4	0	A

Figure 2.38: The first few rows of conversion_rates.csv

3. Group the data by the group **column** and count the number of conversions. Store the result in a DataFrame named **converted_df**:

```
converted_df = data.groupby('group').sum()
converted_df
```

You will get the following output:

	converted
group	
A	90
B	21

Figure 2.39: Count of converted displays

From the preceding output, you can see that group **A** has **90** people who have converted. This means that advertisement **A** is quite successful compared to **B**.

4. We would like to find out how many people have viewed the advertisement. For that use the **groupby** function to group the data and the **count()** function to count the number of times each advertisement was displayed. Store the result in a DataFrame **viewed_df**. Also, make sure you change the column name from **converted** to **viewed**:

```
viewed_df = data.groupby('group').count()\
                .rename({'converted':'viewed'}, \
                    axis = 'columns')
viewed_df
```

You will get the following output:

group	viewed
A	1030
B	970

Figure 2.40: Count of number of views

You can see that around **1030** people viewed advertisement **A** and **970** people viewed advertisement **B**.

5. Combine the **converted_df** and **viewed_df** datasets in a new DataFrame, named **stats** using the following commands:

```
stats = converted_df.merge(viewed_df, on = 'group')
stats
```

This gives the following output:

group	converted	viewed
A	90	1030
B	21	970

Figure 2.41: Combined dataset

From the preceding figure, you can see that group **A** has **1030** people who viewed the advertisement, and **90** of them got converted.

6. Create a new column called **conversion_ratio** that displays the ratio of converted ads to the number of views the ads received:

```
stats['conversion_ratio'] = stats['converted']\
                            /stats['viewed']
stats
```

This gives the following output:

	converted	viewed	conversion_ratio
group			
A	90	1030	0.087379
B	21	970	0.021649

Figure 2.42: Adding a column to stats

From the preceding figure, you can see that group **A** has a better conversion factor when compared with group **B**.

7. Create a DataFrame **df** where group **A**'s conversion ratio is accessed as **df['A'] ['conversion_ratio']**. Use the **stack** function for this operation:

```
df = stats.stack()
df
```

This gives the following output:

```
group
A       converted             90.000000
        viewed              1030.000000
        conversion_ratio       0.087379
B       converted             21.000000
        viewed               970.000000
        conversion_ratio       0.021649
dtype:  float64
```

Figure 2.43: Understanding the different levels of your dataset

From the preceding figure, you can see the group-wise details which are easier to understand.

8. Check the conversion ratio of group **A** using the following code:

```
df['A']['conversion_ratio']
```

You should get a value of **0.08738**.

9. To bring back the data to its original form we can reverse the rows with the columns in the **stats** DataFrame with the **unstack()** function twice:

```
stats.unstack().unstack()
```

This gives the following output:

group	A	B
converted	90.000000	21.000000
viewed	1030.000000	970.000000
conversion_ratio	0.087379	0.021649

Figure 2.44: Reversing rows with columns

This is exactly the information we needed in the goal of the exercise, stored in a neat, tabulated format. It is clear by now that ad **A** is performing much better than ad **B** given its better conversion ratio.

In this exercise, you have reshaped the data in a readable format. pandas also provides a simpler way to reshape the data that allows making comparisons while analyzing data very easy. Let's have a look at it in the next section.

PIVOT TABLES

A pivot table can be used to summarize, sort, or group data stored in a table. You've already seen an example of the pivot table functionality in excel; this one's similar to that. With a pivot table, you can transform rows to columns and columns to rows. The **pivot** function is used to create a pivot table. It creates a new table, whose row and column indices are the unique values of the respective parameters.

For example, consider the **data** DataFrame you saw in *Step 2* of the preceding exercise:

	converted	group
0	0	B
1	0	B
2	0	A
3	0	B
4	0	A

Figure 2.45: The first few rows of the dataset being considered

You can use the **pivot** function to change the columns to rows as follows:

```
data=data.pivot(columns = 'group', values='converted')
data.head()
```

This gives the following output:

group	A	B
0	NaN	0.0
1	NaN	0.0
2	0.0	NaN
3	NaN	0.0
4	0.0	NaN

Figure 2.46: Data after being passed through the pivot command

In the preceding figure, note that the columns and indices have changed but the observations individually have not. You can see that the data that had either a **0** or **1** value remains as it is, but the groups that were not considered have their remaining values filled in as **NaN**.

There is also a function called **pivot_table**, which aggregates fields together using the function specified in the **aggfunc** parameter and creates outputs accordingly. It is an alternative to aggregations such as **groupby** functions. For instance, if we apply the **pivot_table** function to the same DataFrame to aggregate the data:

```
data.pivot_table(index='group', columns='converted', aggfunc=len)
```

This gives the following output:

converted	0	1
group		
A	940	90
B	949	21

Figure 2.47: Applying pivot_table to data

Note that the use of the **len** argument results in columns **0** and **1** that show how many times each of these values appeared in each group. Remember that, unlike pivot, it is essential to pass the **aggfunc** function when using the **pivot_table** function.

In the next section, you will be learning how to understand your data even better by visually representing it.

VISUALIZING DATA

There are a lot of benefits to presenting data visually. Visualized data is easy to understand, and it can help reveal hidden trends and patterns in data that might not be so conspicuous compared to when the data is presented in numeric format. Furthermore, it is much quicker to interpret visual data. That is why you'll notice that many businesses rely on dashboards comprising multiple charts. In this section, you will learn the functions that will help you visualize numeric data by generating engaging plots. Once again, pandas comes to our rescue with its built-in **plot** function. This function has a parameter called **kind** that lets you choose between different types of plots. Let us look at some common types of plots you'll be able to create.

Density plots:

A density plot helps us to find the distribution of a variable. In a density plot, the peaks display where the values are concentrated.

Here's a sample density plot drawn for the **Product cost** column in a **sales** DataFrame:

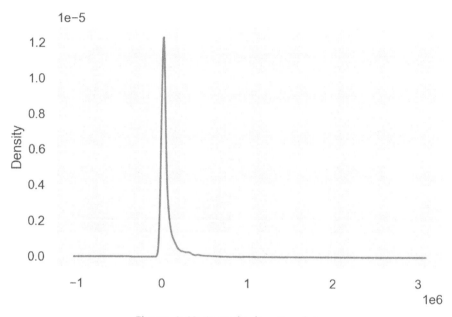

Figure 2.48: Sample density plot

In this plot, the **Product cost** is distributed with a peak very close to **0**. In pandas, you can create density plots using the following command:

```
df['Column'].plot(kind = 'kde',color='gray')
```

> **NOTE**
>
> The value **gray** for the attribute **color** is used to generate graphs in grayscale. You can use other colors like **darkgreen**, **maroon**, etc. as values of **color** parameters to get the colored graphs.

Bar Charts:

Bar charts are used with categorical variables to find their distribution. Here is a sample bar chart:

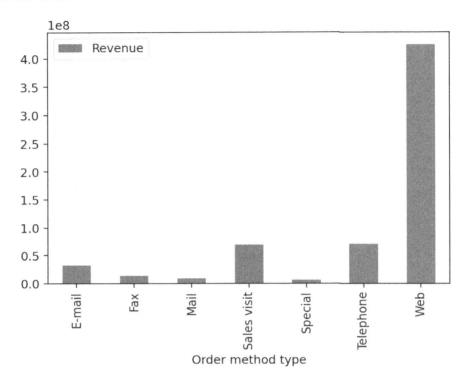

Figure 2.49: Sample bar chart

In this plot, you can see the distribution of revenue of the product via different order methods. In pandas, you can create bar plots by passing **bar** as value to the **kind** parameter.

```
df['Column'].plot(kind = 'bar', color='gray')
```

Box Plot:

A box plot is used to depict the distribution of numerical data and is primarily used for comparisons. Here is a sample box plot:

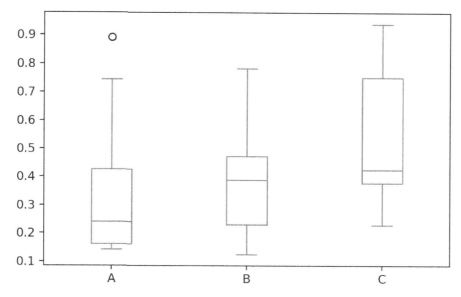

Figure 2.50: Sample box plot

The line inside the box represents the median values for each numerical variable. In pandas, you can create a box plot by passing **box** as a value to the **kind** parameter:

```
df['Column'].plot(kind = 'box', color='gray')
```

Scatter Plot:

Scatter plots are used to represent the values of two numerical variables. Scatter plots help you to determine the relationship between the variables.

Here is a sample scatter plot:

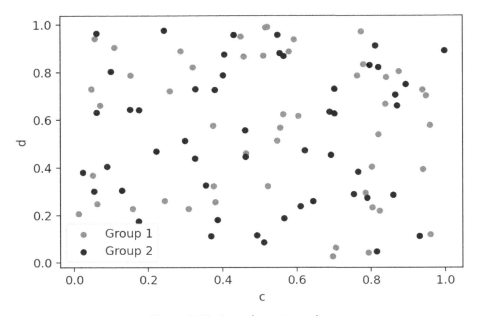

Figure 2.51: Sample scatter plot

In this plot, you can observe the relationship between the two variables. In pandas, you can create scatter plots by passing **scatter** as a value to the **kind** parameter.

```
df['Column'].plot(kind = 'scatter', color='gray')
```

Let's implement these concepts in the exercise that follows.

EXERCISE 2.03: VISUALIZING DATA WITH PANDAS

In this exercise, you'll be revisiting the **sales.csv** file you worked on in *Exercise 2.01, Exploring the Attributes in Sales Data*. This time, you'll need to visualize the sales data to answer the following two questions:

1. Which mode of order generates the most revenue?

2. How have the following parameters varied over four years: Revenue, Planned revenue, and Gross profit?

> **NOTE**
>
> You can find the **sales.csv** file here: https://packt.link/dhAbB.

You will make use of bar plots and box plots to explore the distribution of the **Revenue** column.

1. Open a new Jupyter Notebook to implement this exercise. Save the file as **Exercise2-03.ipnyb**.

2. Import the **pandas** library using the **import** command as follows:

```
import pandas as pd
```

3. Create a new panda DataFrame named **sales** and load the **sales.csv** file into it. Examine if your data is properly loaded by checking the first few values in the DataFrame by using the **head()** command:

```
sales = pd.read_csv("sales.csv")
sales.head()
```

> **NOTE**
>
> Make sure you change the path (highlighted) to the CSV file based on its location on your system. If you're running the Jupyter notebook from the same directory where the CSV file is stored, you can run the preceding code without any modification.

You will get the following output:

	Year	Product line	Product type	Product	Order method type	Retailer country	Revenue	Planned revenue	Product cost	Quantity	Unit cost	Unit price	Gross profit	Unit sale price
0	2004	Golf Equipment	Golf Accessories	Course Pro Golf and Tee Set	Sales visit	United States	5819.70	6586.16	1733.2	619.0	2.8	10.64	4086.50	5.105
1	2004	Golf Equipment	Golf Accessories	Course Pro Golf and Tee Set	Sales visit	United Kingdom	NaN	NaN	NaN	NaN	NaN	NaN	NaN	NaN
2	2005	Golf Equipment	Golf Accessories	Course Pro Golf and Tee Set	Sales visit	United States	10904.28	11363.52	2990.4	1068.0	2.8	10.64	7913.88	10.210
3	2005	Golf Equipment	Golf Accessories	Course Pro Golf and Tee Set	Sales visit	United Kingdom	27987.84	28855.68	7593.6	2712.0	2.8	10.64	20394.24	10.320
4	2006	Golf Equipment	Golf Accessories	Course Pro Golf and Tee Set	Sales visit	United States	NaN	NaN	NaN	NaN	NaN	NaN	NaN	NaN

Figure 2.52: Output of sales.head()

4. Group the **Revenue** by **Order method type** and create a bar plot:

```
sales.groupby('Order method type').sum()\
    .plot(kind = 'bar', y = 'Revenue', color='gray')
```

This gives the following output:

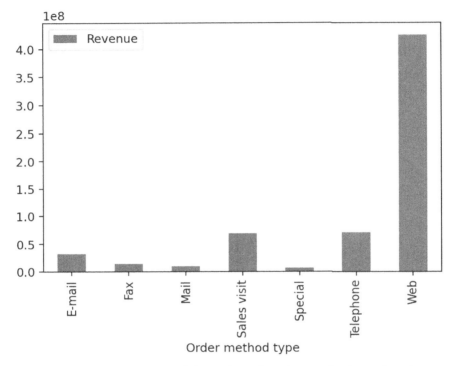

Figure 2.53: Revenue generated through each order method type in sales.csv

From the preceding image, you can infer that web orders generate the maximum revenue.

5. Now group the columns by year and create boxplots to get an idea on a relative scale:

```
sales.groupby('Year')[['Revenue', 'Planned revenue', \
                'Gross profit']].plot(kind= 'box',\
                                color='gray')
```

NOTE

In *Steps 4* and *5*, the value **gray** for the attribute **color** (emboldened) is used to generate graphs in grayscale. You can use other colors like **darkgreen**, **maroon**, etc. as values of **color** parameter to get the colored graphs. You can also refer to the following document to get the code for the colored plot and the colored output: https://packt.link/NOjgT.

You should get the following plots:

The first plot represents the year 2004, the second plot represents the year 2005, the third plot represents the year 2006 and the final one represents 2007.

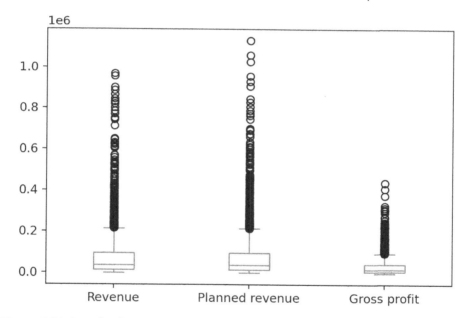

Figure 2.54: Boxplot for Revenue, Planned revenue and Gross profit for year 2004

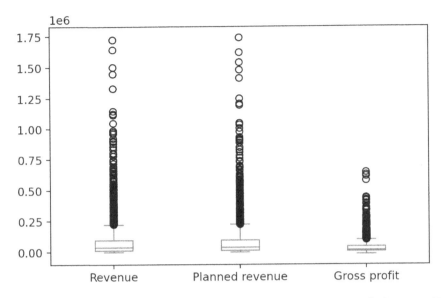

Figure 2.55: Boxplot for Revenue, Planned revenue and Gross profit for year 2005

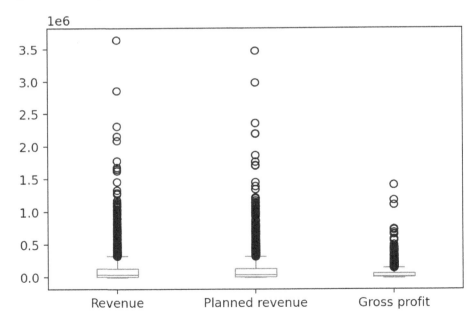

Figure 2.56: Boxplot for Revenue, Planned revenue and Gross profit for year 2006

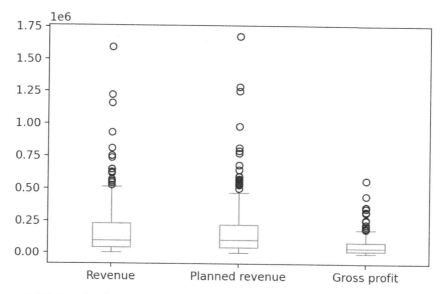

Figure 2.57: Boxplot for Revenue, Planned revenue and Gross profit for year 2007

The bubbles in the plots represent outliers. Outliers are extreme values in the data. They are caused either due to mistakes in measurement or due to the real behavior of the data. Outlier treatment depends entirely on the business use case. In some of the scenarios, outliers are dropped or are capped at a certain value based on the inputs from the business. It is not always advisable to drop the outliers as they can give us a lot of hidden information in the data.

From the above plots, we can infer that **Revenue** and **Planned revenue** have a higher median than **Gross profit** (the median is represented by the line inside the box).

Even though pandas provides you with the basic plots, it does not give you a lot of control over the look and feel of the visualizations.

Python has alternate packages such as seaborn which allow you to generate more fine-tuned and customized plots. Let's learn about this package in the next section.

VISUALIZATION THROUGH SEABORN

Even though pandas provides us with many of the most common plots required for analysis, Python also has a useful visualization library, **seaborn**. It provides a high-level API to easily generate top-quality plots with a lot of customization options.

You can change the environment from regular **pandas/Matplotlib** to **seaborn** directly through the **set** function of **seaborn**. **Seaborn** also supports a **displot** function, which plots the actual distribution of the pandas series passed to. To generate histograms through **seaborn**, you can use the following code:

```
import seaborn as sns
sns.set()
sns.displot(sales['Gross profit'].dropna(),color='gray')
```

The preceding code plots a histogram of the values of the **Gross profit** column. We have set the parameter **dropna()** which tells the plotting function to ignore null values if present in the data. The **sns.set()** function changes the environment from regular **pandas/Matplotlib** to **seaborn**.

The **color** attribute is used to provide colors to the graphs. In the preceding code, **gray** color is used to generate grayscale graphs. You can use other colors like **darkgreen**, **maroon**, etc. as values of **color** parameters to get the colored graphs.

This gives the following output:

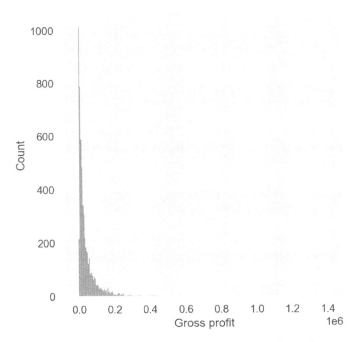

Figure 2.58: Histogram for Gross Profit through Seaborn

From the preceding plot, you can infer that most of the gross profit is around **$1,000**.

Pair Plots:

Pair plots are one of the most effective tools for exploratory data analysis. They can be considered as a collection of scatter plots between the variables present in the dataset. With a pair plot, one can easily study the distribution of a variable and its relationship with the other variables. These plots also reveal trends that may need further exploration.

For example, if your dataset has four variables, a pair plot would generate 16 charts that show the relationship of all the combinations of variables.

To generate a pair plot through **seaborn**, you can use the following code:

```
import seaborn as sns
sns.pairplot(dataframe, palette='gray')
```

The **palette** attribute is used to define the color of the pair plot. In the preceding code, **gray** color is used to generate grayscale graphs.

An example pair plot generated using **seaborn** would look like this:

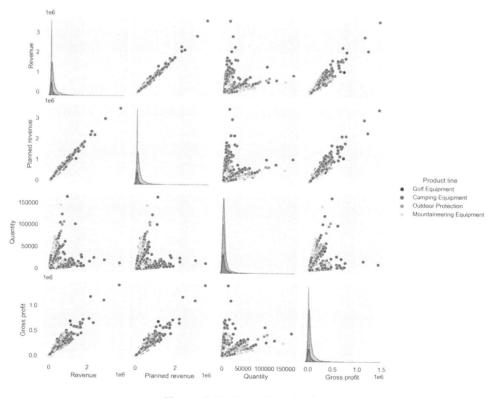

Figure 2.59: Sample pair plot

The following inferences can be made from the above plot.

1. Revenue and Gross profit have a linear relationship; that is, when Revenue increases the Gross Profit increases

2. Quantity and Revenue show no trend; that is, there is no relationship.

> **NOTE**
>
> You can refer to the following link for more details about the **seaborn** library: https://seaborn.pydata.org/tutorial.html.

In the next section, we will understand how to visualize insights using the **matplotlib** library.

VISUALIZATION WITH MATPLOTLIB

Python's default visualization library is **matplotlib**. matplotlib was originally developed to bring visualization capabilities from the MATLAB academic tool into an open-source programming language, Python. matplotlib provides low-level additional features that can be added to plots made from any other visualization library like **pandas** or **seaborn**.

To start using **matplotlib**, you need to first import the **matplotlib. pyplot** object as **plt**. This **plt** object becomes the basis for generating figures in **matplotlib**.

```
import matplotlib.pyplot as plt
```

We can then run any functions on this object as follows:

```
plt.<function name>
```

Some of the functions that we can call on this **plt** object for these options are as follows:

Function	Description
legend(*args, **kwargs)	Place a legend on the axes
grid([b, which, axis])	Configure the grid lines
axes([arg])	Add an axes to the current figure and make it the current axes
xlabel, ylabel	Set the label for the x-axis, y-axis
xticks, yticks	Get or set the current tick locations and labels of the x-axis, y-axis
tick-params	Change the appearance of ticks, tick labels, and grid lines
title(label[, fontdict, loc, pad])	Set a title for the axes

Figure 2.60: Functions that can be used on plt

For example, on the **sales** DataFrame, you can plot a bar graph between products and revenue using the following code.

```python
# Importing the matplotlib library
import matplotlib.pyplot as plt

#Declaring the color of the plot as gray
plt.bar(sales['Product line'], sales['Revenue'], color='gray')

# Giving the title for the plot
plt.title("Products with their corresponding revenue")

# Naming the x and y axis
plt.xlabel('Products')
plt.ylabel('Revenue')


# Rotates X-Axis labels by 45-degrees
plt.xticks(rotation = 45)

# Displaying the bar plot
plt.show()
```

This gives the following output:

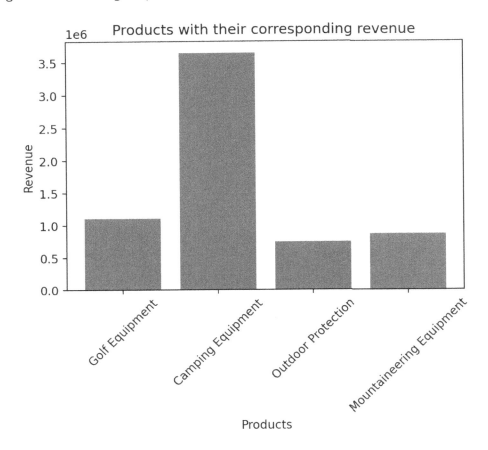

Figure 2.61: Sample bar graph

The color of the plot can be altered with the **color** parameter. We can use different colors such as **blue**, **black**, **red**, and **cyan**.

> **NOTE**
>
> Feel free to explore some of the things you can do directly with Matplotlib by reading up the official documentation at https://matplotlib.org/stable/api/_as_gen/matplotlib.pyplot.html.
>
> For a complete course on data visualization in general, you can refer to the *Data Visualization Workshop*: https://www.packtpub.com/product/the-data-visualization-workshop/9781800568846.

Before we head to the activity, the following table shows some of the key plots along with their usage:

Type of Plot	Usage
Bar Plot	Shows the frequency distribution of a categorical variable
Histogram	Shows the frequency distribution of a numerical variable
Pie Chart	Shows the composition of a group.
Scatter Plot	Shows the relationship between 2 continuous variables. It can be used to understand the distribution of the data
Pair Plot	It is used to understand the relationship between all possible combinations of numerical variables in the dataset
Density Plot	It is used to visualize the distribution of a continuous variable

Figure 2.62: Key plots and their usage

With that, it's time to put everything you've learned so far to test in the activity that follows.

ACTIVITY 2.01: ANALYZING ADVERTISEMENTS

Your company has collated data on the advertisement views through various mediums in a file called **Advertising.csv**. The advert campaign ran through radio, TV, web, and newspaper and you need to mine the data to answer the following questions:

1. What are the unique values present in the **Products** column?

2. How many data points belong to each category in the **Products** column?

3. What are the total views across each category in the **Products** column?

4. Which product has the highest viewership on TV?

5. Which product has the lowest viewership on the web?

To do that, you will need to examine the dataset with the help of the functions you have learned, along with charts wherever needed.

NOTE

You can find the **Advertising.csv** file here: https://packt.link/q1c34.

Follow the following steps to achieve the aim of this activity:

1. Open a new Jupyter Notebook and load **pandas** and the visualization libraries that you will need.

2. Load the data into a pandas DataFrame named **ads** and look at the first few rows. Your DataFrame should look as follows:

	Products	Web	Newspaper	Radio	TV
Date					
01/01/2018	Mobile	230100	69200	37800	22100
01/02/2018	Mobile	44500	45100	39300	10400
01/03/2018	Mobile	17200	69300	45900	9300
01/04/2018	Mobile	151500	58500	41300	18500
01/05/2018	Mobile	180800	58400	10800	12900

Figure 2.63: The first few rows of Advertising.csv

3. Understand the distribution of numerical variables in the dataset using the **describe** function.

4. Plot the relationship between the variables in the dataset with the help of pair plots. You can use the **hue** parameter as **Products**. The **hue** parameter determines which column can be used for color encoding. Using **Products** as a **hue** parameter will show the different products in various shades of gray.

You should get the below output:

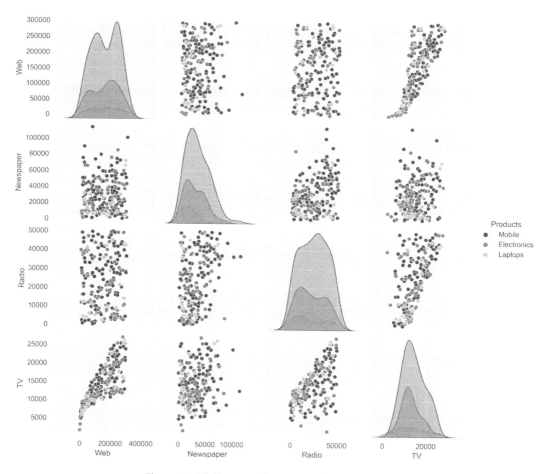

Figure 2.64: Expected output of Activity 2.01

> **NOTE**
>
> The solution for this activity can be found on page 482.

SUMMARY

In this chapter, you have looked at exploratory data analysis. You learned how to leverage pandas to help you focus on the attributes that are critical to your business goals. Later, you learned how to use the tools that helped you fine-tuned these insights to make them more comprehensible to your stakeholders. Toward the end of the chapter, you used visualization libraries like seaborn and matplotlib to visually present your insights. Effective data visualization will also help reveal hidden insights in your data. The skills you've learned so far should help you create a strong foundation for your journey toward mastering marketing analytics.

In the next chapter, you will build upon these skills by learning some of the practical applications of exploratory data analysis through examples you may encounter in practice as a marketing analyst.

3

UNSUPERVISED LEARNING AND CUSTOMER SEGMENTATION

OVERVIEW

In this chapter, you will implement one of the most powerful techniques in marketing – **customer segmentation**. You will begin by understanding the need for customer segmentation, following which you will study and implement the machine learning approach to segmentation. You will use the **k-means** clustering algorithm to segment customers and then analyze the obtained segments to gain an understanding of the results so that businesses can act on them.

By the end of this chapter, you will be able to perform segmentation using relevant tools and techniques and analyze the results of the segmented data. You will also be comfortable with using the **k-means** algorithm, a machine learning approach to segmentation.

INTRODUCTION

Put yourself in the shoes of the marketing head of an e-commerce company with a base of 1 million transacting customers. You want to make the marketing campaigns more effective, reaching the right customer with the right messaging. You know that by understanding the customer and their needs better, marketing campaigns could provide a significant boost to the business. As you begin solving this problem, you think about the customer experience. An average customer receives several communications from your platform about the latest offers and programs. These are relayed via email, push notifications, and social media campaigns. This may not be a great experience for them, especially if these communications are generic/mass campaigns. If the company understood the customers' needs better and sent them the relevant content, they would shop much more frequently.

Several examples like this show that a deep understanding of customers and their needs is beneficial not only to the company but also to the customer. If you are running a small company, understanding the needs of all the customers is as easy as running a quick survey. However, for a company with a large user base with millions of customers, understanding their needs would be extremely difficult, given each customer will have their own different tastes and needs. Moreover, with customers from different backgrounds, cultures, and age groups, this problem becomes even more difficult to solve.

Things would surely be easier if we could simplify this task and condense customers into a few groups. Instead of dealing with a million customers, would it not be easier to deal with, say, five types of customers? Customer segmentation lets you do just that – abstract potentially millions of customers to a few segments and understand their characteristics and needs. With such understanding, the impact you can realize is tremendous. You can send more directed and targeted messaging through marketing campaigns, offer differential services, make better product recommendations, and more to make the overall customer experience better; all these leading to a significant business impact – not just an immediate revenue impact through more efficient marketing campaigns, but also a significant positive impact on the long-term value that customers bring to the platform.

In the previous chapters, you got comfortable working with data and performing detailed analysis on your own. In this chapter, you will understand what customer segmentation is, how it is used, and how to use machine learning to build your own customer segmentation models in Python.

SEGMENTATION

Segmentation, simply put, means grouping similar entities together. The entities of each group are similar to each other, that is, "the groups are homogenous," meaning the entities have similar properties. Before going further, we need to understand two key aspects here – **entities** and **properties**.

What entities can be segmented? You can segment customers, products, offers, vehicles, fruits, animals, countries, or even stars. If you can express, through data, the properties of the entity, you can compare that entity with other entities and segment it. In this chapter, we will focus on customer segmentation – that is, grouping and segmenting present/potential customers, an exercise that has tremendous utility in marketing.

Coming to the second key aspect, what properties are we talking about? We are talking about properties relevant to the grouping exercise. Say you are trying to group customers based on their purchase frequency of a product. In such cases, data such as the customers' gender, even though it may be readily available to you, may not be relevant to your analysis. That's why picking the relevant attributes is critical. We will discuss this aspect in more detail later in this chapter, in the *Choosing Relevant Attributes (Segmentation Criteria)* section.

A general customer segmentation exercise involves the following key steps:

1.   Choosing the relevant attributes for the entities

2.   Clustering/grouping the entities

3.   Understanding and describing the segments

While *steps 1* and *2* are generally discussed and given a fair amount of attention, *step 3* is often ignored. The segments determined as a result of this activity should make sense to the business and be actionable. Business stakeholders, who play the critical role of the "human in the loop," must be able to understand these segments clearly. Then with their feedback, these segments can be refined further, making them even more actionable and business-driven. The marketing team can then readily understand and leverage them to create a successful marketing campaign. That's why describing the obtained segments in a way that the business understands is a necessary step.

We will touch upon all these steps in detail in this chapter. First, let's get our hands dirty by loading some data and begin the entire process, the result of which will be your own segmentation models. You will help a mall gain a better understanding of its customers to enable better targeting and boost sales.

In the exercise that follows, you will load the data, perform some cleanup, and build an understanding that will be critical for performing customer segmentation.

EXERCISE 3.01: MALL CUSTOMER SEGMENTATION – UNDERSTANDING THE DATA

You are a data scientist at a leading consulting company and among their newest clients is a popular chain of malls spread across many countries. The mall wishes to gain a better understanding of its customers to re-design their existing offerings and marketing communications to improve sales in a geographical area. The data about the customers is available in the `Mall_Customers.csv` file.

> **NOTE**
>
> `Mall_Customers.csv` can be found here: https://packt.link/Dgl1z.

Create a fresh Jupyter notebook for this exercise. Unless mentioned otherwise, we will continue using the same Jupyter notebook for future exercises. The goal of this exercise is to perform a basic analysis of the fields in the dataset and perform basic data cleanup. The understanding and the cleanup will be critical in helping us perform customer segmentation:

> **NOTE**
>
> All the exercises in this chapter need to be performed in the same Jupyter Notebook. Similarly, the activities too build upon each other so they need to be performed in a separate, single Jupyter Notebook. You may download the exercises and activities Notebooks for this chapter from here: https://packt.link/89fGH.
>
> The datasets used for these activities and exercises can be found here: https://packt.link/gjMjf.

1. Import **numpy**, **pandas**, and **pyplot** from **matplotlib** and **seaborn** using the following code:

```
import numpy as np, pandas as pd
import matplotlib.pyplot as plt, seaborn as sns
%matplotlib inline
```

2. Using the **read_csv** method from **pandas**, import the **Mall_Customers.csv** file into a **pandas** DataFrame named **data0** and print the first five rows:

```
data0 = pd.read_csv("Mall_Customers.csv")
data0.head()
```

> **NOTE**
>
> Make sure you change the path (highlighted) to the CSV file based on its location on your system. If you're running the Jupyter notebook from the same directory where the CSV file is stored, you can run the preceding code without any modification.

You should see the following output:

	CustomerID	Gender	Age	Annual Income (k$)	Spending Score (1-100)
0	1	Male	19	15	39
1	2	Male	21	15	81
2	3	Female	20	16	6
3	4	Female	23	16	77
4	5	Female	31	17	40

Figure 3.1: First five rows of the dataset

We see that we have information such as the gender and age of the customers, along with their estimated annual income (**Annual Income (k$)**). We also have a spending score calculated by the mall (**Spending Score (1-100)**), which denotes the amount of shopping the customer has done at the mall – a higher score means a higher spend.

3. Use the **info** method of the DataFrame to print information about it:

```
data0.info()
```

You should get the following output:

```
<class 'pandas.core.frame.DataFrame'>
RangeIndex: 200 entries, 0 to 199
Data columns (total 5 columns):
 #   Column                  Non-Null Count  Dtype
---  ------                  --------------  -----
 0   CustomerID              200 non-null    int64
 1   Gender                  200 non-null    object
 2   Age                     200 non-null    int64
 3   Annual Income (k$)      200 non-null    int64
 4   Spending Score (1-100)  200 non-null    int64
dtypes: int64(4), object(1)
memory usage: 7.9+ KB
```

Figure 3.2: Information about the DataFrame

You can observe that the dataset contains the data of **200** customers. You can also see that there are no missing values in the dataset to handle.

4. For convenience, rename the **Annual Income (k$)** and **Spending Score (1-100)** columns to **Income** and **Spend_score** respectively, and print the top five records using the following code:

```
data0.rename({'Annual Income (k$)':'Income', \
              'Spending Score (1-100)':'Spend_score'}, axis=1, \
             inplace=True)
data0.head()
```

The table should look like the following figure, with shorter names for easier handling:

	CustomerID	Gender	Age	Income	Spend_score
0	1	Male	19	15	39
1	2	Male	21	15	81
2	3	Female	20	16	6
3	4	Female	23	16	77
4	5	Female	31	17	40

Figure 3.3: First five rows of the dataset with the renamed columns

5. To get a high-level understanding of the customer data, print out the descriptive summary of the numerical fields in the data using the DataFrame's `describe` method:

```
data0.describe()
```

The descriptive summary should be as follows:

	CustomerID	Age	Income	Spend_score
count	200.000000	200.000000	200.000000	200.000000
mean	100.500000	38.850000	60.560000	50.200000
std	57.879185	13.969007	26.264721	25.823522
min	1.000000	18.000000	15.000000	1.000000
25%	50.750000	28.750000	41.500000	34.750000
50%	100.500000	36.000000	61.500000	50.000000
75%	150.250000	49.000000	78.000000	73.000000
max	200.000000	70.000000	137.000000	99.000000

Figure 3.4: Descriptive summary of the dataset

Overall averages show that the average age of the customer is around **39** and the average income is around **61,000 USD**. The spend scores seem to be calculated based on percentiles – having a minimum value of **1** and a maximum of **99**, which is common with percentiles (scores from **0** to **1** are also common for percentiles). The maximum income is around **137,000** USD. Looking at these values, we do not suspect any outliers in the data. This completes a very high-level understanding of the data.

We will next begin to understand the approaches to use such data for customer segmentation.

APPROACHES TO SEGMENTATION

Every marketing group does, in effect, some amount of customer segmentation. However, the methods they use to do this might not always be clear. These may be based on intuitions and hunches about certain demographic groups, or they might be the output of some marketing software, where the methods used are obscure. There are advantages and disadvantages to every possible method and understanding them allows you to make use of the right tool for the job. In the following sections, we will discuss some of the most commonly used approaches for customer segmentation along with considerations when using such approaches.

TRADITIONAL SEGMENTATION METHODS

A preferred method for marketing analysts consists of coming up with rough groupings based on intuitions and arbitrary thresholds. For this, they leverage whatever data about customers they have at their disposal – typically demographic or behavioral. An example of this would be deciding to segment customers into different income tiers based on $10,000 increments. Another approach could be looking at how the values for the attributes are distributed and looking for natural thresholds from the data.

To understand this concept better, let's apply a simple segmentation approach to the mall customers' data using the income of the customers.

EXERCISE 3.02: TRADITIONAL SEGMENTATION OF MALL CUSTOMERS

The mall wants to segment its customers and plans to use the derived segments to improve its marketing campaigns. The business team has a belief that segmenting based on income levels is relevant for their offerings. You are asked to use a traditional, rule-based approach to define customer segments.

> **NOTE**
>
> Continue in the Jupyter notebook used in the previous exercise. You will need to complete the previous exercise before beginning the current one.

In this exercise, you will perform your first customer segmentation using the income of the customer, employing a traditional rule-based approach to define customer segments. You will plot the distribution for the **Income** variable and assign groups to customers based on where you see the values lying:

1. Plot a histogram of the **Income** column using the DataFrame's **plot** method using the following code:

```
data0.Income.plot.hist(color='gray')
plt.xlabel('Income')
plt.show()
```

> **NOTE**
>
> The **gray** value for the **color** attribute is used to generate graphs in grayscale. You can use other colors such as **darkgreen**, **maroon**, and so on as values of **color** parameters to get the colored graphs. You can also refer to the following document to get the code for the colored plot and the colored output: http://packt.link/NOjgT.

You should see the following histogram:

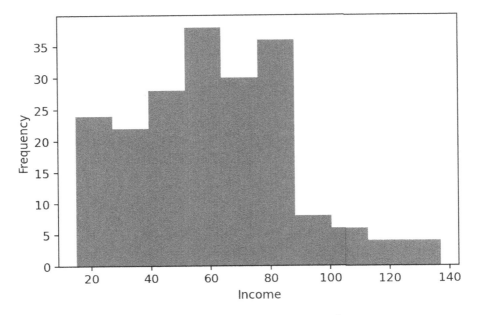

Figure 3.5: Histogram of the Income column

Beyond 90k, the frequency in the bins falls sharply and it seems that these customers can naturally be considered a separate group representing high-income customers. A good proportion of customers seems to lie in the 50k-90k range. These can be considered moderate-income customers. Customers earning less than 40k would be low-income customers. We can use these cutoffs to divide the customers into three groups, as in the following figure. The dotted segments denote the cutoffs/thresholds.

The groups can be named **Low Income**, **Moderate Income**, and **High Earners**:

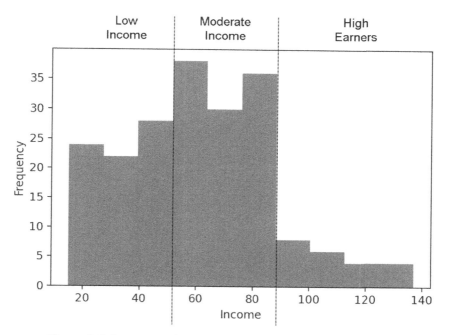

Figure 3.6: Segmentation of the customers based on income

2. Create a new column, **Cluster**, to have the **Low Income**, **Moderate Income**, and **High earners** values for customers with incomes in the ranges **< 50**, **50–90**, and **>= 90** respectively using the following code:

```
data0['Cluster'] = np.where(data0.Income >= 90, 'High earners', \
                   np.where(data0.Income < 50, \
                   'Low Income', 'Moderate Income'))
```

3. To check the number of customers in each cluster and confirm whether the values for the **Income** column in the clusters are in the correct range, get a descriptive summary of **Income** for these groups using the following command:

```
data0.groupby('Cluster')['Income'].describe()
```

The summary should be as follows:

	count	mean	std	min	25%	50%	75%	max
Cluster								
High earners	22.0	108.181818	13.661334	93.0	98.25	103.0	118.25	137.0
Low Income	72.0	33.027778	11.091136	15.0	22.50	33.5	43.00	49.0
Moderate Income	106.0	69.377358	10.651584	50.0	61.00	70.0	78.00	88.0

Figure 3.7: Descriptive summary of the Income column

The maximum and minimum values for each cluster confirm that the clusters have been defined as we intended. Most customers lie in the **Moderate Income** cluster. You can also see that only 22 customers are marked as high earners.

This completes your first customer segmentation exercise. You have successfully created a simple yet extremely useful solution that the marketing team can employ to create a business impact.

These kinds of methods have the advantage of being simple and easy to understand. However, segmentation using traditional approaches becomes much more complex when you add more variables such as age, gender, other relevant demographic information, or other relevant attributes identified by the business. Importantly, as you increase the number of variables, it becomes hard to choose thresholds in a way such that you do not end up with groups with very few customers in them. For example, how many individuals would there be in the group *18- to 25-year-olds making $100,000+?*

This becomes more important when looking at the behavioral data of customers. Creating groups based on intuition can result in underlying patterns in the data being overlooked. For example, there may be segments of the population that respond well to very specific kinds of marketing offers. If the analyst performing the segmentation does not happen to know about this specific group and the types of ads the customers in the group respond to, the analyst may miss out on capturing them as a unique group. For instance, a marketing analyst who separates customers into those who respond to offers for expensive products and those who respond to offers for inexpensive products could miss a group of customers only interested in electronics, regardless of whether they are expensive or inexpensive.

Another important consideration is that even the most careful of humans can bring in unconscious biases from their intuition or experiences. Such considerations necessitate a machine learning-based approach to segmentation, which we will discuss next.

UNSUPERVISED LEARNING (CLUSTERING) FOR CUSTOMER SEGMENTATION

Another method for performing customer segmentation is using unsupervised machine learning. It is often a very powerful technique as it tends to pick up on patterns in data that might otherwise be missed. It is perfect for customer segmentation because it finds data points that are most like each other and groups them together, which is exactly what good customer segmentation techniques should do.

> ### NOTE
>
> Unsupervised learning is the branch of machine learning wherein we do not have some "ground truth" to verify our solutions. In clustering, we do not have a notion of true clusters that the customers belong to, against which we can validate the clusters we obtained.
>
> In contrast, supervised learning is a branch of machine learning where we have some tagged/labeled data, that is, for each sample/record, we have prior knowledge of what the output should be. We will discuss this distinction in greater detail in *Chapter 5, Predicting Customer Revenue Using Linear Regression*.

Clustering is a type of unsupervised machine learning technique that looks for groups or **clusters** in data without knowing them ahead of time. The following are some of the advantages and disadvantages of using clustering for customer segmentation.

Here are the advantages of clustering:

- Can find customer groups that are unexpected or unknown to the analyst
- Flexible and can be used for a wide range of data
- Reduces the need for deep expertise about connections between the demographics of customers and behaviors
- Quick to perform; scalable to very large datasets

Here are the disadvantages of clustering:

- Customer groups created may not be easily interpretable.

- If data is not based on consumer behavior (such as products or services purchased), it may not be clear how to use the clusters that are found.

As you might expect, one downside of clustering is that it may find groups that do not seem to make a lot of sense on the surface. Often this can be fixed by using a better-suited clustering algorithm. Determining how to evaluate and fine-tune clustering algorithms will be covered in the next chapter.

Regardless of the approach to clustering you choose, identifying the right attributes to go into the segmentation is an extremely important step. The output of this exercise is of very little value if the input data is not relevant. Let's discuss this critical step in the following section.

CHOOSING RELEVANT ATTRIBUTES (SEGMENTATION CRITERIA)

To use clustering for customer segmentation (to group customers with other customers who have similar traits), you first have to decide what **similar** means, or in other words, you need to be precise when defining what kinds of customers are similar. Choosing the properties that go into the segmentation process is an extremely important decision as it defines how the entities are represented and directs the nature of the groups formed.

Let's say we wish to segment customers solely by their purchase frequency and transaction value. In such a situation, attributes such as age, gender, or other demographic data would not be relevant. On the other hand, if the intent is to segment customers purely on a demographic basis, their purchase frequency and transaction value would be the attributes that won't be relevant to us.

A good criterion for segmentation could be customer engagement, involving features such as time spent on the site, visits to the platform in a defined time period, pages viewed on a website, days since the last login, and so on. When working with a dataset involving this type of data, we would need to store the data for each entity, say, a customer, in a row. The values for each row in the data would be representative of a customer, more generally, of each entity of interest (time spent on the site, for example) in the dataset. This type of representation helps compare one entity with other entities in the dataset.

For our case study, let's decide on the criteria for segmentation. Regardless of age, let's say we wish to separate customers based on their income level and spending scores. Using these, we could have a differential marketing strategy for customers that have, say, high income and low spending scores versus those with low income and high spending scores. With the segmentation criteria decided, that is, the relevant attributes chosen, let's understand some key concepts that enable the clustering process.

STANDARDIZING DATA

To be able to group customers based on continuous variables, we first need to rescale these parameters such that the data is on similar scales. Why? Take age and income, for instance. These are on very different scales. It is quite common to see annual incomes of two persons that differ by $10,000, but it would be very odd to see their ages differ by 10,000 years. Therefore, we need to better control how the change in one variable impacts the overall similarity between customers. For example, we may want an age difference of 10 years between two customers to be treated equivalent to an income difference of $10,000. However, making these kinds of determinations manually for each variable would be difficult. This is the reason why we typically standardize the data, to put them all on a standard scale.

The scale has a significant impact on the perceived similarity between the entities. To understand the impact of scale and units of measurement in a simple, visual manner, consider the three graphs in *Figure 3.9*. The graphs represent data for four customers (**C1**, **C2**, **C3**, **C4**). The original data is in the following table, where you have the customer age in years and annual income in **000's INR** (**Indian National Rupee**):

Customer	Age	Income (000's INR)
C1	35	3500
C2	40	3500
C3	35	3250
C4	40	3250

Figure 3.8: Data of four customers

If we plot the customers as points on a scatter plot with **Age** on the *x* axis and `Income` on the *y* axis, we see that the incomes of customers **C3** and **C4** are very close to each other and that the incomes of customers **C1** and **C2** form a pair. But what if we converted the annual income to USD (dividing by 70 for simplicity)? Let's look at the middle graph in *Figure 3.9* for this. Surprisingly, now **C1** and **C3** form a pair, with **C2** and **C4** forming another. This is clearly problematic. Our clusters changed drastically by changing the units of measurement (INR to USD):

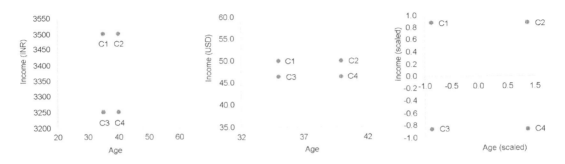

Figure 3.9: Plotting the customers as points on a scatter plot

A natural strategy to handle this issue is to "standardize" the data, that is, get the values to a similar, comparable scale. One such strategy was applied to the preceding four customers' data, resulting in the rightmost plot in *Figure 3.9*. Indeed, it is interesting to notice that after standardizing, none of the points seem to be forming any natural clusters with another. This example illustrates the importance of standardizing and how we can otherwise be fooled into believing there are natural clusters when there are none.

While there are multiple ways to standardize or rescale features, one popular way that is employed for clustering is **standard scaling**, that is, to calculate their **z-score**. This is done in two steps, for each column:

1. First, subtract the mean of the data from each data point. This centers the data around **0**, to make the data easier to look at and interpret, although this is not strictly required for clustering.

2. The second step is to divide the parameters by their **standard deviation**.

The standard deviation is a measure of how spread out our points are. It is calculated by comparing the average of the data to each data point. Data such as income, where the points can be spread out by many thousands, will have much larger standard deviations than data such as age, where the differences between the data points tend to be much smaller. The following formula is used for calculating the standardized value of a data point:

$$Z_i = \frac{x_i - mean\ (x)}{std(x)}$$

Figure 3.10: The standardization equation

Here, Z_i corresponds to the ith standardized value, **x** represents all values, **mean(x)** is the mean value of all **x** values, and **std(x)** is the standard deviation of the **x** values.

In this example, by dividing all the values of **Age** by the standard deviation of the ages, we transform the data such that the standard deviation is equal to **1**. When we do the same thing with the income, the standard deviation of the income will also be equal to **1**. Therefore, a difference of **1** between two customers on either of these measures would indicate a similar level of difference between them. This ensures that all features have a similar influence on the formation of the clusters.

Is there a downside to such an approach? Think about the ease of interpretation of these values. We all have an intuitive sense of what $10,000 or 10 years means, but it is harder to think of what one standard deviation's worth of income means. However, this does not matter for the machine learning algorithm, as it does not have the same intuitive understanding of the data that we do.

For the Python implementation of standardization of data, we will employ the **StandardScaler** utility in scikit-learn. The utility can be imported and instantiated using the following code:

```
from sklearn.preprocessing import StandardScaler
scaler = StandardScaler()
```

The **scaler** object has methods to fit on a given dataset. Fitting here would mean calculating the mean and the standard deviation for each of the columns. To apply the transformation, you simply need to use the **transform** method of the **scaler** object. To perform both of these actions in a single step, calculate the mean and standard deviation (that is, **fit**) and then apply the transformation (that is, **transform**), or you can simply use the **fit_transform** method, as shown in the following code:

```
scaler.fit_transform (data_orig[cols])
```

The preceding command would fit, transform, and return the scaled data. The **cols** variable can be a list of columns to scale in the **data_orig** dataset.

Let's now apply standardization to the mall customer data in the next exercise.

> **NOTE**
>
> Standardizing ensures all variables have a similar influence on cluster formation. While it is standard practice, in business situations you should evaluate whether all variables having a similar influence align with business requirements. Based on the business domain and task at hand, you may sometimes want certain variables to direct and influence the clusters more than the others. Accomplishing this can be done simply by keeping these variables at a different scale than the others.

EXERCISE 3.03: STANDARDIZING CUSTOMER DATA

In this exercise, you will further our segmentation exercise by performing the important step of ensuring that all the variables get similar importance in the exercise, just as the business requires. You will standardize the mall customer data using z-scoring, employing **StandardScaler** from scikit-learn. Continue in the same notebook used for the exercises so far. Note that this exercise works on the modified data from *Exercise 3.02, Traditional Segmentation of Mall Customers*. Make sure you complete all the previous exercises before beginning this exercise:

1. Import the **StandardScaler** method from **sklearn** and create an instance of **StandardScaler** using the following code:

```
from sklearn.preprocessing import StandardScaler
scaler = StandardScaler()
```

2. Create a list named **cols_to_scale** to hold the names of the columns you wish to scale, namely, **Age**, **Income**, and **Spend_score**. Also, make a copy of the DataFrame (to retain original values) and name it **data_scaled**. You will be scaling columns on the copied dataset:

```
cols_to_scale = ['Age', 'Income', 'Spend_score']
data_scaled = data0.copy()
```

3. Using the **fit_transform** method of the scaler, apply the transformation to the chosen columns:

```
data_scaled[cols_to_scale] = scaler.fit_transform\
                               (data0[cols_to_scale])
```

4. To verify that this worked, print a descriptive summary of these modified columns:

```
data_scaled[cols_to_scale].describe()
```

The output should be as follows:

	Age	Income	Spend_score
count	2.000000e+02	2.000000e+02	2.000000e+02
mean	-9.603429e-17	-6.128431e-16	-1.121325e-16
std	1.002509e+00	1.002509e+00	1.002509e+00
min	-1.496335e+00	-1.738999e+00	-1.910021e+00
25%	-7.248436e-01	-7.275093e-01	-5.997931e-01
50%	-2.045351e-01	3.587926e-02	-7.764312e-03
75%	7.284319e-01	6.656748e-01	8.851316e-01
max	2.235532e+00	2.917671e+00	1.894492e+00

Figure 3.11: Descriptive summary of the modified columns

The mean value for all the columns is practically **0** and the standard deviation for all is **1**. This confirms that the standardization has worked. Compare this to the table in *Figure 3.4* to see that the mean value and the standard deviation for each column have been standardized. This ensures that all columns get equal weightage when calculating the similarity or distance between customers.

CALCULATING DISTANCE

You may have understood by now that calculating similarity between entities is a key step for clustering. It helps us quantify how similar two entities are and therefore enables grouping entities. An alternate way of clustering is to calculate the dissimilarity between entities. This way, we can understand how different (or far apart) the entities are. The geometric distance between entities in the feature space is a natural way of measuring dissimilarity. On a two-dimensional scatter plot, the **Euclidean distance** between two customers is just the distance between their points, as you can see in *Figure 3.12*:

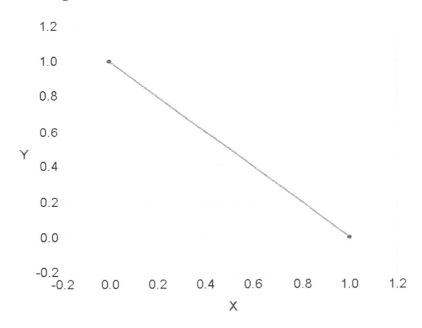

Figure 3.12: Euclidean distance between two points in the XY plane

In the preceding plot, the length of the line is the Euclidean distance between the two points. The greater this distance, the less similar the customers are. While this is easier to think about and visualize in two dimensions, the math for calculating Euclidean distance applies just as well to multiple dimensions.

For two data points, *p* and *q*, the distance between them is calculated as follows:

$$d(p,q) = \sqrt{\sum (p_i - q_i)^2}$$

Figure 3.13: Equation for calculating the Euclidean distance between two points

Here, $\mathbf{p} = (p_1 + p_2 + ... p_n)$, $\mathbf{q} = (q_1 + q_2 + ... q_n)$, and $\mathbf{n}$ is the number of features.

We can therefore find the distance between customers regardless of how many features/dimensions we want to use.

For the Python implementation, we will be using the **cdist** utility in SciPy. The usage of the utility is simple and is demonstrated in the following code example:

```
from scipy.spatial.distance import cdist
cdist(array1, array2, metric='euclidean')
```

In the preceding command, **array1** is the first array of data. It could represent data for one customer or many (two-dimensional array). **array2** is the other array. The distance is calculated between entities of **array1** and those of **array2**. Specifying the metric as **euclidean** calculates the Euclidean distance between **array1** and **array2** entities.

Calculating the distance between points is a key step in clustering. Now, let's shore up our understanding of what we have learned in this section so far by calculating the distance between customers, which is the precursor to clustering them.

> **NOTE**
>
> This section describes finding the Euclidean distance between two points, which is the most common type of distance metric to use for clustering. Another common distance metric is the Manhattan distance. You can read more about different distant metrics here: https://numerics.mathdotnet.com/Distance.html.

EXERCISE 3.04: CALCULATING THE DISTANCE BETWEEN CUSTOMERS

In this exercise, you will calculate the Euclidean distance between three customers. The goal of the exercise is to be able to calculate the similarity between customers. A similarity calculation is a key step in customer segmentation. After standardizing the **Income** and **Spend_score** fields for the first three customers as in the following table (*Figure 3.14*), you will calculate the distance using the **cdist** method from **scipy**.

> **NOTE**
>
> Continue in the same Jupyter notebook. Note that the previous exercises are a prerequisite for this exercise.

1. From the dataset (**data_scaled** created in *Exercise 3.03, Standardizing Customer Data*), extract the top three records with the **Income** and **Spend_score** fields into a dataset named **cust3** and print the dataset, using the following code:

```
sel_cols = ['Income', 'Spend_score']
cust3 = data_scaled[sel_cols].head(3)
cust3
```

The result should be as follows:

	Income	Spend_score
0	-1.738999	-0.434801
1	-1.738999	1.195704
2	-1.700830	-1.715913

Figure 3.14: Income and spend scores of three customers

You can see the top three records. The distance between these three customers will be calculated in this exercise.

2. Next, import the **cdist** method from **scipy.spatial.distance** using the following code:

```
from scipy.spatial.distance import cdist
```

3. The **cdist** function can be used to calculate the distance between each pair of the two collections of inputs. To calculate the distance between the customers in **cust3**, provide the **cust3** dataset as both data inputs to **cdist**, specifying **euclidean** as the metric, using the following code snippet:

    ```
    cdist(cust3, cust3, metric='euclidean')
    ```

    You should get the following result, a two-dimensional grid of distances between each pair of customers:

    ```
    array([[0.        , 1.63050555, 1.28167999],
           [1.63050555, 0.        , 2.91186723],
           [1.28167999, 2.91186723, 0.        ]])
    ```

    Figure 3.15: Output of the cdist function

    The output shows that the distance between the first and the second customer is **1.63** units, while the distance between the first and the third customer is **1.28** units. The distance between the second and the third customer is **2.92** units.

4. Verify that **1.6305** is indeed the **Euclidean distance** between customer 1 and customer 2, by manually calculating it using the following code:

    ```
    np.sqrt((-1.739+1.739)**2 + (-0.4348-1.1957)**2)
    ```

    The result is **1.6305**.

    This matches exactly with the distance calculated by the **cdist** method.

In this exercise, you calculated the distance between three points using the **cdist** package. You saw that points with values that are similar have lower distances. Such distance calculation is a key step in determining the similarity between entities and is used by machine learning algorithms for clustering.

You will now study the most popular machine learning approach for clustering, the **k-means** algorithm.

K-MEANS CLUSTERING

K-means clustering is a very common unsupervised learning technique with a wide range of applications. It is powerful because it is conceptually relatively simple, scales to very large datasets, and tends to work well in practice. In this section, you will learn the conceptual foundations of k-means clustering, how to apply k-means clustering to data, and how to deal with high-dimensional data (that is, data with many different variables) in the context of clustering.

K-means clustering is an algorithm that tries to find the best way of grouping data points into *k* different groups, where *k* is a parameter given to the algorithm. For now, we will choose *k* arbitrarily. We will revisit how to choose *k* in practice in the next chapter. The algorithm then works iteratively to try to find the best grouping. There are two steps to this algorithm:

1. The algorithm begins by randomly selecting *k* points in space to be the centroids of the clusters. Each data point is then assigned to the centroid that is closest to it.

2. The centroids are updated to be the mean of all of the data points assigned to them. The data points are then reassigned to the centroid closest to them.

Step 2 is repeated until none of the data points change the centroid they are assigned to after the centroid is updated.

One point to note here is that this algorithm is not deterministic, that is, the outcome of the algorithm depends on the starting locations of the centroids. Therefore, it is not always guaranteed to find the best grouping. However, in practice, it tends to find good groupings while still being computationally inexpensive even for large datasets. **K-means** clustering is fast and easily scalable and is, therefore, the most common clustering algorithm used.

We will use the **KMeans** module in the scikit-learn package for clustering in the hands-on exercises and activities in this chapter. The **KMeans** module in scikit-learn makes clustering extremely simple to implement. Let's understand the usage. We first need to import **KMeans** and instantiate a **KMeans** object:

```
from sklearn.cluster import KMeans
model = KMeans(n_clusters=N, random_state=random_state)
```

The preceding commands would create a model instance with **N** number of clusters. Note that this command does not perform any clustering. Specifying a random state ensures that we get the same results on repeated executions since the k-means algorithm is not deterministic. Next, the model is fit on the data and the resulting cluster assignments are extracted:

```
model.fit(data[cols])
data['Cluster'] = model.predict(data[cols])
```

In the preceding commands, the **fit** method of the **KMeans** object creates the specified number of clusters from the dataset. **cols** is a list containing the columns from the **data** dataset to be used for clustering. After the model has been fit, the **predict** method is used to extract the cluster assignments for each record in the dataset. The cluster assignments can be added to the original dataset as a new column, as in the preceding example.

For the mall customers, we applied a traditional approach to customer segmentation and created some simple and actionable segments. We are now ready to perform machine learning-based clustering to create groups. In the next exercise, we will perform k-means clustering on the mall customers.

EXERCISE 3.05: K-MEANS CLUSTERING ON MALL CUSTOMERS

In this exercise, you will use machine learning to discover natural groups in the mall customers. You will perform **k-means** clustering on the mall customer data that was standardized in the previous exercise. You will use only the **Income** and **Spend_score** columns. Continue using the same Jupyter notebook from the previous exercises. Perform clustering using the scikit-learn package and visualize the clusters:

1. Create a list called **cluster_cols** containing the **Income** and **Spend_score** columns, which will be used for clustering. Print the first three rows of the dataset, limited to these columns to ensure that you are filtering the data correctly:

```
cluster_cols = ['Income', 'Spend_score']
data_scaled[cluster_cols].head(3)
```

You should get the following output:

	Income	Spend_score
0	-1.738999	-0.434801
1	-1.738999	1.195704
2	-1.700830	-1.715913

Figure 3.16: First three rows of the dataset

2. Visualize the data using a scatter plot with **Income** and **Spend_score** on the *x* and *y* axes respectively with the following code:

```
data_scaled.plot.scatter(x='Income', y='Spend_score', \
                         color='gray')
plt.show()
```

> **NOTE**
>
> In *steps 2* and *5*, the **gray** value for the **color** attribute is used to generate graphs in grayscale. You can use other colors such as **darkgreen**, **maroon**, and so on as values of **color** parameters to get the colored graphs. You can also refer to the following document to get the code for the colored plot and the colored output: http://packt.link/NOjgT.

The resulting plot should look as follows:

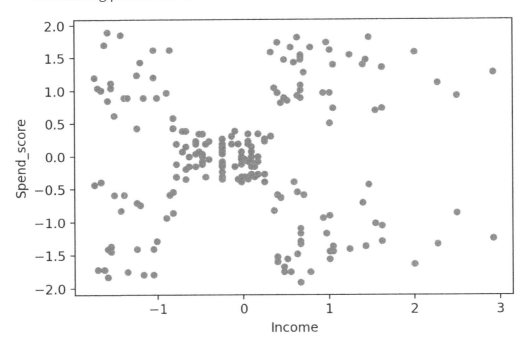

Figure 3.17: A scatter plot of income and spend score

From the plot, there are 5 natural clusters in the data. This tells us that we need to specify **5** as the number of clusters for the k-means algorithm.

3. Import **KMeans** from **sklearn.cluster**. Create an instance of the **KMeans** model specifying **5** clusters (**n_clusters**) and **42** for **random_state**:

```
from sklearn.cluster import KMeans
model = KMeans(n_clusters=5, random_state=42)
```

The model instance is created. Note that no clustering has been performed on the data yet. **n_clusters** specifies the number of clusters to create as **5**. Specifying a random state ensures that we get the same results on repeated executions since the **k-means** algorithm is not deterministic. **42** is an arbitrary choice.

4. Next, fit the model on the data using the columns in **cluster_cols** for the purpose. Using the **predict** method of the k-means model, assign the cluster for each customer to the **'Cluster'** variable. Print the first three records of the **data_scaled** dataset:

```
model.fit(data_scaled[cluster_cols])
data_scaled['Cluster'] = model.predict(data_scaled[cluster_cols])
data_scaled.head(3)
```

You should get the following output:

	CustomerID	Gender	Age	Income	Spend_score	Cluster
0	1	Male	-1.424569	-1.738999	-0.434801	2
1	2	Male	-1.281035	-1.738999	1.195704	3
2	3	Female	-1.352802	-1.700830	-1.715913	2

Figure 3.18: First three records of the data_scaled dataset

You can infer from the first three records that the cluster values are now available to us as a separate column in the dataset.

> **NOTE**
>
> The cluster assignment you see could be different from that in *Figure 3.18*. This is because of some additional randomness in the process introduced by the random cluster center initialization that is done by the k-means algorithm. Unfortunately, the randomness remains even after setting the random seed and we can't control it. Nevertheless, while the assigned cluster number may differ, you should get clusters with the same characteristics and the overall result should be similar.

5. Now you need to visualize it to see the points assigned to each cluster. Plot each cluster with a marker using the following code. You will subset the dataset for each cluster and use a dictionary to specify the marker for the cluster:

```
markers = ['x', '*', '.', '|', '_']

for clust in range(5):
    temp = data_scaled[data_scaled.Cluster == clust]
    plt.scatter(temp.Income, temp.Spend_score, \
                marker=markers[clust], \
                color = 'gray',\
                label="Cluster "+str(clust))
plt.xlabel('Income')
plt.ylabel('Spend_score')
plt.legend()
plt.show()
```

You will get the following output:

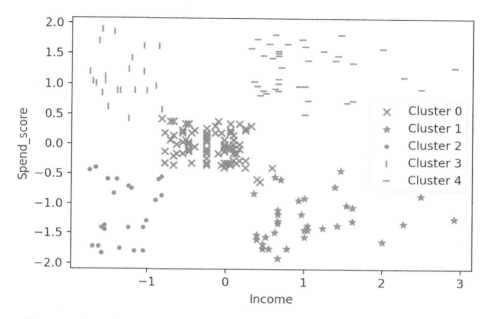

Figure 3.19: A plot of the data with the color/shape indicating which cluster each data point is assigned to

The clusters, represented by the different shapes on the scatter plot, seem to be aligned with the natural groups that we visually identified in *Figure 3.18*. The **k-means** algorithm did a good job of identifying the "natural" clusters in the data.

> **NOTE**
>
> The shapes and colors of the segments you get may vary slightly from the preceding figure. This is because of some additional randomness in the process, introduced by the random cluster center initialization that is done by the k-means algorithm. Unfortunately, the randomness remains even after setting the random seed and we can't control it. Nevertheless, while the assigned shapes may differ, you should get clusters with the same characteristics and the overall result should be similar.

In this exercise, you have successfully performed **k-means** clustering using the **scikit-learn package**. But the segmentation exercise is not over yet. You will still need to understand these clusters and describe them in a way the business understands.

UNDERSTANDING AND DESCRIBING THE CLUSTERS

Marketing analysts need to have a clear understanding of these clusters so that they can explain them to various stakeholders in the business. As mentioned before, business stakeholders play a critical role in the segmentation exercise by reviewing the segments from a business perspective. To understand the clusters, one simple approach is to study the various characteristics of the customers for each cluster. For this purpose, we need not restrict ourselves to the features that went into the clustering. Indeed, supplementing the analysis with other relevant features helps us understand the customer segments and their behavior better. The understanding needs to be conveyed to the business. Additionally, since the business will be referring to the clusters again and again, we need to make sure to label and describe these segments better.

Let's understand the clusters obtained in *Exercise 3.05, K-Means Clustering on Mall Customers*. We will continue in the same Jupyter notebook. Also, note that all the preceding exercises are a prerequisite for running the following code.

To understand the characteristics of the clusters better, we will analyze the features in the original scale and not the standardized features. To do so, let's first add the cluster information to the **data0** dataset that we prepared in *Exercise 3.01, Mall Customer Segmentation – Understanding the Data*. Recall that this is the dataset without the standardization applied and therefore **Income** and **Spend_Score** are available on their original scales. Then, let's see how the values of **Income** and **Spend_score** vary across the clusters. We will group the dataset by **Cluster** and calculate and plot the mean value of these variables using the following code:

```
data0['Cluster'] = data_scaled.Cluster
data0.groupby('Cluster')[['Income', 'Spend_score']].mean()\
    .plot.bar(color=['gray','black'])
plt.show()
```

This results in the following plot:

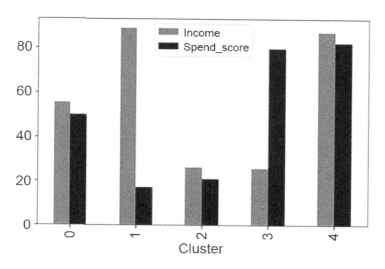

Figure 3.20: Bar chart of the mean values for the Income and Spend_score variables

> **NOTE**
>
> When you run the preceding code, you may encounter some warnings regarding package versions. You can safely ignore the warnings.

The information here is in a way a summary of the plot in *Figure 3.20*. Each cluster can be described as follows:

- **Cluster 0**: Low-income high spenders

- **Cluster 1**: Moderate-income moderate spenders

- **Cluster 2**: High-income low spenders

- **Cluster 3**: Low-income low spenders
- **Cluster 4**: High-income high spenders

> **NOTE**
>
> The cluster order you observe could be different from the order above. This is because of some randomization due to the k-means algorithm. Nevertheless, while the cluster numbers/orders may differ, you should get clusters with the same characteristics and the overall result should be similar.

Additionally, you could assign catchy and/or creative names to these clusters that capture the essence of their behavior. It helps register and convey the understanding better and is just easier to work with. Go ahead, try coming up with creative names for these segments.

> **NOTE**
>
> Another useful approach is giving personas to each segment, that is, representing each customer segment with an imaginary personality. The persona has a name and some attributes to help understand its personality. As an example, **Cluster 1** from the previous exercise could be represented by "Joe." Joe is the quintessential "average customer" whose income level is right at the average, and so is his spend. He does not spend beyond his means. Giving a name and personality helps consolidate the segment understanding into a single, imaginary person, who is much easier to remember than the values of the segments' attributes.

This key step completes the segmentation exercise. This understanding is presented to the business consumers, who, as mentioned earlier, often have some feedback that you can incorporate, leading to more refined segments. Now that you understand all the key steps involved, it is time to put your newly learned skills to the test. In the activity that follows, you will perform an end-to-end segmentation exercise and help create a business impact for a bank.

ACTIVITY 3.01: BANK CUSTOMER SEGMENTATION FOR LOAN CAMPAIGN

Banks often have marketing campaigns for their individual products. Therabank is an established bank that offers personal loans as a product. Most of Therabank's customers have deposits, which is a liability for the bank and not profitable. Loans are profitable for the bank. Therefore, getting more customers to opt for a personal loan makes the equation more profitable. The task at hand is to create customer segments to maximize the effectiveness of their personal loan campaign.

The bank has data for customers including demographics, some financial information, and how these customers responded to a previous campaign (see *Figure 3.21*). Some key columns are described here:

- **Experience**: The work experience of the customer in years

- **Income**: The estimated annual income of the customer (thousands of US dollars)

- **CCAvg**: The average spending on credit cards per month (thousands of US dollars)

- **Mortgage**: The value of the customer's house mortgage (if any)

- **Age**: The age (in years) of the customer

	ID	Age	Experience	Income	ZIP Code	Family	CCAvg	Education	Mortgage	Personal Loan	Securities Account	CD Account	Online	CreditCard
0	1	25	1	49	91107	4	1.6	1	0	0	1	0	0	0
1	2	45	19	34	90089	3	1.5	1	0	0	1	0	0	0
2	3	39	15	11	94720	1	1.0	1	0	0	0	0	0	0
3	4	35	9	100	94112	1	2.7	2	0	0	0	0	0	0
4	5	35	8	45	91330	4	1.0	2	0	0	0	0	0	1

Figure 3.21: First few records of the Therabank dataset

Your goal is to create customer segments for the marketing campaign. You will also identify which of these segments have the highest propensity to respond to the campaign – information that will greatly help optimize future campaigns.

Note that while the previous campaign's response is available to you, if you use it as a criterion/feature for segmentation, you will not be able to segment other customers for whom the previous campaign was never run, thereby severely limiting the number of customers you can target. You will, therefore, exclude the feature (**previous campaign response**) for clustering, but you can use it to evaluate how your clusters overall would respond to the campaign. Execute the following steps in a fresh Jupyter notebook to complete the activity:

> **NOTE**
>
> The file for the activity, **Bank_Personal_Loan_Modelling-1.csv**, can be found here: https://packt.link/IJG24.

1. Import the necessary libraries for data processing, visualization, and clustering.

2. Load the data into a **pandas** DataFrame and display the top five rows. Using the **info** method, get an understanding of the columns and their types.

3. Perform standard scaling on the **Income** and **CCAvg** columns to create new **Income_scaled** and **CCAvg_scaled** columns. You will be using these two variables for customer segmentation. Get a descriptive summary of the processed columns to verify that the scaling has been applied correctly.

4. Perform k-means clustering, specifying **3** clusters using **Income** and **CCAvg** as the features. Specify **random_state** as **42** (an arbitrary choice) to ensure the consistency of the results. Create a new column, **Cluster**, containing the predicted cluster from the model.

5. Visualize the clusters by using different markers for the clusters on a scatter plot between **Income** and **CCAvg**. The output should be as follows:

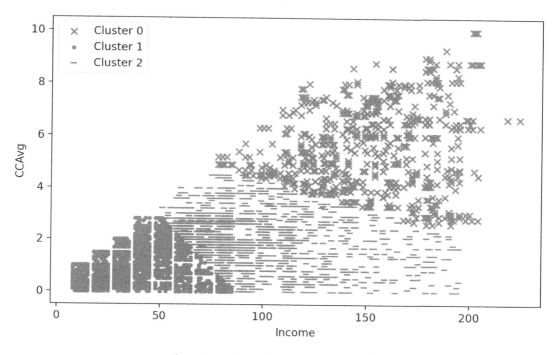

Figure 3.22: Clusters on a scatter plot

6. To understand the clusters, print the average values of **Income** and **CCAvg** for the three clusters.

7. Perform a visual comparison of the clusters using the standardized values for **Income** and **CCAvg**. You should get the following plot:

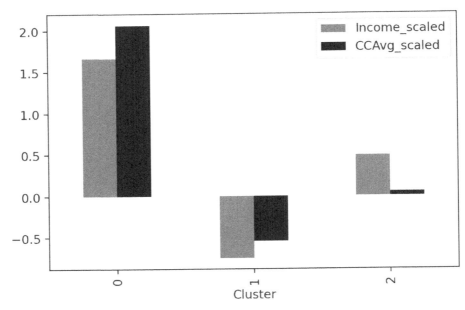

Figure 3.23: Visual comparison of the clusters using the standardized values for Income and CCAvg

8. To understand the clusters better using other relevant features, print the average values against the clusters for the **Age**, **Mortgage**, **Family**, **CreditCard**, **Online**, and **Personal Loan** features. Check which cluster has the highest propensity for taking a personal loan.

9. Based on your understanding of the clusters, assign descriptive labels to the clusters.

> **NOTE**
>
> The solution for this activity can be found on page 490.

If you completed this activity, you must have performed all the key steps to perform the complete segmentation exercise. Not only did you perform the necessary data processing and apply the k-means algorithm, but you also created useful clusters and obtained valuable insights for the business. So far, in the exercises and the activity, you used at most two variables (or dimensions) for clustering. While that was convenient, many business scenarios will require you to deal with numerous customer attributes, thereby requiring you to deal with high-dimensional data. Let's understand the considerations and the process next.

CLUSTERING WITH HIGH-DIMENSIONAL DATA

It is common to have datasets that have more than just two dimensions. In the mall customers dataset that we saw in the previous exercises, we have the age of the customer in addition to income and spending score. We previously used only income and spending scores to perform segmentation. Age could be an interesting feature as we may have differences in behavior and responsiveness to marketing campaigns for customers across different age groups. Additionally, other than the usual demographics, if we had some information about how these customers responded to advertised sales, how many purchases they have made of our products, or how many people live in their household, we could have many more dimensions.

Clustering entities represented in higher dimensions is no different than clustering with two dimensions. The key step is the similarity/distance calculation. Recall that the distance measure we employed, **Euclidean distance**, was defined as follows:

$$d(p, q) = \sqrt{\sum (p_i - q_i)^2}$$

Figure 3.24: Equation for calculating the Euclidean distance between two points

Here, $\mathbf{p} = (p_1 + p_2 + ... p_n)$, $\mathbf{q} = (q_1 + q_2 + ... q_n)$, while $\mathbf{n}$ is the number of features. **Euclidean distance** can very well handle multiple dimensions. Once the distance is defined, the usual machine learning algorithms for clustering, say, k-means, can be employed.

What does change, though, is how we visualize the clusters. In *Exercise 3.05, K-Means Clustering on Mall Customers*, we only had two variables and we could easily visualize data points and the clusters formed. With higher-dimensional data, however, we need to first reduce the data to two dimensions.

Dimensionality reduction techniques are commonly employed for this. The idea of dimensionality reduction is that multi-dimensional data is reduced, usually to two dimensions, for visualization purposes, in a manner that preserves the distance between the points. A simple and intuitive way to understand dimensionality reduction is to consider that pictures and videos we watch on two-dimensional screens are in fact representations of a three-dimensional world, reduced to two dimensions so that they can be visualized on the two-dimensional screen. While we do lose a dimension (depth) in the images, the loss is minimal and does not ruin the viewing experience. Dimensionality reduction, when applied to our multi-dimensional dataset, would condense most of the information into two dimensions to enable visualization.

> **NOTE**
>
> For an overview of some of the numerous techniques for dimensionality reduction, refer to *The Data Science Workshop - Second Edition* at https://www.packtpub.com/product/the-data-science-workshop-second-edition/9781800566927.

The techniques for dimensionality reduction are many. You will study and apply the most popular approach by far – **Principal Component Analysis** (**PCA**). **PCA** is a method of transforming data. It takes the original features/dimensions and creates new features/dimensions that capture the most variance in the data. In other words, it creates dimensions that contain the most amount of information about the data, so that when you take the first two **Principal Components** (**PCs**), that is, dimensions, you are left with most of the information about the data, but reduced to only two dimensions:

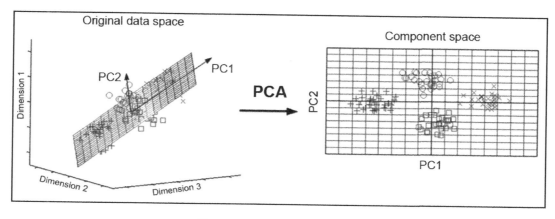

Figure 3.25: How PCA works

For the Python implementation, you will use the **PCA** module from the scikit-learn package. Usage of the package is similar to the usage of the **KMeans** module. Similar to the **KMeans** module, the **PCA** module has `fit` and `transform` methods. Fitting would mean calculating the PCs from the data and transforming would mean representing the data in these new PCs. The `fit_transform` method combines the two methods. The following code illustrates the usage of the **PCA** module:

```
from sklearn import decomposition
pca = decomposition.PCA(n_components=N)
pca_res = pca.fit_transform(data[cols])
```

Here, **N** is the number of PCs to calculate, `cols` is a list of columns to calculate the PCAs from, and **data** is the dataset containing these columns. **pca_res** would contain the transformed data.

To summarize the discussion on PCA, when performing clustering with high-dimensional data, the cluster formation approach remains the same. It is just the visualization that now needs an additional step – reduction to two dimensions using a dimensionality reduction technique such as PCA. In the exercise that follows, you will try this firsthand by clustering the mall customers using age, income, and spend score.

EXERCISE 3.06: DEALING WITH HIGH-DIMENSIONAL DATA

In this exercise, you will perform clustering on the mall customers dataset using the age, income, and spend score. The goal is to find natural clusters in the data based on these three criteria and analyze the customer segments to identify their differentiating characteristics, providing the business with some valuable insight into the nature of its customers. This time though, visualization will not be easy. You will need to use PCA to reduce the data to two dimensions to visualize the clusters:

> **NOTE**
>
> Continue in the same Jupyter notebook used until *Exercise 3.05, K-Means Clustering on Mall Customers*. Alternatively, you can also start a fresh notebook and copy the code until the feature standardization step.

1. Create a list, **cluster_cols**, containing the **Age**, **Income**, and **Spend_score** columns, which will be used for clustering. Print the first three rows of the dataset for these columns:

```
cluster_cols = ['Age', 'Income', 'Spend_score']
data_scaled[cluster_cols].head(3)
```

You should get the following output:

	Age	Income	Spend_score
0	-1.424569	-1.738999	-0.434801
1	-1.281035	-1.738999	1.195704
2	-1.352802	-1.700830	-1.715913

Figure 3.26: First three rows of the dataset

2. Perform **k-means** clustering, specifying **4** clusters using the scaled features. Specify **random_state** as **42**. Assign the clusters to the **Cluster** column:

```
model = KMeans(n_clusters=4, random_state=42)
model.fit(data_scaled[cluster_cols])

data_scaled['Cluster'] = model.predict(data_scaled[cluster_cols])
```

3. Using **PCA** on the scaled columns, create two new columns, **pc1** and **pc2**, containing the data for PC1 and PC2 respectively:

```
from sklearn import decomposition


pca = decomposition.PCA(n_components=2)
pca_res = pca.fit_transform(data_scaled[cluster_cols])


data_scaled['pc1'] = pca_res[:,0]
data_scaled['pc2'] = pca_res[:,1]
```

4. Visualize the clusters by using different markers and colors for the clusters on a scatter plot between **pc1** and **pc2** using the following code:

```
markers = ['x', '*', 'o','|']

for clust in range(4):
    temp = data_scaled[data_scaled.Cluster == clust]
    plt.scatter(temp.pc1, temp.pc2, marker=markers[clust], \
                label="Cluster "+str(clust), \
                color='gray')
plt.xlabel('PC1')
plt.ylabel('PC2')
plt.show()
```

> **NOTE**
>
> The **gray** value for the **color** attribute is used to generate graphs in grayscale. You can use other colors such as **darkgreen**, **maroon**, and so on as values of **color** parameters to get the colored graphs. You can also refer to the following document to get the code for the colored plot and the colored output: http://packt.link/NOjgT.

The following plot should appear:

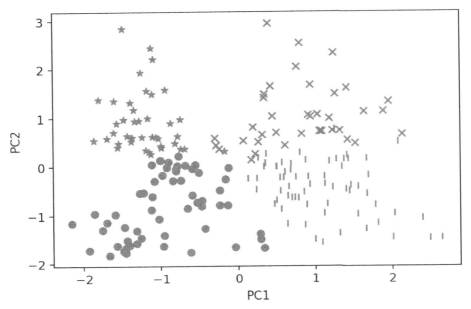

Figure 3.27: A plot of the data reduced to two dimensions denoting the three clusters

Note that the *x* and *y* axes here are the PCs, and therefore are not easily interpretable (as these are derived combinations of the original features). However, by visualizing the clusters, we can get a sense of how good the clusters are based on how much they overlap.

> **NOTE**
>
> The shapes and colors of the segments you get may vary slightly from the preceding figure. This is because of some additional randomness in the process, introduced by the random cluster center initialization that is done by the k-means algorithm. Unfortunately, the randomness remains even after setting the random seed and we can't control it. Nevertheless, while the assigned shapes may differ, you should get clusters with the same characteristics.

5. To understand the clusters, print the average values of the original features used for clustering against the four clusters:

```
data0['Cluster'] = data_scaled.Cluster
data0.groupby('Cluster')[['Age', 'Income', 'Spend_score']].mean()
```

You will get the following output:

Cluster	Age	Income	Spend_score
0	39.368421	86.500000	19.578947
1	32.875000	86.100000	81.525000
2	25.438596	40.000000	60.298246
3	53.984615	47.707692	39.969231

Figure 3.28: Average values for each cluster

From the preceding table, you see that the spend score varies significantly between the clusters. This is true for age as well as income.

6. Next, visualize this information using bar plots. Check which features are the most differentiated for the clusters using the following code:

```
data0.groupby('Cluster')[['Age', 'Income', \
                          'Spend_score']].mean() \
    .plot.bar(color=['lightgray', 'darkgray', 'black'])
plt.show()
```

NOTE

The **lightgray**, **darkgray**, and **black** values for the **color** attribute are used to generate graphs in grayscale. You can use other colors such as **darkgreen**, **maroon**, and so on as values of **color** parameters to get the colored graphs. You can also refer to the following document to get the code for the colored plot and the colored output: http://packt.link/NOjgT.

The output should be as follows:

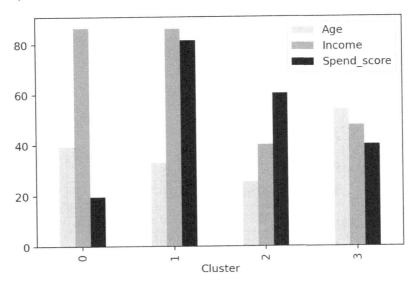

Figure 3.29: Bar plot to check features that are the most differentiated for the clusters

You can see that all three columns vary significantly across the clusters. You have cluster **0** with the highest average income but the lowest spend score and average age. You have cluster **2**, which is average in age, high on income, and the highest on spending. Let's describe these better in the next step.

7. Based on your understanding of the clusters, assign descriptive labels to the clusters.

One way to describe the clusters is as follows:

`Cluster 0`: Middle-aged penny pinchers (high income, low spend)

`Cluster 1`: Young high rollers (younger age, high income, high spend)

`Cluster 2`: Young aspirers (low income, high spend)

`Cluster 3`: Old average Joes (average income, average spend)

> **NOTE**
>
> This is just one example of how to investigate the different clusters. You can also look at the first few examples of data points in each to get a sense of the differences. In more complex cases, using various visualization techniques to probe more deeply into the different clusters may be useful.

In this exercise, you have successfully used **PCA** for **dimensionality reduction** and the visualization of the clusters. With the help of **PCA**, you saw that the clusters are well separated. You also analyzed the clusters and gave them descriptions that businesses can understand and interpret.

With this, we have gone through all the steps that are employed in a customer segmentation exercise. It is important to realize and remember that "clustering," the actual grouping of the customers, is a part of the overall exercise. Standardization of the variables, choosing the right criteria for segmentation, and building a good understanding of the clusters are all critical steps. Not to mention the importance of business stakeholders in getting the most actionable customer segments.

Let's now put all the things we have learned so far to the test in the activity that follows. You will once again work on the Therabank problem statement and help the bank maximize the effectiveness of its marketing campaign for personal loans.

ACTIVITY 3.02: BANK CUSTOMER SEGMENTATION WITH MULTIPLE FEATURES

In this activity, you will be revisiting the Therabank problem statement. You'll need to create customer segments to maximize the effectiveness of their personal loan campaign. You will accomplish this by finding the natural customer types in the data and discovering the features that differentiate them. Then, you'll identify the customer segments that have the highest propensity to take a loan.

In *Activity 3.01*, *Bank Customer Segmentation for Loan Campaign*, you employed just two features of the customer. In this activity, you will employ additional features, namely, **Age**, **Experience**, and **Mortgage**. As you are dealing with high-dimensional data, you will use **PCA** for visualizing the clusters. You will understand the customer segments obtained and provide them with business-friendly labels. As a part of your evaluation and understanding of the segments, you will also check the historical response rates for the obtained segments.

> **NOTE**
>
> Continue in the Jupyter notebook created for *Activity 3.01*, *Bank Customer Segmentation for Loan Campaign*. We will use the datasets created in that activity.

Execute the following steps to complete the activity:

1. Create a copy of the dataset named **bank_scaled**, and perform standard scaling of the **Income, CCAvg, Age, Experience**, and **Mortgage** columns.

2. Get a descriptive summary of the processed columns to verify that the scaling has been applied correctly.

3. Perform **k-means** clustering, specifying **3** clusters using the scaled features. Specify **random_state** as **42**.

4. Using **PCA** on the scaled columns, create two new columns, **pc1** and **pc2**, containing the data for PC1 and PC2 respectively.

5. Visualize the clusters by using different markers for the clusters on a scatter plot between **pc1** and **pc2**. The plot should appear as in the following figure:

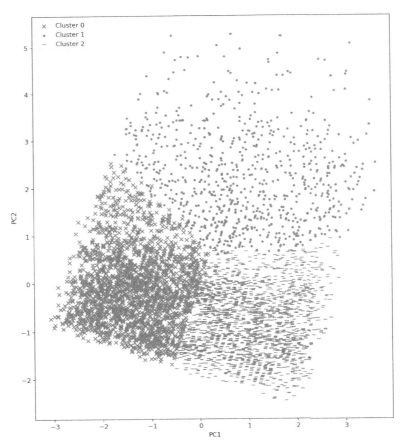

Figure 3.30: A plot of the data reduced to two dimensions denoting the three clusters

6. To understand the clusters, print the average values of the features used for clustering against the three clusters. Check which features are the most differentiated for the clusters.

7. To understand the clusters better using other relevant features, print the average values against the clusters for the **Age**, `Mortgage`, `Family`, `CreditCard`, `Online`, and `Personal Loan` features and check which cluster has the highest propensity for taking a personal loan.

8. Based on your understanding of the clusters, assign descriptive labels to the clusters.

> **NOTE**
>
> The solution for this activity can be found on page 498.

SUMMARY

In this chapter, we explored the idea of segmentation and its utility for business. We discussed the key considerations in segmentation, namely, criteria/features and the interpretation of the segments. We first discussed and implemented a traditional approach to customer segmentation. Noting its drawbacks, we then explored and performed unsupervised machine learning for customer segmentation. We established how to think about the similarity in the customer data feature space, and also learned the importance of standardizing data if it is on very different scales. Finally, we learned about k-means clustering – a commonly used, fast, and easily scalable clustering algorithm. We employed these concepts and techniques to help a mall understand its customers better using segmentation. We also helped a bank identify customer segments and how they have responded to previous marketing campaigns.

In this chapter, we used predefined values for the number of groups we asked the k-means algorithms to look for. In the next chapter, we will learn how to choose the number of groups and evaluate our groupings. We will also discover additional methods for using machine learning to perform customer segmentation.

4

EVALUATING AND CHOOSING THE BEST SEGMENTATION APPROACH

OVERVIEW

In this chapter, you will continue your journey with customer segmentation. You will improve your approach to customer segmentation by learning and implementing newer techniques for clustering and cluster evaluation. You will learn a principled way of choosing the optimal number of clusters so that you can keep the customer segments statistically robust and actionable for businesses. You will apply evaluation approaches to multiple business problems. You will also learn to apply some other popular approaches to clustering such as **mean-shift**, **k-modes**, and **k-prototypes**. Adding these to your arsenal of segmentation techniques will further sharpen your skills as a data scientist in marketing and help you come up with solutions that will create a big business impact.

INTRODUCTION

A large e-commerce company is gearing up for its biggest event for the year – its annual sale. The company is ambitious in its goals and aims to achieve the best sales figures so far, hoping for significant growth over last year's event. The marketing budget is the highest it has ever been. Naturally, marketing campaigns will be a critical factor in deciding the success of the event. From what we have learned so far, we know that for those campaigns to be most effective, an understanding of the customers and choosing the right messaging for them is critical.

In such a situation, well-performed customer segmentation can make all the difference and help maximize the **ROI** (**Return on Investment**) of marketing spend. By analyzing customer segments, the marketing team can carefully define strategies for each segment. But before investing precious resources into a customer segmentation project, data science teams, as well as business teams, need to answer a few key questions to make sure the project bears the desired result.

How should we decide the number of segments the activity should result in? How do we evaluate the robustness of the segments? Surely, before spending millions using these segments, the business would want to ensure that these segments are robust from a technical perspective as well; the fact that they are indeed homogenous must be numerically established. As an analyst, you will also want to explore alternate machine learning techniques for clustering that may be more suitable for the nature of the data. What if most of the features are categorical features? All of these are pertinent questions for any real-world customer segmentation with high stakes.

In the previous chapter, we introduced the concept of clustering and practiced it using **k-means clustering** – a simple and powerful approach to clustering that divides the data points into a pre-specified number of clusters. But we used several assumptions in the previous chapter. We created a pre-determined number of clusters, assuming that we had the right number of clusters with us, either from intuition or business constraints. Also, to evaluate the resulting clusters, we used a business perspective to assess the actionability and quality of the clusters. To complete our understanding of clustering and to ensure we have the right knowledge base to tackle any problem around segmentation, we need to be able to answer the following questions for any segmentation exercise:

- How do we choose the number of clusters?

- How do we evaluate the clusters statistically/numerically?

- Which is the best clustering algorithm for the task?

As with many questions in data science, the short answer to these questions is, "it depends". But we will not stop at that vague answer. Instead, in this chapter, we will understand all the considerations to make a choice. We will start by answering the first question. To choose the right number of clusters, in addition to business considerations, we will look at three different approaches to statistically arrive at a number. We will apply these methods, compare them, and see for ourselves the benefits and drawbacks of each.

Then, we will also explore methods that do not expect us pre-specify the desired number of clusters. These techniques will bring their own tradeoffs that we must understand. Knowing multiple methods and understanding how to choose between them will be an essential addition to your data science repertoire.

So far, we have only worked with data that is fairly easy for **k-means** to deal with: continuous variables or binary variables. In this chapter, we will explain how to deal with data containing categorical variables with many different possible values, using the **k-mode** and **k-prototype** clustering methods.

Finally, we will learn how to tell whether one method of clustering is better than another. For this purpose, we want to be able to tweak the hyperparameters of a modeling algorithm and be able to tell whether that led to a better or worse clustering, as well as compare the completely different types of algorithms to each other. In the process, we will answer the remaining two questions we asked above.

CHOOSING THE NUMBER OF CLUSTERS

While performing segmentation in the previous chapter, we specified the number of clusters to the **k-means** algorithm. In practice, though, we don't typically know the number of clusters to expect in the data. While an analyst or business team may have some intuition that may be very different from the 'natural' clusters that are available in the data. For instance, a business may have an intuition that there are generally three types of customers. But an analysis of the data may point to five distinct groups of customers. Recall that the features that we choose and the scale of those features also play an important role in defining 'similarity' between customers.

There is, hence, a need to understand the different ways we can choose the 'right' number of clusters. In this chapter, we will discuss three approaches. First, we will learn about **simple visual inspection**, which has the advantages of being easy and intuitive but relies heavily on individual judgment and subjectivity. We will then learn about the **elbow method with sum of squared errors**, which is partially quantitative but still relies on individual judgment. We will also learn about using the **silhouette score**, which removes subjectivity from the judgment but is not a very intuitive metric.

As you learn about these different methods, there is one overriding principle you should always keep in mind: the quantitative measures only tell you how well that number of clusters fits the data. They do not tell you how useful those clusters are for business. We discussed in the previous chapter that usually it is the business teams that consume and act upon these segments. The clusters, no matter how good statistically, are useless if they are not actionable by the business. There are two ways in which the clusters can turn out to be non-actionable:

- The clusters don't make business sense

- The cluster are far too many

The clusters must be interpretable by the business for them to be actionable. For instance, for making marketing campaigns most effective, you need to understand well the nature of the clusters and what each cluster cares about so that the messaging can be tuned accordingly. Regarding the number of clusters, creating a differential marketing strategy or customer experience for 30 different clusters is not practical. Often, there is an upper limit to the number of clusters that is practical for a business to act on.

Using fewer clusters and fewer variables can often lead to easier-to-interpret clusters. In general, real-world data is quite messy and there are a lot of judgment calls to be made. Learning about these methods will help you tell how good your clusters are while ensuring the methods themselves are well-founded. But keep in mind that they are only one factor. From a quantitative perspective, the difference between choosing four clusters versus five may be small, and at that point, you should be prepared to use your judgment on deciding what's best.

Now that we understand the considerations in choosing the right number of clusters, let us see these methods in practice. Let us begin by employing the simple visual approach to the mall customers in the next exercise.

NOTE

Unless specified otherwise, you will need to run the exercises in this chapter in the same Jupyter notebook.

EXERCISE 4.01: DATA STAGING AND VISUALIZATION

You will be revisiting the business problem you worked on in *Chapter 3, Unsupervised Learning and Customer Segmentation*. You are a data scientist at a leading consulting company and its new client is a popular chain of malls spread across many countries. The mall wishes to re-design its existing offers and marketing communications to improve sales in one of its key markets. An understanding of their customers is critical for this objective, and for that, good customer segmentation is needed.

The goal of this exercise is to load the data and perform basic clean-up so that you can use it conveniently for further tasks. Also, you will visualize the data to understand better how the customers are distributed on two key attributes – **Income** and **Spend_score**. You will be using these fields later to perform clustering.

> **NOTE**
>
> All the exercises in this chapter need to be performed in the same Jupyter Notebook. Similarly, the activities too build upon each other, so they need to be performed in a separate, single Jupyter Notebook. You may download the exercises and activities Notebooks for this chapter from here: https://packt.link/ZC4An.
>
> The datasets used for these activities and exercises can be found here: https://packt.link/mfNZY.

1. In a fresh Jupyter notebook, import **pandas**, **numpy**, **matplotlib** and **seaborn** libraries and load the mall customer data from the file **Mall_Customers.csv** into a DataFrame (**mall0**) and print the top five records, using the code below.

```
import numpy as np, pandas as pd
import matplotlib.pyplot as plt, seaborn as sns

mall0 = pd.read_csv("Mall_Customers.csv")
mall0.head()
```

> **NOTE**
>
> Make sure you place the CSV file in the same directory from where you are running the Jupyter Notebook. If not, make sure you change the path (emboldened) to match the one where you have stored the file.

You should get the following output:

	CustomerID	Gender	Age	Annual Income (k$)	Spending Score (1-100)
0	1	Male	19	15	39
1	2	Male	21	15	81
2	3	Female	20	16	6
3	4	Female	23	16	77
4	5	Female	31	17	40

Figure 4.1: The top five records of the mall customers dataset

We see that we have information like gender and age of the customers, along with their estimated annual income (**Annual Income (k$)**). We also have a spending score calculated by the mall (**Spending Score (1-100)**), a percentile-based score which denotes the extent of shopping the customer has done at the mall – a higher score means higher spend (highest spender gets a score of **100**).

2. Rename the columns '**Annual Income (k$)**' and '**Spending Score (1-100)**' to '**Income**' and '**Spend_score**' respectively. Print the top five records of the dataset to confirm that the change was completed. The following is the code:

```
mall0.rename({'Annual Income (k$)':'Income', \
              'Spending Score (1-100)':'Spend_score'}, \
             axis=1, inplace=True)
mall0.head()
```

The output will be as follows:

	CustomerID	Gender	Age	Income	Spend_score
0	1	Male	19	15	39
1	2	Male	21	15	81
2	3	Female	20	16	6
3	4	Female	23	16	77
4	5	Female	31	17	40

Figure 4.2: The mall0 DataFrame after renaming the columns

3. Plot a scatterplot of the **Income** and **Spend_score** fields using the following code. You will be performing clustering later using these two features as the criteria.

```
mall0.plot.scatter(x='Income', y='Spend_score', color='gray')
plt.show()
```

> **NOTE**
>
> The value **gray** for the attribute **color** (emboldened) is used to generate graphs in grayscale. You can use other colors like **darkgreen**, **maroon**, and so on as values of **color** parameter to get the colored graphs. You can also refer to the following document to get the code for the colored plot and the colored output: http://packt.link/NOjgT.

The plot you get should look like the one shown here:

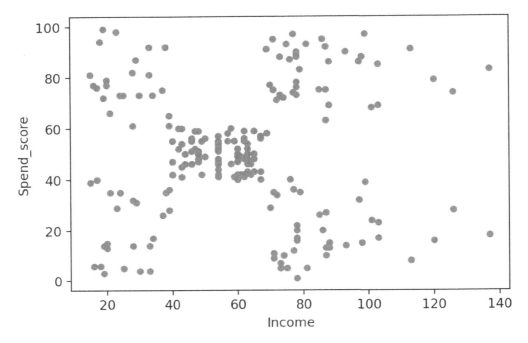

Figure 4.3: Scatterplot of Spend_score vs. Income

Figure 4.3 shows how the customers are distributed on the two attributes. We see that in the middle of the plot we have a bunch of customers with moderate income and moderate spend scores. These customers form a dense group that can be thought of as a natural cluster. Similarly, customers with low income and low spend scores also form a somewhat close group and can be thought of as a natural cluster. Customers with income above 70 and a spend score of less than 40 in the lower right area of the plot are interesting. These customers are thinly spread across and do not form a close group. However, these customers are significantly different from the other customers and can be considered a loose cluster.

Visualizing the data provides good insights into the distribution and can give us a sense of the natural groups in the data. These insights can inform the numbers that we choose for the clustering activity. Let us discuss this idea further in the next section.

SIMPLE VISUAL INSPECTION TO CHOOSE THE OPTIMAL NUMBER OF CLUSTERS

An intuitive and straightforward method of choosing the number of clusters is to perform clustering with a range of clusters and visually inspect the results. You can usually tell by looking at data how well separated the different clusters are.

Clusters are better when they are well separated, without too much overlap, and when they capture the most densely populated parts of the data space. In *Figure 4.3*, the cluster in the center of the chart – with about average income and spend score, is a good tight cluster as the points are close to each other in a dense area. The cluster in the lower right corner, on the other hand, is thinly spread across a larger area. In an ideal scenario, we would only have dense, non-overlapping clusters.

The choice of the number of clusters has a significant effect on how the clusters get allocated. Too few clusters will often lead to plots that look like a single cluster is spanning more than one densely packed space. On the other hand, too many clusters will often look like two are competing for a single densely packed space. When dealing with more than two dimensions, we can use dimensionality reduction techniques to enable the visual assessment. Remember that because two-dimensional representations of the high dimensional space are not perfect, the more dimensions there are, the poorer the visualization is of how the data are actually clustered.

Choosing the number of clusters based on visual inspection is often appealing because it is a decision based on looking at what is happening with the data most directly. People are usually quite good at looking at how much different clusters overlap and deciding whether a given number of clusters leads to too much overlap. This is not a quantitative method; however, as it leaves a lot to subjectivity and individual judgment, for many simple problems, it is a great way to decide how many clusters to use. Let us see this approach in action in the exercise that follows.

EXERCISE 4.02: CHOOSING THE NUMBER OF CLUSTERS BASED ON VISUAL INSPECTION

The goal of the exercise is to further refine the customer segmentation approach by using visual inspection to decide on the optimal number of clusters. You will try different numbers of clusters (ranging from two to six) and use visual inspection to evaluate the results and choose the right number of clusters. Continue in the Jupyter notebook from *Exercise 4.01, Data Staging and Visualization* and perform the following steps.

1. Standardize the columns **Age**, **Income** and **Spend_score**, using the **StandardScaler** from **sklearn**, after copying the information into new dataset named **mall_scaled,** using the following code:

```
mall_scaled = mall0.copy()
cols_to_scale = ['Age', 'Income', 'Spend_score']

from sklearn.preprocessing import StandardScaler
scaler = StandardScaler()

mall_scaled[cols_to_scale] = scaler.fit_transform\
                        (mall_scaled[cols_to_scale])
```

2. Import the **Kmeans** module from the **sklearn** package. Create a list, **'cluster_cols'** that stores the names of the fields (**Income** and **Spend_score**) and define the colors and shapes that you will use for each cluster (since you will be visualizing up to seven clusters in all, define seven different shapes), as follows:

```
from sklearn.cluster import KMeans
cluster_cols = ['Income', 'Spend_score']
markers = ['x', '*', '.', '|', '_', '1', '2']
```

When plotting the obtained clusters, items in the clusters will be represented by the symbols in the list in order. **'x'** will represent the first cluster (Cluster **0**). For the final clustering with **7** clusters, all the shapes in the list will be used and **Cluster 6** will be represented by the marker **'2'** (called the **'tickup'**).

3. Then, using a **for** loop, cluster the data using a different number of clusters, ranging from two to seven, and visualize the resulting plots obtained in a **subplot**. Use a separate **for** loop to plot each **cluster** in each **subplot**, so we can use different shapes for each cluster. Use the following snippet:

```
plt.figure(figsize=[12,8])

for n in range(2,8):
    model = KMeans(n_clusters=n, random_state=42)
    mall_scaled['Cluster']= model.fit_predict\
                            (mall_scaled[cluster_cols])

    plt.subplot(2,3, n-1)
    for clust in range(n):
        temp = mall_scaled[mall_scaled.Cluster == clust]
        plt.scatter(temp.Income, temp.Spend_score, \
                    marker=markers[clust], \
                    label="Cluster "+str(clust), color='gray')
        plt.title("N clusters: "+str(n))
        plt.xlabel('Income')
        plt.ylabel('Spend_score')
        plt.legend()

plt.show()
```

> **NOTE**
>
> The value **gray** for the attribute **color** (emboldened) is used to generate graphs in grayscale. You can use other colors like **darkgreen**, **maroon**, and so on as values of **color** parameter to get the colored graphs. You can also refer to the following document to get the code for the colored plot and the colored output: http://packt.link/NOjgT.

> **NOTE**
>
> If the plots you are getting are overlapping or are not clear, you can try changing the dimensions of the plot by modifying them in the emboldened line of code.

You should see the following plots when this is done:

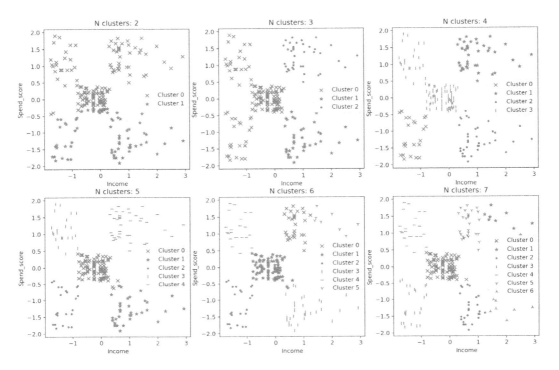

Figure 4.4: Scatterplots of Income and Spend_score with clusters progressing from 2 to 7

By observing the resulting plots, we can see that with too few clusters (**2**, **3** or **4**), we end up with clusters spanning sparse regions in between more densely packed regions. For instance, with **3** clusters, we see that we get one huge cluster for lower-income customers. On the other hand, with too many (**6** or **7**), we end up with clusters that border each other but do not seem separated by a region of sparseness. Five clusters seem to capture things very well with clusters that are non-overlapping and are fairly dense. Five is, therefore, the 'right' number of clusters. This is in line with our expectation that we built in *Exercise 4.01, Data Staging and Visualization*. This simple visual method is effective, but note that it is entirely subjective. Let's now try a quantitative approach, which is the most popular approach for determining the optimal number of clusters.

THE ELBOW METHOD WITH SUM OF SQUARED ERRORS

Often, it is difficult to tell by visualization alone how many clusters should be used to solve a particular problem. Different people may disagree about the number of clusters to use, and there may not be a clear, unanimous answer. With higher dimensional data, there is an additional issue: *dimensionality-reduction techniques are not perfect*. They attempt to take all the information in multiple dimensions and reduce it to only two. In some cases, this can work well, but as the number of dimensions increases, the data becomes more complex, and these visual methods quickly reach their limitations. When this happens, it's not easy to determine through visual inspection what the right number of clusters to use is. In these cases, it's often better to reach for a more quantitative measure. One such classic measure is to look for an *elbow* in a plot of the sum of squared errors, also called an **Inertia Plot**.

The **sum of squared errors** (**SSE**) is the sum of the "errors" (the difference between a data point and the centroid of its assigned cluster) for all data points, squared. Another term for it is inertia. The tighter the clusters, the closer the constituent points to their respective clusters, and the lower the SSE/inertia. The sum of squared errors for the model can be calculated using the following equation:

$$SS = \sum_k \sum_{x_i \in k} (x_i - \mu_k)^2$$

Figure 4.5: Equation for calculating the sum of squared errors of data points in a dataset

Here, μ_k is the location of the centroid of cluster k, and each x_i is a data point assigned to cluster *k*. When all the entities are treated as a single cluster, this SSE value is at its maximum for the dataset. As we increase *k*, we should expect the sum of squared errors to decrease since there are more centroids. In the extreme case, when each point is a cluster, the SSE/inertia value is **0**, as each point is the centroid for its own cluster. In scikit-learn, you will use the '**inertia_**' attribute that is available after fitting a model. For instance, if '**model**' is the name of the Kmeans instance you fit on the data, extracting and printing the SSE is as simple as the following command:

```
print(model.inertia_)
```

This would print the value of the SSE as a simple number. We will see this in action in the next exercise.

> **NOTE**
>
> The Kmeans model in Python calculates the SSE exactly as in the equation in *Figure 4.5*. The value for SSE/inertia is available in the `'inertia_'` attribute of the trained model. The documentation on this can be found at the following link:
> https://scikit-learn.org/stable/modules/generated/sklearn.cluster.KMeans.html.

This intuition helps identify the optimal number of clusters. When SSE/inertia is plotted at different numbers of clusters, there often is an **elbow** in the plot, where the **gain** in terms of reduced errors seems to slow down for each new cluster. An example plot is shown below in *Figure 4.6*.

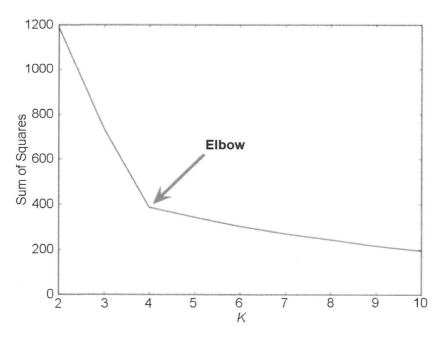

Figure 4.6: SSE/inertia for different values of k, with an "elbow" (inflection point) at k=4

The elbow method is a simple and commonly used method for choosing the number of clusters. With the theory understood, let us now see the method in practice to make our understanding concrete. Let us create an inertia plot for the mall customer data and choose the optimal number of clusters, in the following exercise.

EXERCISE 4.03: DETERMINING THE NUMBER OF CLUSTERS USING THE ELBOW METHOD

In this exercise, you will use the elbow method to identify the optimal number of clusters. The goal is to improve upon the mall customer segmentation approach by using a principled method to determine the number of clusters so that all involved stakeholders, including business teams, gain more confidence in the soundness of the approach and the resulting clusters. Try the range 2 – 10 for the number of clusters using the age and income data. Continue in the same Jupyter notebook you have been using for the exercises so far.

1. On the scaled mall customer data (**mall_scaled**), using the columns '**Income**' and '**Spend_score**', create three clusters using the **KMeans** algorithm:

```
K = 3
model = KMeans(n_clusters=K, random_state=42)
model.fit(mall_scaled[cluster_cols])
```

2. Once the model is fit, the SSE/inertia is available very conveniently in the '**inertia_**' attribute of the model object. Print out the SSE/ inertia for the model with 3 clusters using the following code:

```
print(model.inertia_)
```

You will see that inertia is **157.70**. Note that this number by itself does not mean much to us. We are more interested in how this number changes with the number of clusters.

> **NOTE**
>
> You may observe minor differences in the value owing to randomization in the processes, some of which we can't control. The values should be of a similar order.

3. Next, fit multiple **KMeans** models with the number of clusters ranging from 2 to 10 and store the inertia values for the different models in a list. The code is as follows:

```
X = mall_scaled[cluster_cols]

inertia_scores = []
for K in range(2,11):
    inertia = KMeans(n_clusters=K, random_state=42).fit(X)\
                                                  .inertia_
    inertia_scores.append(inertia)
```

The list **inertia_scores** should now contain the sum of squared errors for different values of **K**.

4. Create the SSE/inertia plot as a line plot with the following code.

```
plt.figure(figsize=[7,5])
plt.plot(range(2,11), inertia_scores, color='gray')
plt.title("SSE/Inertia vs. number of clusters")
plt.xlabel("Number of clusters: K")
plt.ylabel('SSE/Inertia')
plt.show()
```

> **NOTE**
>
> The value **gray** for the attribute **color** is used to generate graphs in grayscale. You can use other colors like **darkgreen**, **maroon**, and so on as values of **color** parameter to get the colored graphs. You can also refer to the following document to get the code for the colored plot and the colored output: http://packt.link/NOjgT.

You should get the following plot.

Figure 4.7: SSE plot for different values of k, showing an "elbow" (inflection point) at k=5

By observing the preceding plot, you will notice that there is an elbow in the plot at **K=5**. So, we take five as the optimal number of clusters, the best value of **K** for the **KMeans** algorithm. Before that, every additional cluster gives us big gains in reducing the sum of squared errors. Beyond five, we seem to be getting extremely low returns.

In this exercise, you created sum of squared error plots to visually identify the optimal number of clusters. You now understand and have implemented two approaches for the task, making your overall approach to clustering, and therefore customer segmentation, technically far more robust. It's time to put your learning to the test in the next activity, where you will employ both approaches for solving a business problem using customer segmentation.

ACTIVITY 4.01: OPTIMIZING A LUXURY CLOTHING BRAND'S MARKETING CAMPAIGN USING CLUSTERING

You are working at a company that sells luxury clothing. Their sales team has collected data on customer age, income, their annual spend at the business, and the number of days since their last purchase. The company wants to start targeted marketing campaigns but doesn't know how many different types of customers they have. If they understood the number of different segments, it would help design the campaign better by helping define the channels to use, the messaging to employ, and more.

Your goal is to perform customer segmentation for the company which will help them optimize their campaigns. To make your approach robust and more reliable to business, you need to arrive at the right number of segments by using the visualization approach as well as the elbow method with the sum of squared errors. Execute the following steps to complete the activity:

> **NOTE**
>
> The file for the activity, `Clothing_Customers.csv`, can be found on GitHub at https://packt.link/rwW7j.

Create a fresh Jupyter notebook for this activity.

1. Import the libraries required for DataFrame handling and plotting (**pandas**, **numpy**, **matplotlib**). Read in the data from the file '`Clothing_Customers.csv`' into a DataFrame and print the top 5 rows to understand it better.

2. Standardize all the columns in the data. You will be using all four columns for the segmentation.

3. Visualize the data to get a good understanding of it. Since you are dealing with four dimensions, use **PCA** to reduce to two dimensions before plotting. The resulting plot should be as follows.

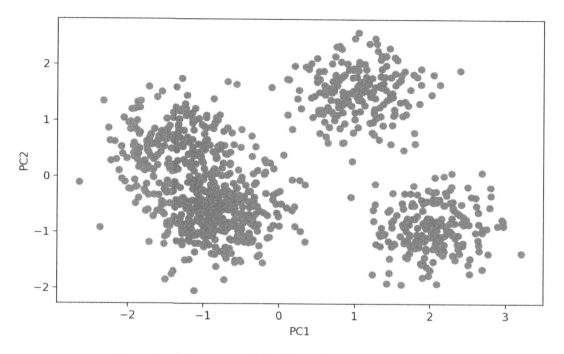

Figure 4.8: Scatterplot of the dimensionality reduced data

4. Visualize clustering with two through seven clusters. You should get the following plot.

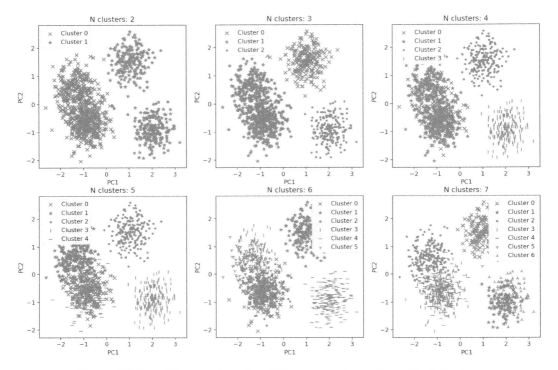

Figure 4.9: Resulting clusters for different number of specified clusters

Choosing clusters using elbow method - create a plot of the sum of squared errors and look for an elbow. Vary the number of clusters from 2 to 11. You should get the following plot.

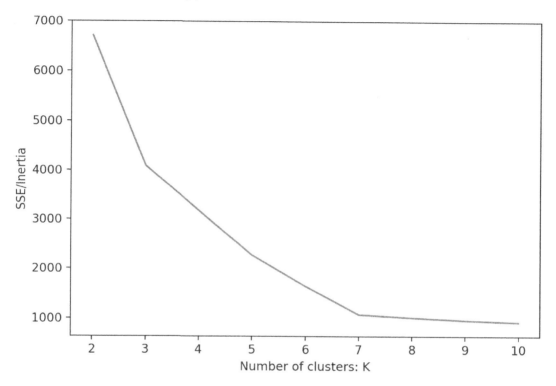

Figure 4.10: SSE plot for different values of k

5. Do both the methods agree on the optimal number of clusters? Looking at the results from both, and based on your business understanding, what is the number of clusters you would choose? Explain your decision.

> **NOTE**
>
> The solution for this activity can be found on page 504.

MORE CLUSTERING TECHNIQUES

If you completed the preceding activity, you must have realized that you had to use a more robust approach to determine the number of clusters. You dealt with high dimensional data for clustering and therefore the visual analysis of the clusters necessitated the use of PCA. The visual assessment approach and the elbow method from the inertia plot however did not agree very well. This difference can be explained by understanding that visualization using PCA loses a lot of information and therefore provides an incomplete picture. Realizing that, you used the learning from the elbow method as well as your business perspective to arrive at an optimal number of clusters.

Such a comprehensive approach that incorporates business constraints helps the data scientist create actionable and therefore valuable customer segments. With these techniques learned and this understanding created, let us look at more techniques for clustering that will make the data scientist even more effective and proficient at customer segmentation.

So far, we have been employing the **k-means** algorithm for clustering on multiple datasets. We saw that **k-means** is a useful clustering algorithm because it is simple, widely applicable, and scales very well to large datasets. However, it is not the only clustering algorithm available. Some techniques don't need to pre-specify the number of clusters, while some other techniques are better equipped to handle different data types. Each clustering algorithm has its own strengths and weaknesses, so it's extremely useful to have more than one in your toolkit. We will look at some of the other popular clustering algorithms in this section.

MEAN-SHIFT CLUSTERING

Mean-shift clustering is an interesting algorithm in contrast to the k-means algorithm because unlike k-means, it does not require you to specify the number of clusters. The intuition of its working is rather simple – it works by starting at each data point and shifting the data points (assigning them to clusters) toward the area of greatest density – that is, towards a natural cluster centroid. When all the data points have found their local density peak, the algorithm is complete. This tends to be computationally expensive, so this method does not scale well to large datasets (k-means clustering, on the other hand, scales very well).

The following diagram illustrates this:

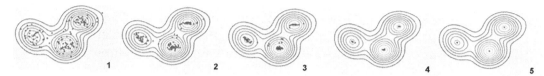

Figure 4.11: Illustration of the workings of the mean-shift algorithm

Figure. 4.11 shows the working of the **mean-shift** algorithm. Note that the 'shifting' of the points does not mean that the points themselves are altered, but rather there is an allocation to a center of high density. Effectively, as we progress from *step 1* to *step 5*, the clusters become more defined and so do the greater density areas.

While not needing to choose the number of clusters sounds great, there is another hyper-parameter that strongly influences the behavior of the algorithm - **bandwidth**. Also referred to as **window size**, bandwidth defines how far each data point will look when searching for a higher density area. As you can expect, a higher bandwidth would allow points to look farther and get linked to farther away clusters and can lead to fewer, looser, larger clusters. Consider the image for *Step 1* in *Figure 4.11*: if an extremely high bandwidth parameter (close to **1**) were employed, all the points would have been lumped into one cluster. On the other hand, a lower value of bandwidth may result in a higher number of tight clusters. Referring again to *Step 1* of *Figure 4.11*, if we used a very low value of bandwidth (close to **0**) we would have arrived at dozens of clusters. The parameter, therefore, has a strong impact on the result and needs to be balanced.

A common method (which we will use shortly) for determining the best bandwidth is to estimate it based on the distances between nearby points (using a quantile parameter which specifies the proportion of data points to look across), but this method requires you to choose a quantile that determines the proportion of points to look at. This is non-trivial. In practice, this ends up being a very similar problem to the problem of choosing a number of clusters where at some point you, the user, have to choose what hyperparameter to use.

For the Python implementation for estimating bandwidth, you will employ the **estimate_bandwidth** utility in scikit-learn. You need to first import the **estimate_bandwidth** utility from sklearn, then simply execute it by providing the data and the **quantile** parameter (discussed in the previous paragraph). The function returns the calculated bandwidth. The commands below demonstrate the usage of **estimate_bandwidth**.

```
from sklearn.cluster import estimate_bandwidth
bandwidth = estimate_bandwidth(data, quantile=quantile_value)
```

Where **data** is the dataset you wish to cluster eventually and **quantile_value** is the value for quantile that you can specify.

Let us make this understanding concrete by applying the **mean-shift** algorithm to the mall customers' data.

> **NOTE**
>
> For the Python implementation for estimating bandwidth, we will employ the **estimate_bandwidth** utility in scikit-learn. More details and usage examples can be found at the official documentation here: https://scikit-learn.org/stable/modules/generated/sklearn.cluster.estimate_bandwidth.html.

EXERCISE 4.04: MEAN-SHIFT CLUSTERING ON MALL CUSTOMERS

In this exercise, you will cluster mall customers using the mean-shift algorithm. You will employ the columns **Income** and **Spend_score** as criteria. You will first manually specify the bandwidth parameter. Then, you will estimate the bandwidth parameter using the **estimate_bandwidth** method and see how it varies with the choice of quantile. Continue in the Jupyter notebook from *Exercise 4.03, Determining the Number of Clusters Using the Elbow Method* and perform the following steps.

1. Import **MeanShift** and **estimate_bandwidth** from **sklearn** and create a variable **'bandwidth'** with a value of **0.9** – the bandwidth to use (an arbitrary, high value). The code is as follows -

```
from sklearn.cluster import MeanShift, estimate_bandwidth
bandwidth = 0.9
```

2. To perform mean-shift clustering on the standardized data, create an instance of **MeanShift**, specifying the bandwidth and setting **bin_seeding** to **True** (to speed up the algorithm). Fit the model on the data and assign the cluster to the variable '**Cluster**'. Use the following code:

```
ms = MeanShift(bandwidth=bandwidth, bin_seeding=True)
ms.fit(mall_scaled[cluster_cols])

mall_scaled['Cluster']= ms.predict(X)
```

3. Visualize the clusters using a scatter plot.

```
markers = ['x', '*', '.', '|', '_', '1', '2']

plt.figure(figsize=[8,6])
for clust in range(mall_scaled.Cluster.nunique()):
    temp = mall_scaled[mall_scaled.Cluster == clust]
    plt.scatter(temp.Income, temp.Spend_score, \
                marker=markers[clust], \
                label="Cluster"+str(clust), \
                color='gray')

plt.xlabel("Income")
plt.ylabel("Spend_score")
plt.legend()
plt.show()
```

> **NOTE**
>
> The value **gray** for the attribute **color** (emboldened) is used to generate graphs in grayscale. You can use other colors like **darkgreen**, **maroon**, etc. as values of **color** parameter to get the colored graphs. You can also refer to the following document to get the code for colored plot and the colored output: http://packt.link/NOjgT.

You should get the following plot:

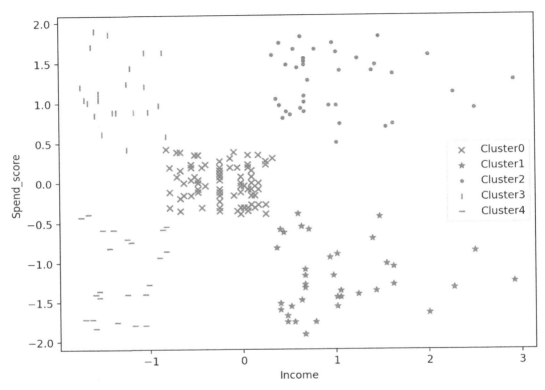

Figure 4.12: Clusters from mean-shift with bandwidth at 0.9

The model has found five unique clusters. They are very much aligned with the clusters you arrived at earlier using **K-means** where you specified **5** clusters. But notice that the clusters on the right have areas of very low density. The choice of bandwidth has led to such loose clusters.

4. Estimate the required bandwidth using the **estimate_bandwidth** method. Use the **estimate_bandwidth** function with a quantile value of **0.1** (an arbitrary choice) to estimate the best bandwidth to use. Print the value, fit the model, and note the number of clusters, using the following code:

```
bandwidth = estimate_bandwidth(mall_scaled[cluster_cols], \
                               quantile=0.1)
print(bandwidth)
```

You will get a value of about **0.649**. Using this, fit the model on the data.

```
ms = MeanShift(bandwidth=bandwidth, bin_seeding=True)
ms.fit(mall_scaled[cluster_cols])
mall_scaled['Cluster']= ms.predict(mall_scaled[cluster_cols])
mall_scaled.Cluster.nunique()
```

The output for the unique number of clusters is **7**.

5. Visualize the obtained clusters using a scatter plot.

```
plt.figure(figsize=[8,6])

for clust in range(mall_scaled.Cluster.nunique()):
    temp = mall_scaled[mall_scaled.Cluster == clust]
    plt.scatter(temp.Income, temp.Spend_score, \
            marker=markers[clust], \
            label="Cluster"+str(clust), \
            color='gray')
plt.xlabel("Income")
plt.ylabel("Spend_score")
plt.legend()
plt.show()
```

> **NOTE**
>
> The value **gray** for the attribute `color` is used to generate graphs in grayscale. You can use other colors like **darkgreen**, **maroon**, and so on as values of `color` parameter to get the colored graphs. You can also refer to the following document to get the code for the colored plot and the colored output: http://packt.link/NOjgT.

The output should look like the following plot:

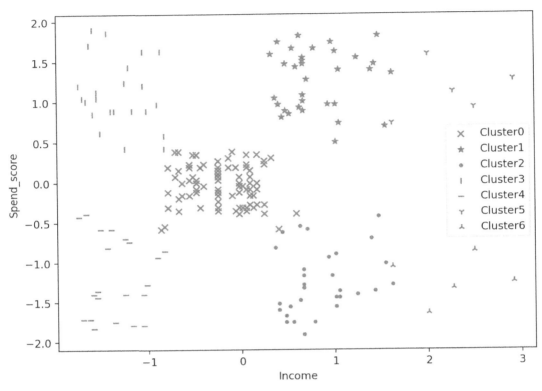

Figure 4.13: mean-shift with estimated bandwidth

6. Estimate the bandwidth again, this time with a quantile value of **0.15**. Print out the number of clusters obtained.

```
bandwidth = estimate_bandwidth(mall_scaled[cluster_cols], \
                               quantile=0.15)
print(bandwidth)
```

The calculated bandwidth is **0.858**.

7. Use the bandwidth calculated in the previous step to fit and extract the number of clusters.

```
ms = MeanShift(bandwidth=bandwidth, bin_seeding=True)
ms.fit(mall_scaled[cluster_cols])
mall_scaled['Cluster']= ms.predict(mall_scaled[cluster_cols])
mall_scaled.Cluster.nunique()
```

The result should be **5**.

8. Visualize the clusters obtained.

```
plt.figure(figsize=[8,6])

for clust in range(mall_scaled.Cluster.nunique()):
    temp = mall_scaled[mall_scaled.Cluster == clust]
    plt.scatter(temp.Income, temp.Spend_score, \
                marker=markers[clust], \
                label="Cluster"+str(clust), \
                color='gray')

plt.xlabel("Income")
plt.ylabel("Spend_score")
plt.legend()
plt.show()
```

NOTE

The value **gray** for the attribute **color** (emboldened) is used to generate graphs in grayscale. You can use other colors like **darkgreen**, **maroon**, and so on as values of **color** parameter to get the colored graphs. You can also refer to the following document to get the code for the colored plot and the colored output: http://packt.link/NOjgT.

The output should be as follows.

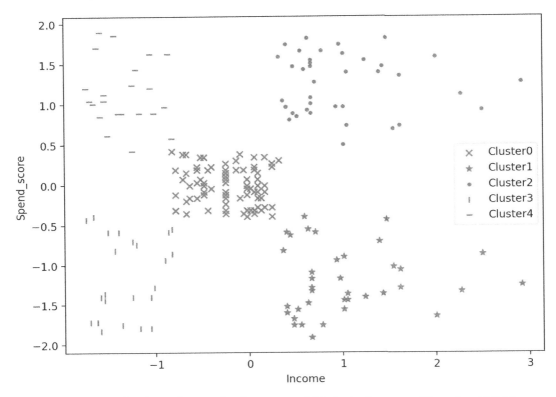

Figure 4.14: The data clustered using mean-shift clustering, quantile value of 0.15

You can see from *Figure 4.14* that you have obtained five clusters. This is the optimal number as you have seen from multiple approaches, including visual inspection.

In this exercise, you successfully used **mean-shift** clustering with varying parameters to make your understanding more concrete. When you used a quantile value of **0.15**, which means you looked at more points to estimate the bandwidth required, you ended up with a bandwidth of about **0.86** and obtained **5** clusters. When you used a quantile value of **0.1**, though, the estimated bandwidth was about **0.65** and obtained **7** clusters. This demonstrates the impact of the **bandwidth** parameter, alternatively, the **quantile** parameter used to estimate the bandwidth.

BENEFITS AND DRAWBACKS OF THE MEAN-SHIFT TECHNIQUE

In the previous exercise, we saw that the mean-shift algorithm too had its own key hyper-parameters. This is again a choice to be made by the user. Why, then, bother with mean-shift clustering? To answer this let us understand the benefits and drawbacks of the mean-shift algorithm.

Benefits of mean-shift algorithm

1. We don't need to pre-specify the number of clusters.

2. The single parameter, **bandwidth**, has a physical meaning and its effects are easy to interpret.

3. It can identify complex-shaped clusters (**k-means** only gave spherical/globular clusters).

4. Robust to outliers.

Drawbacks of mean-shift algorithm

1. Computationally expensive, doesn't scale well to large datasets.

2. Does not work well with a high number of dimensions (leads to unstable clusters).

3. No direct control over the number of clusters, which is problematic when we have business constraints on the number of clusters.

We can see that the **mean-shift** algorithm is another powerful, density-based approach to clustering. While it has its own hyper-parameter and some issues with scalability, it does have its merits which can be extremely useful in certain situations. But both approaches we saw so far work only for quantitative data. In practice, we come across many situations that need us to work with non-numeric data. Let us now explore another technique for clustering, that helps us handle different types of data better.

K-MODES AND K-PROTOTYPES CLUSTERING

k-means clustering is great when you are dealing exclusively with quantitative data. However, when you have categorical data (that is, data that can't be converted into numerical order, such as race, language, and country) with more than two categories, the representation of this data using numbers becomes a key consideration. In statistics, one common strategy for dealing with categorical data is to use dummy variables—the practice of creating a new **indicator** variable for each category - so that each of these dummy variables is a binary. When clustering, this can lead to complications, because if you have many different categories, you are adding many different dimensions for each categorical variable and the result will often not properly reflect the kinds of groupings you're looking for.

To handle such situations, two related methods make dealing with categorical data more natural. k-modes is a clustering algorithm that uses the mode of a cluster rather than the mean, but otherwise performs just like the k-means algorithm. Like mean is a good measure for the typical/ central value for a continuous variable, 'mode' or the most commonly occurring category is the typical value for a categorical variable. The K-modes algorithm is a great choice for categorical data.

k-prototypes clustering allows you to deal with cases where there is a mix of categorical and continuous variables. Instead of defining a centroid for each cluster like k-means or k-modes, k-prototypes clustering chooses a data point to be the prototype and uses that as if it is the centroid of the cluster, updating to a new data point closer to the center of all data points assigned to that cluster using the same process as k-means or k-modes.

For the Python implementation, you will be using the **kmodes** package. Make sure you install the package, which can be done using the **pip** command:

```
!pip install kmodes
```

The package contains the **kmodes** and **Kprototypes** techniques, which can be employed using the same syntax that we used for the Kmeans technique. For example, **Kprototypes** can be imported and an instance of it created using the following command:

```
from kmodes.kprototypes import KPrototypes
kp = KPrototypes(n_clusters=N, random_state=seed_value)
```

Where **N** is the number of clusters and **seed_value** is the **random_state** to ensure reproducibility of results. The model can then be fit on any dataset using a command like the one below:

```
kp.fit(dataset)
```

Where **dataset** contains the data you wish to cluster. Note that the syntax is consistent with the Kmeans package and **fit_predict** and **predict** methods will work the same way. A similar syntax will work for the Kmodes technique as well.

EXERCISE 4.05: CLUSTERING DATA USING THE K-PROTOTYPES METHOD

For this exercise, you will revisit the customer segmentation problem for Therabank, that you encountered in *Activity 3.01, Bank Customer Segmentation for Loan Campaign*. The business goal is to get more customers to opt for a personal loan to increase the profitability of the bank's portfolio. Creating customer segments will help the bank identify the types of customers, tune their messaging in the marketing campaigns for the personal loan product. The dataset provided contains data for customers including demographics, some financial information, and how these customers responded to a previous campaign.

> **NOTE**
>
> The file for the exercise, **Bank_Personal_Loan_Modelling-2.csv** can be found here: https://packt.link/b0J5j.

An important feature for business is the education level of the customer and needs to be included in the segmentation. The values in the data are **Primary**, **Secondary**, and **Tertiary**. Since this is a categorical feature, K-means is not a suitable approach. You need to create customer segmentation with this data by applying **k-prototype** clustering to data that has a mix of categorical (**education**) and continuous (**income**) variables.

You can continue using the same Jupyter notebook from the previous exercises, or feel free to use a new one. Execute the following steps.

> **NOTE**
>
> If all variables were categorical, we would use **k-modes** instead of **k-prototypes** clustering. The code would be the same, except all references to `kprototypes` would be changed to `kmodes`. You will use `kmodes` in the next activity.

1. Import pandas and read in the data from the file **Bank_Personal_Loan_Modelling-2.csv** into a pandas DataFrame named **bank0**:

```
import pandas as pd
bank0 = pd.read_csv("Bank_Personal_Loan_Modelling-2.csv")
bank0.head()
```

> **NOTE**
>
> Make sure you place the CSV file in the same directory from where you are running the Jupyter Notebook. If not, make sure you change the path (emboldened) to match the one where you have stored the file.

The output should be:

	ID	Age	Experience	Income	ZIP Code	Family	CCAvg	Education	Mortgage	Personal Loan	Securities Account	CD Account	Online	CreditCard
0	1	25	1	49	91107	4	1.6	Primary	0	0	1	0	0	0
1	2	45	19	34	90089	3	1.5	Primary	0	0	1	0	0	0
2	3	39	15	11	94720	1	1.0	Primary	0	0	0	0	0	0
3	4	35	9	100	94112	1	2.7	Secondary	0	0	0	0	0	0
4	5	35	8	45	91330	4	1.0	Secondary	0	0	0	0	0	1

Figure 4.15: First five rows of the DataFrame

2. Standardize the **Income** column:

```
from sklearn.preprocessing import StandardScaler
scaler = StandardScaler()


bank_scaled = bank0.copy()
bank_scaled['Income'] = scaler.fit_transform(bank0[['Income']])
```

3. Import **KPrototypes** from the **kmodes** module. Perform **k-prototypes** clustering using three clusters, specifying the **education** column (in column index **1**) as **categorical**, and save the result of the clustering as a new column called **cluster**. Specify a **random_state** of **42** for consistency.

```
from kmodes.kprototypes import KPrototypes
cluster_cols = ['Income', 'Education']


kp = KPrototypes(n_clusters=3, random_state=42)


bank_scaled['Cluster'] = kp.fit_predict\
                         (bank_scaled[cluster_cols],\
                          categorical=[1])
```

4. To understand the obtained clusters, get the proportions of the different education levels in each cluster using the following code.

```
res = bank_scaled.groupby('Cluster')['Education']\
              .value_counts(normalize=True)


res.unstack().plot.barh(figsize=[9,6], \
                        color=['black','lightgray','dimgray'])
plt.show()
```

> **NOTE**
>
> The values **black**, **lightgray**, and **dimgray** for the attribute **color** (emboldened) are used to generate graphs in grayscale. You can use other colors like **darkgreen**, **maroon**, etc. as values of **color** parameter to get the colored graphs. You can also refer to the following document to get the code for the colored plot and the colored output: http://packt.link/NOjgT.

You should get the following plot:

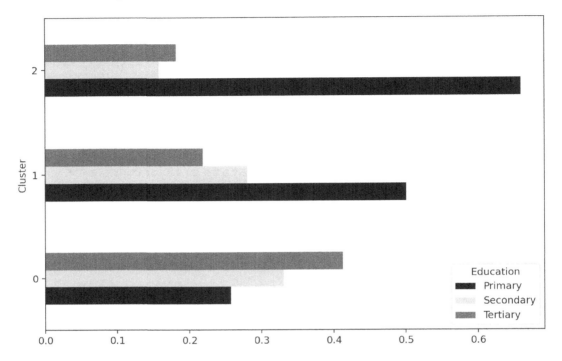

Figure 4.16: The proportions of customers of different educational levels in each cluster

> **NOTE**
>
> You can get a different order for the clusters in the chart. The proportions should be the same, though. This is because the clusters that you get would be the same. The order in which the clusters are numbered, in other words, which cluster becomes `Cluster 0` is affected by randomization that we cannot control by setting the seed. Therefore, while the numbers assigned to the clusters can differ, the resulting groups and their respective attributes will not.

You can see in *Figure 4.16* that `cluster 2` is dominated by customers with primary education. In `cluster 1`, the number of primary educated customers roughly equals the number of secondary and tertiary educated customers together. In `cluster 0`, customers with higher education (secondary or tertiary) significantly outnumber those with primary education.

> **NOTE**
>
> We used this method of visualizing the education data instead of the usual scatterplots because the categorical data increases the dimensionality. If we used dimensionality reduction to visualize the data, we would not be able to visualize how the clusters capture the different education levels.

With this exercise, you have successfully used **k-prototypes** clustering to segment people based on their Income and Education levels. A visual analysis gave insight into the nature of the clusters. Visual analysis is good but brings a lot of subjectivity and isn't always a good idea when dealing with high-dimensional data. It is always good to have quantitative measures for evaluating clusters. Let's discuss some approaches in the next section.

EVALUATING CLUSTERING

We have seen various ways of performing clustering so far, each approach having its merits. For the same task, we saw that the approaches provided varying results. Which of them is better? Before we answer that, we need to be able to evaluate how good the results from clustering are. Only then can we compare across segmentation approaches. We need to have, therefore, ways to evaluate the quality of clustering.

Another motivation for cluster evaluation methods is the reiteration that clustering is a part of a bigger segmentation exercise, of which clustering is a key part, but far from the whole. Recall from the discussion in the previous chapter that in segmentation exercises, business is often the end consumer of the segments and acts on them. The segments, therefore, need to make sense to the business as well and be actionable. That is why we need to be able to evaluate clusters from a business perspective as well. We have discussed this aspect in the previous chapter and stated the involved considerations. Let us further the discussion on the technical evaluation of clusters.

A principled, objective way of evaluating clusters is essential. Subjective methods, such as visual inspection, can always be used, but we acknowledge that they have serious limitations. Quantitative methods for cluster evaluation remove subjectivity and have the added advantage of enabling some level of automation. One such measure is the **silhouette score** - a powerful objective method that can be used with data that is more difficult to visualize. We will learn more about this in the next section.

Note that the silhouette score is a general measure of how well a clustering fits the data, so it can be used to not only compare two different models of different types but also choose hyperparameters, such as the number of clusters or choice of quantile for calculating bandwidth for mean-shift clustering.

SILHOUETTE SCORE

A natural way to evaluate clusters is as follows: if the clusters are well-separated, then any point in a cluster should be closer to most of the points in the same cluster than to a point from another cluster.

This intuition is quantified through the silhouette score. The silhouette score is a formal measure of how well a clustering fits the data. The higher the score, the better the clusters are. The score is calculated for each data point separately, and the average is taken as a measure of how well the model fits the whole dataset altogether.

Let us understand the score better. There are two main components to the score. The first component measures how well the data point fits into the cluster that it is assigned to. This is defined as the average distance between it and all other members of that same cluster. The second component measures how well the data point fits into the next nearest cluster. It is calculated in the same way by measuring the average distance between the data point and all the data points assigned to the next nearest cluster. The difference between these two numbers can be taken as a measure of how well the data point fits into the cluster it is assigned to as opposed to a different cluster. Therefore, when calculated for all data points, it's a measure of how well each data point fits into the particular cluster it's been assigned to.

More formally, given data point x_i, where a_{xi} is the average distance between that data point and all other data points in the same cluster and b_{xi} is the average distance between data point x_i and the data points in the next nearest cluster, the **silhouette score** is defined as follows:

$$s(x_i) = \frac{b_{x_i} - a_{x_i}}{\max\left(a_{x_i}, b_{x_i}\right)}$$

Figure 4.17: Equation for calculating the silhouette score for a data point

Note that since we divide by the maximum of a_{x_i} and b_{x_i}, we end up with a number between **−1** and **1**. A negative score means that this data point is actually on average closer to the other cluster, whereas a high positive score means it's a much better fit to the cluster it is assigned to. A value close to **0** would mean that the sample is close to both clusters. When we take the average score across all data points, we will therefore still get a number between **−1** and **1**, where the closer we are to one the better the fit.

Silhouette score in Python is calculated using the **silhouette_score** utility in scikit-learn, which calculates the value exactly as described in *Figure. 4.17*. To calculate the silhouette score, you need the data and the assigned clusters. You can import the **silhouette_score** utility and calculate the score like in the commands below –

```
from sklearn.metrics import silhouette_score
silhouette_avg = silhouette_score(data, cluster_assignments)
```

where **data** contains the data you clustered and **cluster_assignments** are the clusters assigned to the rows.

Note that the silhouette score is a general measure of how well a clustering fits the data, so it can be used to choose the optimal number of clusters for the dataset. We can also use the measure to compare clusters from different algorithms, an idea that we will explore later in this chapter. Let us proceed and use silhouette score for choosing the number of clusters.

EXERCISE 4.06: USING SILHOUETTE SCORE TO PICK OPTIMAL NUMBER OF CLUSTERS

In this exercise, you will continue working on the mall customer segmentation case. The objective of the exercise is to identify the right number of clusters using a statistical approach that is, the silhouette score. You will perform k-means clustering on mall customers using different numbers of clusters and use the silhouette score to determine the best number of clusters to use. You will need to continue in the Jupyter notebook used for the exercises so far.

1. On the scaled mall customer dataset (**mall_scaled**) created in *Exercise 4.02, Choosing the Number of Clusters Based on Visual Inspection*, fit a **KMeans** model using the features '**Income**' and '**Spend_score**', specifying **3** clusters. Extract the assigned cluster for each point, using the **fit_predict** method of the model as in the following code:

```
cluster_cols = ['Income', 'Spend_score']
X = mall_scaled[cluster_cols]

model = KMeans(n_clusters=3, random_state=42)
cluster_assignments = model.fit_predict(X)
```

2. Import the **silhouette_score** method from **sklearn** and calculate the average silhouette score for the current cluster assignments with three clusters using the code that follows:

```
from sklearn.metrics import silhouette_score
silhouette_avg = silhouette_score(X, cluster_assignments)
print(silhouette_avg)
```

You should get the value **0.467**. Note that this number by itself is not intuitive and may not mean much, but is useful as a relative measure, as we will see in the next step.

3. Now that you know how to calculate the silhouette score, you can calculate the scores, looping over different values of **K (2-10)**, as follows:

```
silhouette_scores = []

for K in range(2, 11):
    model = KMeans(n_clusters=K, random_state=42)
    cluster_assignments = model.fit_predict(X)
    silhouette_avg = silhouette_score(X, cluster_assignments)
    silhouette_scores.append(silhouette_avg)
```

4. Make a line plot with the silhouette score for the different values of **K**. Then identify the best value of **K** from the plot.

```
plt.figure(figsize=[7,5])
plt.plot(range(2,11), silhouette_scores, color='gray')
plt.xlabel("Number of clusters: K")
plt.ylabel('Avg. Silhouette Score')
plt.show()
```

Your plot will look as follows:

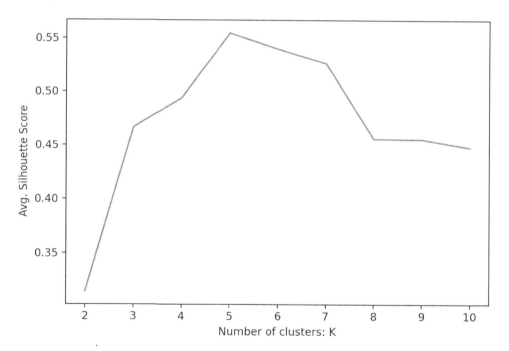

Figure 4.18: Average silhouette score vs. K. K=5 has the best value.

From the preceding plot, you can infer that **K=5** has the best **silhouette score** and is therefore the optimal number of clusters.

In this exercise, you used **silhouette score** to choose the optimal number of clusters. This was the third approach you saw and applied for choosing the number of clusters.

> **NOTE**
>
> The three approaches to choosing optimal clusters may not agree for many datasets, especially high dimensional, where the visual inspection method may not be reliable. In such cases, supplement the **silhouette scores** and **elbow method** with your business understanding/ inputs from business teams to choose the right number of clusters.

TRAIN AND TEST SPLIT

The methods discussed so far were around examining, either visually or through numbers, how well separated the clusters were. Another important aspect of the quality of the clusters is how generalizable they are to new data. A quite common concern in machine learning is the problem of overfitting. **Overfitting** is when a machine learning model fits so well to the data that was used to create it, that it doesn't generalize to new data. This problem is usually a larger concern with supervised learning, where there is a label with the correct result expected from the algorithm.

However, it can also be a concern with clustering when you are trying to choose the best clustering technique or hyperparameters that fit the data. One of the problems is getting a good result merely by chance. Because we try many combinations of parameters and algorithms, there is a possibility that one set came out on top just because of some peculiarity in the data on which it was trained. The same set may not work well on a similar dataset that the model hasn't seen before. We want the model to generalize well and identify clusters equally well on newer data.

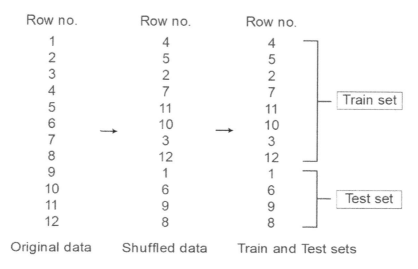

Figure 4.19: The train test split process illustrated

It is therefore considered a best practice to evaluate your models using a held-out portion of the data called the **test set**. *Figure 4.19* shows the steps employed in the process. The dataset is first shuffled so that there is no order in the rows and therefore any underlying logic that was employed to order the rows in the data is no longer applicable. This would ensure that in the next step, where some records are allocated to the train and test sets, the allocation happens randomly. Such random sampling helps make each of the sets representative of the entire dataset. This is useful because if any model you make performs well on the test set as well (which it has never seen before), then you can be sure the model would generalize well to other unseen data as well.

Before doing any kind of clustering, the data is divided into the **training set** and the **test set**. The model is then fit using the training set, meaning that the centroids are defined based on running the **k-means** algorithm on that portion of the data. Then, the test data is assigned to clusters based on those centroids, and the model is evaluated based on how well that test data is fit. Since the model has not been trained using the test set, this is just like the model encountering new data, and you can see how well your model generalizes to this new data, which is what matters the most.

For the Python implementation of the train-test split, we will be employing the `train_test_split` function from scikit-learn. The function is simple to use and returns train and test sets from any dataset provided to it. You first import the utility from scikit-learn using the following command:

```
from sklearn.model_selection import train_test_split
```

Next, you execute the function by supplying to it the dataset to split, the proportion of data to go into the train set and a `random_state` for consistency of results, like in the command below:

```
data_train, data_test = train_test_split\
                        (data, train_size = 0.8, \
                         random_state=seed_value)
```

In the example above, 80% of the data points are assigned to the train set and 20% to the test set. The function returns two datasets corresponding to the train and test datasets respectively. The train and test datasets will then be available to you to continue the modeling process. Let us now see the train test split in action and use it to evaluate clustering performance.

EXERCISE 4.07: USING A TRAIN-TEST SPLIT TO EVALUATE CLUSTERING PERFORMANCE

In this exercise, you will use a **train-test split** approach to evaluate the performance of the clustering. The goal of the exercise is to ensure reliable and robust customers segments from the mall customers. You will need to separate the data into train and test sets first. Then, you will fit a **K-means** model with a sub-optimal number of clusters. If the clusters are good, the **silhouette score** should be consistent between the train and test data. Continue in the same Jupyter notebook used so far for all the preceding exercises.

> ### NOTE
>
> The scaling of the data needs to be performed after the **train test split**. Performing scaling before the split would leak data from the test set in the calculation of mean and standard deviation. Later, when we apply the model on the test data, it wouldn't really be 'unseen'. This is an example of 'data leakage' and should be carefully avoided.

1. Import the **train_test_split** function from **sklearn** and perform the split on the mall customer data. Specify the **train size** as **0.75** and a **random_state** of **42**. Print the shapes of the resulting datasets.

```
from sklearn.model_selection import train_test_split
df_train, df_test = train_test_split\
                        (mall0, train_size=0.75, \
                         random_state=42)
```

Specifying a **train_size** of **0.75** assigns 75% of the records to the train set and the remaining to the test set. Using **random_state** ensures that the results are reproducible.

```
print(df_train.shape)
print(df_test.shape)
```

The shapes would be printed as follows:

```
(150, 5)
(50, 5)
```

2. Fit a **Kmeans** mode with **6** clusters on the **train data**. Calculate the average **silhouette score**. Ignore the warnings (if any) resulting from this step.

```
model = KMeans(n_clusters=6, random_state=42)
df_train['Cluster'] = model.fit_predict(df_train[cluster_cols])
silhouette_avg = silhouette_score\
                    (df_train[cluster_cols], df_train['Cluster'])
print(silhouette_avg)
```

The score should be **0.545**. Next, find out the score when the model is applied to the test set.

3. Using the **predict** method of the model, predict the clusters for the test data. Then, calculate the average **silhouette score** for the test data using the following code. Ignore warnings, if any, from the code.

```
df_test['Cluster'] = model.predict(df_test[cluster_cols])
silhouette_avg = silhouette_score\
                    (df_test[cluster_cols],df_test['Cluster'])
print(silhouette_avg)
```

The **silhouette score** is **0.495**, which is a big drop from **0.545** on the train set. To understand the cause for this drop, you'll need to visualize the clusters on the test data.

4. Visualize the predicted clusters on the test data using a scatter plot, marking the different clusters.

```
for clust in range(df_test.Cluster.nunique()):
    temp = df_test[df_test.Cluster == clust]
    plt.scatter(temp.Income, temp.Spend_score, \
                marker=markers[clust], \
                color='gray')
plt.xlabel("Income")
plt.ylabel("Spend_score")
plt.show()
```

> **NOTE**
>
> The value **gray** for the attribute **color** (emboldened) is used to generate graphs in grayscale. You can use other colors like **darkgreen**, **maroon**, etc. as values of **color** parameter to get the colored graphs. You can also refer to the following document to get the code for colored plot and the colored output: http://packt.link/NOjgT.

You should get the following plot:

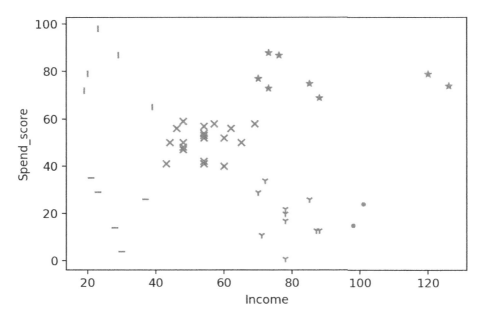

Figure 4.20: The clusters on the test data

What do you gather from the plot? First, the top right cluster doesn't seem to be a good one. There are two points that are far from the dense part of the cluster. This is not a tight cluster. Second, the bottom right cluster contains just two points, both of which are very close to another cluster. This cluster should be merged with the adjacent cluster.

In this exercise, you saw that if your clusters are not optimal and are fitting the train data too well, the clusters don't generalize well on unseen data. The performance on unseen data can very effectively be measured using the **train-test split** approach.

ACTIVITY 4.02: EVALUATING CLUSTERING ON CUSTOMER DATA

You are a data science manager in the marketing division at a major multinational alcoholic beverage company. Over the past year, the marketing team launched **32** initiatives to increase its sales. Your team has acquired data that tells you which customers have responded to which of the **32** marketing initiatives recently (this data is present within the **customer_offers.csv** file). The business goal is to improve future marketing campaigns by targeting them precisely, so they can provide offers customized to groups that tend to respond to similar offers. The solution is to build customer segments based on the responses of the customers to past initiatives.

In this activity, you will employ a thorough approach to clustering by trying multiple clustering techniques. Additionally, you will employ statistical approaches to cluster evaluation to ensure your results are reliable and robust. Using the cluster evaluation techniques, you will also tune the hyperparameters, as applicable, for the clustering algorithms. Start in a new Jupyter notebook for the activity.

> **NOTE**
>
> **customer_offers.csv** can be found here: https://packt.link/nYpaw.

Execute the following steps to complete this activity:

1. Import the necessary libraries for data handling, clustering, and visualization. Import data from **customer_offers.csv** into a pandas DataFrame.

2. Print the top five rows of the DataFrame, which should look like the table below.

	1	2	3	4	5	6	7	8	9	10	...	23	24	25	26	27	28	29	30	31	32
0	0	0	0	0	0	0	0	0	0	0	...	0	0	0	0	0	0	1	1	0	0
1	0	0	0	0	0	0	0	0	1	0	...	0	0	0	0	1	0	0	0	0	0
2	0	0	0	0	0	0	0	0	0	0	...	0	1	0	1	0	0	0	0	0	0
3	0	0	0	0	0	0	0	1	0	0	...	0	0	0	0	0	0	0	1	0	0
4	0	0	0	0	0	0	1	0	0	1	...	0	0	0	0	0	0	0	0	1	0

Fig. 4.21: First five records of the customer_offers data

3. Divide the dataset into train and test sets by using the **train_test_split** method from scikit-learn. Specify **random_state** as **100** for consistency.

4. Perform k-means on the data. Identify the optimal number of clusters by using the silhouette score approach on the train data by plotting the score for the different number of clusters, varying from **2** through **10**. The plot for silhouette scores should be as follows:

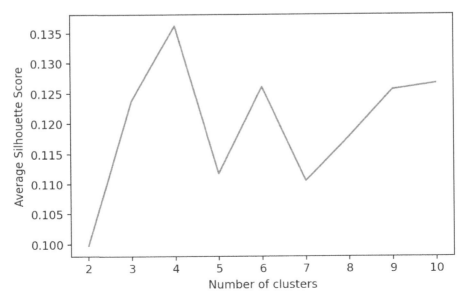

Fig. 4.22: Silhouette scores for different number of clusters

5. Perform K means using **k** found in the previous step. Print out the **silhouette score** on the test set.

6. Perform **mean-shift** clustering on the data, using the `estimate_bandwidth` method with a quantile value of **0.1** to estimate the bandwidth. Print out the silhouette score from the model on the test set.

7. Perform k-modes on the data. Identify the optimal number of clusters by using the silhouette score approach on the train data by plotting the score for the different number of clusters, varying from **3** through **10**. You should get the following output.

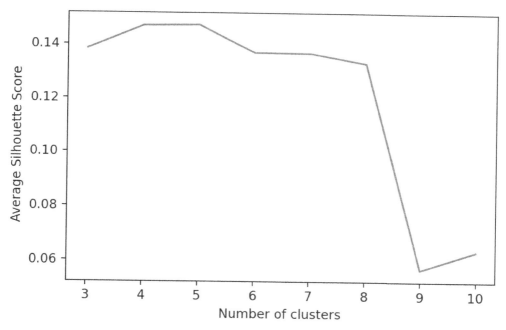

Fig 4.23: Silhouette scores for different K for K-modes

8. Using **K** found in the previous step, perform K-modes on the data. Print out the **silhouette score** on the test set.

9. Which of the three techniques gives you the best result? What is the final number of clusters you will go with?

> **NOTE**
>
> The solution for this activity can be found on page 510.

THE ROLE OF BUSINESS IN CLUSTER EVALUATION

By now, we understand that the clusters need to be sensible and actionable for the business. Machine learning-based approaches identify the naturally occurring clusters in the data. We also know that there is some subjectivity in this process and identifying the right number of clusters is not trivial. Even if the algorithms have correctly identified the true, natural clusters in the data, they may not be feasible for action. Statistical measures may suggest 20 optimal clusters, but the business may be able to act on only four clusters.

Consider another situation in which the clustering activity outputs 2 clusters of a certain nature. Businesses may come back with a strong point of view on the validity of those clusters. For example, a business may assert that, by knowing their own business and the customers so thoroughly, they expect at least 4 distinct clusters with certain behaviors. Or in a different scenario, they may disagree with at least one of the features you have used for the clustering. Or maybe they strongly believe that a particular feature should get a much higher weight among all features.

All of these are cases where business inputs can lead to significant changes in your clusters. Business review of the clustering process and therefore the segments is imperative. Business plays the role of not only the important 'human in the loop' in the segmentation process, but also provides indispensable inputs to make your segments much more useful to the organization and create business impact.

SUMMARY

Machine learning-based clustering techniques are great in that they help speed up the segmentation process and can find patterns in data that can escape highly proficient analysts. Multiple techniques for clustering have been developed over the decades, each having its merits and drawbacks. As a data science practitioner in marketing, understanding different techniques will make you far more effective in your practice. However, faced with multiple options in techniques and hyper-parameters, it's important to be able to compare the results from the techniques objectively. This, in turn, requires you to quantify the quality of clusters resulting from a clustering process.

In this chapter, you learned various methods for choosing the number of clusters, including judgment-based methods such as visual inspection of cluster overlap and elbow determination using the sum of squared errors/ inertia, and objective methods such as evaluating the silhouette score. Each of these methods has strengths and weaknesses - the more abstract and quantified the measure is, the further removed you are from understanding why a particular clustering seems to be failing or succeeding. However, as we have seen, making judgments is often difficult, especially with complex data, and this is where quantifiable methods, in particular the silhouette score, tend to shine. In practice, sometimes one measure will not give a clear answer while another does; this is all the more reason to have multiple tools in your toolkit.

In addition to learning new methods for evaluating clustering, we also learned new methods for clustering, such as the mean-shift algorithm, and k-modes and k-prototypes algorithms. Finally, we learned one of the basic concepts of evaluating a model, which will be important as we move forward: using a test set. By separating data into training and testing sets, we are treating the test set as if it's new data that we didn't have at the time that we developed the model. This allows us to see how well our model does with this new data. As we move into examples of supervised learning, this concept becomes even more important.

In the next chapter, we will learn about using regression, a type of supervised learning, for making predictions about continuous outcomes such as revenue.

5

PREDICTING CUSTOMER REVENUE USING LINEAR REGRESSION

OVERVIEW

In this chapter, you will learn how to solve business problems that require the prediction of quantities. You will learn about regression, a supervised learning approach to predict continuous outcomes. You will explore linear regression, a simple yet powerful technique that is the workhorse for predictive modeling in the industry. Then you will learn how to implement some key steps in the modeling process – feature engineering and data cleaning. Later, you will implement your linear regression models and finally interpret the results to derive business insights.

INTRODUCTION

Azra, a large, high-end, fast-fashion retailer that has operations all over the world, has approved its marketing budget for the latest campaign in a particular country. The marketing team is now looking to allocate the budget to each marketing channel, but they have many questions:

- How much should they spend on email? Read rates are low, but the quality of conversions is high.

- How about social media? It seems to be an effective channel in general.

- Should they do any offline promotions? If so, to what extent?

- How about paid search as a channel?

The company understands that each channel provides a different **return on investment (ROI)** – that is, some channels are more effective than others. However, all channels should be considered, nonetheless. Naturally, different distributions of allocation to these channels would provide different results. Incredibly low spending on a channel with great ROI is missed potential and high spending on an extremely low-ROI channel is a waste of resources. Surely, this task is not trivial. If the company understood well how the amount spent on various channels affects sales, that would be a great help. More concretely, if the company could mathematically model the impact of various channels on sales, or in other words, model the relationship between channel spends and sales, they could predict the sales for any allocation and accordingly choose the right levels. Thankfully, machine learning comes to our aid once again – a machine learning based sales prediction approach would do the trick.

In the previous two chapters, you used machine learning to find natural groups of entities from the data; something that would be challenging to perform through manual calculations. You have used unsupervised learning in the previous chapters. That is, you did not have any pre-defined target label/quantity that you were trying to predict. You were just looking at the hidden structures in the data and using them to group data points. You had no *ground truth* to *supervise* the learning done by the machine – there was no notion of *true segments* of the customers. For example, when you created segments of the mall's customers in *Chapter 3, Unsupervised Learning and Customer Segmentation*, and *Chapter 4, Evaluating and Choosing the Best Segmentation Approach*, you did not have the segments given to you beforehand. You had no ground truth for these segments to verify their correctness.

You will now explore another machine learning style – **supervised learning** – where, in contrast, you have historical data that you can leverage and some examples that the machine can learn from. In supervised learning, you train the machine to perform a certain task – learn from historical data to make predictions. You can predict quantities – revenue, stock prices, house prices, credit lines, ratings of a product, and so on. Or you can predict categories/classes – clicking on an ad, customer churn (customer not returning to a website), purchases of a product, the opening of a promotional push notification, the preferred traffic channel, and so on. Using historical transaction data for customers, you can use supervised learning to make the machine learn how to predict the future revenue that a customer will bring based on past activity. This is exactly what you will do in this chapter to help a multi-national e-commerce chain, Azra, evaluate the potential revenue from customers. This will in turn help Azra identify high-value customers for whom a differential marketing experience can be defined. In this chapter, you will explore and apply linear regression, a supervised ML approach that helps predict quantities, and understand its utility for marketing decisions.

You will work on multiple business problems. You will use linear regression to help the company understand how advertising spend on various channels impacts revenue. The understanding will help the company in budget allocation to the channels and help maximize their ROI on marketing. You will also help the retail chain identify and target high-value customers. To accomplish this, you will use regression to predict the future revenue from customers by analyzing their purchase history.

Now, let us begin by investigating what regression problems are in the section that follows.

REGRESSION PROBLEMS

The prediction of quantities is a recurring task in marketing. Predicting the units sold for a brand based on the spend on the visibility (impressions) allocated to the brand's products is an example. Another example could be predicting sales based on the advertising spend on television campaigns. Predicting the lifetime value of a customer (the total revenue a customer brings over a defined period) based on a customer's attributes is another common requirement. All these situations can be formulated as **regression problems**.

> **NOTE**
>
> A common misconception is that regression is a specific algorithm/technique. Regression is a much broader term that refers to a class of problems. Many equate regression to linear regression, which is only one of the many techniques that can be employed to solve a regression problem.

Regression refers to a class of problems where the value to predict is a quantity. There are various techniques available for regression, ranging from the simple and easy to interpret (for example, simple linear regression) to the extremely complex, black-box approaches (where how the model makes a prediction is practically not possible to understand; for example, deep neural networks, or ensemble methods such as gradient boosting). Since regression is a supervised learning formulation, it relies on historical data to make predictions about the new data. It learns patterns from the historical data to make predictions for new data. The understanding that the way the regression technique develops can be expressed in a mathematical form is what we refer to as a **model**.

> **NOTE**
>
> It is important to separate the notion of a model from a modeling technique. We may employ a certain algorithm or technique on a dataset. The result, that is, the understanding of the patterns or the relationships between the different variables in the data with the outcome, is called a **model**.

We can think of models as ways to mathematically describe the relationships between the **target/outcome/dependent** variables and the **predictor/feature/independent** variables. Let us understand these terms better. A **dependent variable** is a variable you are trying to predict. For example, if you want to predict revenue based on marketing spend on social media, then revenue would be the target/dependent variable. Social media spend, the variable that is being used to predict the revenue is the predictor/independent variable.

You can have different kinds of relationships between the dependent and the independent variables. Indeed, in practice, you may encounter relationships of all sorts. *Figure 5.1* illustrates a few types of relationships that you may encounter in data.

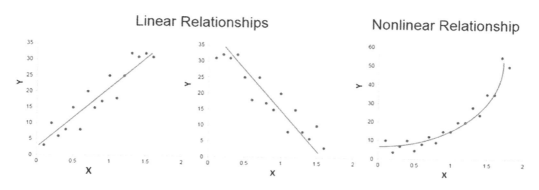

Figure 5.1: Regression problems

The first two plots in the preceding figure show linear relationships, where the dependent variable (on the vertical axis) is related to the independent variable (on the horizontal axis) in a simple linear fashion – a line on a graph can describe the relationship very well. The third plot shows a more complex, nonlinear relationship, where a curve captures the relationship better.

For the social media spend example, consider the data in *Figure 5.2*, where you have plotted some hypothetical data representing the relationship between **Revenue** and **Spend** – each point on the graph represents some time period in the past where a certain revenue was obtained corresponding to the social media spend.

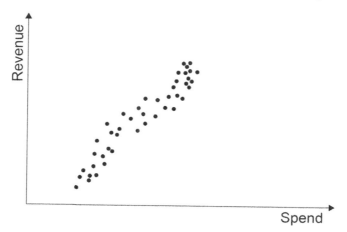

Figure 5.2: Revenue versus social media spend

If you describe the preceding relationship mathematically, you can do the following:

- Predict the revenue for any level of spending on social media.

- Calculate the required spend on social media to attain the desired revenue.

This can be extremely useful for the marketing team. What kind of relationship, do you reckon, describes the observed data the best? Here is where you can have multiple approaches, and therefore need to make a decision. Look at *Figure 5.3* where you have visualized three possible choices of relations to describe the data. Some of us would prefer the simple line (*a*) as a sufficient fit to the data, while others would prefer the complex curve denoted by *c*. Some may prefer *b* as it is somewhat of a balance between *a* and *c*. All three are valid choices for modeling the relationship.

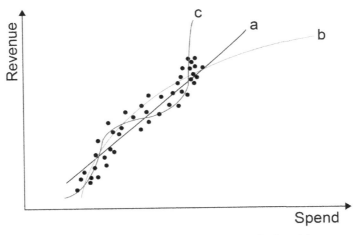

Figure 5.3: Choices in modeling the relationship

In this chapter, you will focus on the simple, linear model (**a**), that is, describing the relationships using lines. This approach to using a line to describe the relationship between target/outcome and predictor variables is called **linear regression**. Alternatively stated, in linear regression, you predict the target from the predictor variables by modeling their relationship as a line.

> **NOTE**
>
> You will learn how to model nonlinear relationships in *Chapter 6, More Tools and Techniques for Evaluating Regression Models*.

The mathematical form of the linear regression model is simple. For a single predictor/independent variable, the model can be described in a simple equation, as follows:

$$Y = b_0 + b_1 . X_1$$

Here, **Y** is the predicted value of the dependent variable and X_1 represents the independent variable. Let us look at *Figure 5.4* to understand this equation and do a quick recap of some basic coordinate geometry. b_0 is the intercept (where the line crosses the *y* axis) – the predicted outcome when the independent variable is 0. b_1 is the slope of the line and captures how sharply the value of the dependent variables increases on a unit change in the independent variable. b_1 is also called the **coefficient** for the independent variable. With multiple independent variables, the geometric interpretation becomes complex. We will discuss this again in a later section, *Performing and Interpreting Linear Regression*.

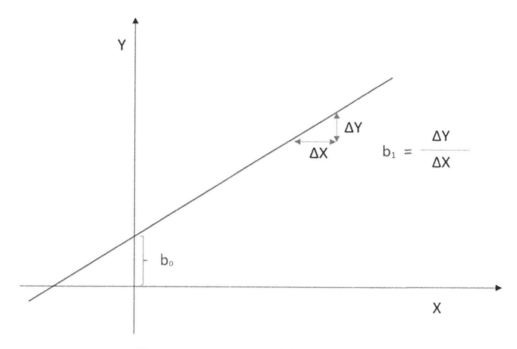

Figure 5.4: Parameters of the regression line

This seemingly simple approach of linear regression is extremely powerful. It is also quite popular, often considered the workhorse for predictive modeling of quantities in the industry. Some reasons for its popularity are the following:

- Easy to interpret even by non-technical stakeholders (business teams)

- Mathematically simple

- Quick in execution

We will keep touching upon the benefits throughout the chapter and discover for ourselves how useful this approach is. For now, let us first get comfortable with the idea of regression and build our linear regression model using scikit-learn, a package that has made predictive modeling possible in just a few lines of code.

You will employ the **LinearRegression** model from scikit-learn, which has an extremely easy syntax. The syntax is similar to the **fit** and **predict** approach you used for the clustering techniques in *Chapter 3, Unsupervised Learning and Customer Segmentation*, and *Chapter 4, Evaluating and Choosing the Best Segmentation Approach*. First, you have to import and create an instance of the **LinearRegression** class, using the following code:

```
from sklearn.linear_model import LinearRegression
lr = LinearRegression()
```

Then, you simply use the **fit** method, supplying to it the dependent and independent variables:

```
lr.fit(independent_variable, dependent_variable)
```

That should *fit* the model. To make predictions, just use the **predict** method as you did for clustering. That is all it takes to train a linear regression model in Python.

Let us go ahead and train our first linear regression model to help a **fast-moving consumer goods** (**FMCG**) giant predict sales in the following exercise.

EXERCISE 5.01: PREDICTING SALES FROM ADVERTISING SPEND USING LINEAR REGRESSION

HINA Inc. is a large FMCG company that is streamlining its marketing budget. This involves taking stock of all its marketing strategies. This, in turn, means re-assessing the effectiveness of its existing spend on various marketing channels. As a marketing analyst, you need to figure out if spending money on TV advertising campaigns results in a direct increase in sales. In other words, you need to find out if the TV advertising spend and the sales figures share a linear relationship. Linear regression seems perfect for the job as it models the relationship as a line.

You are provided with historical advertising data – weekly sales and spend on each channel – for almost the 4 previous years. Using linear regression, you will make a model that predicts sales based on TV channel spend and study the obtained relationship.

> **NOTE:**
>
> The dataset for this exercise, **advertising.csv**, can be found at https://packt.link/CsvBU.

1. Import the relevant libraries for plotting and data manipulation, load **advertising.csv** dataset into a **pandas** DataFrame, and print the top five records using the following code:

```
import numpy as np, pandas as pd
import matplotlib.pyplot as plt, seaborn as sns
advertising = pd.read_csv("advertising.csv")
advertising.head()
```

> **NOTE**
>
> Make sure you change the path (highlighted) to the CSV file based on its location on your system. If you're running the Jupyter notebook from the same directory where the CSV file is stored, you can run the preceding code without any modification.

The dataset should get printed as follows:

	TV	Radio	Newspaper	Sales
0	230.1	37.8	69.2	22.1
1	44.5	39.3	45.1	10.4
2	17.2	45.9	69.3	12.0
3	151.5	41.3	58.5	16.5
4	180.8	10.8	58.4	17.9

Figure 5.5: Top five records of the advertising dataset

2. Visualize the association between **TV** and **Sales** through a scatter plot using the following code:

```
plt.scatter(advertising.TV, advertising.Sales, \
            marker="+", color='gray')
plt.xlabel("TV")
plt.ylabel("Sales")
plt.show()
```

> **NOTE**
>
> In *steps 2* and *6*, the value **gray** for the attribute **color** (emboldened) is used to generate graphs in grayscale. You can use other colors such as **darkgreen**, **maroon**, and so on as values of **color** parameters to get colored graphs. You can also refer to the following document to get the code for the colored plot and the colored output: http://packt.link/NOjgT.

You should get the following plot:

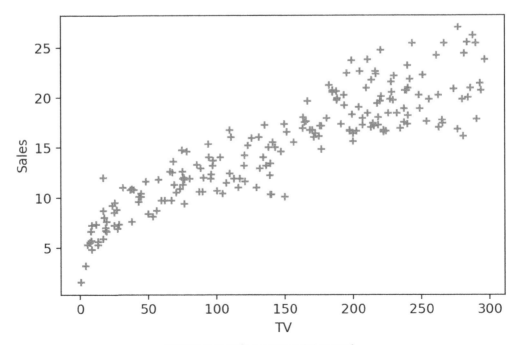

Figure 5.6: Sales versus TV spend.

As you can see from the preceding figure, **TV** spend clearly has a close association with **Sales** – sales seem to increase as TV spend increases. Let us use **Sales** to build the linear regression model.

3. Import **LinearRegression** from **sklearn** and create an instance of **LinearRegression** using the following code:

```
from sklearn.linear_model import LinearRegression
lr = LinearRegression()
```

4. Fit a linear regression model, supplying the **TV** column as the features and **Sales** as the outcome, using the **fit** method of **LinearRegression**:

```
lr.fit(advertising[['TV']], advertising[['Sales']])
```

5. Using the **predict** method of the model, create a **sales_pred** variable containing the predictions from the model:

```
sales_pred = lr.predict(advertising[['TV']])
```

6. Plot the predicted sales as a line over the scatter plot of **Sales** versus **TV** (using the simple line plot). This should help you assess how well the line fits the data and if it indeed is a good representation of the relationship:

```
plt.plot(advertising.TV, sales_pred,"k--")
plt.scatter(advertising.TV, advertising.Sales, \
            marker='+', color='gray')
plt.xlabel("TV")
plt.ylabel('Sales')
plt.show()
```

You should get the following output:

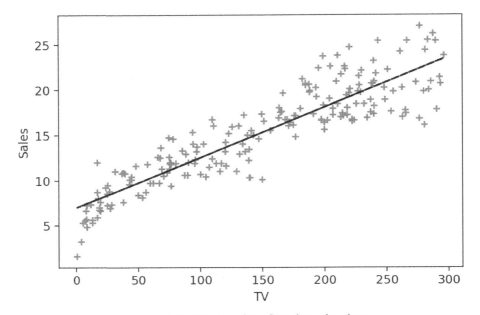

Figure 5.7: Regression line fitted on the data

As you can see, the regression line does a decent job of describing the relationship between sales and advertising spend on TV as a channel. From the line, you see that the sales increase very well together with the spend on TV advertising and that TV advertising can be a decent predictor of the expected sales. This tells HINA Inc. that this is a great channel for marketing investment.

In this exercise, you built a quick and simple linear regression model to model the relationship between sales and TV spend. The dataset you have used was convenient to build a model straightaway. We did not discuss any of the workings of the model, something that we will do in detail in this chapter.

> **NOTE**
>
> The exercise was to familiarize you with the **sklearn** package and the **LinearRegression** method. The entire process of predictive modeling has many nuances and steps involved, which we will discuss shortly.

Many problems in marketing are related to predicting a continuous outcome. Therefore, regression has many different use cases in marketing. Predicting how much a customer will spend in the next year to assess customer value is one example. Predicting the sales for the next month for a store or all stores in a chain is another. Indeed, being able to predict quantities using machine learning is one of the most useful skills a data science professional in the marketing domain must possess. However, before you can perform the mathematical modeling through linear regression, you need to perform some other critical steps in the general predictive modeling process pipeline.

Let us begin by transforming the data and creating features/variables that will be useful for predicting your outcome. You will learn how to do this in the following section.

FEATURE ENGINEERING FOR REGRESSION

Raw data is a term that is used to refer to the data as you obtain it from the source – without any manipulation from your side. Rarely, a raw dataset can directly be employed for a modeling activity. Often, you perform multiple manipulations on data and the act of doing so is termed **feature engineering**. In simple terms, **feature engineering** is the process of taking data and transforming it into features for use in predictions. There can be multiple motivations for feature engineering:

- Creating features that capture aspects of what is important to the outcome of interest (for example, creating an average order value, which could be more useful for predicting revenue from a customer, instead of using the number of orders and total revenue)

- Using your domain understanding (for example, flagging certain high-value indicators for predicting revenue from a customer)

- Aggregating variables to the required level (for example, creating customer-level features for predicting revenue from customers)

This process requires both data expertise and domain knowledge – you need to know what can be done with the data that you have, as well as knowledge of what might be predictive of the outcome you're interested in.

Once the features are created, they need to be assessed from the lens of not just a data analyst but also from a business perspective. In most marketing cases, the outcome of the modeling activity must make sense to businesses that will be making decisions using the model. This can be done by simply looking for relationships between the features and the outcome of interest.

You will first look at how to transform data to create features, and then how to clean the data of the resulting features to ensure models are trained on high-quality data in the following sections.

FEATURE CREATION

To perform a regression, you first need data to be in a format that allows regression. In many cases, data is in the form of customer transactions. The data needs to be transformed into features that can be used to perform a prediction. These features then become your predictors.

Features are transformed versions of the data that capture what you think is possibly predictive of the outcome of interest. Let's say you are trying to predict the future value of a customer (that is, how much you expect a customer to spend on a company's product in the future), examples of useful features might include the number of purchases a customer has made previously, the amount they have spent, or the time since their last order.

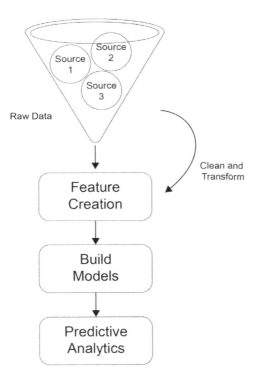

Figure 5.8: Role of feature engineering in a machine learning workflow

Figure 5.8 illustrates the role of feature engineering in a machine learning workflow. You begin with raw data – data that you accumulate from, in the general case, multiple sources. The raw data is rarely conducive to model building. It could have many issues – errors, imperfections such as missing values or erroneous values, or could just need to be aggregated. The data needs to be cleaned and transformed and from the transformation results the features of the model. The model then learns from these features. The predictions or understanding from the model then are employed to take business decisions.

Let us first discuss the imperfections in the data. Indeed, datasets in real-world scenarios have imperfections such as garbage values or missing values. You may also have unexpectedly high/low values that may throw off your analyses/models. You need to fix these before the modeling, and that's where data cleaning comes in handy.

DATA CLEANING

Generally, feature creation and data cleaning go hand in hand. As you create your features, you might notice problems with the data that need to be dealt with. The following are common problems you will notice with data:

- **Missing Data**: The easiest way to deal with missing data is to just remove the data points that are missing some data if it makes sense to do so. Otherwise, you can attempt to insert a value for a missing variable based on the average or median of the other data points.

- **Outliers**: Outliers are data points that lie far outside the normal range of a variable, or in other words, far from the norm. A common definition is that an outlier is any data point that is more than three standard deviations above/below the median. They are dangerous because they might not reflect normal behavior but can have a disproportionate effect on your model.

The following figure illustrates an outlier:

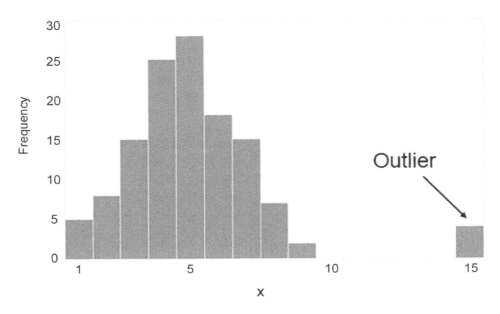

Figure 5.9: A histogram showing an outlier value

The preceding histogram shows that for the variable **X**, most values are in the
0 to **9** range. But a few values are much higher than the rest. These values
are considered outliers. These could be due to some error in the data, or valid
values that are just way higher than the rest due to some peculiarity in the data.
It is recommended that you understand the source for these high values and
choose the right strategy for handling them, depending on the analysis and the
significance of these high values. In general, an easy and extremely common
method of dealing with outliers is to simply remove them.

Now that you understand the significance and need for data cleaning and feature
creation, it's time to see these ideas in action. In the next exercise, you will perform
extensive feature engineering. This will be the first of the steps in a process through
which you will help a giant retail company evaluate its customers by predicting their
future revenue.

EXERCISE 5.02: CREATING FEATURES FOR CUSTOMER REVENUE PREDICTION

Azra is a big high-fashion retailer with operations in multiple countries. To optimize their marketing activities, Azra seeks to identify high-value customers – customers that are expected to bring high revenue to the retailer – and have a differential marketing strategy for them. You are a marketing analytics manager at Azra and have a solution to this business problem. The key idea is that a predictive model can be employed to predict the next year's revenue of the customer based on the previous year's purchases. A customer with higher predicted revenue is naturally a higher-value customer.

To validate this approach, you plan to build a model to predict the revenue of the customer in 2020 based on the purchases made in 2019. If the model performs well, the approach gets validated. The 2020 purchase data can then be used to predict customer revenue for 2021 and help the company identify high-value customers.

You have historical transaction data for the years 2019 and 2020 in the file `azra_retail_transactions.csv`.

> **NOTE**
>
> `azra_retail_transactions.csv` can be found here:
> https://packt.link/WqWMe.

The first few records are shown in *Figure 5.10*. For each transaction, you have the following:

- Customer identifier (`CustomerID`)

- The number of units purchased (`Quantity`)

- The date and time of the purchase (`InvoiceDate`)

- The unit cost (`UnitPrice`)

- Some other information about the item purchased (`StockCode`, `Description`) and the customer (`Country`)

The dataset looks like the following:

InvoiceNo	StockCode	Description	Quantity	InvoiceDate	UnitPrice	CustomerID	Country
546729	22775	PURPLE DRAWERKNOB ACRYLIC EDWARDIAN	12	16-03-2020 11:36	1.25	18231	United Kingdom
559898	21868	POTTING SHED TEA MUG	6	13-07-2020 12:18	1.25	16225	United Kingdom
548648	71459	HANGING JAM JAR T-LIGHT HOLDER	24	01-04-2020 13:20	0.85	12949	United Kingdom
540543	22173	METAL 4 HOOK HANGER FRENCH CHATEAU	4	09-01-2020 15:23	2.95	14395	United Kingdom

Figure 5.10: Sample records from the file azra_retail_transactions.csv

The goal of this exercise is to manipulate the data and create variables that will allow you to model the customer spend for the year 2020, based on the past activity. The total customer spends for 2020 will therefore be the dependent variable. The independent variables will be features that capture information about the customer's past purchase behavior. Note that this also requires aggregation of the data in order to get one record for each customer.

More concretely, you will be creating the following variables from the transactions data:

- **revenue_2019** (total revenue for the year 2019)

- **days_since_first_purchase** (the number of days since the first purchase by the customer)

- **days_since_last_purchase** (the number of days since the customer's most recent purchase)

- **number_of_purchases** (the total number of purchases by the customer in 2019)

- **avg_order_cost** (the average value of the orders placed by the customer in 2019)

- **revenue_2020** (the total revenue for the year 2020)

revenue_2020 will be the dependent variable in the model, the rest being the independent variables. The modified dataset with the created features should look like the table in *Figure 5.11*.

CustomerID	revenue_2019	days_since_first_purchase	days_since_last_purchase	number_of_purchases	avg_order_cost	revenue_2020
12347.0	711.79	23.0	23.0	1.0	711.79	3598.21
12348.0	892.80	14.0	14.0	1.0	892.80	904.44
12370.0	1868.02	16.0	13.0	2.0	934.01	1677.67
12377.0	1001.52	10.0	10.0	1.0	1001.52	626.60
12383.0	600.72	8.0	8.0	1.0	600.72	1249.84

Figure 5.11: The expected result with the created variables

Perform the following steps to complete this exercise. Continue in the same Jupyter notebook you used in the preceding exercise:

1. Import **pandas** and load the data from **retail_transactions.csv** into a DataFrame named **df**, then print the first five records of the DataFrame. Also, import the **datetime** module as it will come in handy later:

```
import pandas as pd
import datetime as dt
df = pd.read_csv('azra_retail_transactions.csv')
df.head()
```

> **NOTE**
>
> Make sure you change the path (highlighted) to the CSV file based on its location on your system. If you're running the Jupyter notebook from the same directory where the CSV file is stored, you can run the preceding code without any modification.

The first five instances of your dataset should appear as follows:

	InvoiceNo	StockCode	Description	Quantity	InvoiceDate	UnitPrice	CustomerID	Country
0	546729	22775	PURPLE DRAWERKNOB ACRYLIC EDWARDIAN	12	2020-03-16 11:36:00	1.25	18231.0	United Kingdom
1	559898	21868	POTTING SHED TEA MUG	6	2020-07-13 12:18:00	1.25	16225.0	United Kingdom
2	548648	71459	HANGING JAM JAR T-LIGHT HOLDER	24	2020-04-01 13:20:00	0.85	12949.0	United Kingdom
3	540543	22173	METAL 4 HOOK HANGER FRENCH	4	2020-01-09 15:23:00	2.95	14395.0	United Kingdom

Figure 5.12: The truncated output of first five rows of the retail transactions data

The first five records displayed in the figure contain the same information as the table in *Figure 5.10*. This confirms that the data has been loaded correctly. **InvoiceDate** has the date and time to the minute for the invoice. The time of the invoice is too much information, and we can work with just the date part. Also, note that while we have the unit price and the item quantity, we do not have a total transaction value (revenue) for the transaction. We can derive this by simply multiplying the unit price with the item quantity.

2. Convert the **InvoiceDate** column to date format using the **to_datetime** method from pandas:

```
df['InvoiceDate'] = pd.to_datetime(df['InvoiceDate'])
```

3. Calculate the **revenue** for each row, by multiplying **Quantity** by **UnitPrice**. Print the first five records of the dataset to verify the result:

```
df['revenue'] = df['UnitPrice']*df['Quantity']
df.head()
```

The first five records get printed as follows:

	InvoiceNo	StockCode	Description	Quantity	InvoiceDate	UnitPrice	CustomerID	Country	revenue
0	546729	22775	PURPLE DRAWERKNOB ACRYLIC EDWARDIAN	12	2020-03-16 11:36:00	1.25	18231.0	United Kingdom	15.0
1	559898	21868	POTTING SHED TEA MUG	6	2020-07-13 12:18:00	1.25	16225.0	United Kingdom	7.5
2	548648	71459	HANGING JAM JAR T-LIGHT HOLDER	24	2020-04-01 13:20:00	0.85	12949.0	United Kingdom	20.4
3	540543	22173	METAL 4 HOOK HANGER FRENCH CHATEAU	4	2020-01-09 15:23:00	2.95	14395.0	United Kingdom	11.8
4	561390	20726	LUNCH BAG WOODLAND	10	2020-07-27 09:52:00	1.65	17068.0	United Kingdom	16.5

Figure 5.13: Top five records after creating a column for the revenue

Revenue seems to be correctly calculated as a product of values of the **UnitPrice** and **Quantity** columns.

4. In the dataset, each invoice could be spread over multiple rows, one for each type of product purchased (since the row is for each product, and a customer can buy multiple products in an order). These can be combined such that data for each transaction is on a single row. To do so, perform a **groupby** operation on **InvoiceNo**. However, before that, you need to specify how to combine those rows that are grouped together. Use the following code:

```
operations = {'revenue':'sum',\
              'InvoiceDate':'first',\
              'CustomerID':'first'}
df = df.groupby('InvoiceNo').agg(operations)
```

In the preceding code snippet, you have first specified the aggregation functions that you will use for each column and then performed a **groupby** operation. **InvoiceDate** and **CustomerID** will be the same for all rows for the same invoice, so you can just take the first entry for them. For **revenue**, you need to add the revenue across all items for the same invoice to get the total revenue for that invoice.

5. Finally, use the **head** function to display the result:

```
df.head()
```

Your DataFrame should now appear as follows:

InvoiceNo	revenue	InvoiceDate	CustomerID
536365	139.12	2019-12-01 08:26:00	17850.0
536366	22.20	2019-12-01 08:28:00	17850.0
536367	278.73	2019-12-01 08:34:00	13047.0
536368	70.05	2019-12-01 08:34:00	13047.0
536369	17.85	2019-12-01 08:35:00	13047.0

Figure 5.14: The first five rows of the data after aggregating by invoice number

6. You will be using the year of the transaction to derive features for 2019 and 2020. Create a separate column named **year** for the year. To do that, use the **year** attribute of the **InvoiceDate** column, as follows:

```
df['year'] = df['InvoiceDate'].dt.year
```

7. For each transaction, calculate how many days' difference there is between the last day of 2019 and the invoice date using the following code. Use the **datetime** module we imported earlier:

```
df['days_since'] = (dt.datetime(year=2019, month=12, day=31) \
                    - df['InvoiceDate']).apply(lambda x: x.days)
```

8. Next, create the features for days since the first and last purchase, along with the number of purchases and total revenue for 2019. Define a set of aggregation functions for each of the variables and apply them using the **groupby** method. You will calculate the sum of revenue. For the **days_since** column, you will calculate the maximum and the minimum number of days, as well as the number of unique values (giving you how many separate days this customer made a purchase on). Since these are your predictors, store the result in a variable, **X**, using the following code:

```
operations = {'revenue':'sum',\
              'days_since':['max','min','nunique']}

X = df[df['year'] == 2019].groupby('CustomerID').agg(operations)
```

9. Now, use the **head** function to see the results:

```
X.head()
```

You should see the following:

CustomerID	revenue sum	days_since max	min	nunique
12347.0	711.79	23	23	1
12348.0	892.80	14	14	1
12370.0	1868.02	16	13	2
12377.0	1001.52	10	10	1
12383.0	600.72	8	8	1

Figure 5.15: The first five rows of data after aggregating by customer ID

As you can see from the preceding figure, because you performed multiple types of aggregation on the **days_since** column, you ended up with multi-level column labels.

10. To simplify this, reset the names of the columns to make them easier to refer to later. Use the following code and print the results using the **head** function:

```
X.columns = [' '.join(col).strip() for col in X.columns.values]

X.head()
```

Your columns should now appear as follows:

CustomerID	revenue sum	days_since max	days_since min	days_since nunique
12347.0	711.79	23	23	1
12348.0	892.80	14	14	1
12370.0	1868.02	16	13	2
12377.0	1001.52	10	10	1
12383.0	600.72	8	8	1

Figure 5.16: The first five rows after simplifying the column names

You can see that the names have been successfully modified and are more convenient to work with.

11. Derive one more feature: the average spend per order. Calculate this by dividing **revenue sum** by **days_since nunique** (note that this is the average spend per day. For simplicity, assume that a customer only makes one order in a day):

```
X['avg_order_cost'] = X['revenue sum']/X['days_since nunique']
```

12. You need the outcome that you will be predicting, which is just the sum of revenue for 2020. Calculate this with a simple **groupby** operation and store the values in the **y** variable, as follows:

```
y = df[df['year'] == 2020].groupby('CustomerID')['revenue'].sum()
```

13. Put your predictors and outcomes into a single DataFrame, **wrangled_df**, and rename the columns to have more intuitive names. Finally, look at the resulting DataFrame, using the **head** function:

```
wrangled_df = pd.concat([X,y], axis=1)
wrangled_df.columns = ['revenue_2019',\
                       'days_since_first_purchase',\
                       'days_since_last_purchase',\
                       'number_of_purchases',\
                       'avg_order_cost',\
                       'revenue_2020']
wrangled_df.head()
```

Your DataFrame will appear as follows:

CustomerID	revenue_2019	days_since_first_purchase	days_since_last_purchase	number_of_purchases	avg_order_cost	revenue_2020
12346.0	NaN	NaN	NaN	NaN	NaN	77183.60
12347.0	711.79	23.0	23.0	1.0	711.79	3598.21
12348.0	892.80	14.0	14.0	1.0	892.80	904.44
12349.0	NaN	NaN	NaN	NaN	NaN	1757.55
12350.0	NaN	NaN	NaN	NaN	NaN	334.40

Figure 5.17: The first five rows of the data after feature creation

Note that many of the values in our DataFrame are **NaN**. This is caused by customers who were active either only in 2019 or only in 2020, so there is no data for the other year. In Chapter 7, *Supervised Learning: Predicting Customer Churn*, you will work on predicting which of your customers will churn, but for now, you will just drop all customers not active in both years. Note that this means that your model will predict the spending of customers in the next year assuming that they remain active customers.

14. To drop the customers without values, drop rows where either of the **revenue** columns are null, as follows:

```
wrangled_df = wrangled_df[~wrangled_df.revenue_2019.isnull()]
wrangled_df = wrangled_df[~wrangled_df.revenue_2020.isnull()]
```

15. As a final data-cleaning step, it's often a good idea to get rid of outliers. A standard definition is that an outlier is any data point more than three standard deviations above the median. Use this criterion to drop customers that are outliers in terms of 2019 or 2020 revenue:

```
wrangled_df = wrangled_df[wrangled_df.revenue_2020 \
                < ((wrangled_df.revenue_2020.median()) \
                + wrangled_df.revenue_2020.std()*3)]
wrangled_df = wrangled_df[wrangled_df.revenue_2019 \
                < ((wrangled_df.revenue_2019.median()) \
                + wrangled_df.revenue_2019.std()*3)]
```

16. It's often a good idea after you've done your data cleaning and feature engineering, to save the new data as a new file, so that, as you're developing your model, you don't need to run the data through the whole feature engineering and cleaning pipeline each time you want to rerun your code. You can do this using the **to_csv** function. Also, take a look at your final DataFrame using the **head** function:

```
wrangled_df.to_csv('wrangled_transactions.csv')
wrangled_df.head()
```

Your DataFrame will now look as follows:

	revenue_2019	days_since_first_purchase	days_since_last_purchase	number_of_purchases	avg_order_cost	revenue_2020
CustomerID						
12347.0	711.79	23.0	23.0	1.0	711.79	3598.21
12348.0	892.80	14.0	14.0	1.0	892.80	904.44
12370.0	1868.02	16.0	13.0	2.0	934.01	1677.67
12377.0	1001.52	10.0	10.0	1.0	1001.52	626.60
12383.0	600.72	8.0	8.0	1.0	600.72	1249.84

Figure 5.18: The final, cleaned dataset

The output in *Figure 5.18* confirms that you have successfully manipulated the data and created the variables (dependent and independent) from the raw transaction data. This dataset is now in a format conducive to the steps involved in the modeling process.

ASSESSING FEATURES USING VISUALIZATIONS AND CORRELATIONS

Once you have created your features of interest, the next step is to assess those features. The motivations for assessment could be many – performing sanity checks (basic checks to ensure that values are within the expected ranges), understanding the individual columns better, understanding the associations between the features and patterns in the data that add information and can be potentially leveraged for the task. A commonly followed sequence is as follows:

1. First, perform a sanity check of your features to make sure their values are what you would expect. You can plot a histogram of each feature to make sure the distribution of the feature is also what you would expect. This can often reveal unexpected problems with your data – for example, presence of the value **1000** in a field that is supposed to have only **True** or **False** values.

2. The next step is to examine the relationships between your features and the outcome of interest. This can be done in the following two ways:

a) Creating scatter plots: Often, the most effective means of assessing a relationship is to create a scatter plot that plots a feature against the outcome of interest and see whether there is any obvious relationship.

b) Assessing correlations: Another quick and effective method for assessing a relationship is to see whether there is a correlation between the variables. A correlation is a quantification of the linear association between two variables. Correlations can be positive, meaning that as one variable increases, the other increases. For example, you expect sales to have a positive correlation with the marketing spend. A correlation can also be negative, that is, as one variable increases in value, the other decreases. As an example, you expect customers with higher mortgages to spend less on a luxury goods platform.

The correlation value quantifies the association between the variables in a single number. The magnitude and the sign of the value tell us about the nature of the association, or lack of it, between the variables.

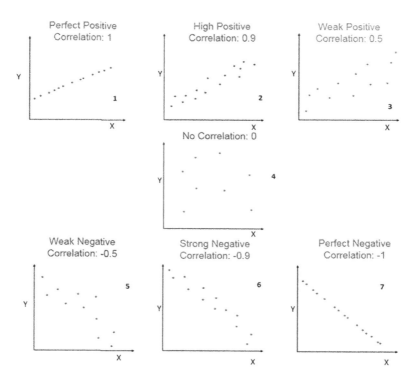

Figure 5.19: A visualization of the different levels of correlation

Figure 5.19 shows various relationships on scatter plots and their corresponding correlation values. In *Plot 1*, **X** and **Y** have a perfect linear relationship with **Y** increasing with **X**. The correlation value for this relationship is **1**, the highest possible value corresponding to a perfect positive correlation. The other extreme is *Plot 7*, where **X** and **Y** have a perfect negative correlation with a value of **−1**. **Y** decreases as **X** increases. In both *Plots 1* and *7*, the relationship could be well described by a line where not a single point would be deviating from that line. *Plot 2* is a case with a strong positive correlation too. But this time, if you drew a line for the relationship, some points would deviate from the line. The deviations would be small but present. The correlation value, therefore, is not **1** but is a high value close to **1**. In *Plot 3*, **Y** increases with **X**, but the points would significantly deviate from a line. The correlation value is **0.5**, signifying a positive but weak correlation. *Plots 5* and *6* have patterns similar to *2* and *3* respectively, albeit with a negative association between **X** and **Y**. When there is no relation between **X** and **Y**, that is, changes in **X** have no impact on **Y**, you get a plot like *Plot 4*. The correlation value for such a relation, or lack thereof, is **0**. Correlation can be calculated easily using statistical packages, resulting in a single number that can often reveal whether there is a strong relationship between two variables.

Calculating the correlation in Python can be done in many ways. One of the simplest approaches is through the **corr** method of the pandas DataFrame. If you wish to calculate correlations for all the variable pairs in a DataFrame, **df**, you can simply use the **corr** method as in the following code:

```
df.corr()
```

If you just want to calculate the correlation between any two series/lists/arrays of numbers, you can use the **corrcoef** function of the **numpy** library. The following command shows how to import **numpy** and calculate the correlation between two variables, **var1** and **var2**:

```
import numpy as np
np.corrcoef(var1, var2)
```

var1 and **var2** could be pandas series, NumPy arrays, or even lists.

Correlation is an extremely useful measure of the association between two quantitative variables. You saw how the magnitude and the sign of the correlation value can reveal the association between variables. A value close to 0 would mean there is no correlation between the variables, while magnitudes closer to 1 indicate strong associations. The sign of the correlation coefficient tells you whether both variables increase together.

Now that you understand this important measure, it is time to apply it to a business problem and help the e-commerce company progress in its approach to predicting customer revenue. You will further the model-building process by examining the relationships between the predictors and the outcome.

EXERCISE 5.03: EXAMINING RELATIONSHIPS BETWEEN PREDICTORS AND THE OUTCOME

In *Exercise 5.02*, *Creating Features for Customer Revenue Prediction*, you helped the e-commerce company Azra to transform the raw transaction data into a transformed dataset that has useful dependent and independent features that can be used for model building. In this exercise, you will continue the model-building process by analyzing the relationship between the predictors (independent variables) and the outcome (dependent variable). This will help you identify how the different purchase history-related features affect the future revenue of the customer. This will also help you assess whether the associations in the data make business sense.

You will use scatter plots to visualize the relationships and use correlations to quantify them. Continue in the same Jupyter notebook you used for the previous exercises. Perform the following steps:

1. Use **pandas** to import the data you saved at the end of the last exercise (**wrangled_transactions.csv**). The **CustomerID** field is not needed for the analysis. Assign **CustomerId** as the index for the DataFrame:

```
df = pd.read_csv('wrangled_transactions.csv', \
                 index_col='CustomerID')
```

> **NOTE**
>
> **wrangled_transactions.csv** can be found here:
> http://packt.link/5NcUX.
>
> Also, make sure you change the path (highlighted) to the CSV file based on its location on your system. If you're running the Jupyter notebook from the same directory where the CSV file is stored, you can run the preceding code without any modification.

2. Using the **plot** method of the pandas DataFrame, make a scatter plot with **days_since_first_purchase** on the *x* axis and **revenue_2020** on the *y* axis to examine the relationship between them:

```
df.plot.scatter(x="days_since_first_purchase", \
                y="revenue_2020", \
                figsize=[6,6], color='gray')
plt.show()
```

> **NOTE**
>
> The value **gray** for the attribute **color** (emboldened) is used to generate graphs in grayscale. You can use other colors such as **darkgreen**, **maroon**, and so on as values of **color** parameters to get colored graphs. You can also refer to the following document to get the code for the colored plot and the colored output: http://packt.link/NOjgT.

The output should be as follows:

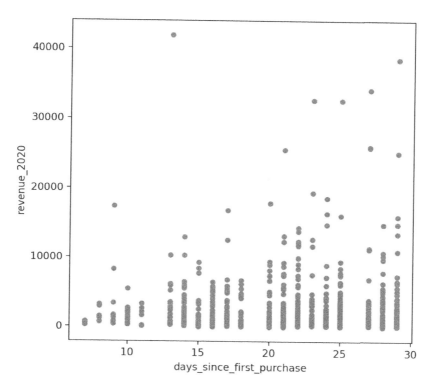

Figure 5.20: revenue_2020 versus days_since_first_purchase in a scatter plot

You can see that while there is not a very strong correlation between them, in general, we see higher instances of high revenue for customers with higher tenure (a higher value for **days_since_first_purchase**).

3. Using the **pairplot** function of the **seaborn** library, create pairwise scatter plots of all the features. Use the following code:

```
import seaborn as sns
sns.set_palette('Greys_r')
sns.pairplot(df)
plt.show()
```

NOTE

The value `Greys_r` (emboldened) is used to generate graphs in grayscale. You can also refer to the following document to get the code for the colored plot and the colored output: http://packt.link/NOjgT.

You will get the following plot:

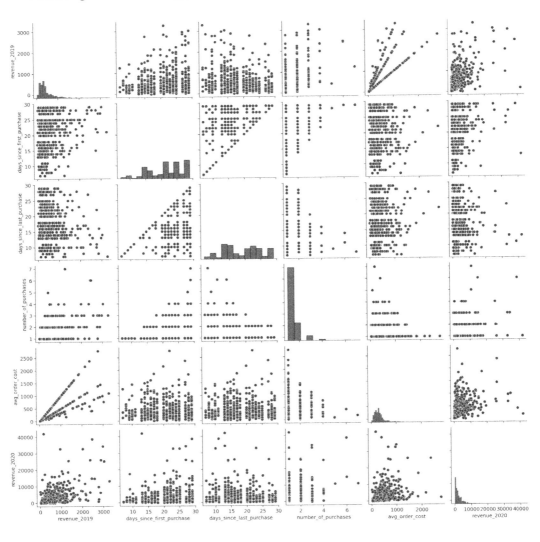

Figure 5.21: The seaborn pairplot of the entire dataset

In *Figure 5.21*, the diagonal shows a histogram for each variable, whereas each row shows the scatter plot between one variable and each other variable. The bottom row of the figures shows the scatter plots of the 2020 revenue (our outcome of interest) against each of the other variables. Because the data points are overlapping and there is a fair amount of variance, the relationships do not look very clear in the visualizations. Spend some time on this image and understand the associations in the data.

4. Using the **pairplot** function and the **y_vars** parameter, limit the view to the row for your target variable, that is, **revenue_2020**:

```
sns.pairplot(df, x_vars=df.columns, y_vars="revenue_2020")
plt.show()
```

You should get the following output:

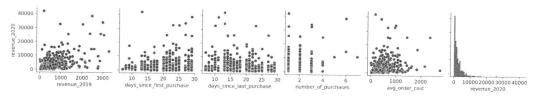

Figure 5.22: Pairplot limited to include the target variable

From this view focused on the associations between **revenue_2020** and the independent variables, you visually assess that none of the predictors have a strong relationship with the customer revenue for 2020. The strongest relationship seems to be with **revenue_2019** and it is a positive relationship.

5. Next, use correlations to quantify the associations between the variables. Use the **corr** method on the pandas DataFrame, as in the following code:

```
df.corr()
```

Your output should appear as follows:

	revenue_2019	days_since_first_purchase	days_since_last_purchase	number_of_purchases	avg_order_cost	revenue_2020
revenue_2019	1.000000	0.109692	-0.254964	0.504438	0.779401	0.548234
days_since_first_purchase	0.109692	1.000000	0.641574	0.327502	-0.074321	0.061743
days_since_last_purchase	-0.254964	0.641574	1.000000	-0.398268	-0.054051	-0.171294
number_of_purchases	0.504438	0.327502	-0.398268	1.000000	-0.012466	0.355751
avg_order_cost	0.779401	-0.074321	-0.054051	-0.012466	1.000000	0.357384
revenue_2020	0.548234	0.061743	-0.171294	0.355751	0.357384	1.000000

Figure 5.23: The correlations between each variable and each other variable in the dataset

Again, you can look at the last row to see the relationships between your predictors and the outcome of interest (2020 revenue). Positive numbers indicate a positive relationship – for instance, the higher the 2019 revenue from a customer, the greater the expected revenue from them in 2020 should be. Negative numbers mean the reverse – for example, the more days there have been since a customer's last purchase, the lower you would expect the 2020 revenue from them to be. The correlation values agree with the visual assessment that **revenue_2019** has the strongest relationship with **revenue_2020**.

In this exercise, you saw how you can use correlations to quantify the associations between variables. The single value of correlation can tell us about the strength as well as the nature of the relationship that is, whether they move in the same or opposite directions (one increases as the other decreases). It is an extremely useful tool for data analysis. Let us now apply these concepts to a different problem statement and see how correlation can help us get significant insights from data.

ACTIVITY 5.01: EXAMINING THE RELATIONSHIP BETWEEN STORE LOCATION AND REVENUE

The fashion giant Azra also has several physical retail stores where customers can try and buy apparel and fashion accessories. With increased internet penetration and higher adoption of e-commerce among customers, the footfall to the physical stores has been decreasing. To optimize operation costs, the company wishes to understand the factors that affect the revenue of a store. This will help them take better calls regarding setting up future stores and making decisions about the existing ones.

The data for the activity is in the file **location_rev.csv**. The file has data on several storefront locations and information about the surrounding area. This information includes the following:

- **revenue** (the revenue of the storefront at each location)
- **location_age** (the number of years since the store opened)
- **num_competitors** (the number of competitors in a 20-mile radius)
- **median_income** (the median income of the residents in the area)

- **`num_loyalty_members`** (the members enrolled in the loyalty program in the area)

- **`population_density`** (the population density of the area)

The goal of the activity is to use the data to uncover some business insights that will help the company decide on the locations for its stores. You will visualize the different associations in the data and then quantify them using correlations. You will interpret the results and answer some questions pertinent to the business:

- Which variable has the strongest association with the revenue?

- Are all the associations intuitive and make business sense?

Perform these steps to complete the activity. Start in a fresh Jupyter notebook:

1. Load the necessary libraries (**pandas**, **pyplot** from **matplotlib**, and **seaborn**), read the data from **location_rev.csv** into a DataFrame, and examine the data by printing the top five rows.

> **NOTE**
>
> **location_rev.csv** can be found here: https://packt.link/FPXO2.

You should get the following output:

revenue	num_competitors	median_income	num_loyalty_members	population_density	location_age
42247.80	3.0	30527.57	1407.0	3302.0	12.0
38628.37	3.0	30185.49	1025.0	4422.0	11.0
39715.16	1.0	32182.24	1498.0	3260.0	12.0
35593.30	5.0	29728.65	2340.0	4325.0	10.0
35128.18	4.0	30691.17	847.0	3774.0	11.0

Figure 5.24: First five records of the storefront data

2. Using the pandas DataFrame's **plot** method, create a scatter plot between **median_income** and the revenue of the store. The output should look like the following:

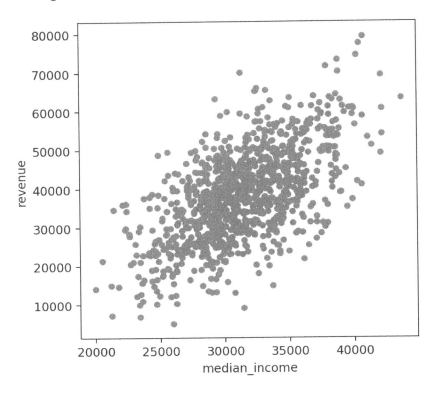

Figure 5.25: Scatter plot of median_income and revenue

3. Use seaborn's `pairplot` function to visualize the data and its relationships. You should get the following plot:

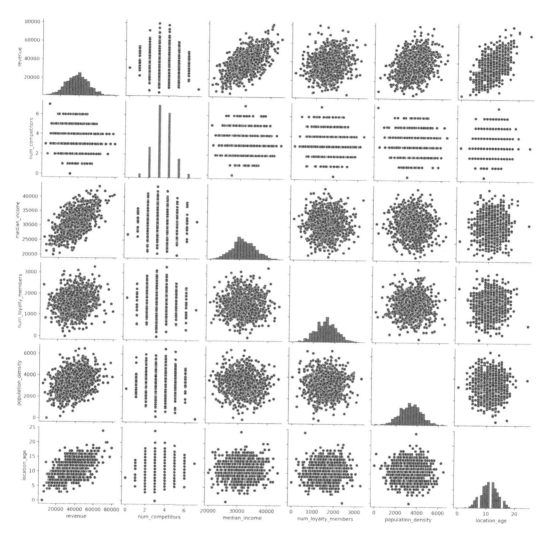

Figure 5.26: The seaborn pairplot of the entire dataset

4. Using the **y_vars** parameter, plot only the row for associations with the **revenue** variable. The output should be as follows:

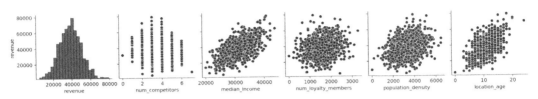

Figure 5.27: Associations with revenue

5. Finally, calculate correlations using the appropriate method(s) to quantify the relationships between the different variables and location revenue. Analyze the data so that you can answer the following questions:

a) Which variables have the highest association with revenue?

b) Do the associations make business sense?

> **NOTE**
>
> The solution for this activity can be found on page 517.

So far, we have discussed and implemented some key steps in the predictive modeling process. We began with data cleanup and feature engineering and saw how it can help us go from raw data to features that can be used in a model. We then saw how correlations can be used to analyze and quantify the different types of relationships between the variables. With these two steps done, we are now ready to approach the core technique for modeling the relationship – linear regression. Let us now understand linear regression and see it in action.

PERFORMING AND INTERPRETING LINEAR REGRESSION

In *Exercise 5.01, Predicting Sales from Advertising Spend Using Linear Regression*, we implemented and saw the output of a linear regression model without discussing the inner workings. Let us understand the technique of linear regression better now. Linear regression is a type of regression model that predicts the outcome using linear relationships between predictors and the outcome. Linear regression models can be thought of as a line running through the feature space that minimizes the distance between the line and the data points.

The **model** that a linear regression learns is the equation of this line. It is an equation that expresses the dependent variable as a linear function of the independent variables. This is best visualized when there is a single predictor (see *Figure 5.28*). In such a case, you can draw a line that best fits the data on a scatter plot between the two variables.

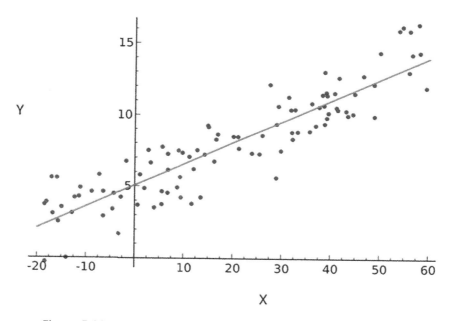

Figure 5.28: A visualization of a linear regression line fit to data

The line is generated by trying to find the *line of best fit*. This will be the line that best minimizes the error (difference) between itself and the data points.

> **NOTE**
>
> You will learn more about types of errors in the next chapter, where you will learn how to use them to evaluate models, but it is important to note that errors are also used in the process of fitting the model.

One of the big benefits of linear regression is that it is an extremely simple model. The model can be described in a simple equation, as follows:

$$Y = b_0 + b_1X_1 + b_2X_2 \ldots b_iX_i$$

Here, Y is the predicted value of the outcome variable, b_0 is the intercept (where the line crosses the *x* axis), each X is the value of a variable, and each b is the respective weight assigned to that variable.

Advantages of Linear Regression

A big advantage of this equation is that it makes the model easy to interpret. By looking at the coefficients, you can easily see how much you would predict Y to change for each unit change in the predictor. For example, if you had a model predicting sales revenue from each customer for the next year and the coefficient for the number of purchases in the previous year predictor was **10**, you could say that for each purchase in the previous year, you could expect the revenue from a customer to be **$10** higher.

Disadvantages of Linear Regression

Linear regression models also have significant weaknesses that stem from their simplicity. *They can only model linear relationships*, while relationships in the real world are often more complex. Linear models assume that no matter how high the value of a predictor is, adding more to it will have the same effect as if the predictor were lower. In real-world scenarios, this is often not the case. If a product appeals to customers in a middle-income range, you would expect that a boost in income for a customer with low income would increase sales to that customer, while a boost in income for a customer with high income could very well decrease sales to that customer. This would be a nonlinear relationship, examples of which can be seen in the following figure.

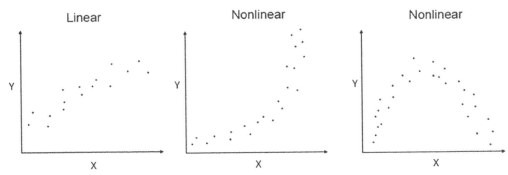

Figure 5.29: Some examples of linear and nonlinear relationships

In addition to nonlinear relationships, *linear models are unable to capture interactions between variables easily*. In statistics, interaction is a situation in which, when two variables are combined, their effect is larger than (or less than) the sum of their effect alone. For example, it could be the case that while television advertisements and radio advertisements both have a positive effect on sales in an area when both are done at once, the sum of their effect is less than the effect each would have alone due to saturation of the market with ads. Linear models do not have a built-in way of dealing with these kinds of effects, since they assume a simple linear relationship between the predictors and the outcome.

This does not mean that linear models are completely unable to account for nonlinear relationships or interactions. By performing transformations on predictors, a nonlinear relationship can be turned into a linear one, and interaction terms can be created by multiplying two predictors together; these terms can then be added to the model. However, this can be difficult and time-consuming to do and increases the complexity of the model, which makes it harder to interpret, thereby eliminating many of the benefits of using linear models, to begin with.

For the Python implementation, we will be using **LinearRegression** from the scikit-learn package. The **LinearRegression** object in scikit-learn follows a syntax identical to what we used for clustering earlier. We use the **fit** method to train the model with the provided data. The following commands will import **LinearRegression**, create an instance, and fit it on the supplied data (independent and dependent variables):

```
from sklearn.linear_model import LinearRegression
model = LinearRegression()
model.fit(X_train, y_train)
```

Here, **X_train** contains the independent variables and **y_train** contains the dependent variable.

After the model is fit, predictions on any new data can be made by simply using the **predict** method of the model and storing it in a variable, as shown in the following command:

```
predictions = model.predict(new_data)
```

In the preceding command, the variable predictions will hold the predicted outcome for each record in **new_data**. Once the model is trained, the coefficients for the different independent variables are available in the **coef_** attribute of the model. The values can be displayed using the following command:

```
model.coef_
```

The intercept of the linear regression equation is available in the **intercept_** attribute and can be displayed using the following command:

```
model.intercept_
```

With these few, straightforward commands, you can easily build a regression model. This is how simple training a linear regression model in scikit-learn is.

Linear regression models are simple but powerful models that execute quickly and provide a result that businesses can easily interpret. In the next exercise, you will use this model to help the fashion company estimate the future revenue for the customer and help identify high-value customers.

EXERCISE 5.04: BUILDING A LINEAR MODEL PREDICTING CUSTOMER SPEND

Predicting the future revenue for a customer based on past transactions is a classic problem that linear regression can solve. In this exercise, you will create a linear regression model to predict customer revenue for 2020 for the high-fashion company Azra. In the previous exercises, you performed feature engineering to get the data ready for modeling and analyzed the relationships in the data. Now, using linear regression, you will create a model that describes how future revenue relates to the features based on past transactions.

You will train a linear regression model with **revenue_2020** as the dependent variable and the rest of the variables as the independent variables. You will use the train-test approach to make sure you train the model on part of the data and assess it on the unseen test data. You will interpret the coefficients from the trained model and check whether they make business sense. To mathematically assess the performance of the model, you will check the correlation between the predicted values of **revenue_2020** and the actual values. A higher correlation would indicate a higher performance of the model.

You will use the file **wrangled_transactions.csv** created in *Exercise 5.02, Creating Features for Transaction Data.*

> **NOTE**
>
> **wrangled_transactions.csv** can be found here:
> https://packt.link/5NcUX.

Continue working in the Jupyter notebook used for the previous exercises and perform the following tasks:

1. Import **pandas** and **numpy** using the following code:

    ```
    import pandas as pd, numpy as np
    ```

2. Create a new DataFrame named **df** and read the data from **wrangled_transactions.csv** with **CustomerID** as the index:

    ```
    df = pd.read_csv('wrangled_transactions.csv', \
                     index_col='CustomerID')
    ```

    > **NOTE**
    >
    > Make sure you change the path (highlighted) to the CSV file based on its location on your system. If you're running the Jupyter notebook from the same directory where the CSV file is stored, you can run the preceding code without any modification.

3. Look at the correlations between the variables again using the **corr** function:

    ```
    df.corr()
    ```

Your DataFrame will look as follows:

	revenue_2019	days_since_first_purchase	days_since_last_purchase
revenue_2019	1.000000	0.109692	-0.254964
days_since_first_purchase	0.109692	1.000000	0.641574
days_since_last_purchase	-0.254964	0.641574	1.000000
number_of_purchases	0.504438	0.327502	-0.398268
avg_order_cost	0.779401	-0.074321	-0.054051
revenue_2020	0.548234	0.061743	-0.171294

Figure 5.30: The correlations between each pair of variables

NOTE

The preceding image does not contain all the columns of the DataFrame. The image is for demonstration purposes only.

Recall that there is only a weak relationship between **days_since_first_purchase** and **revenue_2020** (correlation close to **0**). We will therefore not include that predictor in our model.

4. Store the independent and dependent variables in the **X** and **y** variables, respectively:

```
X = df[['revenue_2019',\
        'days_since_last_purchase',\
        'number_of_purchases',\
        'avg_order_cost']]
y = df['revenue_2020']
```

5. Use **sklearn** to perform a train-test split on the data, so that you can assess the model on a dataset it was not trained on:

```
from sklearn.model_selection import train_test_split

X_train, X_test, y_train, y_test = train_test_split\
                                   (X, y, random_state = 100)
```

6. Import **LinearRegression** from **sklearn** using the following code:

```
from sklearn.linear_model import LinearRegression
```

7. Create a **LinearRegression** model, and fit it on the training data:

```
model = LinearRegression()
model.fit(X_train,y_train)
```

8. Examine the model coefficients by checking the **coef_** property. Note that these are in the same order as your **X** columns: **revenue_2019**, **days_since_last_purchase**, **number_of_purchases**, and **avg_order_cost**:

```
model.coef_
```

This should result in an array with the values **5.788**, **7.477**, **336.608**, and **-2.056**.

9. Check the intercept term of the model by checking the **intercept_** property:

```
model.intercept_
```

This should give a value of **264.86**. From *steps 8* and *9*, you can arrive at the model's full equation:

```
revenue_2020= 264.86.74 + 5.79*(revenue_2019) + 7.477*(days_since_
last_purchase) + 336.61*(number_of_purchases) - 2.056*(avg_order_
cost)
```

10. You can now use the fitted model to make predictions about a customer outside of your dataset. Make a DataFrame that holds data for one customer, where revenue for 2019 is **1,000**, the number of days since the last purchase is **20**, the number of purchases made is **2**, and the average order cost is **500**. Have the model make a prediction on this one customer's data:

```
single_customer = pd.DataFrame({'revenue_2019': [1000],\
                                'days_since_last_purchase': [20],\
                                'number_of_purchases': [2],\
                                'avg_order_cost': [500]})

model.predict(single_customer)
```

The result should be an array with a single value of about **5847.67**, indicating the predicted revenue for 2020 for a customer with this data.

11. You can plot the model's predictions on the test set against the true value. First, import **matplotlib**, and make a scatter plot of the model predictions on **X_test** against **y_test**. Limit the *x* and *y* axes to a maximum value of **10,000** so that we get a better view of where most of the data points lie. Finally, add a line with slope **1**, which will serve as your reference—if all the points lie on this line, it means you have a perfect relationship between your predictions and the true answer:

```
import matplotlib.pyplot as plt
%matplotlib inline

plt.scatter(model.predict(X_test), y_test, color='gray')
plt.xlim(0,10000)
plt.ylim(0,10000)
plt.plot([0, 10000], [0, 10000], 'k-')
plt.xlabel('Model Predictions')
plt.ylabel('True Value')
plt.show()
```

NOTE

The value **gray** for the attribute **color** is used to generate graphs in grayscale. You can use other colors such as **darkgreen**, **maroon**, and so on as values of the **color** parameter to get colored graphs. You can also refer to the following document to get the code for the colored plot and the colored output: http://packt.link/NOjgT.

Your plot will look as follows:

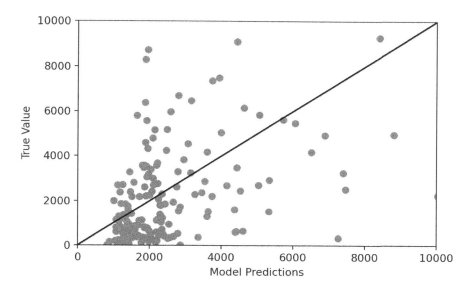

Figure 5.31: The model predictions plotted against the true values

In the preceding plot, the line indicates where points would lie if the prediction was the same as the true value. Since many of your points are quite far from the line, this indicates that the model is not completely accurate. However, there does seem to be some relationship, with higher model predictions having higher true values.

12. To further examine the relationship, you can use correlation. Use the **corrcoef** method from NumPy to calculate the correlation between the predicted and the actual values of **revenue_2020** for the test data:

```
np.corrcoef(model.predict(X_test), y_test)
```

You should get the following output (the same convention as the **corr** method on the pandas DataFrame):

```
array([[1.        , 0.61257401],
       [0.61257401, 1.        ]])
```

Figure 5.32: Correlation between the predicted and the actual values
of revenue_2020 for the test data

The correlation value is roughly **0.613**. This is a fairly strong relationship, telling us that the model does a decent job of predicting the future revenue for the customer based on the past year's transactions.

> **NOTE**
>
> R-squared is another common metric that is used to judge the fit of a model and is calculated by simply squaring the correlation between the model's prediction and the actual result. You will learn more about it in *Chapter 6, More Tools and Techniques for Evaluating Regression Models*.

In this exercise, you completed the last part of the entire predictive modeling process – the actual model building. Note that thanks to scikit-learn, the actual model building part is greatly simplified. You also saw that you can very easily derive an equation from the linear regression model that can be easily interpreted by the business.

You also now understand that besides training the model on the data, there are other important steps in the modeling process. Feature engineering is a key step that transforms raw data into something that a predictive model can work on. Correlation analysis is another important tool that can help us identify variables that have a high association with the dependent variable, and also variables that have little to no association.

With all this understanding and hands-on practice, let us now solve another problem using linear regression. You will help the fashion company Azra choose the right locations for upcoming stores by building a model that predicts store revenue based on information about the store locations.

ACTIVITY 5.02: PREDICTING STORE REVENUE USING LINEAR REGRESSION

Revisit the problem you were solving earlier for the high-fashion company Azra. A good understanding of which factors drive the revenue for a storefront will be critical in helping the company decide the locations for upcoming stores in a way that maximizes the overall revenue.

You will continue working on the dataset you explored in *Activity 5.01, Examining the Relationship between Store Location and Revenue*. You have, for each store, the revenue along with information about the location of the store. In *Activity 5.01, Examining the Relationship between Store Location and Revenue*, you analyzed the relationship between the store revenue and the location-related features.

Now, you will build a predictive model using linear regression to predict the revenue of a store using information about its location. You will use a train-test split approach to train the model on part of the data and assess the performance on unseen test data. You will assess the performance of the test data by calculating the correlation between the actual values and the predicted values of revenue. Additionally, you will examine the coefficients of the model to ensure that the model makes business sense.

Complete the following tasks. Continue in the Jupyter notebook used for *Activity 5.01, Examining the Relationship between Store Location and Revenue.*

1. Import the necessary libraries and the data from **location_rev.csv** and view the first few rows, which should look as follows:

	revenue	num_competitors	median_income	num_loyalty_members	population_density	location_age
0	42247.80	3.0	30527.57	1407.0	3302.0	12.0
1	38628.37	3.0	30185.49	1025.0	4422.0	11.0
2	39715.16	1.0	32182.24	1498.0	3260.0	12.0
3	35593.30	5.0	29728.65	2340.0	4325.0	10.0
4	35128.18	4.0	30691.17	847.0	3774.0	11.0

Figure 5.33: The first five rows of the location revenue data

2. Create a variable, **X**, with the predictors (all columns except **revenue**) in it, and store the outcome (**revenue**) in a separate variable, **y**.

3. Split the data into a training and test set. Use **random_state = 100**.

4. Create a linear regression model and fit it on the training data.

5. Print out the model coefficients.

6. Print out the model intercept.

7. Produce a prediction for a location that has three competitors; a median income of **30,000**; **1,200** loyalty members; a population density of **2,000**; and a location age of **10**. The result should be an array with a single value of **27573.21782447**, indicating the predicted revenue for a customer with this data.

8. Plot the model's predictions versus the true values on the test data. Your plot should look as follows:

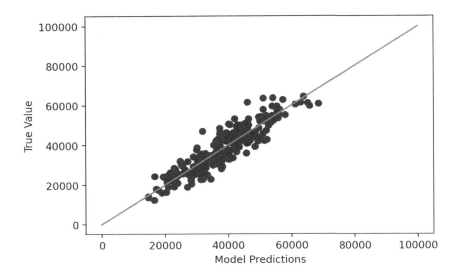

Figure 5.34: The model predictions plotted against the true value

9. Calculate the correlation between the model predictions and the true values of the test data.

    The result should be around **0.91**.

> **NOTE**
>
> The solution for this activity can be found on page 522.

SUMMARY

In this chapter, you explored a new approach to machine learning, that is, supervised machine learning, and saw how it can help a business make predictions. These predictions come from models that the algorithm learns. The models are essentially mathematical expressions of the relationship between the predictor variables and the target. You learned about linear regression – a simple, interpretable, and therefore powerful tool for businesses to predict quantities. You saw that feature engineering and data cleanup play an important role in the process of predictive modeling and then built and interpreted your linear regression models using scikit-learn. In this chapter, you also used some rudimentary approaches to evaluate the performance of the model. Linear regression is an extremely useful and interpretable technique, but it has its drawbacks.

In the next chapter, you will expand your repertoire to include more approaches to predicting quantities and will explore additional numeric methods for model evaluation.

6

MORE TOOLS AND TECHNIQUES FOR EVALUATING REGRESSION MODELS

OVERVIEW

This chapter explains how to evaluate various regression models using common measures of accuracy. You will learn how to calculate the **Mean Absolute Error (MAE)** and **Root Mean Squared Error (RMSE)**, which are common measures of the accuracy of a regression model. Later, you will use **Recursive Feature Elimination (RFE)** to perform feature selection for linear models. You will use these models together to predict how spending habits in customers change with age and find out which model outperforms the rest. By the end of the chapter, you will learn to compare the accuracy of different tree-based regression models, such as regression trees and random forest regression, and select the regression model that best suits your use case.

INTRODUCTION

You are working in a marketing company that takes projects from various clients. Your team has been given a project where you have to predict the percentage of conversions for a Black Friday sale that the team is going to plan. The percentage of conversion as per the client refers to the number of people who actually buy products vis-à-vis the number of people who initially signed up for updates regarding the sale by visiting the website. Your first instinct is to go for a regression model for predicting the percentage conversion. However, you have millions of rows of data with hundreds of columns. In scenarios like these, it's very common to encounter issues of multi-collinearity where two or more features effectively convey the same information. This can then end up affecting the robustness of the model. This is where solutions such as **Recursive Feature Selection** (**RFE**) can be of help.

In the previous chapter, you learned how to prepare data for regression modeling. You also learned how to apply linear regression to data and interpret the results.

In this chapter, you will learn how to evaluate a regression model to judge its performance. Specifically, you will target metrics such as the **Mean Absolute Error** (**MAE**) and **Root Mean Squared Error** (**RMSE**).

You will build on this knowledge by learning how to evaluate a model. Learning this skill will help you choose the right features to use for a model, as well as to compare different models based on their MAE and RMSE values. Later on in the chapter, you will learn about RFE, which is a powerful and commonly used technique for selecting only the most relevant features for building a regression model, thereby removing the redundant ones. Finally, you will learn about tree-based regression methods, and why they sometimes outperform linear regression techniques.

Let's begin this chapter by learning how to evaluate the accuracy of a regression model.

EVALUATING THE ACCURACY OF A REGRESSION MODEL

To evaluate regression models, you first need to define some metrics. The common metrics used to evaluate regression models rely on the concepts of *residuals* and *errors*, which are quantifications of how much a model incorrectly predicts a particular data point. In the following sections, you will first learn about residuals and errors. You will then learn about two evaluation metrics, the MAE and RMSE, and how they are used to evaluate regression models.

RESIDUALS AND ERRORS

An important concept in understanding how to evaluate regression models is the **residual**. The residual refers to the difference between the value predicted by the model and the true value for a data point. It can be thought of as by how much your model missed a particular value. In the following diagram, we can see a best-fit (or regression) line with data points scattered above and below it. The distance between a data point and the line signifies how far away the prediction (x_i, y_i) is from the actual value $(x_j, \mathbf{y}_j)$. This difference is known as a **residual**. The data points below the line will take negative values, while the ones above will take positive values:

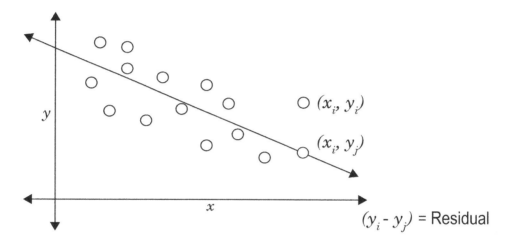

Figure 6.1: Estimating the residual

The residual is taken to be an estimate of the error of a model, where the error is the difference between the true process underlying the data generation and the model or, in other words, the difference between the actual value and the predicted value. We cannot directly observe the error because we do not know the true process, and therefore, we use the residual values as our best guess at the error. For this reason, error and residual are closely related and are often used interchangeably. For example, if you were asked to build a machine learning model for predicting the average age of all the people in a country, the *error* would mean the difference between the actual average age and the predicted average age. However, finding the actual average would be a difficult task as you would need to collect data for the whole country. Still, you could make the best guess at the average by taking the mean of the ages of some of the people in the country. This guess can then be used to find the residual, and hence serve as the error.

At this point, you might be thinking, why do we need any other evaluation metric? Why not just take the average of residuals? Let's try to understand this with the help of an example. The following table presents the actual selling price of some items and the selling prices for the same items predicted by a machine learning model (all prices are in Indian National Rupee):

Actual Selling Price	Predicted Selling Price	Residual (=Actual SP – Predicted SP)
INR 650	INR 660	-10
INR 540	INR 500	40
INR 200	INR 210	-10
INR 500	INR 520	-20
Sum of residuals		0
Average residuals = (sum of residuals)/ (number of entries)		0

Figure 6.2: Average residual calculation

As you can observe in *Figure 6.2*, the average residual is zero; however, notice that the model is not performing well. It is missing every data point. Therefore, we know for sure that the error is non-zero. The reason we are getting the average residual as zero is that the negative and positive values of residuals are canceling out, and therefore we must go for absolute or squared values of residuals. This helps in focusing only on the **magnitude of residuals**.

Let's discuss two of the most commonly used evaluation metrics – the MAE and RMSE, both of which follow the reasoning we discussed in the earlier paragraph. Instead of focusing on the positive or negative signs of the residuals, both the MAE and RMSE convert the residuals into magnitudes, which gives the correct estimate of the model's performance.

MEAN ABSOLUTE ERROR

There are multiple ways to use residuals to evaluate a model. One way is to simply take the absolute value of all residuals and calculate the average. This is called the **Mean Absolute Error (MAE)**, and can intuitively be thought of as the average difference you should expect between your model's predictions and the true value:

$$MAE = \frac{1}{n} \sum_{j=1}^{n} |y_j - \hat{y}_j|$$

Figure 6.3: Equation for calculating the MAE of a model

In the preceding equation, $\mathbf{y}_j$ is the true value of the outcome variable for the data point $\mathbf{j}$, and $\hat{\mathbf{y}}_j$ is the prediction of the model for that data point. By subtracting these terms and taking the absolute value, we get the residual. $\mathbf{n}$ is the number of data points, and thus by summing over all data points and dividing by $\mathbf{n}$, we get the mean of the absolute error.

Therefore, a value of **zero** would mean that your model predicts everything perfectly, and larger values mean a less accurate model. If we have multiple models, we can look at the MAE and prefer the model with the lower value.

We can implement MAE using the scikit-learn library, as shown here:

1. We will import the **mean_absolute_error** metric from the **sklearn.metrics** module:

    ```
    from sklearn.metrics import mean_absolute_error
    ```

2. Next, we just need to call the **mean_absolute_error** function with two arguments – **predictions**, and the **ground_truth** values:

    ```
    MAE = mean_absolute_error(predictions, ground_truth)
    ```

One issue with the MAE is that it accounts for all errors equally. For many real-world applications, small errors are acceptable and expected, whereas large errors could lead to larger issues. However, with MAE, two medium-sized errors could add up and outweigh one large error. This means that the MAE may prefer a model that is fairly accurate for most predictions but is occasionally extremely inaccurate over a model with more consistent errors over all predictions. For this reason, instead of using the absolute error, a common technique is to use the **squared error**.

ROOT MEAN SQUARED ERROR

As we discussed earlier, another way of focusing only on the magnitudes of residuals is by squaring their values, which helps in getting rid of the positive or negative signs. This concept serves as the core of the RMSE metric. Before we jump into the details of the metric, let's try to understand why we need to take the square root (as the name suggests) of the squared residuals.

By squaring the error term, large errors are weighted more heavily than small ones that add up to the same total amount of error. If we then try to optimize the **Mean Squared Error** (**MSE**) rather than the MAE, we will end up with a preference for models with more consistent predictions, since those large errors are going to be penalized so heavily. The following figure illustrates how, as the size of the residual increases, the squared error grows more quickly than the absolute error:

Residual	Absolute Error	Squared Error
+1 or -1	1	1
+2 or -2	2	4
+3 or -3	3	9
+4 or -4	4	16

Figure 6.4: Squared error versus absolute error

One downside of this, however, is that the error term becomes harder to interpret. The MAE gives us an idea of how much we should expect the prediction to differ from the true value on average, while the MSE is more difficult to interpret. For example, in the case of the previous age prediction problem, MSE would be in the units of "year squared", assuming the age is in years. You can see how difficult it is to comprehend saying that a model has an error of 5 years squared. Therefore, it is common to take the root of the MSE, resulting in the RMSE, as shown by the following equation:

$$\text{RMSE} = \sqrt{\frac{1}{n}\sum_{j=1}^{n}\left(y_j - \hat{y}_j\right)^2}$$

Figure 6.5: Equation for calculating the RMSE of a model

Like the MAE, we can implement the RMSE using the scikit-learn library, as shown here:

1. We will import the **mean_squared_error** metric from the **sklearn.metrics** module:

```
From sklearn.metrics import mean_squared_error
```

2. Next, we just need to call the **mean_squared_error** function with two arguments – **predictions**, and the **ground_truth** values:

```
RMSE = mean_squared_error(predictions, ground_truth)
```

Now that we have discussed both the RMSE and MAE in detail, it is time to implement them using the scikit-learn library and understand how the evaluation metrics help in understanding the model performance. We will also use the same concept to compare the effect of the removal of a predictor (feature or column in the data) on the performance of the model.

EXERCISE 6.01: EVALUATING REGRESSION MODELS OF LOCATION REVENUE USING THE MAE AND RMSE

A chain store has narrowed down five predictors it thinks will have an impact on the revenue of one of its store outlets. Those are the number of competitors, the median income in the region, the number of loyalty scheme members, the population density in the area, and the age of the store. The marketing team has had the intuition that the number of competitors may not be a significant contributing factor to the revenue. Your task is to find out if this intuition is correct.

In this exercise, you will calculate both the MAE and RMSE for models built using the store location revenue data used in *Chapter 5, Predicting Customer Revenue Using Linear Regression*. You will compare models built using all the predictors to a model built excluding one of the predictors. This will help in understanding the importance of the predictor in explaining the data. If removing a specific predictor results in a high drop in performance, this means that the predictor was important for the model, and should not be dropped.

Perform the following steps to achieve the aim of the exercise:

1. Import **pandas** and use it to create a DataFrame from the data in **location_rev.csv**. Call this DataFrame **df**, and view the first five rows using the **head** function:

```
import pandas as pd

df = pd.read_csv('location_rev.csv')
df.head()
```

> **NOTE**
>
> You can get **location_rev.csv** at the following link:
> https://packt.link/u8vHg. If you're not running the **read_csv** command from the same directory as where your Jupyter notebook is stored, you'll need to specify the correct path instead of the one emboldened.

You should see the following output:

	revenue	num_competitors	median_income	num_loyalty_members	population_density	location_age
0	42247.80	3.0	30527.57	1407.0	3302.0	12.0
1	38628.37	3.0	30185.49	1025.0	4422.0	11.0
2	39715.16	1.0	32182.24	1498.0	3260.0	12.0
3	35593.30	5.0	29728.65	2340.0	4325.0	10.0
4	35128.18	4.0	30691.17	847.0	3774.0	11.0

Figure 6.6: The first five rows of the data in location_rev.csv

2. Import **train_test_split** from **sklearn**. Define the **y** variable as **revenue**, and **X** as **num_competitors**, **median_income**, **num_loyalty_members**, **population_density**, and **location_age**:

```
from sklearn.model_selection import train_test_split

X = df[['num_competitors',\
        'median_income'\,
        'num_loyalty_members',\
        'population_density',\
        'location_age']]

y = df['revenue']
```

3. Perform a train-test split on the data, using **random_state=15**, and save the results in **X_train**, **X_test**, **y_train**, and **y_test**:

```
X_train, X_test, y_train, y_test = train_test_split\
                                 (X, y, random_state = 15)
```

4. Import **LinearRegression** from **sklearn**, and use it to fit a linear regression model to the training data:

```
from sklearn.linear_model import LinearRegression

model = LinearRegression()
model.fit(X_train,y_train)
```

5. Get the model's predictions for the **X_test** data, and store the result in a variable called **predictions**:

```
predictions = model.predict(X_test)
```

6. Instead of calculating the RMSE and the MAE yourselves, you can import functions from **sklearn** to do this for you. Note that **sklearn** only contains a function to calculate the MSE, so we need to take the root of this value to get the RMSE (that's where the **0.5** comes in). Use the following code to calculate the RMSE and MAE:

```
from sklearn.metrics import mean_squared_error, \
mean_absolute_error
print('RMSE: ' + \
    str(mean_squared_error(predictions, y_test)**0.5))
print('MAE: ' + \
    str(mean_absolute_error(predictions, y_test)))
```

This should result in the following values:

```
RMSE: 5133.736391468814
MAE: 4161.387875602789
```

7. Now, rebuild the model after dropping **num_competitors** from the predictors and evaluate the new model. Create **X_train2** and **X_test2** variables by dropping **num_competitors** from **X_train** and **X_test**. Train a model using **X_train2** and generate new predictions from this model using **X_test2**:

```
X_train2 = X_train.drop('num_competitors', axis=1)
X_test2 = X_test.drop('num_competitors', axis=1)

model.fit(X_train2, y_train)
predictions2 = model.predict(X_test2)
```

8. Calculate the RMSE and MAE for the new model's predictions and print them out, as follows:

```
print('RMSE: ' + \
    str(mean_squared_error(predictions2, y_test)**0.5))
print('MAE: ' + \
    str(mean_absolute_error(predictions2, y_test)))
```

This should result in the following output:

```
RMSE: 5702.030002037039
MAE: 4544.416946418695
```

Note that both values are higher than the values we calculated for the previous model. This means that dropping **num_competitors** from our model increased the error in our model on the test set. In other words, our model was more accurate when it contained **num_competitors**. Thus, the intuition by the marketing team was not correct.

Thus, we can see how the MAE and the RMSE can be used to determine the features that are important to have in a model and those that have little impact on performance and can therefore be left out.

In the next activity, you will use the same concept on a marketing dataset to find out the most important variables. Recall that finding the important variables means that less important variables can be dropped, which will add up to the robustness of the model and also reduce the computation time.

ACTIVITY 6.01: FINDING IMPORTANT VARIABLES FOR PREDICTING RESPONSES TO A MARKETING OFFER

You have been given some data regarding a company's marketing campaign, wherein discounts were offered for various products. You are interested in building a model that predicts the number of responses to an offer. It should also provide information about how much of a discount the offer included (**offer_discount**), how many customers the offer reached (**offer_reach**), and a value representing the offer quality that the marketing team assigned to that offer (**offer_quality**). You want to build a model that is accurate but does not contain unnecessary variables. Use the RMSE to evaluate how the model performs when all variables are included and compare this to what happens when each variable is dropped from the model. This will then help in finding the most important variables for predicting the number of responses to a marketing offer. Follow the steps given here:

1. Import **pandas**, read in the data from **offer_responses.csv**, and use the **head** function to view the first five rows of the data. Your output should appear as follows:

	responses	offer_discount	offer_quality	offer_reach
0	4151.0	26.0	10.257680	31344.0
1	3397.0	35.0	15.194380	24016.0
2	3274.0	21.0	13.971468	28832.0
3	3426.0	27.0	6.054338	26747.0
4	5745.0	42.0	16.801365	46968.0

Figure 6.7: The first five rows of the offer_responses data

> **NOTE**
>
> You can download **offer_responses.csv** by clicking the following link: https://packt.link/M0wuH.

2. Import **train_test_split** from **sklearn** and use it to split the data into training and test sets, using responses as the **y** variable and all others as the predictor (**X**) variables. Use **random_state=10** for the train-test split.

3. Import **LinearRegression** and **mean_squared_error** from **sklearn**. Fit the model to the training data (using all the predictors), get predictions from the model on the test data, and print out the calculated RMSE on the test data. The RMSE with all variables should be approximately **966.2461828577945**.

4. Create **X_train2** and **X_test2** by dropping **offer_quality** from **X_train** and **X_test**. Train and evaluate the RMSE of the model using **X_train2** and **X_test2**. The RMSE without **offer_quality** should be approximately **965.5346123758474**.

5. Perform the same sequence of steps from *step 4*, but this time dropping **offer_discount** instead of **offer_quality**. The RMSE without **offer_discount** should be approximately **1231.6766556327284**.

6. Perform the same sequence of steps, but this time dropping **offer_reach**. The RMSE without **offer_reach** should be approximately **1185.8456831644114**.

> **NOTE**
>
> The solution for this activity can be found on page 526.

USING RECURSIVE FEATURE SELECTION FOR FEATURE ELIMINATION

So far, we have discussed two important evaluation metrics – the MAE and RMSE. We also saw how these metrics can be used with the help of the scikit-learn library and how a change in the values of these metrics can be used as an indicator of a feature's importance. However, if you have a large number of features, removing one feature at a time would become a very tedious job, and this is where RFE comes into the picture. When a dataset contains features (all columns, except the column that we want to predict) that either are not related to the target column or are related to other columns, the performance of the model can be adversely affected if all the features are used for model training. Let's understand the basic reasoning behind this.

For example, consider that you want to predict the number of sales of a product given the cost price of the product, the discount available, the selling price of the product, and the date when the product was first launched on the market. As you can expect, the launch date of the original product will not affect the current sales of the product. It means that the feature (launch date of the original product) is not related to the target column (sales of the product). Similarly, the cost price of the product becomes a piece of redundant information if the selling price and discount are already available, which is an example of the second case, in which one column is related to other columns.

When one or more features have a low correlation (dependency between two columns) with the target column, this means that these columns are not going to provide any useful information to the model. However, if we still include them while training the model, the model will be forced to (incorrectly) learn that these columns have some effect on the target column. This can result in **overfitting**, in which the model will work very well for the training dataset; however, it will show poor performance on the test dataset.

A similar scenario can occur when features have a high correlation. In such a case, the model will overfit the redundant information provided by correlated columns. To avoid such situations, it is recommended to remove extraneous columns (variables that are not related to the outcome of interest) from the dataset before training the model.

In this chapter, we will discuss a powerful technique of feature elimination referred to as RFE. As the name suggests, RFE is a recursive technique that works by removing one feature at a time and compares the effect of removing a feature on the performance of the model. Based on this comparison, the feature that has a minimum adverse effect (or a maximum positive effect) on the model performance is removed, and the process goes on. As you may have understood, this is very similar to the process we followed in the previous activity. In terms of implementation, RFE is part of the scikit-learn package and can be used as follows:

1. First, import **RFE** from the scikit-learn package:

```
from sklearn.feature_selection import RFE
```

2. Next, create an RFE instance while specifying how many features you want to select. For example, if you want to select **5** features, you will use the following code:

```
rfe = RFE(estimator=LinearRegression(), n_features_to_select=5)
```

3. Fit the RFE model on the training dataset:

```
rfe.fit(X_train,y_train)
```

4. You can then find out which columns were selected by RFE, and which were not, using the following code:

```
for featureNum in range(X_train.shape[1]):
  # If feature was selected
  if rfe.support_[featureNum] == True:
    # Print feature name and rank
    print("Feature: {}, Rank:{}"\
          .format(X_train.columns[featureNum],\
                  rfe.ranking_[featureNum]))
```

You will get the following output:

```
Feature: offer_quality, Rank:1 Feature: offer_discount, Rank:1 Feature:
offer_reach, Rank:1
```

Now, let's get some hands-on experience of using RFE in the next exercise. We will reuse the code we studied here for RFE in this next exercise.

EXERCISE 6.02: USING RFE FOR FEATURE SELECTION

For this exercise, you've been given data of the revenue of stores at different locations, and a series of 20 scores based on internal metrics in the **20scores.csv** file. You aren't told what the scores mean, but are asked to build a predictive model that uses as few of these scores as possible without sacrificing the ability to predict the location revenue.

> **NOTE**
>
> You can get the **20scores.csv** file at the following link:
> https://packt.link/KfBrK.

1. Import **pandas**, read the data from **20scores.csv** into a DataFrame called **df**, and display the first five rows of data using the **head** function:

```
import pandas as pd

df = pd.read_csv('20scores.csv')
df.head()
```

> **NOTE**
>
> Make sure you change the path (emboldened) to the CSV file based on its location on your system. If you're running the Jupyter notebook from the same directory where the CSV file is stored, you can run the preceding code without any modifications.

You should see the following output:

	revenue	score0	score1	score2	score3	score4	score5	score6	score7
0	30698.74	0.067763	1.762772	0.211119	0.619655	-1.586284	0.051320	-0.529940	-0.177908
1	46813.75	0.943657	-0.696100	3.503075	1.323145	-0.579567	-1.379598	0.013465	1.061996
2	39493.35	-0.070838	-1.817580	-0.156724	-0.159741	-1.564338	-0.817489	0.125174	-1.053015
3	48130.55	-0.133306	0.815997	2.261204	0.794839	-0.947440	0.049189	-0.042403	1.657086
4	35129.09	0.452780	1.529394	0.085364	-0.787245	1.351148	-0.340774	0.354099	-0.319731

Figure 6.8: The first five rows of the 20scores.csv data

> **NOTE**
>
> The preceding image does not contain all the columns of the DataFrame. The image is for demonstration purposes only.

2. Extract the target variable (**y**) and the predictor variable (**X**) from the data:

```
x_cols = df.columns[1:]
X = df[x_cols]

y = df['revenue']
```

3. Import **train_test_split** and perform a train-test split on the data with **random_state=10**, storing revenue in the **y** variable and all other features in the **X** variable:

```
from sklearn.model_selection import train_test_split

X_train, X_test, y_train, y_test = train_test_split\
                            (X, y, random_state = 10)
```

4. Import **LinearRegression** from **sklearn** and fit a linear regression model on the training data:

```
from sklearn.linear_model import LinearRegression

model = LinearRegression()
model.fit(X_train,y_train)
```

5. Look at the model's coefficients using the following code:

```
model.coef_
```

You should get the following result:

```
array([ 3.10465458e+01,  1.35929333e+00, -1.71996170e+01, -4.26396854e+00,
       -4.56514104e+00,  2.71178012e+01,  1.12523398e+01, -9.62768549e+00,
        1.28097189e+01, -3.82102937e+01, -3.92691076e+00, -4.49267755e+00,
        9.12581579e+03,  2.81237962e+01,  1.26722148e+01,  1.99096955e+01,
       -1.73401880e+01,  3.77047162e+03, -7.57356369e+00,  4.99844116e+03])
```

Figure 6.9: Model's coefficients

Note that all of these values are non-zero. Therefore, the model is using all variables.

6. Now import **RFE** from **sklearn**. Use a **LinearRegression** model as the estimator, which RFE will use in every iteration. Moreover, you will need to specify the number of features you want to select. For now, keep only five features:

```
from sklearn.feature_selection import RFE
rfe = RFE(estimator=LinearRegression(), n_features_to_select=5)
```

7. Train the RFE model you just created in the previous step on the training data using the following command:

```
rfe.fit(X_train,y_train)
```

This will provide the following output:

```
RFE(estimator=LinearRegression(copy_X=True, fit_intercept=True,
n_jobs=None, normalize=False), n_features_to_select=5, step=1,
verbose=0)
```

> **NOTE**
>
> The output may vary from system to system.

8. Print the columns that were selected by RFE along with their ranks:

```
for featureNum in range(X_train.shape[1]):
  # If feature was selected
  if rfe.support_[featureNum] == True:
    # Print feature name and rank
```

```
print("Feature: {}, Rank: {}"\
    .format(X_train.columns[featureNum],\
        rfe.ranking_[featureNum]))
```

The output obtained for this code is given here:

```
Feature: score0, Rank: 1
Feature: score9, Rank: 1
Feature: score12, Rank: 1
Feature: score17, Rank: 1
Feature: score19, Rank: 1
```

Notice that only five features were selected by RFE and that all of those features were given a rank **1**, meaning that RFE considered all five features to be equally important.

9. Using the preceding information, now create a reduced dataset having only the columns selected by RFE:

```
X_train_reduced = X_train[X_train.columns[rfe.support_]]
X_test_reduced = X_test[X_train.columns[rfe.support_]]
```

10. Next, use the reduced training dataset to fit a new linear regression model:

```
rfe_model = LinearRegression()
rfe_model.fit(X_train_reduced, y_train)
```

11. Import **mean_squared_error** from **sklearn** and use it to calculate the RMSE of the linear regression model on the test data:

```
from sklearn.metrics import mean_squared_error

predictions = model.predict(X_test)
print(mean_squared_error(predictions, y_test)**0.5)
```

The output should be similar to **491.78833768572633**.

12. Similarly, calculate the RMSE of the model generated in *step 9* on the test data:

```
rfe_predictions = rfe_model.predict(X_test_reduced)
print(mean_squared_error(rfe_predictions, y_test)**0.5)
```

The output should be similar to **487.6184171986599**.

You can observe that, although the reduced dataset obtained using RFE only has five features, its RMSE is lower than the linear model that uses all of them. This shows that it has not lost any predictive power, even though it has greatly simplified the model by removing variables.

In the next activity, we will use RFE to find out the top three features for predicting customer spend. This will give you an insight into how RFE can be used in marketing problems where a larger number of columns are commonly present.

ACTIVITY 6.02: USING RFE TO CHOOSE FEATURES FOR PREDICTING CUSTOMER SPEND

You've been given the following information (features) regarding various customers:

prev_year_spend: How much they spent in the previous year

days_since_last_purchase: The number of days since their last purchase

days_since_first_purchase: The number of days since their first purchase

total_transactions: The total number of transactions

age: The customer's age

income: The customer's income

engagement_score: A customer engagement score, which is a score created based on customers' engagement with previous marketing offers.

You are asked to investigate which of these is related to the customer spend in the current year (**cur_year_spend**). You'll also need to create a simple linear model to describe these relationships.

Follow the steps given here:

1. Import **pandas**, use it to read in the data in **customer_spend.csv**, and use the **head** function to view the first five rows of data. The output should appear as follows:

	cur_year_spend	prev_year_spend	days_since_last_purchase	days_since_first_purchase
0	5536.46	1681.26	7	61
1	871.41	1366.74	12	34
2	2046.74	1419.38	10	81
3	4662.70	1561.21	12	32
4	3539.46	1397.60	17	72

Figure 6.10: The first five rows of customer_spend.csv

> **NOTE**
>
> You can download the **customer_spend.csv** file by clicking the following link: https://packt.link/tKJn8.

2. Use **train_test_split** from **sklearn** to split the data into training and test sets, with **random_state=100** and **cur_year_spend** as the **y** variable:

3. Use RFE to obtain the three most important features and obtain the reduced versions of the training and test datasets by using only the selected columns.

4. Train a linear regression model on the reduced training dataset and calculate the RMSE value on the test dataset.

   The RMSE value should be approximately **1075.9083016269915**.

> **NOTE**
>
> The solution for this activity can be found on page 530.

TREE-BASED REGRESSION MODELS

In the preceding activity, you were able to identify the three most important features that could be used to predict customer spend. Now, imagine doing the same by removing each feature one at a time and finding out the RMSE. RFE aims to remove the redundant task of going over each feature by doing it internally, without forcing the user to put in the effort to do it manually.

So far, we have covered linear regression models. Now it's time to take it up a notch by discussing some tree-based regression models.

Linear models are not the only type of regression models. Another powerful technique is the use of **regression trees**. Regression trees are based on the idea of a **decision tree**. A decision tree is a bit like a flowchart, where, at each step, you ask whether a variable is greater than or less than some value. After *flowing* through several of these steps, you reach the end of the tree and receive an answer for what value the prediction should be. The following figure illustrates the working of regression trees. For example, if you want to predict the age of a person with a height of 1.7 m and a weight of 80 kg, then using the regression tree (left), since the height is less than 1.85m, you will follow the left branch. Similarly, since the weight is less than 90 kg, you will follow the left branch and end at 18. This means that the age of the person is 18 years:

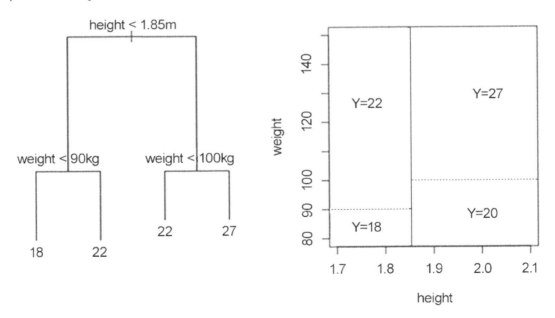

Figure 6.11: A regression tree (left) and how it parses the feature space into predictions

Decision trees are interesting because they can pick up on trends in data that linear regression might miss or capture poorly. Whereas linear models assume a simple linear relationship between predictors and an outcome, regression trees result in more complex functions, which can fit certain kinds of relationships more accurately.

The implementation stays the same as the linear regression model in scikit-learn, the only difference being that this time, instead of importing **LinearRegression**, you will need to import **DecisionTreeRegressor**, as shown here:

```
from sklearn.tree import DecisionTreeRegressor
```

You can then create an instance of the decision tree regressor. In the following code, you can change the maximum depth of the tree as per requirements:

```
tree_model = DecisionTreeRegressor(max_depth=2)
```

One important parameter for regression trees is the *maximum depth of the tree*. The more depth that a tree is allowed, the more complex a relationship it can model. While this may sound like a good thing, choosing too high a maximum depth can lead to a model that is highly overfitted to the data. In fact, the tendency to overfit is one of the biggest drawbacks of regression trees. That's where random forests come in handy.

RANDOM FORESTS

To overcome the issue of overfitting, instead of training a single tree to find patterns in data, many trees are trained over random subsets of the data. The predictions of these trees are then averaged to produce a prediction. Combining trees together in this way is called a **random forest**. This technique has been found to overcome many of the weaknesses associated with regression trees. The following figure illustrates an ensemble of tree models, each of whose predictions are averaged to produce the ensemble's predictions. We see that **n** number of trees are trained over random subsets of data. Then, the mean of the predictions from those trees is the desired prediction:

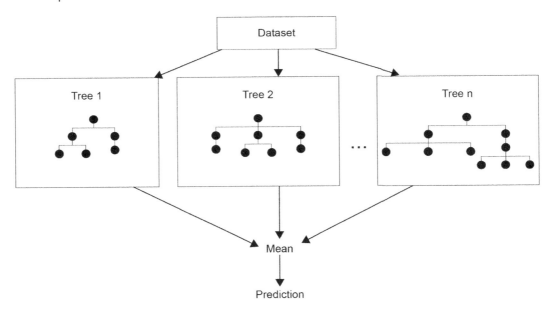

Figure 6.12: An ensemble of tree models

Random forests are based on the idea of creating an **ensemble**, which is where multiple models are combined to produce a single prediction. This is a powerful technique that can often lead to very good outcomes. In the case of random forests, creating an ensemble of regression trees together in this way has been shown to not only decrease overfitting but also to produce very good predictions in a wide variety of scenarios.

Similar to the regression trees discussed in the previous section, random forests can be created using the following steps with the help of the scikit-learn library.

First, import **RandomForestRegressor** from the scikit-learn module:

```
from sklearn.module import RandomForestRegressor
```

You can then create an instance of the random forest regressor. In the following code, you can change the maximum depth of the trees present in the random forest as per your requirements:

```
forest_model = RandomForestRegressor(max_depth=2)
```

Because tree-based methods and linear regression are so drastically different in the way they fit to data, they often work well in different circumstances. When the relationships in data are linear (or close to it), linear models will tend to produce more accurate predictions, with the bonus of being easy to interpret. When relationships are more complex, tree-based methods may perform better. For example, the profit made by a firm and the profit made by each advertisement run by them is a linear relationship. If the profit made by each ad doubles, the overall profit of the firm will also double. However, the number of ads doesn't necessarily have to follow a linear relationship with the profit, as you can have 100 ads performing poorly, versus only one ad performing really well. This is a complex, or non-linear, relationship. Testing each and choosing the best model for the job requires evaluating the models based on their predictive accuracy with a metric such as the RMSE. The choice is ultimately dependent on the data you are working on.

For example, if you realize during the initial stages of data analysis (let's say you notice that the data points are approximately following a linear curve) that a linear model will fit the data accurately, it's better to go for a linear regression model rather than the more complex tree-based regression models. In the worst-case scenario, you can try out both approaches and choose the most accurate one.

Now it is time to put the skills we learned to use by using tree-based regression models to predict the customers' spend given their ages.

EXERCISE 6.03: USING TREE-BASED REGRESSION MODELS TO CAPTURE NON-LINEAR TRENDS

In this exercise, you'll look at a very simple dataset where you have data on customers' spend and their ages. You want to figure out how spending habits change with age in your customers, and how well different models can capture this relationship. Having a model like this can help in building age-specific website patterns for your customers since you will be able to recommend products that suit the customers' spend levels.

Perform the following steps to achieve the aim of this exercise:

1. Import **pandas** and use it to read in the data in **age_spend.csv**. Use the **head** function to view the first five rows of the data:

```
import pandas as pd

df = pd.read_csv('age_spend.csv')
df.head()
```

> **NOTE**
>
> Make sure you change the path (emboldened) to the CSV file based on its location on your system. If you're running the Jupyter notebook from the same directory where the CSV file is stored, you can run the preceding code without any modifications.

Your output will appear as follows:

	spend	age
0	2725.0	20.0
1	3010.0	38.0
2	2782.0	25.0
3	2809.0	31.0
4	2774.0	54.0

Figure 6.13: The first five rows of the age_spend data

> **NOTE**
>
> You can download the **age_spend.csv** file from the following link:
> https://packt.link/NxEiK.

2. Extract the target variable (**y**) and the predictor variable (**X**) from the data:

```
X = df[['age']]

y = df['spend']
```

3. Import **train_test_split** from **sklearn** and use it to perform a train-test split of the data, with **random_state=10** and **y** being the spend and **X** being the age:

```
from sklearn.model_selection import train_test_split

X_train, X_test, y_train, y_test = train_test_split\
                                (X, y, random_state = 10)
```

4. Import **DecisionTreeRegressor** from **sklearn** and fit two decision trees to the training data, one with **max_depth=2** and one with **max_depth=5**:

```
from sklearn.tree import DecisionTreeRegressor

max2_tree_model = DecisionTreeRegressor(max_depth=2)
max2_tree_model.fit(X_train,y_train)

max5_tree_model = DecisionTreeRegressor(max_depth=5)
max5_tree_model.fit(X_train,y_train)
```

5. Import **LinearRegression** from **sklearn** and fit a linear regression model to the training data, as shown:

```
from sklearn.linear_model import LinearRegression

model = LinearRegression()
model.fit(X_train,y_train)
```

You will get the following output:

```
LinearRegression(copy_X=True, fit_intercept=True, n_jobs=None,
normalize=False)
```

> **NOTE**
>
> The output may vary from system to system.

6. Import **mean_squared_error** from **sklearn**. For the linear model and the two regression tree models, get predictions from the model for the test set and use these to calculate the RMSE. Use the following code:

```
from sklearn.metrics import mean_squared_error

linear_predictions = model.predict(X_test)
print('Linear model RMSE: ' + \
        str(mean_squared_error(linear_predictions, y_test)**0.5))

max2_tree_predictions = max2_tree_model.predict(X_test)
print('Tree with max depth of 2 RMSE: ' + \
        str(mean_squared_error(max2_tree_predictions, y_test)**0.5))

max5_tree_predictions = max5_tree_model.predict(X_test)
print('tree with max depth of 5 RMSE: ' + \
        str(mean_squared_error(max5_tree_predictions, y_test)**0.5))
```

You should get the following RMSE values for the linear and decision tree models with maximum depths of **2** and **5**, respectively: **159.07639273785358**, **125.1920405443602**, and **109.73376798374653**.

Notice that the linear model has the largest error, the decision tree with a maximum depth of **2** does better, and the decision tree with a maximum depth of **5** has the lowest error of the three.

7. Import **matplotlib**. Create a variable called **ages** to store a DataFrame with a single column containing ages from 18 to 70, so that we can have our models give us their predictions for all these ages:

```
import matplotlib.pyplot as plt
%matplotlib inline

ages = pd.DataFrame({'age':range(18,70)})
```

8. Create a scatter plot with the test data and, on top of it, plot the predictions from the linear regression model for the range of ages. Plot with **color='k'** and **linewidth=5** to make it easier to see:

```
plt.scatter(X_test.age.tolist(), y_test.tolist(), color='gray')
plt.plot(ages,model.predict(ages), color='k', linewidth=5, \
         label="Linear Regression")
plt.xlabel("age")
plt.ylabel("spend")
plt.show()
```

> **NOTE**
>
> In *Steps 8*, *9*, *10*, *13*, and *14*, the values **gray** and **k** for the attribute **color** (emboldened) is used to generate graphs in grayscale. You can also refer to the following document to get the code for the colored plot and the colored output: http://packt.link/NOjgT.

The following plot shows the predictions of the linear regression model across the **age** range plotted on top of the actual data points:

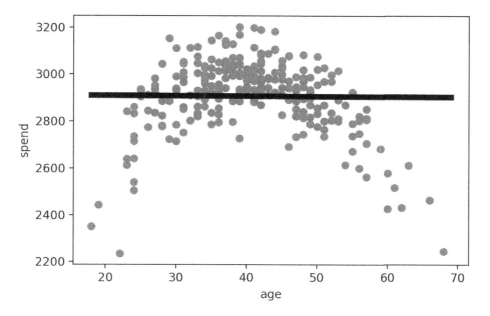

Figure 6.14: The predictions of the linear regression model

You can see that the linear regression model just shows a flat line across the ages; it is unable to capture the fact that people aged around 40 spend more, while people younger and older than 40 spend less.

9. Create another scatter plot with the test data, this time plotting the predictions of the **max2_tree** model on top with **color='k'** and **linewidth=5**:

```
plt.scatter(X_test.age.tolist(), y_test.tolist(), color='gray')
plt.plot(ages,max2_tree_model.predict(ages), \
         color='k',linewidth=5,label="Tree with max depth 2")
plt.xlabel("age")
plt.ylabel("spend")
plt.show()
```

The following plot shows the predictions of the regression tree model with **max_depth** of 2 across the **age** range plotted on top of the actual data points:

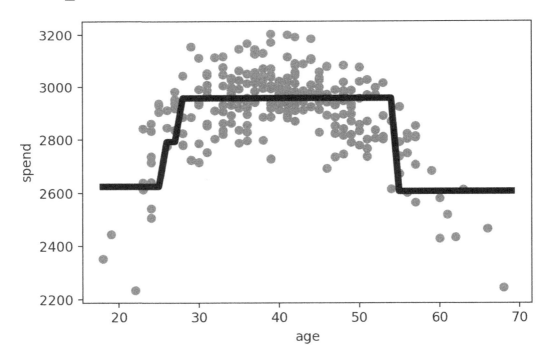

Figure 6.15: The predictions of the regression tree model with max_depth of 2

This model does a better job of capturing the relationship, though it does not capture the sharp decline in the oldest or youngest populations.

10. Create one more scatter plot with the test data, this time plotting the predictions of the **max5_tree** model on top with **color='k'** and **linewidth=5**:

```
plt.scatter(X_test.age.tolist(), y_test.tolist(), color='gray')
plt.plot(ages,max5_tree_model.predict(ages), color='k',\
        linewidth=5, label="Tree with max depth 5")
plt.xlabel("age")
plt.ylabel("spend")
plt.show()
```

The following plot shows the predictions of the regression tree model with **max_depth** of 5 across the **age** range plotted on top of the actual data points:

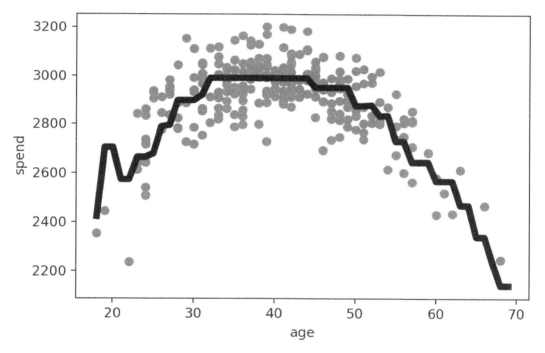

Figure 6.16: The predictions of the regression tree model with max_depth of 5

This model does an even better job of capturing the relationship, properly capturing a sharp decline in the oldest or the youngest population.

11. Let's now perform random forest regression on the same data. Import **RandomForestRegressor** from **sklearn**. Fit two random forest models with **random_state=10**, one with **max_depth=2** and the other with **max_depth=5**, and save these as **max2_forest_model** and **max5_forest_model**, respectively:

```
from sklearn.ensemble import RandomForestRegressor

max2_forest_model = RandomForestRegressor\
                    (max_depth=2, random_state=10)
max2_forest_model.fit(X_train,y_train)

max5_forest_model = RandomForestRegressor\
                    (max_depth=5, random_state=10)
max5_forest_model.fit(X_train,y_train)
```

You will get the following output:

```
RandomForestRegressor(max_depth=5, random_state=10)
```

12. Calculate and print the RMSE for the two random forest models using the following code:

```
max2_forest_predictions = max2_forest_model.predict(X_test)
print('Max depth of 2 RMSE: ' + \
      str(mean_squared_error(max2_forest_predictions, \
                             y_test)**0.5))

max5_forest_predictions = max5_forest_model.predict(X_test)
print('Max depth of 5 RMSE: ' + \
      str(mean_squared_error(max5_forest_predictions, \
                             y_test)**0.5))
```

The following RMSE values should be obtained for the random forest models with maximum depths of **2** and **5**, respectively: **115.51279667457273** and **109.61188562057568**. Please note that there might be some minute differences in these values.

Based on the RMSE values obtained, we can see that the random forest models performed better than regression tree models of the same depth. Moreover, all tree-based regression models outperformed the linear regression model.

13. Create another scatter plot with the test data, this time plotting the predictions of the **max2_forest_model** model on top with **color='k'** and **linewidth=5**:

```
plt.scatter(X_test.age.tolist(), y_test.tolist(),color='gray')
plt.plot(ages,max2_forest_model.predict(ages), color='k',\
        linewidth=5, label="Forest with max depth 2")
plt.xlabel("age")
plt.ylabel("spend")
plt.show()
```

The following plot shows the predictions of the random forest model with **max_depth** of **2** across the **age** range plotted on top of the actual data points:

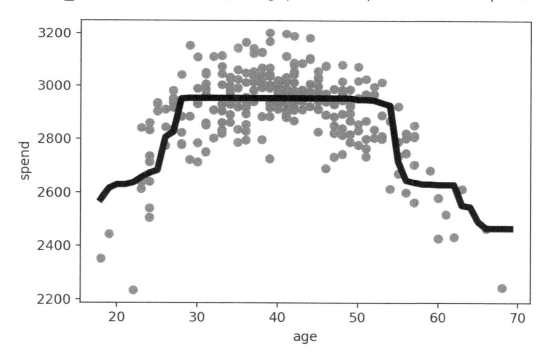

Figure 6.17: The predictions of the random forest model with max_depth of 2

We can see that this model captures the data trend better than the decision tree, but still doesn't quite capture the trend at the very high or low ends of our range.

14. Create another scatter plot with the test data, this time plotting the predictions of the **max2_forest_model** model on top with **color='k'** and **linewidth=5**:

```
plt.scatter(X_test.age.tolist(), y_test.tolist(), color='gray')
plt.plot(ages,max5_forest_model.predict(ages), color='k',\
        linewidth=5, label="Forest with max depth 5")
plt.xlabel("age")
plt.ylabel("spend")
plt.show()
```

The following plot shows the predictions of the random forest model with **max_depth** of 5 across the **age** range plotted on top of the actual data points:

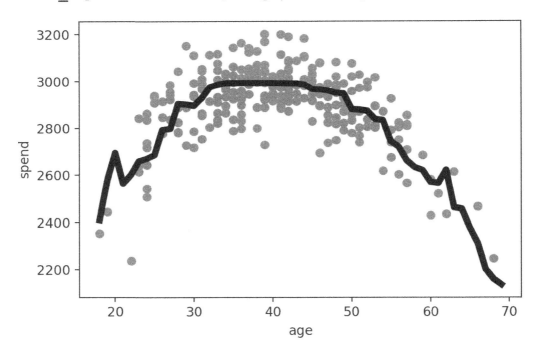

Figure 6.18: The predictions of the random forest model with max_depth of 5

Again, in the model, the greater maximum depth does an even better job of capturing the relationship, properly capturing the sharp decline in the oldest and youngest population groups.

The preceding results can easily be clubbed together to create the plot shown here, which presents a nice comparison of using different **max_depth** attributes while training the random forest model.

The code used to generate the plot is given here:

```
plt.figure(figsize=(12,8))
plt.scatter(X_test.age.tolist(), y_test.tolist())
plt.plot(ages,model.predict(ages), color='r', linewidth=5, \
        label="Linear Regression")
plt.plot(ages,max2_tree_model.predict(ages), color='g',\
        linewidth=5,label="Tree with max depth 2")
plt.plot(ages,max5_tree_model.predict(ages), color='k',\
        linewidth=5, label="Tree with max depth 5")
plt.plot(ages,max2_forest_model.predict(ages), color='c',\
        linewidth=5, label="Forest with max depth 2")
plt.plot(ages,max5_forest_model.predict(ages), color='m',\
        linewidth=5, label="Forest with max depth 5")
plt.legend()
plt.xlabel("age")
plt.ylabel("spend")
plt.show()
```

You should get the following output:

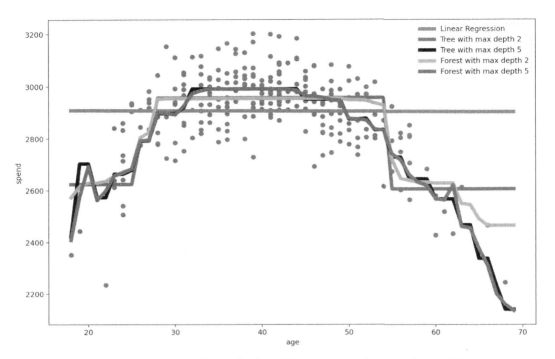

Figure 6.19: Comparison of using different max_depth values while training the random forest model

In this exercise, you saw that the tree-based models outperformed the linear regression model since the data was non-linear. Among the tree-based models, the random forest model had the lowest RMSE value. You also saw that by increasing the maximum depth from **2** to **5**, the curve started fitting the training dataset more tightly. You will explore this part in detail in later chapters. You also saw that for people aged between 20 and 40, the total expenditure increased with age; however, for people aged over 50, the trend was completely the opposite.

Now, let's use the knowledge gained so far to build a regression model to predict the customer spend based on the user data given. You will again have to fit different kinds of regression models and choose the best among those.

ACTIVITY 6.03: BUILDING THE BEST REGRESSION MODEL FOR CUSTOMER SPEND BASED ON DEMOGRAPHIC DATA

You are given data of customers' spend at your business and some basic demographic data regarding each customer (age, income, and years of education). You are asked to build the best predictive model possible that can predict, based on these demographic factors, how much a given customer will spend at your business. The following are these high-level steps to solve this activity:

1. Import **pandas**, read the data in **spend_age_income_ed.csv** into a DataFrame, and use the **head** function to view the first five rows of the data. The output should be as follows:

	spend	age	income	years_of_education
0	3304.0	36.0	45125.0	12
1	3709.0	43.0	41695.0	10
2	3305.0	47.0	39253.0	17
3	2170.0	33.0	32384.0	13
4	2113.0	30.0	33182.0	10

Figure 6.20: The first five rows of the spend_age_income_ed data

> **NOTE**
>
> You can get the **spend_age_income_ed.csv** file at the following link: https://packt.link/LGGyB.

2. Perform a train-test split with **random_state=10**.

3. Fit a linear regression model to the training data.

4. Fit two regression tree models to the data, one with **max_depth=2** and one with **max_depth=5**.

5. Fit two random forest models to the data, one with **max_depth=2**, one with **max_depth=5**, and **random_state=10** for both.

6. Calculate and print out the RMSE on the test data for all five models.

The following table summarizes the expected output for all the models. The values you get may not be an exact match with these expected values. You may get a deviation of within 5% of these values.

Model	RMSE
Linear model	348.19771532747865
Decision tree with max depth of 2	268.51069264082935
Decision tree with max depth of 5	125.53257106419696
Random forest with max depth of 2	267.88627970886233
Random forest with max depth of 5	115.88545042221628

Figure 6.21: Expected outputs for all five models

NOTE

The solution for this activity can be found on page 533.

SUMMARY

In this chapter, we learned how to evaluate regression models. We used residuals to calculate the MAE and RMSE, and then used those metrics to compare models. We also learned about RFE and how it can be used for feature selection. We were able to see the effect of feature elimination on the MAE and RMSE metrics and relate it to the robustness of the model. We used these concepts to verify that the intuitions about the importance of the "number of competitors" feature were wrong in our case study. Finally, we learned about tree-based regression models and looked at how they can fit some of the non-linear relationships that linear regression is unable to handle. We saw how random forest models were able to perform better than regression tree models and the effect of increasing the maximum tree depth on model performance. We used these concepts to model the spending behavior of people with respect to their age.

In the next chapter, we will learn about classification models, the other primary type of supervised learning models.

7

SUPERVISED LEARNING: PREDICTING CUSTOMER CHURN

OVERVIEW

In this chapter, you will perform classification tasks using logistic regression and implement the most widely used data science pipeline – **Obtain, Scrub, Explore, Model**, and **iNterpret (OSEMN)**. You will interpret the relationship between the target and explanatory variables by performing data exploration. This will in turn help in selecting features for building predictive models. You will use these concepts to train your churn model. You will also perform logistic regression as a baseline model to predict customer churn.

INTRODUCTION

The success of a company is highly dependent on its ability to attract new customers while holding on to the existing ones. **Churn** refers to the situation where a customer of a company stops using its product and leaves the company. Churn can be anything—employee churn from a company, customer churn from a mobile subscription, and so on. Predicting customer churn is important for an organization because acquiring new customers is easy but retaining them is more difficult. Similarly, high employee churn can also affect a company, since the companies spend a huge sum of money on grooming talent. Also, organizations that have high retention rates benefit from consistent growth, which can also lead to high referrals from existing customers. Churn prediction is one of the most common use cases of machine learning.

You learned about supervised learning in the previous chapters, where you gained hands-on experience in solving regression problems. When it comes to predicting customer churn, you will find that most of the use cases involve supervised classification tasks. That is why you will begin this chapter by learning about classification problems. Then you will learn about the logistic regression algorithm. You'll not only understand the intuition behind this algorithm but also its implementation. Next, you will see how to organize data to build a churn model, followed by an exploration of the data to see if statistical inferences can be drawn from it. You will find out what the important features are for building your churn model, and finally, you'll apply logistic regression to predict customer churn. Throughout the chapter, you will be working with a case study of customer churn prediction to understand and implement the preceding concepts. By the end of the chapter, you would have built a model that, given some attributes of a customer, can predict the chances of the customer churning.

CLASSIFICATION PROBLEMS

Consider a situation where you have been tasked to build a model to predict whether a product bought by a customer will be returned or not. Since we have focused on regression models so far, let's try and imagine whether these will be the right fit here. A regression model will give continuous values as output (for example, 0.1, 100, 100.25, and so on), but in our case study we just have two values as output – a product will be returned, or it won't be returned. In such a case, except for these two values, all other values will be incorrect/invalid. While we can say that *product returned* can be considered as the value **0**, and *product not returned* can be considered as the value **1**, we still can't define what a value of 1.5 means.

In scenarios like these, classification models come into the picture. Classification problems are the most common type of machine learning problem. Classification tasks are different from regression tasks in the sense that in classification tasks, we predict a discrete class label (for example, the product will be returned, or not returned), whereas, in the case of regression, we predict continuous values (for example, the price of a house, the age of a person, and so on). Another notable difference between classification problems and regression problems lies in the choice of performance metrics. With classification problems, accuracy is commonly chosen as a performance metric, while the root mean square is quite common in the case of regression.

There are many important business use cases for classification problems where the dependent variable (also referred to as the target variable, which is the value we are trying to predict) is discrete, such as *churn* or *fraud detection*. In these cases, the response variable has only two values, that is, churn or not churn, and fraud or not fraud. For example, suppose we wanted to predict whether a customer will churn ($y = 1$) or won't churn ($y = 0$) after signing up for a mobile service contract. Here, the probability that a customer churns is indicated as $\mathbf{p} = \mathbf{P(Churn)}$, and the possible explanatory variable x includes the account age, current billing amount, and average days of delinquency (that is, the average number of days a person misses making their payment). The following figure illustrates how a supervised classification task works:

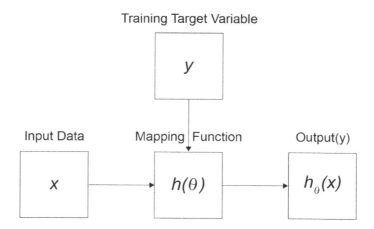

Figure 7.1: The workflow of a supervised classification task

As a supervisor, we provide the model with the variables **(x,y)**, which lets the model calculate the parameter theta (**θ**). This parameter is learned from the training data and is also termed a **coefficient**. **x** includes the explanatory variables and **y** is the target label that we provide to the model so that the model learns the parameters. Using this, the model produces a function **h(θ)**, which maps input **x** to a prediction **h₍(x)**.

For the churn prediction case study, **x** will refer to the attributes of the customer, which will be fed into the mapping function **h(θ)** for predicting the likelihood of the customer churning (target variable **y**).

Classification problems can generally be divided into two types:

- **Binary classification**: The target variable can have only two categorical values or classes. For example, given an image, classify whether it's a cat or not a cat.

- **Multiclass classification**: The target variable can have multiple classes. For example, given an image, classify whether it's a cat, dog, rabbit, or bird.

Now that we have gone over the basics of a supervised classification task, let's start with learning the commonly used baseline model in classification – logistic regression.

UNDERSTANDING LOGISTIC REGRESSION

Logistic regression is one of the most widely used classification methods, and it works well when data is linearly separable. The objective of logistic regression is to squash the output of linear regression to classes **0** and **1**. Let's first understand the "regression" part of the name and why, despite its name, logistic regression is a classification model.

REVISITING LINEAR REGRESSION

In the case of linear regression, our mapping function would be as follows:

$$h_\theta(x) = \theta_0 + \theta_1 * x$$

Figure 7.2: Equation of linear regression

Here, **x** refers to the input data and **θ₀** and **θ₁** are parameters that are learned from the training data.

Also, the cost function in the case of linear regression, which is to be minimized, is the **root mean squared error** (**RMSE**), which we discussed in the previous chapter.

This works well for continuous data, but the problem arises when we have a categorical target variable, such as **0** or **1**. When we try to use linear regression to predict the target variable, we can get a value anywhere between $-\infty$ to $+\infty$, which is not what we need. Now that we know why linear regression can't be used in classification tasks, let's understand how logistic regression can be used as a classification model.

LOGISTIC REGRESSION

If a response variable has binary values, the assumptions of linear regression are not valid for the following reasons:

- The relationship between the independent variable and the predictor variable is not linear.

- The error terms are heteroscedastic. Recall that heteroscedastic means that the variance of the error terms is not the same throughout the range of x (input data).

- The error terms are not normally distributed.

If we proceed, considering these violations, the results would be as follows:

- The predicted probabilities could be greater than 1 or less than 0.

- The magnitude of the effects of independent variables may be underestimated.

With logistic regression, we are interested in modeling the mean of the response variable, **p**, in terms of an explanatory variable, **x**, as a probabilistic model in terms of the **odds ratio**. The odds ratio is the ratio of two probabilities – the probability of the event occurring, and the probability of the event not occurring. A high odds ratio signifies that the chances of the event occurring are high. Similarly, a rarely occurring event will have a low odds ratio. A simple logistic regression model formula, utilizing the concept of odds ratio, is as follows:

$$\boldsymbol{logit(p)} = \boldsymbol{log}\left(\frac{p}{1-p}\right) = \theta_0 + \theta_1 * x_1 + \theta_2 * x_2 + \theta_3 * x_3 \ldots$$

$$\text{Where, } p \text{ is the probability that an event } y \text{ occurs}, p(y = 1)$$

$$\frac{p}{1-p} \text{ is the odd ratio}$$

$$log\left(\frac{p}{1-p}\right) \text{ is the log odds, or logit}$$

Figure 7.3: Simple logistic regression model formula

With logistic regression, we still use the linear regression formula. However, we will be squashing the output of the linear function to a range of **0** and **1** using the sigmoid function. The sigmoid function is the inverse of the logit function:

$$p = g(z) = \frac{1}{1 + e^{-z}}$$

Figure 7.4: Sigmoid function

Here, **z** is any real number.

Squash the output of the linear equation as follows:

$$linear\ function:\ \boldsymbol{h_\theta}(\boldsymbol{x}) = \theta_0 + \theta_1 * x_1 + \theta_2 * x_2 + \theta_3 * x_3 \ldots$$

$$taking\ (\theta_0 + \theta_1 * x_1 + \theta_2 * x_2 + \theta_3 * x_3 \ldots)\ as\ \boldsymbol{\theta^T x}$$

$$g(\boldsymbol{\theta^T x}) = \frac{1}{1 + e^{-\theta^T x}}$$

Figure 7.5: Squashing output of linear equation using sigmoid

Here, we take the output of $\mathbf{h}_\theta(\mathbf{x})$ and give it to the **g(z)** function, which returns the squashed function in the range of **0** to **1**.

If we now try to plot the sigmoid function, we will end up with an S-shaped curve, as shown in *Figure 7.6*:

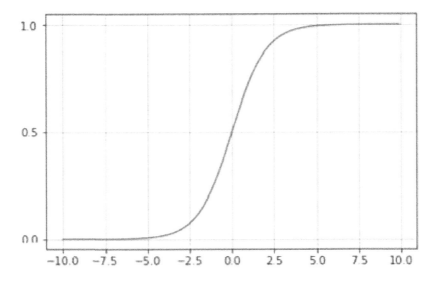

Figure 7.6: A plot of the sigmoid function

From the preceding graph, it is evident that the sigmoid function squashes the values of **−10** to **+10** to between **0** and **1**, whereas the linear function is unable to do so.

So far, we have covered the concept of the sigmoid function. However, we are yet to discuss the cost function that we can use here. All machine learning algorithms aim to minimize the value of the cost function to come up with the best fit. We also discussed why RMSE is not a good cost function in the case of classification tasks. Let's discuss the cost function used in logistic regression in the next section.

COST FUNCTION FOR LOGISTIC REGRESSION

The sigmoid function that we described previously contains a non-linear term. We must convert it into a linear term, else we would have a complex function that would be difficult to optimize. The **cost** function of logistic regression can be defined as follows:

$$cost(g(\theta^T x), y) = \begin{cases} -log\left(g(\theta^T x)\right) & y = 1 \\ -log\left(1 - g(\theta^T x)\right) & y = 0 \end{cases}$$

Figure 7.7: Logistic regression cost function

It is easy for the algorithm to optimize the **cost** function when we have a linear term (see the plot to the left in the following figure), whereas it becomes difficult for the algorithm to optimize if our cost function is non-linear (see the plot to the right in the following figure):

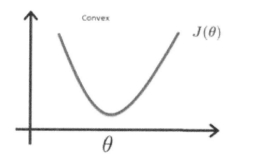
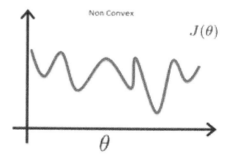

Figure 7.8: Difference between plots with linear and non-linear terms

After converting our cost function ($\mathbf{J(\theta)}$) for logistic regression to a linear term, we finally get the following equation:

$$J(\theta) = -\frac{1}{no\ of\ rows} \sum_{i=0}^{i=no\ of\ rows} y^i * \log\left(g(\theta^T x) + \left(1 - y^i\right) * \log\left(1 - g(\theta^T x)\right)\right)$$

Figure 7.9: Optimized logistic regression cost function

Here, θ is the parameter the model learns from the training data. Now that we have covered both the mapping function and the cost function for logistic regression, let's go over the assumptions of the logistic regression algorithm, which will help us understand the scenarios where it can be applied.

> **NOTE**
>
> The derivation of the cost function is beyond the scope of this book. We recommend you go through the derivation separately. You can find the derivation here: https://mathworld.wolfram.com/SigmoidFunction.html.

ASSUMPTIONS OF LOGISTIC REGRESSION

The following are the assumptions of the logistic regression algorithm:

- Unlike linear regression, logistic regression does not assume linearity between the independent variables (**x**) and the target variable (**y**).

- The dependent variable must be binary (that is, have two categories).

- The independent variable need not have intervals, be normally distributed, linearly related, or have equal variance within each group.

- The categories must be mutually exclusive and exhaustive.

Now that we have gone over the theory and assumptions of logistic regression, let's see how we can implement it using the scikit-learn module. Here are the steps that we need to follow:

1. Import the **linear_model** module from scikit-learn:

```
from sklearn import linear_model
```

2. Create a logistic regression model:

```
logit = linear_model.LogisticRegression()
```

3. Next, we can train the model on the training dataset as follows:

```
logit.fit(X_train, y_train)
```

4. Finally, similar to linear regression, we can use **logit.predict(X)** to make predictions for a specific value. Moreover, we can use **logit.score(X_train, y_train)** to get the training score and **logit.score(X_test, y_test)** to get the test score for the trained model.

In the previous sections, we have discussed the assumptions along with the mapping function, and the cost function of logistic regression. We also saw how to implement logistic regression using the scikit-learn library in Python. Now it's time to use these concepts in a real-life problem statement.

EXERCISE 7.01: COMPARING PREDICTIONS BY LINEAR AND LOGISTIC REGRESSION ON THE SHILL BIDDING DATASET

Consider the **Shill_Bidding_Dataset.csv** dataset, which contains details regarding auctions done for various products on eBay.com. The target column, **Class**, provides information about the bidding behavior, **0** being normal and **1** being abnormal behavior. Abnormal behavior can be similar to malicious clicks or automatic bidding. You have been asked to develop a machine learning model that can predict whether the bidding behavior in a particular auction is normal (**0**) or not (**1**). Apply linear and logistic regression to predict the output and check which one of them is useful in this situation:

> **NOTE**
>
> The **Shill_Bidding_Dataset.csv** dataset can be found here:
> https://packt.link/eLnAi.

1. Import the **pandas**, **numpy**, **sklearn**, and **matplotlib** libraries using the following code:

```
import pandas as pd
import numpy as np
from sklearn.model_selection import train_test_split
from sklearn import linear_model
import matplotlib.pyplot as plt
```

2. Create a new DataFrame and name it **data**. Look at the first few rows using the following code:

```
data = pd.read_csv("Shill_Bidding_Dataset.csv")
data.head()
```

> **NOTE**
>
> Make sure you change the path (emboldened in the preceding code snippet) to the CSV file based on its location on your system. If you're running the Jupyter notebook from the same directory where the CSV file is stored, you can run the preceding code without any modification.

You will get the following output. You may notice that we have some ID columns unique to each row:

	Record_ID	Auction_ID	Bidder_ID	Bidder_Tendency	Bidding_Ratio	Successive_Outbidding	Last_Bidding	Auction_Bids
0	1	732	_***i	0.200000	0.400000	0.0	0.000028	0.0
1	2	732	g***r	0.024390	0.200000	0.0	0.013123	0.0
2	3	732	t***p	0.142857	0.200000	0.0	0.003042	0.0
3	4	732	7***n	0.100000	0.200000	0.0	0.097477	0.0
4	5	900	z***z	0.051282	0.222222	0.0	0.001318	0.0

Figure 7.10: The first five rows of the data

> **NOTE**
>
> The preceding image does not contain all the columns of the DataFrame. The image is for demonstration purposes only.

3. Next, remove the columns that are irrelevant to the case study; that is, remove the **Record_ID**, **Auction_ID**, and **Bidder_ID** columns. This is because these columns contain unique IDs and thus do not add any new information to the model:

```
data.drop(["Record_ID","Auction_ID","Bidder_ID"],axis=1,\
        inplace=True)
```

4. Now view the first five rows of the revised data:

```
data.head()
```

You should get the following output. From the following output, you can see that the dataset is now devoid of the unwanted columns we removed in *Step 3*:

	Bidder_Tendency	Bidding_Ratio	Successive_Outbidding	Last_Bidding	Auction_Bids	Starting_Price_Average
0	0.200000	0.400000	0.0	0.000028	0.0	0.993593
1	0.024390	0.200000	0.0	0.013123	0.0	0.993593
2	0.142857	0.200000	0.0	0.003042	0.0	0.993593
3	0.100000	0.200000	0.0	0.097477	0.0	0.993593
4	0.051282	0.222222	0.0	0.001318	0.0	0.000000

Figure 7.11: The first five rows of the reduced data

> **NOTE**
>
> The preceding image does not contain all the columns of the DataFrame. The image is for demonstration purposes only.

5. Split the data into **training** and **testing** sets as follows. We are sticking to the default value for test data size (30% of the entire data). Moreover, to add reproducibility, we are using a **random_state** of **1**, and to account for any class imbalance, we will use stratified splitting. Reproducibility will ensure that when someone else runs the code, they will get similar results. Stratified splitting will ensure that we take into account the class distribution of the target column while splitting the data into train and test sets:

```
X = data.drop("Class",axis=1)
y = data["Class"]
# Split the dataset into training and testing sets
X_train,X_test,y_train,y_test = train_test_split\
                        (X,y,test_size=0.3,\
                         random_state=1, stratify=y)
```

6. Print the size of training and testing datasets:

```
print("Training dataset size: {}, Testing dataset size: {}"\
      .format(X_train.shape,X_test.shape))
```

The preceding code will generate the following output:

```
Training dataset size: (4424, 9), Testing dataset size: (1897, 9)
```

Notice that the ratio of training and testing dataset size is 7:3, which matches our calculation on the test set size (30% test set size, 70% train set size).

7. Fit the model using linear regression:

```
linear = linear_model.LinearRegression()
linear.fit(X_train,y_train)
```

The preceding code will generate the following output. The output you get might vary slightly depending on your system:

```
LinearRegression(copy_X=True, fit_intercept=True, n_jobs=None,
normalize=False)
```

8. Predict on the first 10 test data points using the following code:

```
linear.predict(X_test)[:10]
```

This gives the following output:

```
array([-0.00375542, -0.00248633, -0.01090699, -0.02753235,
0.01939224,
        0.99493654,  0.02761226, -0.00565047,  0.48101551,
0.00471959])
```

9. Now check the actual target values using **`y_test[:10].values`**:

```
y_test[:10].values
```

Your output will be as follows:

```
array([0, 0, 0, 0, 0, 1, 0, 0, 0, 0])
```

You can observe that linear regression was unable to predict the values as **1** and **0** and rather gave continuous values as output (as we saw in the previous step). Therefore, the model is not able to distinguish the classes correctly.

10. Evaluate the score of the linear regression model on the training and testing datasets:

```
print("Score on training dataset: {}, "\
        "Score on testing dataset: {}"\
        .format(linear.score(X_train,y_train),\
                linear.score(X_test,y_test)))
```

Your output will be as follows:

```
Score on training dataset: 0.8166836356918417, Score on testing
dataset: 0.8119909602893055
```

We'll now compare this result against a model fit using the logistic regression algorithm.

11. Fit the model using logistic regression as follows:

```
logit = linear_model.LogisticRegression()
logit.fit(X_train,y_train)
```

12. Predict on the test data:

```
logit.predict(X_test)[:10]
```

You should get the following output:

```
array([0, 0, 0, 0, 0, 1, 0, 0, 0, 0])
```

Notice how the values obtained using logistic regression are discrete values of **0** and **1**, unlike the continuous values obtained using linear regression.

13. Check the actual target values with **`y_test[:10].values`**:

```
y_test[:10].values
```

You should get the following output:

```
array([0, 0, 0, 0, 0, 1, 0, 0, 0, 0])
```

14. Similar to linear regression, find the score on the training and testing datasets as follows:

```
print("Score on training dataset: {}, "\
      "Score on testing dataset: {}"\
      .format(logit.score(X_train,y_train),\
              logit.score(X_test,y_test)))
```

You should get the following output:

```
Score on training dataset: 0.9794303797468354, Score on testing
dataset: 0.9715340010542962
```

We can note a couple of things regarding the logistic regression algorithm from this case study. First, logistic regression can predict discrete classes as outputs, unlike linear regression, which gave us non-discrete values. Second, note that logistic regression was able to obtain a much higher score compared to linear regression. This means that logistic regression was able to perform much better than linear regression and is more suited for classification tasks.

So far, we have worked on a dataset that did not require any cleaning or pre-processing. However, most of the datasets that we will come across in real life will have some quality issues that need to be addressed before they can be used for model training. In the next section, we will cover the various steps of a data science pipeline and how they can be applied.

CREATING A DATA SCIENCE PIPELINE

"Pipeline" is a commonly used term in data science, and it means that a pre-defined list of steps is performed in a proper sequence – one after another. The clearer the instructions, the better the standard of results obtained, in terms of quality and quantity. OSEMN is one of the most common data science pipelines used for approaching any kind of data science problem. The acronym is pronounced *awesome*.

The following figure provides an overview of the typical sequence of actions a data analyst would follow to create a data science pipeline:

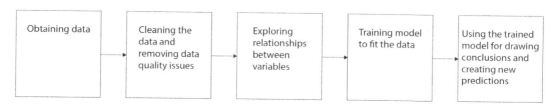

Figure 7.12: The OSEMN pipeline

Let's understand the steps in the OSEMN pipeline in a little more detail:

1. **O**btaining the data, which can be from any source: structured, unstructured, or semi-structured.

2. **S**crubbing the data, which means getting your hands dirty and cleaning the data, which can involve renaming columns and imputing missing values.

3. **E**xploring the data to find out the relationships between each of the variables. This means searching for any correlation among the variables and finding the relationship between the explanatory variables and the response variable.

4. **M**odeling the data, which can include prediction, forecasting, and clustering.

5. **IN**terpreting the data, which is combining all the analyses and results to draw a conclusion.

You'll be learning more about these steps and also implementing them in the case study that follows.

CHURN PREDICTION CASE STUDY

You work at a multinational bank that is aiming to increase its market share in Europe. Recently, the number of customers using banking services has declined, and the bank is worried that existing customers have stopped using them as their main bank. As a data scientist, you are tasked with finding out the reasons behind customer churn and predicting future customer churn. The marketing team is interested in your findings and wants to better understand existing customer behavior and possibly predict future customer churn. Your results will help the marketing team to use their budget wisely to target potential churners.

Before you start analyzing the problem, you'll first need to have the data at you disposal.

OBTAINING THE DATA

This step refers to collecting data. Data can be obtained from a single source or multiple sources. In the real world, collecting data is not always easy since the data is often divided. It can be present in multiple departments of an organization and might have to be collected from various sources and then merged. Data collection in a large organization is done by gathering data from both internal sources (such as company fact sheets and internal reports) and external sources (such as social media or news reports). In the following exercise, you will obtain the data from a **.csv** file.

EXERCISE 7.02: OBTAINING THE DATA

In this exercise, you will import the banking data (**Churn_Modelling.csv**) provided by the bank and do some initial checks, such as seeing how many rows and columns are present. This will give you a quick peek into the real-life problem statements that a marketing analyst and a data scientist will work on, where the dataset is not always clean. The more time you spend improving and getting familiar with the dataset, the better the observations you can make about the trend will be:

1. Import the **pandas**, **numpy**, **matplotlib**, and **seaborn** libraries:

```
import pandas as pd
import numpy as np
import matplotlib.pyplot as plt
import seaborn as sns
```

2. Read the data into a pandas DataFrame named **data**. Also, view the first five rows of the dataset:

```
data= pd.read_csv('Churn_Modelling.csv')
data.head(5)
```

> **NOTE**
>
> Make sure you change the path (emboldened in the preceding code snippet) to the CSV file based on its location on your system. If you're running the Jupyter notebook from the same directory where the CSV file is stored, you can run the preceding code without any modification.

You should get the following output:

	CustomerId	CredRate	Geography	Gender	Age	Tenure	Balance	Prod Number	HasCrCard	ActMem	EstimatedSalary	Exited
0	15634602	619	France	Female	42.0	2	0.00	1	1	1	101348.88	1
1	15647311	608	Spain	Female	41.0	1	83807.86	1	0	1	112542.58	0
2	15619304	502	France	Female	42.0	8	159660.80	3	1	0	113931.57	1
3	15701354	699	France	Female	39.0	1	0.00	2	0	0	93826.63	0
4	15737888	850	Spain	Female	43.0	2	125510.82	1	1	1	79084.10	0

Figure 7.13: The first few rows of the churn modeling data

3. Check the number of rows and columns in the dataset:

```
len(data)
data.shape
```

The dataset has **10,000** rows and **12** columns.

Now, you have a basic idea of what the data is like. You know how many rows and columns it contains. Let's see if it has any missing or incorrect values.

SCRUBBING THE DATA

Scrubbing the data typically involves missing value imputation (the process of filling in the missing values), data type conversion, standardization of features, and renaming columns. You will perform these steps in the next exercise.

EXERCISE 7.03: IMPUTING MISSING VALUES

After reading the banking data, you have to find any missing values in the data and perform imputation on the missing values:

> **NOTE**
>
> You will need to continue in the same Jupyter notebook as the preceding exercise. Alternatively, if you skipped that exercise, you may use the Jupyter notebook at https://packt.link/ezFqO, which includes all the code of *Exercise 7.02, Obtaining the Data*. Continue this exercise by creating a new cell at the end of the notebook (make sure you select **Cell** from the toolbar and then select **Run All** before you begin).

1. Check for any missing values first using the following code:

```
data.isnull().values.any()
```

This will give you an output of **True**. This means that there are some columns with missing values. Let's see which are the columns with missing values in the next step.

2. Explore the columns that have these missing values by using the following code:

```
data.isnull().any()
```

You should get the following output:

```
CustomerId          False
CredRate            False
Geography           False
Gender               True
Age                  True
Tenure              False
Balance             False
Prod Number         False
HasCrCard           False
ActMem              False
EstimatedSalary      True
Exited              False
dtype: bool
```

Figure 7.14: Checking for missing values

It seems that the **Gender**, **Age**, and **EstimatedSalary** columns have missing values.

3. Use **describe** function to explore the data in the **Age** and **EstimatedSalary** columns:

> **NOTE**
>
> Since **Gender** is a categorical variable with only two values, we have used only **Age** and **EstimatedSalary** for our **describe** function.

```
data[["EstimatedSalary","Age"]].describe()
```

You should get the following output:

	EstimatedSalary	Age
count	9996.000000	9994.000000
mean	100074.744083	38.925255
std	57515.774555	10.489248
min	11.580000	18.000000
25%	50974.077500	32.000000
50%	100168.240000	37.000000
75%	149388.247500	44.000000
max	199992.480000	92.000000

Figure 7.15: Description statistics for the EstimatedSalary and Age columns

4. Now use **describe** function for the entire DataFrame as well. This will help in understanding the statistical description of the columns:

```
data.describe()
```

You should get the following output:

	CustomerId	CredRate	Age	Tenure	Balance	Prod Number	HasCrCard	ActMem	EstimatedSalary	Exited
count	1.000000e+04	10000.000000	9994.000000	10000.000000	10000.000000	10000.000000	10000.00000	10000.000000	9996.000000	10000.000000
mean	1.569094e+07	650.528800	38.925255	5.012800	76485.889288	1.530200	0.70550	0.515100	100074.744083	0.203700
std	7.193619e+04	96.653299	10.489248	2.892174	62397.405202	0.581654	0.45584	0.499797	57515.774555	0.402769
min	1.556570e+07	350.000000	18.000000	0.000000	0.000000	1.000000	0.00000	0.000000	11.580000	0.000000
25%	1.562853e+07	584.000000	32.000000	3.000000	0.000000	1.000000	0.00000	0.000000	50974.077500	0.000000
50%	1.569074e+07	652.000000	37.000000	5.000000	97198.540000	1.000000	1.00000	1.000000	100168.240000	0.000000
75%	1.575323e+07	718.000000	44.000000	7.000000	127644.240000	2.000000	1.00000	1.000000	149388.247500	0.000000
max	1.581569e+07	850.000000	92.000000	10.000000	250898.090000	4.000000	1.00000	1.000000	199992.480000	1.000000

Figure 7.16: Descriptive statistics

From the descriptive statistics, we can observe that the **HasCrCard** column has a minimum value of **0** and a maximum value of **1**. It seems that this variable is categorical.

5. Now, check the count of 0s and 1s in this column using the following syntax:

```
data['HasCrCard'].value_counts()
```

You should get an output that shows the number of 1s is **7055** and the number of 0s is **2945**. This shows that approximately 70% of the customers have a credit card and 29% of them do not have a credit card.

6. Use the following syntax to find out the total number of missing values:

```
data.isnull().sum()
```

You should get the following output:

```
CustomerId          0
CredRate            0
Geography           0
Gender              4
Age                 6
Tenure              0
Balance             0
Prod Number         0
HasCrCard           0
ActMem              0
EstimatedSalary     4
Exited              0
dtype: int64
```

Figure 7.17: Checking for missing values in the dataset

The preceding output indicates that the **Gender**, **Age**, and `EstimatedSalary` columns have **4**, **6**, and **4** missing values, respectively.

At this point, you might be wondering why there is a sudden change from finding missing values to working on categorical variables. This is because by exploring the categorical variables, we can find out which values can be used to replace the missing values for the categorical variables. This ensures that all the missing value treatment/imputing can be done at the same time.

7. Find out the percentage of missing values using the following code:

```
round(data.isnull().sum()/len(data)*100,2)
```

You should get the following output:

```
CustomerId           0.00
CredRate             0.00
Geography            0.00
Gender               0.04
Age                  0.06
Tenure               0.00
Balance              0.00
Prod Number          0.00
HasCrCard            0.00
ActMem               0.00
EstimatedSalary      0.04
Exited               0.00
dtype: float64
```

Figure 7.18: Percentages of missing values in the dataset

The output indicates that the missing values constitute **4**, **6**, and **4** percent of the total values in the **Gender**, **Age**, and **EstimatedSalary** columns, respectively.

8. Check the data types of the missing columns:

```
data[["Gender","Age","EstimatedSalary"]].dtypes
```

Your output should be as follows. As you can see, all the columns are of the correct data types – **age** and **salary** are of floating-point data type, and **gender** is a string or object:

```
Gender               object
Age                  float64
EstimatedSalary      float64
dtype: object
```

Figure 7.19: Data type of columns that have missing values

9. Now you need to impute the missing values. You can do that by dropping the rows that have missing values, filling in the missing values with a test statistic (such as mean, mode, or median), or predicting the missing values using a machine learning algorithm. For **EstimatedSalary**, fill in the missing values with the mean of the data in that column using the following code:

```
mean_value=data['EstimatedSalary'].mean()
data['EstimatedSalary']=data['EstimatedSalary']\
                        .fillna(mean_value)
```

> **NOTE**
>
> For **EstimatedSalary**, since the column is continuous, you can use the mean of the values for the estimated salary to replace the missing values.

10. For **Gender**, use **value_count()** to see how many instances of each gender are present:

```
data['Gender'].value_counts()
```

Your output should be:

```
Male      5457
Female    4543
Name: Gender, dtype: int64
```

Figure 7.20: Distribution of people with respect to gender

As you can see, there are more males (**5453**) than females (**4543**). As a rule of thumb, you fill the missing values with the more frequently occurring entry, which in this case is **Male**:

```
data['Gender']=data['Gender'].fillna(data['Gender']\
                        .value_counts().idxmax())
```

11. For **Age**, use **mode()** to get the mode of the data, which is **37**, and then replace the missing values with the mode of the values in the column using the following code:

```
data['Age'].mode()
mode_value=data['Age'].mode()
data['Age']=data['Age'].fillna(mode_value[0])
```

12. Check whether the missing values have been imputed:

```
data.isnull().any()
```

You should get the following output. As you can see, there are no missing values left in your dataset:

```
CustomerId          False
CredRate            False
Geography           False
Gender              False
Age                 False
Tenure              False
Balance             False
Prod Number         False
HasCrCard           False
ActMem              False
EstimatedSalary     False
Exited              False
dtype: bool
```

Figure 7.21: Check for missing values

In this exercise, you first used the **describe()** function to find out the descriptive stats of the data. Then, you learned how to find missing values, and performed missing value imputation for the **EstimatedSalary**, **Gender**, and **Age** columns.

In the next exercise, you will focus on changing the names and data types of columns. This not only ensures that the column names give more clarity about the data they contain, but also improves the overall work quality of the project.

EXERCISE 7.04: RENAMING COLUMNS AND CHANGING THE DATA TYPE

Scrubbing data also involves renaming columns in the right format and can include removing any special characters and spaces in the column names, shifting the target variable either to the extreme left or right for better visibility, and checking whether the data types of the columns are correct. In this exercise, you have to convert the column names into a more human-readable format. For example, you must have noticed column names such as **ActMem** and **CredRate**. These can be renamed to give a clearer idea of what the columns represent. The main reason behind doing this is that if someone else is going over your work, ambiguous column names can reduce the clarity. Therefore, in this exercise, you will rename some of the columns, change the data types, and shift the **Churn** column to the rightmost position. This will help differentiate the independent features from the dependent ones:

> **NOTE**
>
> You will need to continue in the same Jupyter notebook as the preceding exercise. Alternatively, if you skipped the previous exercise, you may use the Jupyter notebook at https://packt.link/GdDU5, which includes all the code up to *Exercise 7.03*, *Imputing Missing Values*. Continue this exercise by creating a new cell at the end of the notebook (make sure you select **Cell** from the toolbar and then select **Run All** before you begin).

1. Rename the **CredRate**, **ActMem**, **Prod Number**, and **Exited** columns using the following command:

```
data = data.rename(columns={'CredRate': 'CreditScore',\
                            'ActMem' : 'IsActiveMember',\
                            'Prod Number': 'NumOfProducts',\
                            'Exited':'Churn'})
```

2. Check that the preceding columns have been appropriately renamed using the **columns** command:

```
data.columns
```

You should get the following output:

```
Index(['CreditScore', 'Geography', 'Gender', 'Age', 'Tenure', 'Balance',
       'NumOfProducts', 'HasCrCard', 'IsActiveMember', 'EstimatedSalary',
       'Churn'],
      dtype='object')
```

Figure 7.22: Renamed columns

3. Move the **Churn** column to the right and drop the **CustomerId** column using the following code. You will need to drop the **CustomerId** column since it is unique for each entry and thus, does not provide any useful information:

```
data.drop(labels=['CustomerId'], axis=1,inplace = True)


column_churn = data['Churn']
data.drop(labels=['Churn'], axis=1,inplace = True)
data.insert(len(data.columns), 'Churn', column_churn.values)
```

4. Check whether the order of the columns has been fixed using the following code:

```
data.columns
```

The preceding code will give the following output:

```
Index(['CreditScore', 'Geography', 'Gender', 'Age', 'Tenure', 'Balance',
       'NumOfProducts', 'HasCrCard', 'IsActiveMember', 'EstimatedSalary',
       'Churn'],
      dtype='object')
```

Figure 7.23: Output of the data.columns command

Notice that the **CustomerId** column has been removed and the **Churn** column has been shifted to the rightmost position, as desired.

5. Change the data type of the **Geography**, **Gender**, **HasCrCard**, **Churn**, and **IsActiveMember** columns to **category** as shown. Recall that these columns were initially strings or objects. However, since these are distinct values, you will need to convert them to categorical variables by converting the data type to **category**:

```
data["Geography"] = data["Geography"].astype('category')
data["Gender"] = data["Gender"].astype('category')
data["HasCrCard"] = data["HasCrCard"].astype('category')
data["Churn"] = data["Churn"].astype('category')
data["IsActiveMember"] = data["IsActiveMember"]\
                         .astype('category')
```

6. Now check whether the data types have been converted or not using the following code:

```
data.dtypes
```

You should get the following output. Notice that the data types of the columns have been updated:

```
CreditScore               int64
Geography              category
Gender                 category
Age                     float64
Tenure                    int64
Balance                 float64
NumOfProducts             int64
HasCrCard              category
IsActiveMember         category
EstimatedSalary         float64
Churn                  category
dtype: object
```

Figure 7.24: Data type of the columns

In this exercise, you successfully renamed a few columns to give more clarity about their description. You converted the **Geography**, **Gender**, **HasCrCard**, **Churn**, and **IsActiveMember** columns to the **category** type to convert them to categorical features. Next, you shifted the **Churn** column to the extreme right to differentiate between the target variable (**Churn**) and other columns.

So far, you have loaded and cleaned the data, but you are yet to explore the relationship between the columns themselves and with the target column. You will see how to do this in the next section.

EXPLORING THE DATA

Data exploration is one of the most important steps before building a machine learning model. It is important to know the data well before applying any kind of machine learning algorithm. Typically, the data exploration phase consists of the following steps: **statistical overview**, **correlation**, and **visualization**. These steps can be performed in any order. Let's discuss the steps one by one:

a) Statistical Overview

This step typically involves inspecting the data using general descriptive statistics. In a statistical overview, we summarize the data using the central tendency and distribution of the data and inspect the target variable using **mean**, **count**, and other functions studied in previous chapters.

b) Correlation

The correlation coefficient measures the linear relationship between two variables. It is usually represented by **r** and varies from **+1** to **−1**. We can interpret the correlation value as given in the following table. For example, if there is a positive correlation between the salary of a person and their monthly expenditure, we would infer that if the salary increases, the person would tend to spend more, and vice versa:

Correlation Value	Interpretation
−1	Perfect negative linear relationship between the two variables
−0.80	Strong negative linear relationship
−0.50	Moderate negative linear relationship
−0.30	Weak negative linear relationship
0	No linear relationship
+0.30	Weak positive relationship
+0.50	Moderate positive relationship
+0.80	Strong positive relationship
+1	Perfect positive linear relationship between the two variables

Figure 7.25: Correlation coefficient

We use a correlation plot to visualize the relationships between variables better, though a detailed explanation on visualization is covered in the section that follows. We can obtain the visualization plot using the following steps:

1. Import the **seaborn** and **matplotlib** modules:

```
import matplotlib.pyplot as plt
import seaborn as sns
```

2. We can then use **data.corr()** to obtain the correlation between variables in the DataFrame data.

3. In order to create a heatmap visualizing how strongly or weakly correlated the variables are, we can use the following code:

```
corr = data.corr()
sns.heatmap(corr, \
            xticklabels=corr.columns.values,\
            yticklabels=corr.columns.values,annot=True)
corr
```

> **NOTE**
>
> When finding out the correlation coefficient, one of our assumptions is that there is a linear relationship between the two variables. However, in reality, there may or may not be any linear relationship between them. Hence, it is wise to plot your data and visually verify it.

Before we explore the third step, which is visualization, let's first practice the first two steps (statistical overview and correlation) in the next exercise.

EXERCISE 7.05: OBTAINING THE STATISTICAL OVERVIEW AND CORRELATION PLOT

You are requested to find out the number of customers that churned using basic exploration techniques. The **churn** column has two attributes: **0** indicates that the customer did not churn and **1** implies that the customer churned. You will be required to obtain the percentage of customers who churned, the percentage of customers who have a credit card, and more. This information will be valuable at a later stage to make inferences about consumer behavior. You are also required to plot the correlation matrix, which will give you a basic understanding of the relationship between the target variable and the rest of the variables.

> **NOTE**
>
> You will need to continue in the same Jupyter notebook as the preceding exercise. Alternatively, if you skipped the previous exercise, you may use the Jupyter notebook at https://packt.link/Lz7fB, which includes all the code up to *Exercise 7.04, Renaming Columns and Changing the Data Type*. Continue this exercise by creating a new cell at the end of the notebook (make sure you select **Cell** from the toolbar and then select **Run All** before you begin).

1. Inspect the target variable to see how many of the customers have churned using the following code:

```
data['Churn'].value_counts(0)
```

The following output tells you that **7963** customers did not churn, whereas **2037** customers churned:

```
0    7963
1    2037
Name: Churn, dtype: int64
```

Figure 7.26: Number of customers who churned

2. Inspect the percentage of customers who left the bank using the following code:

```
data['Churn'].value_counts(1)*100
```

This will again give us an output of **79.63** and **20.37** percent corresponding to the customers that did not churn and those that churned, respectively. Hence, you can infer that the proportion of customers that churned is 20.37% (2,037), and the proportion of those that did not churn is 79.63% (7,963):

```
0    79.63
1    20.37
Name: Churn, dtype: float64
```

Figure 7.27: Percentage of customers who left the bank

3. Inspect the percentage of customers that have a credit card using the following code:

```
data['HasCrCard'].value_counts(1)*100
```

You should get an output of **70.55** for the number of 1s and **29.45** for the number of 0s, implying that 70.55% of the customers have a credit card, whereas 29.25% do not have a credit card. Information like this helps us understand whether there is some imbalance in features. Let's assume that all the members had an active credit card. In that case, it wouldn't make any sense to use that feature. Such a feature would not have added any value to the model. However, that is not the case here:

```
1    70.55
0    29.45
Name: HasCrCard, dtype: float64
```

Figure 7.28: Percentage of customers that have a credit card

4. Get a statistical overview of the data:

```
data.describe()
```

You should get the following output:

	CreditScore	Age	Tenure	Balance	NumOfProducts	EstimatedSalary
count	10000.000000	10000.000000	10000.000000	10000.000000	10000.000000	10000.000000
mean	650.528800	38.924100	5.012800	76485.889288	1.530200	100074.744083
std	96.653299	10.486207	2.892174	62397.405202	0.581654	57504.269099
min	350.000000	18.000000	0.000000	0.000000	1.000000	11.580000
25%	584.000000	32.000000	3.000000	0.000000	1.000000	51002.110000
50%	652.000000	37.000000	5.000000	97198.540000	1.000000	100134.325000
75%	718.000000	44.000000	7.000000	127644.240000	2.000000	149382.097500
max	850.000000	92.000000	10.000000	250898.090000	4.000000	199992.480000

Figure 7.29: Statistical overview of the data

Inspect some of the statistics, such as **mean** and **max**, in the preceding figure. These statistics will help you answer questions such as the average age, salary, and the number of products purchased by your customers, or the maximum and minimum numbers of products purchased by your customer base. These statistics should also help the marketing team and senior management to understand whether a feature is important for model training, and what kind of data they are dealing with.

5. Inspect the mean attributes of customers who churned compared to those who did not churn:

```
summary_churn = data.groupby('Churn')
summary_churn.mean()
```

You should get the following output:

	CreditScore	Age	Tenure	Balance	NumOfProducts	EstimatedSalary
Churn						
0	651.853196	37.411277	5.033279	72745.296779	1.544267	99718.932023
1	645.351497	44.837997	4.932744	91108.539337	1.475209	101465.677531

Figure 7.30: Mean attributes of the customer with respect to churn

From the preceding figure, you can infer that the average credit score of customers that churned is **645.35**, and the average age of the customers that churned is **44.83** years. The average balance and the estimated salary of the customers that churned are **911108.53** USD and **101465.67** USD respectively, which is greater than the values for customers that didn't churn.

6. Also, find the median attributes of the customers:

```
summary_churn.median()
```

You should get the following output:

	CreditScore	Age	Tenure	Balance	NumOfProducts	EstimatedSalary
Churn						
0	653	36.0	5	92072.68	2	99645.04
1	646	45.0	5	109349.29	1	102460.84

Figure 7.31: Median attributes of the customer with respect to churn

Note that the median number of products bought by customers that churned is **1**.

7. Now use the **seaborn** library to plot the correlation plot using the following code:

```
corr = data.corr()
plt.figure(figsize=(15,8))
sns.heatmap(corr, \
            xticklabels=corr.columns.values,\
            yticklabels=corr.columns.values,\
            annot=True,cmap='Greys_r')
corr
```

> **NOTE**
>
> The **Greys_r** value for the **cmap** attribute (emboldened in the preceding code snippet) is used to generate the graphs in grayscale. You can remove this attribute to get the colored graphs. The code would then look like the following:
>
> ```
> sns.heatmap(corr, \
>             xticklabels=corr.columns.values,\
>             yticklabels=corr.columns.values,\
>             annot=True)
> ```
>
> You can also refer to the following document to get the code for the colored plot and the corresponding colored output: http://packt.link/NOjgT.

The correlation statistics and plot provide the correlation between our continuous features. It tells us how each of these variables is related to the others. For example, referring to *Figure 7.32*, **NumOfProducts** and **Balance** have a negative correlation of −**0.304**, whereas **Balance** and **Age** have a positive correlation of **0.028**. A negative correlation means that if one value increases, the other will decrease, whereas the magnitude of correlation decides to what extent the change in value in one feature affects the change in value in the second feature. Thus, a change in **NumOfProducts** will have a stronger effect on **Balance** than it will on **Age**.

However, because of the negative correlation, the effect would be reversed:

	CreditScore	Age	Tenure	Balance	NumOfProducts	EstimatedSalary
CreditScore	1.000000	-0.004179	0.000842	0.006268	0.012238	-0.001352
Age	-0.004179	1.000000	-0.009996	0.028141	-0.030590	-0.007215
Tenure	0.000842	-0.009996	1.000000	-0.012254	0.013444	0.007407
Balance	0.006268	0.028141	-0.012254	1.000000	-0.304180	0.013129
NumOfProducts	0.012238	-0.030590	0.013444	-0.304180	1.000000	0.014132
EstimatedSalary	-0.001352	-0.007215	0.007407	0.013129	0.014132	1.000000

Figure 7.32: Correlation statistics of features

The correlation plot should look like the following:

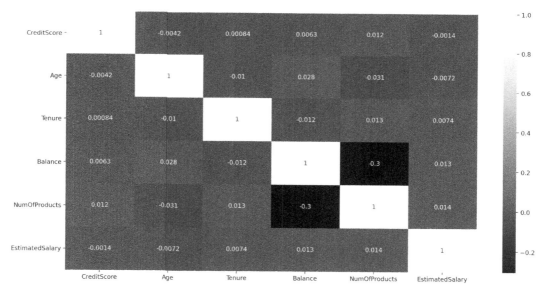

Figure 7.33: Correlation plot of different features

In the correlation plot, it appears that there is a negative (-0.3%) relationship between the number of products purchased and the balance.

> **NOTE**
>
> A word of warning for interpreting the results of the correlation. Correlation does not imply causation. Even if the matrix shows a relationship, do not assume that one variable caused the other. Both may be influenced by a third variable.
>
> Many other interesting observations can be obtained from this analysis. You are encouraged to find out some more useful insights from the statistical overview. It is always good practice to perform an initial statistical review.

So far, we have discussed how the statistical overview of the features helps us understand the relationship between features and the target variable. However, as we know, a picture is worth a thousand words. This is why we will see how we can use data visualization to get a better idea of the dataset we are working on. We will go over these details in the next section.

VISUALIZING THE DATA

The best way to perform data exploration is to visualize the data to find out how each of the variables interacts with the other variables. As pointed out by William S. Cleveland, a professor of statistics at Purdue University, "*data analysis without data visualization is no data analysis.*" In statistics, the use of graphical methods (refer to *Figure 7.31*) to reveal the distribution and/or statistics of a selected variable is popularly known as **Exploratory Data Analysis** (**EDA**).

As a quick recap, univariate data analysis requires focusing only on one variable, whereas bivariate data analysis requires understanding the effect of one variable on another.

EDA, for a marketing analyst, helps in exploring the data and coming up with some statements regarding the data distribution. These statements or hypotheses can help in creating better models. Based on the number of features that are being explored, several graphical methods can be used. For example, a bar chart and histogram help in understanding the distribution of a feature in the dataset (for example, the gender distribution in a marketing dataset), and that's why they are part of the EDA methods for univariate data. On the other hand, a scatter plot helps in analyzing two continuous variables present in the dataset (for example, the relationship between the salary of a person and their age) and that's why it is a part of EDA methods for bivariate data.

The following figure provides a summary of the EDA methods belonging to the two categories:

EDA for Univariate Data	EDA for Bivariate Data

1. Distribution Analysis
    a. Bar Chart
    b. Histogram
	1. Tow categorical Variables Analysis
	    a. Mosaic Plot
	    b. Trellis Bar chart

2. Deviation Analysis
    a. Boxplot
	2. Two Continuous Variables
	    a. Scatter Plot
	    b. Scatter Plot Matrix
	    c. Trellis Scatter Plots

3. Part Whole Analysis
    a. Pie Chart
    b. Pareto Chart
	3. Part Whole Analysis
	    a. Pie Chart
	    b. Pareto Chart

4. Trend Patterns
    a. Line Graph
	4. One Categorical and One Continuous
	    a. Trellis Box Plot/Histogram

Figure 7.34: EDA graphs for univariate and bivariate data

Before we move on to the exercise where we will use these graphs, let's quickly see how we can implement them using the **seaborn** and **matplotlib** libraries:

1. Import the **seaborn** and **matplotlib** libraries:

```
import seaborn as sns
import matplotlib.pyplot as plt
```

2. Next, you can use the **seaborn** library to plot all the kinds of plots specified in *Figure 7.34*:

    sns.distplot for distribution plot, which is commonly used for univariate analysis of continuous variables. You can read more about it in the documentation at https://seaborn.pydata.org/generated/seaborn.distplot.html.

    sns.countplot for showing the distribution of categorical/discrete variables, which is a part of bivariate analysis. You can read more about it at https://seaborn.pydata.org/generated/seaborn.countplot.html.

    sns.kdeplot to show the distribution of observations for continuous variables as part of univariate analysis. You can read more about it at https://seaborn.pydata.org/generated/seaborn.kdeplot.html.

Similarly, `sns.barplot` can be used to plot bar plots as part of bivariate analysis. You can read more about it at https://seaborn.pydata.org/generated/seaborn.barplot.html.

> **NOTE**
>
> Because of the scope of the book, we will not be covering all the EDA techniques. You are encouraged to explore them further, though. An interesting book covering the EDA techniques in detail can be found at https://www.packtpub.com/product/hands-on-exploratory-data-analysis-with-python/9781789537253.

EXERCISE 7.06: PERFORMING EXPLORATORY DATA ANALYSIS (EDA)

In this exercise, you will perform EDA, which includes univariate analysis and bivariate analysis, on the **Churn_Modelling.csv** dataset. You will use this analysis to come up with inferences regarding the dataset, and the relationship between features such as geography, customer age, customer bank balance, and more with respect to churn:

> **NOTE**
>
> You will need to continue in the same Jupyter notebook as the preceding exercise. Alternatively, if you skipped the previous exercise, you may use the Jupyter notebook at https://packt.link/QFQFT, which includes all the code up to *Exercise 7.05*, *Obtaining the Statistical Overview and Correlation Plot*. Continue this exercise by creating a new cell at the end of the notebook (make sure you select **Cell** from the toolbar and then select **Run All** before you begin).

1. Start with univariate analysis. Plot the distribution graph of the customers for the **EstimatedSalary**, **Age**, and **Balance** variables using the following code:

```
f, axes = plt.subplots(ncols=3, figsize=(15, 6))

sns.distplot(data.EstimatedSalary, kde=True, color="gray", \
             ax=axes[0]).set_title('EstimatedSalary')
axes[0].set_ylabel('No of Customers')

sns.distplot(data.Age, kde=True, color="gray", \
```

```
                ax=axes[1]).set_title('Age')
axes[1].set_ylabel('No of Customers')

sns.distplot(data.Balance, kde=True, color="gray", \
                ax=axes[2]).set_title('Balance')
axes[2].set_ylabel('No of Customers')
```

> **NOTE**
>
> The **gray** value for the **color** attribute is used to generate the graphs in grayscale. You can use other colors, such as **darkgreen**, **maroon**, and so on, as values of the **color** parameter to get colored graphs. You can also refer to the following document to get the code for the colored plot and the colored output: http://packt.link/NOjgT.

Your output should look as follows:

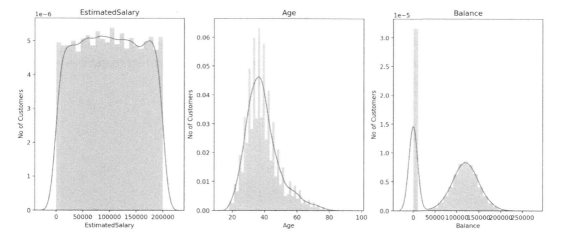

Figure 7.35: Univariate analysis

The following are the observations from the univariate analysis:

EstimatedSalary: The distribution of the estimated salary seems to be a plateau distribution – meaning that for a significant range of estimated salary, the number of customers is more or less constant.

Age: This has a normal distribution that is right-skewed. Most customers lie in the range of 30-45 years of age.

Balance: This has a bimodal distribution – this means that there exist two values of balance for which the number of customers is unusually high. A considerable number of customers with a low balance are there, which seems to be an outlier.

2. Now, move on to bivariate analysis. Inspect whether there is a difference in churn for **Gender** using bivariate analysis. Use the following code:

```
plt.figure(figsize=(15,4))
p=sns.countplot(y="Gender", hue='Churn', data=data,\
                palette="Greys_r")
legend = p.get_legend()
legend_txt = legend.texts
legend_txt[0].set_text("No Churn")
legend_txt[1].set_text("Churn")
p.set_title('Customer Churn Distribution by Gender')
```

> **NOTE**
>
> In *Steps 1* to *8*, the **Greys_r** value of the **palette** attribute is used to generate the graphs in grayscale. You can use **palette="Set2"** to get colored bar charts. You can also refer to the following document to get the code for the colored plot and the colored output: http://packt.link/NOjgT.

Your output should look as follows:

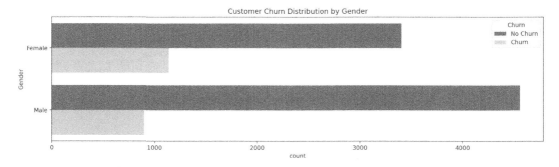

Figure 7.36: Number of customers churned, plotted by gender

You will observe that comparatively, more female customers have churned.

3. Plot **Geography** versus **Churn**:

```
plt.figure(figsize=(15,4))
p=sns.countplot(x='Geography', hue='Churn', data=data, \
                palette="Greys_r")
legend = p.get_legend()
legend_txt = legend.texts
legend_txt[0].set_text("No Churn")
legend_txt[1].set_text("Churn")
p.set_title('Customer Geography Distribution')
```

You should get the following output:

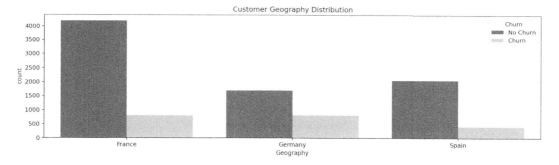

Figure 7.37: Number of customers churned, plotted by geography

Note that the difference between the number of customers that churned and those that did not churn is less for Germany and Spain in comparison with France. France has the highest number of customers compared to the other countries.

4. Plot **NumOfProducts** versus **Churn**:

```
plt.figure(figsize=(15,4))
p=sns.countplot(x='NumOfProducts', hue='Churn', data=data, \
                palette="Greys_r")
legend = p.get_legend()
legend_txt = legend.texts
legend_txt[0].set_text("No Churn")
legend_txt[1].set_text("Churn")
p.set_title('Customer Distribution by Product')
```

You should get the following output. Note that the largest proportion of churned customers were found where the number of products was one:

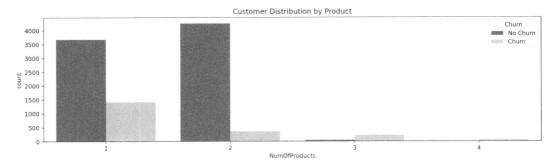

Figure 7.38: Number of customers churned, plotted by product

5. Inspect **Churn** versus **Age**:

```
plt.figure(figsize=(15,4))
ax=sns.kdeplot(data.loc[(data['Churn'] == 0),'Age'] , \
                color=sns.color_palette("Greys_r")[0],\
                shade=True,label='no churn', \
                linestyle='--')
ax=sns.kdeplot(data.loc[(data['Churn'] == 1),'Age'] , \
                color=sns.color_palette("Greys_r")[1],\
                shade=True, label='churn')
ax.set(xlabel='Customer Age', ylabel='Frequency')
plt.title('Customer Age - churn vs no churn')
plt.legend()
```

You should get the following output. The peak on the left represents the distribution plot for the **no churn** category, whereas the peak on the right (around the age of 45) represents the **churn** category distribution.

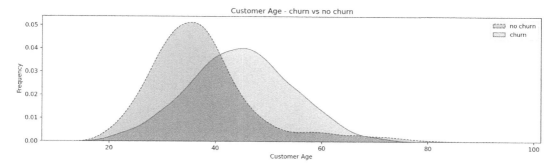

Figure 7.39: Distribution of customer age (churn versus no churn)

Customers in the 35 to 45 age group seem to churn more. As the age of customers increases, they usually churn more.

6. Plot **Balance** versus **Churn**:

```
plt.figure(figsize=(15,4))
ax=sns.kdeplot(data.loc[(data['Churn'] == 0),'Balance'] , \
               color=sns.color_palette("Greys_r")[0],\
               shade=True,label='no churn',linestyle='--')
ax=sns.kdeplot(data.loc[(data['Churn'] == 1),'Balance'] , \
               color=sns.color_palette("Greys_r")[1],\
               shade=True, label='churn')
ax.set(xlabel='Customer Balance', ylabel='Frequency')
plt.title('Customer Balance - churn vs no churn')
plt.legend()
```

You should get the following output:

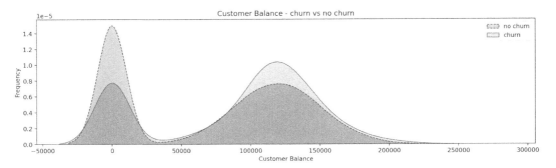

Figure 7.40: Distribution of customer balance (churn versus no churn)

Customers with a negative to low balance churn less than customers with a balance between 75,000 and 150,000.

7. Plot **CreditScore** versus **Churn**:

```
plt.figure(figsize=(15,4))
ax=sns.kdeplot(data.loc[(data['Churn'] == 0),'CreditScore'] , \
            color=sns.color_palette("Greys_r")[0],\
            shade=True,label='no churn',linestyle='--')
ax=sns.kdeplot(data.loc[(data['Churn'] == 1),'CreditScore'] , \
            color=sns.color_palette("Greys_r")[1],\
            shade=True, label='churn')
ax.set(xlabel='CreditScore', ylabel='Frequency')
plt.title('Customer CreditScore - churn vs no churn')
plt.legend()
```

You should get the following output. Notice that the largest proportion of customers who churned have a credit score around 600, whereas those who didn't have a credit score around 650:

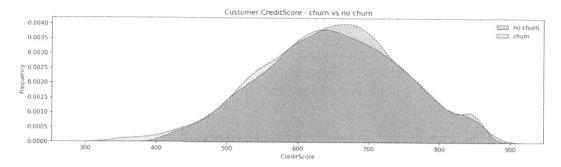

Figure 7.41: Distribution of customer credit score (churn versus no churn)

8. So far you have been analyzing two variables at a time. Compare three variables by plotting **Balance** versus **NumOfProducts** by **Churn**:

```
plt.figure(figsize=(16,4))
p=sns.barplot(x='NumOfProducts',y='Balance',hue='Churn',\
              data=data, palette="Greys_r")
p.legend(loc='upper right')
legend = p.get_legend()
legend_txt = legend.texts
legend_txt[0].set_text("No Churn")
legend_txt[1].set_text("Churn")
p.set_title('Number of Product VS Balance')
```

You should get the following output:

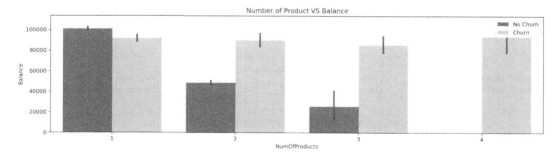

Figure 7.42: Number of products versus balance by churn

In the preceding figure, it appears that as the number of products increases, the balance for churned customers remains very high.

In this exercise, you saw how to carry out univariate, bivariate, and multivariate analyses with the help of different kinds of graphs and how to come up with inferences from those graphs. You will test the knowledge you have gained so far in the activity that follows.

ACTIVITY 7.01: PERFORMING THE OSE TECHNIQUE FROM OSEMN

A large telecom company wants to know why customers are churning. You are tasked with first finding out the reason behind the customer churn and then preparing a plan to reduce it. For this purpose, you have been provided with some data regarding the current bill amounts of customers (**Current Bill Amt**), the average number of calls made by each customer (**Avg Calls**), the average number of calls made by customers during weekdays (**Avg Calls Weekdays**), how long each account has been active (**Account Age**), and the average number of days the customer has defaulted on their bill payments (**Avg Days Delinquent**). To solve the first problem, you will use the OSE technique from OSEMN to carry out an initial exploration of the data.

Follow these steps:

1. Import the necessary libraries.

2. Download the dataset from https://packt.link/g3yft and save it in a file called **Telco_Churn_Data.csv**.

3. Read the **Telco_Churn_Data.csv** dataset and look at the first few rows of the dataset. You should get the following output:

	Target Churn	Target Code	Current Bill Amt	Avg Calls	Avg Calls Weekdays	Account Age	Percent Increase MOM	Acct Plan Subtype	Complaint Code	Avg Days Delinquent	Current TechSupComplaints
0	No Churn	0	14210	17950.000000	30297.0000	24	-0.334193	Gold	Billing Problem	6.2	0
1	Churn	1	14407	0.000000	0.0000	28	0.000000	Silver	Moving	1.0	0
2	Churn	1	12712	204.666667	10393.6667	23	0.000000	Gold	Billing Problem	17.6	0
3	No Churn	0	13807	15490.333300	41256.3333	39	0.148986	Silver	Billing Problem	0.0	0
4	No Churn	0	3805	5075.000000	12333.3333	23	-0.686047	Gold	Billing Problem	3.8	0

Figure 7.43: The first few rows of read.csv

4. Check the length and shape of the data (the number of rows and columns). The length should be **4708** and the shape should be (**4708, 15**).

5. Rename all the columns in a readable format. Make the column names look consistent by separating them with _ instead of spaces, for example, rename `Target Code` to `Target_Code`. Also, fix the typo in the `Avg_Hours_WorkOrderOpenned` column. Your column names should finally look as follows.

```
Index(['Target_Churn', 'Target_Code', 'Current_Bill_Amt', 'Avg_Calls',
       'Avg_Calls_Weekdays', 'Account_Age', 'Percent_Increase_MOM',
       'Acct_Plan_Subtype', 'Complaint_Code', 'Avg_Days_Delinquent',
       'Current_TechSupComplaints', 'Current_Days_OpenWorkOrders',
       'Equipment_Age', 'Condition_of_Current_Handset',
       'Avg_Hours_WorkOrderOpened'],
      dtype='object')
```

Figure 7.44: Renamed column names

> **HINT**
>
> You can use the following code for renaming columns:
> `data.columns=data.columns.str.replace(' ','_')`.

Check the descriptive statistics of the data and the categorical variable.

6. Change the data type of the `Target_Code`, `Condition_of_Current_Handset`, and `Current_TechSupComplaints` columns from continuous to the categorical object type.

7. Check for any missing values.

> **NOTE**
>
> Use `count()` to replace missing values for categorical values and `mean()` to replace missing values for continuous variables. The columns to be imputed are `Complaint_Code` and `Condition_of_Current_Handset`.

8. Perform data exploration by initially exploring the **Target_Churn** variable. You should get the following summary:

	Target_Code	Current_Bill_Amt	Avg_Calls	Avg_Calls_Weekdays	Account_Age	Percent_Increase_MOM
Target_Churn						
Churn	1.0	20182.709226	9348.878298	37524.030899	25.418452	-0.281309
No Churn	0.0	19494.510120	9194.885309	38698.530221	26.704254	0.255769

Figure 7.45: Summary of Target_Churn

9. Find the correlation among different variables and explain the results. You should get the following statistics:

	Target_Code	Current_Bill_Amt	Avg_Calls	Avg_Calls_Weekdays	Account_Age
Target_Code	1.000000	0.019995	0.007375	-0.014987	-0.089890
Current_Bill_Amt	0.019995	1.000000	0.352535	0.428040	0.003292
Avg_Calls	0.007375	0.352535	1.000000	0.727226	-0.023758
Avg_Calls_Weekdays	-0.014987	0.428040	0.727226	1.000000	0.029957
Account_Age	-0.089890	0.003292	-0.023758	0.029957	1.000000
Percent_Increase_MOM	-0.059899	-0.015588	-0.040899	-0.044496	-0.004022
Avg_Days_Delinquent	0.460092	0.024285	0.019407	0.017134	-0.047542
Current_Days_OpenWorkOrders	0.002891	0.076418	0.078428	0.065318	-0.026270
Equipment_Age	0.042373	-0.040732	-0.099348	-0.103769	0.073503
Avg_Hours_WorkOrderOpened	0.002611	0.016852	0.013441	0.013577	0.005059

Figure 7.46: Correlation statistics of the variables

You should get the following plot:

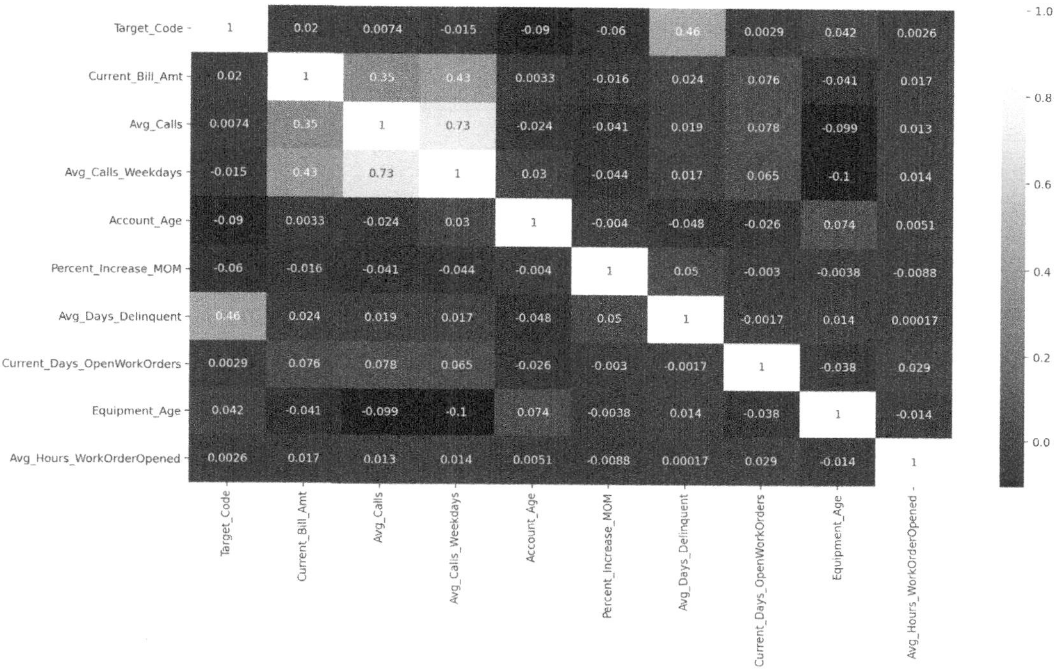

Figure 7.47: Correlation plot of different features

NOTE

Correlation is only obtained for continuous variables, not categorical variables.

10. Perform univariate and bivariate analyses.

For univariate analysis, use the following columns: **Avg_Calls_Weekdays**, **Avg_Calls**, and **Current_Bill_Amt**. You should get the following plots:

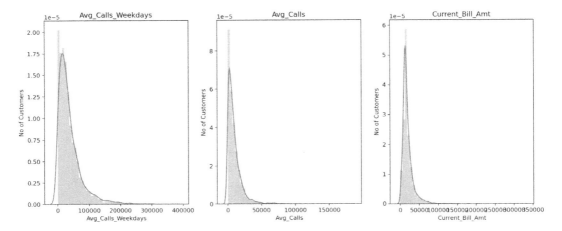

Figure 7.48: Univariate analysis

For bivariate analysis, you should get the following plots.

First, the plot of **Complaint_Code** versus **Target_Churn**:

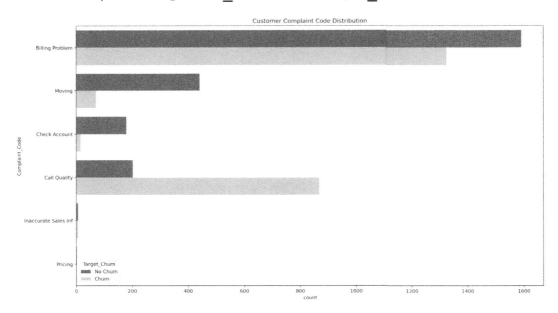

Figure 7.49: Customer complaint code distribution by churn

Then, the plot of **Acct_Plan_Subtype** versus **Target_Churn**:

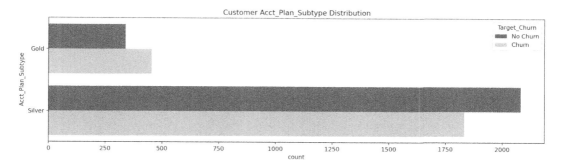

Figure 7.50: Customer account plan subtype distribution by churn

Then, the plot of **Current_TechSupComplaints** versus **Target_Churn**:

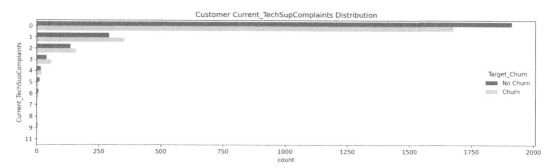

Figure 7.51: Customer technical support complaints distribution by churn

Next, the plot of **Avg_Days_Delinquent** versus **Target_Code**:

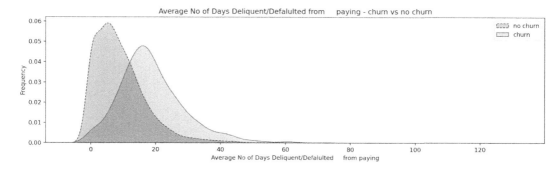

Figure 7.52: Distribution of the average number of days delinquent by churn

Then, the plot of **Account_Age** versus **Target_Code**:

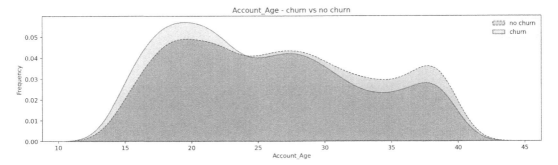

Figure 7.53: Distribution of account age by churn

Lastly, the plot of **Percent_Increase_MOM** versus **Target_Code**:

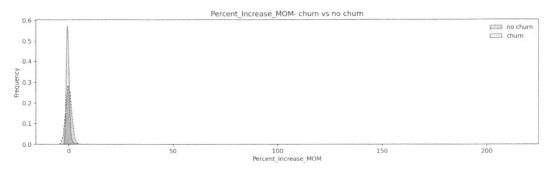

Figure 7.54: Distribution of the percentage increase of month-on-month usage by churn/no churn

NOTE

The solution for this activity can be found on page 538.

MODELING THE DATA

Data modeling, as the name suggests, refers to the process of creating a model that can define the data and can be used to draw conclusions and predictions for new data points. Modeling the data not only includes building your machine learning model but also selecting important features/columns that will go into your model. This section will be divided into two parts: *Feature Selection* and *Model Building*. For example, when trying to solve the churn prediction problem, which has a large number of features, feature selection can help in selecting the most relevant features. Those relevant features can then be used to train a model (in the model-building stage) to perform churn prediction.

FEATURE SELECTION

Before building our first machine learning model, we have to do some feature selection. Consider a scenario of churn prediction where you have a large number of columns and you want to perform prediction. Not all the features will have an impact on your prediction model. Having irrelevant features can reduce the accuracy of your model, especially when using algorithms such as linear and logistic regression.

The benefits of feature selection are as follows:

- **Reduces training time**: Fewer columns mean less data, which in turn makes the algorithm run more quickly.

- **Reduces overfitting**: Removing irrelevant columns makes your algorithm less prone to noise, thereby reducing overfitting.

- **Improves the accuracy**: This improves the accuracy of your machine learning model.

The methods for selecting features are as follows:

- **Univariate feature selection**: This works by selecting the best feature based on the univariate statistical tests. It finds features that have the strongest relationship with the output variable.

- **Recursive feature selection**: This works by recursively removing features and building a machine learning model based on the features remaining. It then uses the model's accuracy to find the combination of features that contribute most to predicting the target.

- **Principal component analysis** (**PCA**): PCA is a method that creates new variables that have a very low correlation with each other. This helps make sure that each feature provides additional information rather than redundant information.

- **Tree-based feature selection**: Tree-based estimators such as random forest, bagging, and boosting can be used to compute feature importance, which in turn can be used to discard irrelevant features.

From the various methods mentioned in the preceding list, let's see how we can use tree-based feature selection in our processed churn prediction dataset in the next exercise.

> **NOTE**
>
> A detailed explanation of the feature selection method will be provided in the next chapter.

EXERCISE 7.07: PERFORMING FEATURE SELECTION

In this exercise, you will be performing feature selection using a tree-based selection method that performs well on classification tasks. By the end of this exercise, you will be able to extract the most relevant features that can then be used for model building.

You will be using a different kind of classifier called **random forest** in this exercise. While we will go into the details of this in the next chapter, the intention is to show how to perform feature selection using a given model. The process for using the random forest classifier is the same as logistic regression using scikit-learn, with the only difference being that instead of importing **linear_model**, you will need to use the **sklearn.ensemble** package to import **RandomForestClassifier**. The steps given in this exercise will provide more details about this.

> **NOTE**
>
> You will need to continue in the same Jupyter notebook as the preceding exercise. Alternatively, if you skipped the previous exercise, you may use the Jupyter notebook at https://packt.link/r0YYz, which includes all the code up to *Exercise 7.06*, *Performing Exploratory Data Analysis (EDA)*. Continue this exercise by creating a new cell at the end of the notebook (make sure you select **Cell** from the toolbar and then select **Run All** before you begin).

1. Import **RandomForestClassifier** and **train_test_split** from the **sklearn** library:

```
from sklearn.ensemble import RandomForestClassifier
from sklearn.model_selection import train_test_split
```

2. Encode the categorical variable using the following code:

```
data.dtypes
### Encoding the categorical variables
data["Geography"] = data["Geography"].astype('category')\
                    .cat.codes
data["Gender"] = data["Gender"].astype('category').cat.codes
data["HasCrCard"] = data["HasCrCard"].astype('category')\
                    .cat.codes
data["Churn"] = data["Churn"].astype('category').cat.codes
```

You will get the following output from the code:

```
CreditScore              int64
Geography             category
Gender                category
Age                    float64
Tenure                   int64
Balance                float64
NumOfProducts            int64
HasCrCard             category
IsActiveMember        category
EstimatedSalary        float64
Churn                 category
dtype: object
```

Figure 7.55: Encoding the categorical values

3. Split the data into training and testing sets as follows:

```
target = 'Churn'
X = data.drop('Churn', axis=1)
y=data[target]

X_train, X_test, y_train, y_test = train_test_split\
                             (X,y,test_size=0.15, \
                              random_state=123, \
                              stratify=y)
```

4. Fit the model using the random forest classifier for feature selection with the following code:

```
forest=RandomForestClassifier(n_estimators=500,random_state=1)

forest.fit(X_train,y_train)
```

> **NOTE**
>
> The random forest classifier is used here for feature selection. A random forest model can provide excellent results since it uses a large number of classifiers and also takes into account overfitting.

5. Call the random forest **feature_importances_** attribute to find the important features and store them in a variable named **importances**:

```
importances=forest.feature_importances_
```

6. Create a variable named **features** to store all the columns, except the target **Churn** variable. Sort the important features present in the **importances** variable using NumPy's **argsort** function:

```
features = data.drop(['Churn'],axis=1).columns

indices = np.argsort(importances)[::-1]
```

7. Plot the important features obtained from the random forest using Matplotlib's **plt** attribute:

```
plt.figure(figsize=(15,4))
plt.title("Feature importances using Random Forest")
plt.bar(range(X_train.shape[1]), importances[indices],\
        color="gray", align="center")
plt.xticks(range(X_train.shape[1]), features[indices], \
            rotation='vertical',fontsize=15)
plt.xlim([-1, X_train.shape[1]])
plt.show()
```

> **NOTE**
>
> The **gray** value for the **color** attribute is used to generate the graph in grayscale. You can use values such as **red**, **r**, and so on as values for the **color** parameter to get the colored graphs. You can also refer to the following document to get the code for the colored plot and the colored output: http://packt.link/NOjgT.

You should get the following plot:

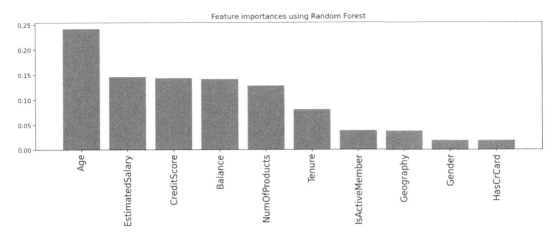

Figure 7.56: Feature importance using random forest

From the preceding figure, you can see that the five most important features selected from tree-based feature selection are **Age**, **EstimatedSalary**, **CreditScore**, **Balance**, and **NumOfProducts**.

You can also display the feature importance as a pandas DataFrame, which will be of more use than the bar plots when you have a large number of features since you will end up with a large number of bars in that case. In situations like these, it's much easier to infer feature importance using a tabular view of the pandas DataFrame.

8. Place the features and their importance in a pandas DataFrame using the following code:

```
feature_importance_df = pd.DataFrame({"Feature":features,\
                                      "Importance":importances})
print(feature_importance_df)
```

You should obtain the following output. You can see that **Age** feature has the highest importance, which is the same information that can be inferred from the bar graph plotted earlier:

	Feature	Importance
0	CreditScore	0.143886
1	Geography	0.038548
2	Gender	0.019299
3	Age	0.241954
4	Tenure	0.081503
5	Balance	0.141760
6	NumOfProducts	0.128461
7	HasCrCard	0.019139
8	IsActiveMember	0.038878
9	EstimatedSalary	0.146571

Figure 7.57: Placing the features and their importance in a pandas DataFrame

Now that we have extracted the importance of all the features, we can select the most important features and use them for training a model. This model-building step will be discussed in the next section.

MODEL BUILDING

So far, the OSEMN pipeline steps have helped in obtaining and cleaning the data, performing EDA, and extracting the most relevant features. Now, based on the problem we are trying to solve, we can use these features to train classification or regression-based models. For example, in the case of churn prediction, we can fit a logistic regression model on the most relevant features.

Unlike in the previous exercises, we will use the **statsmodel** package for fitting a logistic regression model since it provides additional features such as **summary** and **params**. Let's take a quick look at its implementation:

1. Import the **statsmodel** package:

```
import statsmodels.api as sm
```

2. Create a logistic regression model and train it on the training dataset:

```
logReg = sm.Logit(y_train, X_train)
logistic_regression = logReg.fit()
```

3. Now we can easily obtain the summary and model parameters as follows:

```
logistic_regression.summary
logistic_regression.params
```

Let's see how to do this in the next exercise.

EXERCISE 7.08: BUILDING A LOGISTIC REGRESSION MODEL

In the previous exercise, you extracted the importance values of all the features. Next, you are asked to build a logistic regression model using the five most relevant features for predicting the churning of a customer. The customer's attributes are as follows:

*   **Age**: 50
*   **EstimatedSalary**: 100,000
*   **CreditScore**: 600
*   **Balance**: 100,000
*   **NumOfProducts**: 2

Logistic regression has been chosen as the base model for churn prediction because of its easy interpretability.

> **NOTE**
>
> You will need to continue in the same Jupyter notebook as the preceding exercise. Alternatively, if you skipped the previous exercise, you may use the Jupyter notebook at https://packt.link/T5n4Z, which includes all the code up to *Exercise 7.07, Performing Feature Selection*. Continue this exercise by creating a new cell at the end of the notebook (make sure you select **Cell** from the toolbar and then select **Run All** before you begin).

Implement the following steps:

1. Import the **statsmodel** package and select only the top five features that you got from the previous exercise to fit your model. Use the following code:

```
import statsmodels.api as sm

top5_features = ['Age','EstimatedSalary','CreditScore',\
                 'Balance','NumOfProducts']
logReg = sm.Logit(y_train, X_train[top5_features])
logistic_regression = logReg.fit()
```

> **NOTE**
>
> **statsmodels** is a Python module that provides classes and functions for the estimation of many different statistical models, as well as for conducting statistical tests and statistical data exploration.

2. Once the model has been fitted, obtain the summary and your parameters:

```
logistic_regression.summary
logistic_regression.params
```

You will get the following output:

```
Age                0.048335
EstimatedSalary   -0.000001
CreditScore       -0.004470
Balance            0.000003
NumOfProducts     -0.361678
dtype: float64
```

Figure 7.58: Coefficients for each of the features

Notice that the parameters for **EstimatedSalary** and **Balance** are negligible, showing that they have a much smaller effect on the target variable than the other three features.

3. Create a function to compute the coefficients. This function will first multiply each feature by its coefficient (obtained in the previous step) and then finally add up the values for all the features in order to compute the final target value:

```
coef = logistic_regression.params
def y (coef, Age, EstimatedSalary, CreditScore, Balance, \
      NumOfProducts) : return coef[0]*Age+ coef[1]\
                      *EstimatedSalary+coef[2]*CreditScore\
                      +coef[1]*Balance+coef[2]*NumOfProducts
```

4. Calculate the chance of a customer churning by inputting the following values:

    Age: 50

    EstimatedSalary: 100,000

    CreditScore: 600

    Balance: 100,000

    NumOfProducts: 2

    Use the following code (here, we are implementing the formula we saw in *Figure 7.4*):

```
import numpy as np
y1 = y(coef, 50, 100000, 600,100000,2)
p = np.exp(y1) / (1+np.exp(y1))
p
```

    Your output will be approximately **0.38**, implying that a customer who is *50 years* of age, having an estimated salary of *$100,000*, a credit score of *600*, a balance of *$100,000*, and who has purchased *2* products, would have a *38.23%* likelihood of churning.

5. In the previous steps, you learned how to use the **statsmodel** package. In this step, you will implement scikit-learn's **LogisticRegression** module to build your classifier and predict on the test data to find out the accuracy of our model:

```
from sklearn.linear_model import LogisticRegression
```

6. Fit the logistic regression model on the partitioned training data that was prepared previously:

```
clf = LogisticRegression(random_state=0, solver='lbfgs')\
      .fit(X_train[top5_features], y_train)
```

7. Call the **predict** and **predict_proba** functions on the test data:

```
clf.predict(X_test[top5_features])
clf.predict_proba(X_test[top5_features])
```

You will get the following output:

```
array([[0.61565033, 0.38434967],
       [0.76717157, 0.23282843],
       [0.78137389, 0.21862611],
       ...,
       [0.552548  , 0.447452  ],
       [0.85311964, 0.14688036],
       [0.75851722, 0.24148278]])
```

Figure 7.59: Predicted probability of the test data with the top five features

Consider the first set of values – **[0.61565033, 0.38434967]**. A higher value in the first index means that there is a 61.56% chance of the customer not churning, and a 38.44% chance that the customer will churn.

8. Calculate the accuracy of the model by calling the **score** function:

```
clf.score(X_test[top5_features], y_test)
```

Your output will be **0.79**. This shows that the model trained has a 79% accuracy on the testing dataset.

> **NOTE**
>
> We used **lbfgs** as an optimization algorithm that approximates the **Broyden–Fletcher–Goldfarb–Shanno** algorithm and is recommended for smaller datasets. More details can be found in the scikit-learn documentation at https://scikit-learn.org/stable/modules/linear_model.html.

You have successfully implemented logistic regression using the **statsmodel** package. The coefficients of the regression model were obtained in *Step 2*, the logistic regression equation was created in *Step 3*, and the probability for a customer to churn was calculated using the sigmoid function in *Step 4*. Lastly, you used scikit-learn's logistic regression to predict your test data and scored an accuracy of **79%**, which implied that your model was able to accurately predict **79%** of the test data correctly. You will study more about how to check the accuracy of a model in the next chapter.

INTERPRETING THE DATA

The last part of the analysis is interpreting the data, which means summarizing the insights that you have obtained from your analysis. This is also the last step in the OSEMN pipeline, which we have followed throughout our case study:

- The percentage of customers that churned is 20.37% (2,037) and the percentage that did not churn is 79.63% (7,963).

- Overall, the average credit score of the customers who churned is 645.35 and the average age of the customers who churned is 44.83 years.

- The average balance and the estimated salary of the customers who churned are 911,108.53 and 101,465.67 respectively, which is greater than the customers who didn't churn.

- The median number of products purchased by the customers who churned is 1.

- Customer age and churn are 29% positively correlated.

- Balance and churn are 12% positively correlated.

- The number of products purchased and the customer's balance are 30% negatively correlated.

- The difference between churn and non-churning customers in Germany and Spain is less than in France.

- Comparatively, more female customers have churned. The amount of churn is greater for customers who have purchased 3-4 products.

- Customers within the 35-45 age group seem to churn more. As the age of customers increases, they usually churn more.

- The amount of churn is less with customers with a negative to low balance compared to customers having a balance of 75,000–150,000.

- The most important features selected from tree-based feature selection are **Age**, **EstimatedSalary**, **CreditScore**, **Balance**, and **NumOfProducts**.

Now that you have learned how to train your own model on a given dataset and interpret the data, it's time to carry out the same steps on a churn prediction problem in the next activity.

ACTIVITY 7.02: PERFORMING THE MN TECHNIQUE FROM OSEMN

You are working as a data scientist for a large telecom company. The marketing team wants to know the reasons behind customer churn. Using this information, they want to prepare a plan to reduce customer churn. Your task is to analyze the reasons behind the customer churn and present your findings.

After you have reported your initial findings to the marketing team, they want you to build a machine learning model that can predict customer churn. With your results, the marketing team can send out discount coupons to customers who might otherwise churn. Use the MN technique from OSEMN to construct your model.

> **NOTE**
>
> We will be using the results of our *Activity 7.01*, *Performing the OSE technique from OSEMN*, in this activity. You can download the notebook from https://packt.link/ogN5G. Please use this same notebook as a starter file for this activity.

1. Import the necessary libraries.

2. Encode the **Acct_Plan_Subtype** and **Complaint_Code** columns using the **the.astype('category').cat.codes** command.

3. Split the data into training (80%) and testing sets (20%).

4. Perform feature selection using the random forest classifier. You should get the following output:

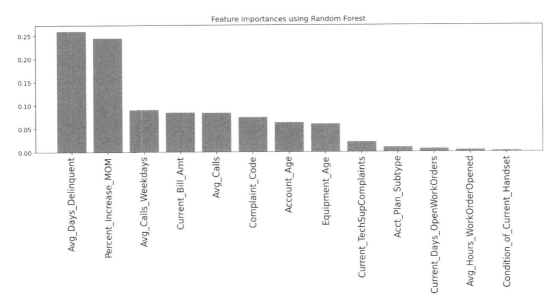

Figure 7.60: Feature importance using random forest

5. Select the top seven features and save them in a variable named **top7_features**.

6. Fit a logistic regression using the **statsmodel** package.

7. Find out the probability that a customer will churn when the following data is used: **Avg_Days_Delinquent**: 40, **Percent_Increase_MOM**: 5, **Avg_Calls_Weekdays**: 39000, **Current_Bill_Amt**: 12000, **Avg_Calls**: 9000, **Complaint_Code**: 0, and **Account_Age**: 17.

The given customer should have a value of around 81.939% likelihood of churning.

> **NOTE**
>
> The solution for this activity can be found on page 555.

SUMMARY

Predicting customer churn is one of the most common use cases in marketing analytics. Churn prediction not only helps marketing teams to better strategize their marketing campaigns but also helps organizations to focus their resources wisely.

In this chapter, we explored how to use the data science pipeline for any machine learning problem. We also learned the intuition behind using logistic regression and saw how it is different from linear regression. We looked at the structure of the data by reading it using a pandas DataFrame. We then used data scrubbing techniques such as missing value imputation, renaming columns, and data type manipulation to prepare our data for data exploration. We implemented various data visualization techniques, such as univariate and bivariate analysis and a correlation plot, which enabled us to find useful insights from the data. Feature selection is another important part of data modeling. We used a tree-based classifier to select important features for our machine learning model. Finally, we implemented logistic regression to find out the likelihood of customer churn.

In the next chapter, we will learn how to evaluate our model, how to tune our model, and how to apply other more powerful machine learning algorithms.

8

FINE-TUNING CLASSIFICATION ALGORITHMS

OVERVIEW

This chapter will help you optimize predictive analytics using classification algorithms such as **support vector machines**, **decision trees**, and **random forests**, which are some of the most common classification algorithms from the scikit-learn machine learning library. Moreover, you will learn how to implement **tree-based classification models**, which you have used previously for regression. Next, you will learn how to choose appropriate performance metrics for evaluating the performance of a classification model. Finally, you will put all these skills to use in solving a customer churn prediction problem where you will optimize and evaluate the best classification algorithm for predicting whether a given customer will churn or not.

INTRODUCTION

Consider a scenario where you are the machine learning lead in a marketing analytics firm. Your firm has taken over a project from Amazon to predict whether or not a user will buy a product during festive season sale campaigns. You have been provided with anonymized data about customer activity on the Amazon website – the number of products purchased, their prices, categories of the products, and more. In such scenarios, where the target variable is a discrete value – for example, the customer will either buy the product or not – the problems are referred to as **classification problems**. There are a large number of classification algorithms available now to solve such problems and choosing the right one is a crucial task. So, you will first start exploring the dataset to come up with some observations about it. Next, you will try out different classification algorithms and evaluate the performance metrics for each classification model to understand whether the model is good enough to be used by the company. Finally, you will end up with the best classification algorithm out of the entire pool of models you trained, and this model will then be used to predict whether a user will buy a product during the sale.

In this chapter, you'll be working on problems like these to understand how to choose the right classification algorithm by evaluating its performance using various metrics. Picking the right performance metrics and optimizing, fine-tuning, and evaluating the model is an important part of building any supervised machine learning model. Moreover, choosing an appropriate machine learning model is an art that requires experience, and each algorithm has its advantages and disadvantages.

In the previous chapter, you learned about the most common data science pipeline: **OSEMN**. You also learned how to preprocess, explore, model, and finally, interpret data. This chapter builds upon the skills you learned therein. You will start by using the most common Python machine learning API, scikit-learn, to build a logistic regression model, then you will learn different classification algorithms and the intuition behind them, and finally, you will learn how to optimize, evaluate, and choose the best model.

SUPPORT VECTOR MACHINES

When dealing with data that is linearly separable, the goal of the **Support Vector Machine (SVM)** learning algorithm is to find the boundary between classes so that there are fewer misclassification errors. However, the problem is that there could be several decision boundaries ($\mathbf{B}_1$, $\mathbf{B}_2$), as you can see in the following figure:

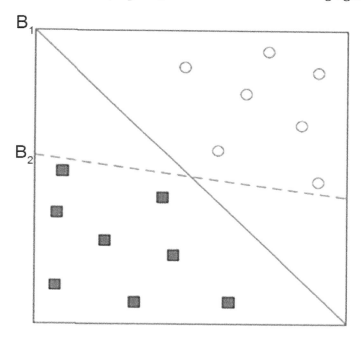

Figure 8.1: Multiple decision boundary

As a result, the question arises as to which of the boundaries is better, and how to define *better*. The solution is to use a **margin** as the optimization objective. A margin can be described as the distance between the boundary and two points (from different classes) lying closest to the boundary. *Figure 8.2* gives a nice visual definition of the margin.

The objective of the SVM algorithm is to maximize the margin. You will go over the intuition behind maximizing the margin in the next section. For now, you need to understand that the objective of an SVM linear classifier is to increase the width of the boundary before hitting a data point. The algorithm first finds out the width of the hyperplane and then maximizes the margin. It chooses the decision boundary that has the maximum margin.

While it might seem too daunting in the beginning, you don't need to worry about this since the algorithm will internally carry out all these tasks and will be able to give you the target class for a given data point. For instance, in the preceding figure, it chooses **B**₁ because it had a larger margin compared to **B**₂. You can refer to the margins for the decision boundaries of **B**₁ and **B**₂ in *Figure 8.2*:

> **NOTE**
>
> In geometry, a hyperplane is a subspace whose dimension is one less than that of its ambient space. For example, in the case of a 2D space (for example, *Figure 8.1*), the hyperplane would be a line.

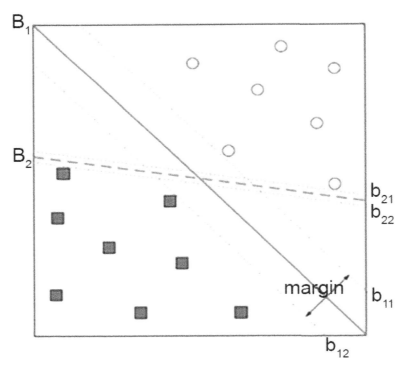

Figure 8.2: Decision boundary with a different width/margin

The following are the advantages and disadvantages of the SVM algorithm:

Advantages

- SVMs are effective when dealing with high-dimensional data, where the number of dimensions is more than the number of training samples.

- SVMs are known for their use of the **kernel** function, making it a very versatile algorithm.

> **NOTE**
>
> Kernel methods are mathematical functions used to convert data from lower-dimensional space to higher-dimensional space, or vice versa. The idea behind kernel functions is that data that is not linearly separated in one-dimensional space might be linearly separated in a higher-dimensional space.

Disadvantages

- SVMs do not calculate probability directly, and instead use five-fold cross-validation to calculate probability, which can make the algorithm considerably slow.

- With high-dimensional data, it is important to choose the **kernel** function and regularization term, which can make the process very slow.

INTUITION BEHIND MAXIMUM MARGIN

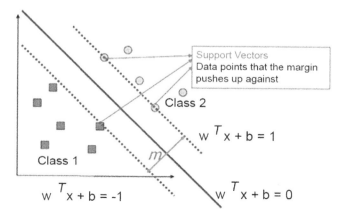

Figure 8.3: Geometrical interpretation of maximum margin

The logic behind having large margins in the case of an SVM is that they have a lower generalization error compared to small margins, which can result in overfitted data.

Consider *Figure 8.3*, where you have data points from two classes –squares and circles. The data points that are closest to the boundary are referred to as support vectors as they are used for calculating the margin. The margin on the left side of the boundary is referred to as the negative hyperplane and the margin on the right side of the boundary is referred to as the positive hyperplane.

Let's consider the positive and negative hyperplane as follows:

$$w^T x_{pos} + b_0 = 1$$

$$w^T x_{neg} + b_1 = -1$$

Figure 8.4: Positive and negative hyperplane equation

In the preceding equations:

- **w** refers to the slope of the hyperplane.
- **b**$_0$ and **b**$_1$ refer to the intercepts of the hyperplanes.
- **T** refers to the transpose.
- **x**$_{pos}$ and **x**$_{neg}$ refer to the points through which the positive and negative hyperplanes are passing, respectively.

The preceding equations can also be thought of as an equation of a line: **y = mx + c**, where **m** is the slope and **c** is the intercept. Because of this similarity, SVM is referred to as the SVM **linear** classifier.

Subtracting the preceding two equations, you get the following:

$$w^T (x_{pos} - x_{neg}) = 2$$

Figure 8.5: Combined equation of two separate hyperplanes

Normalizing the equation by the vector **w**, you get the following, where **m** refers to the data points you have and **i** refers to the ith data point:

$$||w|| = \sqrt{\sum_{i=1}^{m} w_i{}^2}$$

Figure 8.6: Normalized equation

You reduce the preceding equation as follows:

$$margin = \frac{w^T(x_{pos} - x_{neg})}{||w||} = \frac{2}{||w||}$$

Figure 8.7: Equation for margin m

Now, the **objective function** is obtained by maximizing the margin within the constraint that the decision boundary should classify all the points correctly.

Now once you have the decision boundary ready, you can use the following equation to classify the points based on which side of the decision boundary they lie on:

$$w^T x_i + b_0 \geq 1 \quad if \ y_i = 1$$

$$w^T x_i + b_0 \leq -1 \quad if \ y_i = -1$$

Figure 8.8: Equation for separating the data points on a hyperplane

To implement an SVM-based classifier, you can use the scikit-learn module as follows:

1. Import **svm** from scikit-learn:

```
from sklearn import svm
```

2. Create an instance of the SVM model that will then be used for training on the dataset:

```
model = svm.SVC()
```

In the preceding function, you can also specify the kernel type (**linear**, **sigmoid**, **rbf**, and so on), the regularization parameter **C**, the gamma value for the kernel, and so on. You can read the entire list of the parameters available along with their default values here: https://scikit-learn.org/stable/modules/generated/sklearn.svm.SVC.html#sklearn.svm.SVC.

3. Once you have the model instance, you can use **model.fit(X_train, y_train)** to train the model and **model.predict(X)** to get the prediction.

So far you have been dealing with the hard margin, which does not leave any space for mistakes. In other words, all instances from one class have to lie on one side of the margin. However, this rigid behavior can affect the generalizability of the model. To resolve this, you can use a soft margin classifier.

LINEARLY INSEPARABLE CASES

With linearly inseparable cases, such as the one illustrated in the following figure, you cannot use a hard-margin classifier. The solution is to introduce a new kind of classifier, known as a soft-margin classifier, using the slack variable ξ. The slack variable converts the equations discussed in the previous section into inequalities by allowing for some mistakes, as shown in *Figure 8.9*:

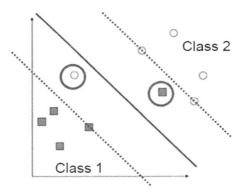

Figure 8.9: Linearly inseparable data points

NOTE

The hard margin refers to the fitting of a model with zero errors; hence you cannot use a hard-margin classifier for the preceding figure. A soft margin, on the other hand, allows the fitting of a model with some error, as highlighted by the points circled in blue in the preceding figure.

A soft-margin SVM works by doing the following:

1. Introducing the slack variable

2. Relaxing the constraints

3. Penalizing the relaxation

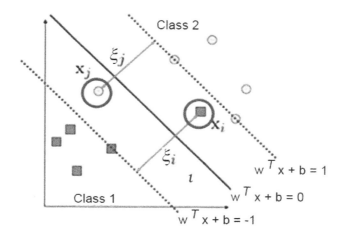

Figure 8.10: Using the slack variable ξ for linearly inseparable data

The linear constraints can be changed by adding the slack variable to the equation in *Figure 8.5* as follows:

$$w^T x_i + b_0 \geq 1 - \xi_i \quad if \ y_i = 1$$
$$w^T x_i + b_0 \leq -1 + \xi_i \quad if \ y_i = -1$$
$$for \ i = 1 \ ... . N \ where \ N \ is \ the \ no \ of \ sample$$

Figure 8.11: Linear constraints for maximizing margin with slack variable ξ

The **objective function** for linearly inseparable data points is obtained by minimizing the following:

$$\frac{1}{2}||w||^2 + C\left(\sum_i \xi_i\right)$$

Figure 8.12: Objective function to be minimized

Here, **C** is the penalty cost parameter (regularization). This parameter **C** can be specified as a parameter when calling the **svm.SVC()** function, as discussed in the previous section.

LINEARLY INSEPARABLE CASES USING THE KERNEL

In the preceding example, you saw how you can use a soft-margin SVM to classify datasets using the slack variable. However, there can be scenarios where it is quite hard to separate data. For example, in the following figure, it would be impossible to have a decision boundary using the slack variable and a linear hyperplane:

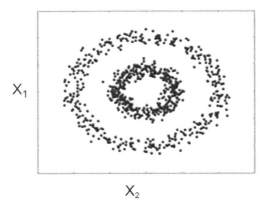

Figure 8.13: Linearly inseparable data points

In this scenario, you can use the concept of a kernel, which creates a nonlinear combination of original features ($\mathbf{X}_1$, $\mathbf{X}_2$) to project to a higher-dimensional space via a mapping function, φ, to make it linearly separable:

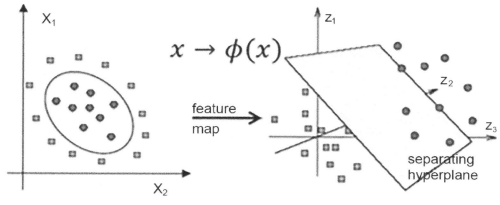

Complex in low dimensions   Simple in higher dimensions

Figure 8.14: Geometric interpretation and equation for projection from a low to a high dimension

The problem with this explicit feature mapping is that the dimensionality of the feature can be very high, which makes it hard to represent it explicitly in memory. This is mitigated using the kernel trick. The **kernel trick** basically replaces the dot product $\mathbf{x}_i^T \mathbf{x}_j$ with a kernel $\varphi \; \mathbf{x}_i^T \varphi (\mathbf{x}_j)$, which can be defined as follows:

$$\frac{1}{2}||w||^2 + c\left(\sum_i \xi_i\right)$$

Figure 8.15: Kernel function

There are different types of kernel functions, namely:

- Linear kernel: $\varkappa(x_i, x_j) = (x_i, x_j) = (x_i)^T(x_j)$

- Polynomial kernel (degree d): $\varkappa(x_i, x_j) = (x_i^T x_j + 1)^d$

- Gaussian kernel: $\varkappa(x_i, x_j) = exp\left(-\dfrac{\|x_i - x_j\|^2}{2\sigma^2}\right)$

  This is also represented as $\varkappa(x_i, x_j) = exp\left(-\gamma\|x_i - x_j\|^2\right)$

  Where $\gamma = \dfrac{1}{2\sigma^2}$ is a free parameter to be optimized, also known as gamma.

Figure 8.16: Different kernel functions

A kernel can also be interpreted as a similarity function and lies between 0 (an exactly dissimilar sample) and 1 (a sample that is exactly the same).

In scikit-learn, the following kernel functions are available:

linear: (x, x')

polynomial: $(\gamma(x, x') + r)^d$. d is specified by keyword degree, r by coef0.

rbf: $exp(-\gamma\|x - x'\|^2)$. gamma is specified by keyword gamma, must be greater than 0.

sigmoid $(tanh(\gamma(x, x') + r))$, where r is specified by coef0.

Figure 8.17: Different kernel functions implemented in scikit-learn

So, you can use them as follows:

```
svm.SVC(kernel='poly', C=1)
```

Here, you can change the kernel using different kernel functions such as `'linear'`, `'poly'`, and so on, which is similar to what we have described in *Figure 8.17*.

Now that you have gone through the details of the SVM algorithm and how to implement the SVM classifier using the scikit-learn module, it's time to put the skills to use by training an SVM classifier on the Shill Bidding dataset.

EXERCISE 8.01: TRAINING AN SVM ALGORITHM OVER A DATASET

In this exercise, you will work with the Shill Bidding dataset, the file for which is named **Shill_Bidding_Dataset.csv**. You can download this dataset from the following link: https://packt.link/GRn3G. This is the same dataset you were introduced to in *Exercise 7.01, Comparing Predictions by Linear and Logistic Regression on the Shill Bidding Dataset*. Your objective is to use this information to predict whether an auction depicts normal behavior or not (0 means normal behavior and 1 means abnormal behavior). You will use the SVM algorithm to build your model:

1. Import **pandas, numpy, train_test_split**, **cross_val_score**, and **svm** from the **sklearn** library:

    ```
    import pandas as pd
    from sklearn.model_selection import train_test_split
    from sklearn import svm
    from sklearn.model_selection import cross_val_score
    import numpy as np
    ```

2. Read the dataset into a DataFrame named **data** using pandas, as shown in the following snippet, and look at the first few rows of the data:

    ```
    data=pd.read_csv("Shill_Bidding_Dataset.csv")
    ```

    > **NOTE**
    >
    > If the CSV file you downloaded is stored in a different directory from where you're running the Jupyter notebook, you'll need to change the emboldened path in the preceding command.

3. First, remove the columns that are irrelevant to the case study. These are ID columns and thus will be unique to every entry. Because of their uniqueness, they won't add any value to the model and thus can be dropped:

    ```
    # Drop irrelevant columns
    data.drop(["Record_ID","Auction_ID","Bidder_ID"],axis=1,\
            inplace=True)

    data.head()
    ```

Your output will look as follows:

	Bidder_Tendency	Bidding_Ratio	Successive_Outbidding	Last_Bidding	Auction_Bids	Starting_Price_Average	Early_Bidding
0	0.200000	0.400000	0.0	0.000028	0.0	0.993593	0.000028
1	0.024390	0.200000	0.0	0.013123	0.0	0.993593	0.013123
2	0.142857	0.200000	0.0	0.003042	0.0	0.993593	0.003042
3	0.100000	0.200000	0.0	0.097477	0.0	0.993593	0.097477
4	0.051282	0.222222	0.0	0.001318	0.0	0.000000	0.001242

Figure 8.18: First few rows of auction data

4. Check the data types, as follows:

```
data.dtypes
```

You'll get the following output. Glancing at it, you can see that all the columns have an appropriate data type so you don't have to do any further preprocessing here:

```
Bidder_Tendency          float64
Bidding_Ratio            float64
Successive_Outbidding    float64
Last_Bidding             float64
Auction_Bids             float64
Starting_Price_Average   float64
Early_Bidding            float64
Winning_Ratio            float64
Auction_Duration         int64
Class                    int64
dtype: object
```

Figure 8.19: Data type of the auction dataset

5. Look for any missing values using the following code:

```
data.isnull().sum()    ### Check for missing values
```

You should get the following output:

```
Bidder_Tendency            0
Bidding_Ratio              0
Successive_Outbidding      0
Last_Bidding               0
Auction_Bids               0
Starting_Price_Average     0
Early_Bidding              0
Winning_Ratio              0
Auction_Duration           0
Class                      0
dtype: int64
```

Figure 8.20: Checking for missing values

Now that there are no missing values, train the SVM algorithm over the dataset.

6. Split the data into train and test sets and save them as **X_train, X_test, y_train**, and **y_test** as shown:

```
target = 'Class'
X = data.drop(target,axis=1)
y = data[target]
X_train, X_test, y_train, y_test = train_test_split\
                                (X.values,y,test_size=0.50,\
                                 random_state=123, \
                                 stratify=y)
```

7. Fit a linear SVM model with **C=1**:

> **NOTE**
>
> C is the penalty cost parameter for regularization. Please refer to the objective function for linearly inseparable data points in the SVM algorithm mentioned in *Figure 8.12*.

```
clf_svm=svm.SVC(kernel='linear', C=1)
clf_svm.fit(X_train,y_train)
```

You will get the following output:

```
SVC(C=1, kernel='linear')
```

> **NOTE**
>
> The output may vary slightly depending on your system.

8. Calculate the accuracy score using the following code:

```
clf_svm.score(X_test, y_test)
```

You will get the following output:

```
0.9775387535590003
```

For the auction dataset, the SVM classifier will score an accuracy of around 97.75%. This implies it can predict **97.75%** of the test data accurately.

DECISION TREES

Decision trees are mostly used for classification tasks. They are a non-parametric form of supervised learning method, meaning that unlike in SVM where you had to specify the **kernel type**, **C**, **gamma**, and other parameters, there are no such parameters to be specified in the case of decision trees. This also makes them quite easy to work with. Decision trees, as the name suggests, use a tree-based structure for making a decision (finding the target variable). Each "branch" of the decision tree is made by following a rule, for example, "is some feature more than some value? – yes or no." Decision trees can be used both as regressors and classifiers with minimal changes. The following are the advantages and disadvantages of using decision trees for classification:

Advantages

- Decision trees are easy to understand and visualize.

- They can handle both numeric and categorical data.

- The requirement for data cleaning in the case of decision trees is very low since they can handle missing data.

- They are non-parametric machine learning algorithms that make no assumptions regarding space distribution and classifier structures.

- It's a white-box model, rather than a black-box model like neural networks, and can explain the logic of the split using Boolean values.

Disadvantages

- Decision trees tend to overfit data very easily, and pruning is required to prevent overfitting of the model. As a quick recap, overfitting occurs when the model starts to learn even the randomness in the data points, instead of focusing only on the inherent pattern in the data points. This results in the model losing its generalizability.

- They are not suitable for imbalanced data, where you may have a biased decision tree. A decision tree would try to split the node based on the majority class and therefore doesn't generalize very well. The remedy is to balance your data before applying decision trees. Most medical datasets, for example, the dataset on the number of polio patients in India, are imbalanced datasets. This is because the percentage of people who have the illness is extremely small compared to those who don't have the illness.

Similar to SVM classifiers, it is very easy to implement a decision tree classifier using the scikit-learn module:

1. Import the **tree** sub-module from the scikit-learn module:

```
from sklearn import tree
```

2. Also, import the **export_graphviz** function that will be used to visualize the created tree:

```
from sklearn.tree import export_graphviz
```

3. To plot the tree in Jupyter Notebooks, import the **Image** submodule:

```
from IPython.display import Image
```

4. You will also need to import the **StringIO** module to convert the text into an image:

```
from sklearn.externals.six import StringIO
```

5. Create a decision tree classifier instance:

```
clf_tree = tree.DecisionTreeClassifier()
```

You can fit the decision tree classifier on the training dataset using **clf_tree.fit(X_train,y_train)**.

6. Similarly, in order to find the prediction using the classifier, use `clf_tree.predict(X)`.

7. Once the decision tree is trained, use the following code to plot it using the `export_graphviz` function:

```
dot_data = StringIO()
export_graphviz(clf_tree, out_file=dot_data, \
                filled=True, rounded=True, \
                class_names=['Positive','Negative'], \
                max_depth = 3, \
                special_characters=True, \
                feature_names=X.columns.values)
graph = pydotplus.graph_from_dot_data(dot_data.getvalue())
Image(graph.create_png())
```

Here, **class_names** is a list that stores the names of the target variable classes. For example, if you want to predict whether a given person has polio or not, the target class names can be **Positive** or **Negative**.

Now that we have discussed decision trees and their implementation, let's use them in the next exercise on the same Shill Bidding dataset we used earlier.

EXERCISE 8.02: IMPLEMENTING A DECISION TREE ALGORITHM OVER A DATASET

In this exercise, you will use decision trees to build a model over the same auction dataset that you used in the previous exercise. This practice of training different classifiers on the same dataset is very common whenever you are working on any classification task. Training multiple classifiers of different types makes it easier to pick the right classifier for a task.

> **NOTE**
>
> Ensure that you use the same Jupyter notebook as the one used for the preceding exercise.

1. Import **tree, graphviz, StringIO, Image, export_graphviz**, and **pydotplus**:

```
import graphviz
from sklearn import tree
from sklearn.externals.six import StringIO
from IPython.display import Image
from sklearn.tree import export_graphviz
import pydotplus
```

2. Fit the decision tree classifier using the following code:

```
clf_tree = tree.DecisionTreeClassifier()
clf_tree = clf_tree.fit(X_train, y_train)
```

3. Plot the decision tree using a graph. In this plot, you will be using **export_graphviz** to visualize the decision tree. You will use the output of your decision tree classifier as your input **clf**. The target variable will be the **class_names**, that is, **Normal** or **Abnormal**.

```
dot_data = StringIO()
export_graphviz(clf_tree, out_file=dot_data,\
                filled=True, rounded=True,\
                class_names=['Normal','Abnormal'],\
                max_depth = 3,
                special_characters=True,\
                feature_names=X.columns.values)
graph = pydotplus.graph_from_dot_data(dot_data.getvalue())
Image(graph.create_png())
```

The output of the preceding snippet will be a graphic visualization of the decision tree to a depth of 3. While it might not seem very intuitive in beginning, it serves an interesting purpose of displaying what rules are being used at each node. For example, in the very beginning, the **Successive_Outbidding** feature is compared. If the value is less than or equal to 0.25, you follow the left branch, otherwise, you follow the right branch. Please note that the output can vary slightly since decision trees use randomness to fit the model.

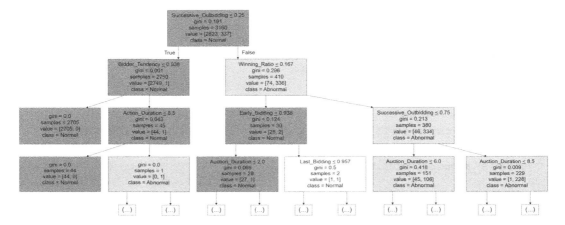

Figure 8.21: Graphic visualization of the decision tree

4. Calculate the accuracy score using the following code:

```
clf_tree.score(X_test, y_test)
```

You should get an output close to 0.9981, which means that our decision tree classifier scores an accuracy of around 99.81%. Hence our classifier can predict 99.81% of the test data correctly.

While we have discussed the basics of decision trees and their implementation, we are yet to go into the theoretical details of the algorithm. In the following sections, we will first cover the terminology related to decision trees and how the decision tree algorithm works.

IMPORTANT TERMINOLOGY FOR DECISION TREES

Decision trees get their name from the inverted tree-like structure they follow. Now, in a normal tree, the bottom part is the root, and the topmost part is the leaf of the tree. Since a decision tree follows the reverse structure, the topmost node is referred to as the **root node**. A node, in simple terms, is the smallest block in the decision tree. Every node has a certain rule that decides where to go next (which **branch** to follow). The last nodes or the **terminal nodes** of the decision tree are called **leaves**. This is where the target variable prediction happens. When a new input is provided for prediction, it first goes to the root node and then moves down to the leaf node for prediction.

As you can understand here, there is a large number of decision trees that can be created out of the features available in a dataset. In the next section, you will see how a specific feature is selected at a node, which then helps in selecting one decision tree out of the large sample space.

DECISION TREE ALGORITHM FORMULATION

Decision trees use multiple algorithms to split at the root node or sub-node. A decision tree goes through all of the features and picks the feature on which it can get the most homogeneous sub-nodes. For classification tasks, it decides the most homogeneous sub-nodes based on the information gained. Let's discuss information gain first. In short, each of the nodes in a decision tree represents a feature, each of the branches represents a decision rule, and each of the leaves represents an outcome. It is a flow-like structure.

Information gain

This gives details on how much "information" a feature will hold about the class. Features that are perfectly separable or partitioned will give us maximum information, while features that are not perfectly separable or partitioned will give us less information:

$$IG(D_p, f) = I(D_p) - \frac{N_{left}}{N_p} I(D_{left}) - \frac{N_{right}}{N_p} I(D_{right})$$

Figure 8.22: Information gain formula

Here, **IG** = information gain, **I** = impurity, **f** = feature, **D**$_p$ = parent dataset, **D**$_{left}$ = left child dataset, **D**$_{right}$ = right child dataset, **N**$_p$ = total number of samples in the parent dataset, **N**$_{left}$ = number of samples in the left child dataset, and **N**$_{right}$ = number of samples in the right child dataset.

The impurity can be calculated using any of the following three criteria:

- Gini impurity

- Entropy

- Misclassification rate

Let's look into each criterion one by one.

Gini impurity

The Gini index can be defined as the criterion that would minimize the probability of misclassification:

$$I_g(t) = \sum_{i=1}^{k} p(i|t)\big(1 - p(i|t)\big) = 1 - \sum_{i=1}^{k} p(i|t)^2$$

Figure 8.23: Gini impurity

Here, **k** = number of classes and **p(i|t)** = proportion of samples that belong to class **k** for a particular node **t**.

For a two-class problem, you can simplify the preceding equation as follows:

$$I_g(t) = 1 - (p^2 + q^2)$$

Where

$$p = probability\ of\ success$$

$$q = probability\ of\ failure$$

Figure 8.24: Simplified Gini impurity formula for binary classification

Entropy

Entropy can be defined as the criterion that maximizes mutual information:

$$I_h(t) = -\sum_{i=1}^{k} p(i|t) log_2 \, p(i|t)$$

Figure 8.25: Entropy formula

Here, **p(i|t)** = the proportion of samples that belong to class **k** for a particular node **t**. The entropy is zero if all the samples belong to the same class, whereas it has maximum value if you have uniform class distribution.

For a two-class problem, you can simplify the preceding equation as follows:

$$I_h(t) = -p \log_2 p - q \log_2 q$$
$$\text{Where,}$$
$$p = \text{probability of success}$$
$$q = \text{probability of failure}$$

Figure 8.26: Simplified equation

Misclassification error

The formula of the misclassification error is as follows:

$$I_e(t) = 1 - max\{p(i|t)\}$$

Figure 8.27: Misclassification formula

Gini impurity and entropy typically give the same results, and either one of them can be used to calculate the impurity. To prune the tree, you can use the misclassification error.

Example: Let's refer to a very popular dataset – the Titanic dataset. The dataset provides data about the unfortunate incident where the Titanic ship sank in the Atlantic Ocean in the year 1912. While the dataset has a large number of features – for example, the sex of the passengers, their embarkation records, and how much fare they paid – to keep things simple, you will only consider two features, **Sex** and **Embarked**, to find out whether a person survived or not:

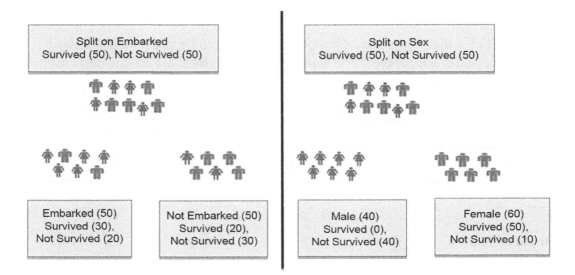

Figure 8.28: Visual representation of tree split

The Gini index impurity for **Embarked** is as follows:

$$I_g(D_p) = 1 - (0.5^2 + 0.5^2) = 0.5$$

$$I_g\left(D_{\frac{left}{embarked}}\right) = 1 - \left(\left(\frac{30}{50}\right)^2 + \left(\frac{20}{50}\right)^2\right) = 0.48$$

$$I_g\left(D_{\frac{right}{Not\ embarked}}\right) = 1 - \left(\left(\frac{20}{50}\right)^2 + \left(\frac{30}{50}\right)^2\right) = 0.48$$

$$IG(D_p, embarked) = I(D_p) - \frac{N_{left}}{N_p}I(D_{left}) - \frac{N_{right}}{N_p}I(D_{right}) = 0.5 - \frac{50}{100}0.48 - \frac{50}{100}0.48 = 0.02$$

Figure 8.29: Information gain calculated using Gini impurity (Embarked)

The Gini index impurity for **Sex** is as follows:

$$I_g(D_p) = 1 - (0.5^2 + 0.5^2) = 0.5$$

$$I_g\left(D_{\frac{left}{male}}\right) = 1 - \left(\left(\frac{0}{40}\right)^2 + \left(\frac{40}{40}\right)^2\right) = 0$$

$$I_g\left(D_{\frac{right}{female}}\right) = 1 - \left(\left(\frac{50}{60}\right)^2 + \left(\frac{10}{60}\right)^2\right) = 0.28$$

$$IG(D_p, sex) = I(D_p) - \frac{N_{left}}{N_p}I(D_{left}) - \frac{N_{right}}{N_p}I(D_{right}) = 0.5 - \frac{40}{100}*0 - \frac{60}{100}*0.28 = 0.33$$

Figure 8.30: Information gain calculated using Gini impurity (Sex)

From the information gain calculated, the decision tree will split based on the **Sex** feature, for which the information gain value is **0.33**.

> **NOTE**
>
> Similarly, information gain can be calculated using entropy and misclassification. You are encouraged to try these two calculations on your own.

So far, we have covered two popular classification algorithms – SVMs and decision tree classifiers. Now it's time to take things up a notch and discuss a very powerful classification algorithm – random forest. As the name suggests, random forest classifiers are nothing but a forest or a collection of decision trees. Let's go into more detail in the next section.

RANDOM FOREST

The decision tree algorithm that you saw earlier faced the problem of overfitting. Since you fit only one tree on the training data, there is a high chance that the tree will overfit the data without proper pruning. For example, referring to the Amazon sales case study that we discussed at the start of this chapter, if your model learns to focus on the inherent randomness in the data, it will try to use that as a baseline for future predictions. Consider a scenario where out of 100 customers, 90 bought a beard wash, primarily because most of them were males with a beard.

However, your model started thinking that this is not related to gender, so the next time someone logs in during the sale, it will start recommending beard wash, even if that person might be female. Unfortunately, these things are very common but can really harm the business. This is why it is important to treat the overfitting of models. The **random forest** algorithm reduces variance/overfitting by averaging multiple decision trees, which individually suffer from high variance.

Random forest is an ensemble method of supervised machine learning. Ensemble methods combine predictions obtained from multiple base estimators/classifiers to improve the robustness of the overall prediction. Ensemble methods are divided into the following two types:

- **Bagging**: The data is randomly divided into several subsets and the model is trained over each of these subsets. Several estimators are built independently from each other and then the predictions are averaged together, which ultimately helps to reduce variance (overfitting). Random forests belong to this category.

- **Boosting**: In the case of boosting, base estimators are built sequentially and each model built is very weak. The objective, therefore, is to build models in sequence, where the latter models try to reduce the error from the previous model and thereby reduce bias (underfitting). Advanced machine learning algorithms like CatBoost and XGBoost belong to this category.

Let's understand how the random forest algorithm works with the help of *Figure 8.31*:

1. A random bootstrap sample (a sample drawn with replacement) of size *m* is chosen from the training data. This splits the training data into subsets such as **Data1**, **Data2**, and so on.

2. Decision trees are grown on each instance of the bootstrap. These decision trees can be referred to as **Learner1**, **Learner2**, and so on.

3. *d* features are chosen randomly without replacement.

4. Each node is split using the *d* features selected based on objective functions, which could be information gain.

5. *Steps 1-4* are repeated *k* times. Eventually, this generates **Model1**, **Model2**, and so on for each subset.

6. All of the predictions from the multiple trees are aggregated and assigned a class label by majority vote. This step is referred to as **Model Combiner** in *Figure 8.31*:

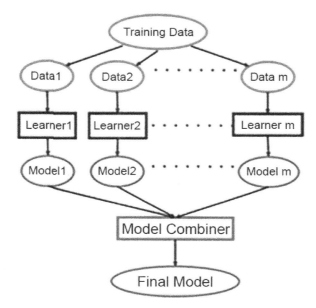

Figure 8.31: The working of a random forest model

The following are the advantages and disadvantages of the random forest algorithm:

Advantages

- It does not suffer from overfitting, since you take the average of all the predictions.
- It can be used to get feature importance.
- It can be used for both regression and classification tasks.
- It can be used for highly imbalanced datasets.
- It can handle missing data.

Disadvantages

- It suffers from bias, although it reduces variance.
- It's mostly a black-box model and is difficult to explain.

Similar to the decision tree algorithm, you can implement a random forest classifier using the scikit-learn module as follows:

1. Import **RandomForestClassifier** from scikit-learn:

```
from sklearn.ensemble import RandomForestClassifier
```

2. Create an instance of the random forest classifier. You can specify the number of trees (**n_estimators**), the maximum depth of the trees, a random state (to add reproducibility to the results), and so on. A complete list of parameters can be found at https://scikit-learn.org/stable/modules/generated/sklearn.ensemble. RandomForestClassifier.html.

```
clf = RandomForestClassifier(n_estimators=20, max_depth=None,\
                             min_samples_split=7, \
                             random_state=0)
```

3. Next, you can fit the classifier on the training dataset using **clf.fit(X_train,y_train)** and use it for prediction on input data using **clf.predict(X)**.

Now that we have discussed the implementation of random forests using scikit-learn, let's train a random forest model on the Shill Bidding dataset and see how it compares to the accuracies obtained from the other classifiers we have trained so far.

EXERCISE 8.03: IMPLEMENTING A RANDOM FOREST MODEL OVER A DATASET

In this exercise, you will use a random forest to build a model over the same auction dataset used previously. Ensure that you use the same Jupyter notebook as the one used for the preceding exercise:

1. Import the random forest classifier:

```
from sklearn.ensemble import RandomForestClassifier
```

2. Fit the random forest classifier to the training data using the following code:

```
clf = RandomForestClassifier(n_estimators=20, max_depth=None,\
                             min_samples_split=7, random_state=0)
clf.fit(X_train,y_train)
```

You will get the following output by running the preceding code. Please note the output may vary on your system.

```
RandomForestClassifier(min_samples_split=7, n_estimators=20, random_
state=0)
```

3. Calculate the accuracy score:

```
clf.score(X_test, y_test)
```

You should get an output close to **0.9896**, which means that the random forest classifier scores an accuracy of around 99%.

Now that you have implemented all three classical algorithms on the same dataset, let's do a quick comparison of their accuracies.

CLASSICAL ALGORITHMS – ACCURACY COMPARED

In the previous sections, we covered the mathematics behind each algorithm and learned about their advantages and their disadvantages. Through three exercises, you implemented each algorithm on the same dataset. In *Figure 8.32*, you can see a summary of the accuracy percentages you got. Circling back to the Amazon case study we discussed at the start of the chapter, it is clear that you would choose the decision tree classifier to predict whether a customer will buy a product during sales:

Classifier	Accuracy Percentage
SVM	97.75%
Decision Tree	99.81%
Random Forest	98.96%

Figure 8.32: Accuracy percentages compared

Let's test the skills you have learned so far to perform an activity where you will implement all the algorithms you have learned so far. Later, you will learn why accuracy is not necessarily the only factor in choosing the model.

ACTIVITY 8.01: IMPLEMENTING DIFFERENT CLASSIFICATION ALGORITHMS

In this activity, you will continue working with the telecom dataset (**Telco_Churn_Data.csv**) that you used in the previous chapter and will build different models from this dataset using the scikit-learn API. Your marketing team was impressed with the initial findings, and they now want you to build a machine learning model that can predict customer churn. This model will be used by the marketing team to send out discount coupons to customers who may churn. To build the best prediction model, it is important to try different algorithms and come up with the best-performing algorithm for the marketing team to use. In this activity, you will use the logistic regression, SVM, and random forest algorithms and compare the accuracies obtained from the three classifiers.

> **NOTE**
>
> In *Activity 7.02*, *Performing MN of OSEMN*, you saved the seven most important features to the **top7_features** variable. You will use these features to build our machine learning model. Please continue from the **Activity8.01_starter.ipynb** notebook present at https://packt. link/buxSG to implement the steps given in the following section.

Follow these steps:

1. Import the libraries for the logistic regression, decision tree, SVM, and random forest algorithms.

2. Fit individual models to the **clf_logistic**, **clf_svm**, **clf_decision**, and **clf_random** variables.

   Use the following parameters to ensure your results are more or less close to ours: for the logistic regression model, use **random_state=0** and **solver='lbfgs'**; for the SVM, use **kernel='linear'** and C=1; and for the random forest model, use **n_estimators=20**, **max_depth=None**, **min_samples_split=7**, and **random_state=0**.

3. Use the **score** function to get the accuracy for each of the algorithms.

You should get accuracy scores similar to the ones listed in the following figure for each of the models at the end of this activity:

Algorithm	Accuracy
Logistic Regression	0.745
SVM	0.765
Decision Tree	0.748
Random Forest	0.810

Figure 8.33: Comparison of different algorithm accuracies on the telecom dataset

> **NOTE**
>
> The solution for this activity can be found on page 560.

PREPROCESSING DATA FOR MACHINE LEARNING MODELS

Preprocessing data before training any machine learning model can improve the accuracy of the model to a large extent. Therefore, it is important to preprocess data before training a machine learning algorithm on the dataset. Preprocessing data consists of the following methods: standardization, scaling, and normalization. Let's look at these methods one by one.

STANDARDIZATION

Most machine learning algorithms assume that all features are centered at zero and have variance in the same order. In the case of linear models such as logistic and linear regression, some of the parameters used in the objective function assume that all the features are centered around zero and have unit variance. If the values of a feature are much higher than some of the other features, then that feature might dominate the objective function and the estimator may not be able to learn from other features. In such cases, standardization can be used to rescale features such that they have a mean of 0 and a variance of 1. The following formula is used for standardization:

$$x^i(std) = \frac{x^i - \mu_x}{\sigma_x}$$

Figure 8.34: Standardization

Here, x^i is the input data, μ_x is the mean, and σ_x is the standard deviation. Standardization is most useful for optimization algorithms such as gradient descent. The scikit-learn API has the **StandardScalar** utility class. Let's see how you can standardize the data using the **StandardScalar** utility class in the next exercise, where you will use the churn prediction data used in *Chapter 7, Supervised Learning: Predicting Customer Churn*. We provide the following sample implementation using the **StandardScalar** utility class:

1. Import the **preprocessing** library from scikit-learn. This has the **StandardScalar** utility class' implementation:

```
from sklearn import preprocessing
```

2. Next, fit the scaler on a set of values – these values are typically the attributes of the training dataset:

```
scaler = preprocessing.StandardScalar().fit(X_train)
```

3. Once you have the scaler ready, you can use it to transform both the training and test dataset attributes:

```
X_train_scalar=scaler.transform(X_train)
X_test_scalar=scaler.transform(X_test)
```

Now, you will use these same steps for standardizing the data in the bank churn prediction problem in the next exercise.

EXERCISE 8.04: STANDARDIZING DATA

For this exercise, you will use the bank churn prediction data that was used in *Chapter 7, Supervised Learning: Predicting Customer Churn*. In the previous chapter, you performed feature selection using a random forest. The features selected for your bank churn prediction data are **Age**, **EstimatedSalary**, **CreditScore**, **Balance**, and **NumOfProducts**.

In this exercise, your objective will be to standardize the data after you have carried out feature selection. On exploring the previous chapter, it was clear that data is not standardized; therefore in this exercise, you will implement **StandardScalar** to standardize the data to zero mean and unit variance. Ensure that you use the same notebook as the one used for the preceding two exercises. You can copy the notebook from this link: https://packt.link/R0vtb:

1. Import the **preprocessing** library:

```
from sklearn import preprocessing
```

2. View the first five rows, which have the **Age**, **EstimatedSalary**, **CreditScore**, **Balance**, and **NumOfProducts** features:

```
X_train[top5_features].head()
```

You will get the following output:

	Age	EstimatedSalary	CreditScore	Balance	NumOfProducts
490	29.0	196356.17	591	97541.24	1
5555	39.0	164018.98	614	0.00	2
9235	27.0	80587.27	462	176913.52	1
6594	40.0	57817.84	747	0.00	1
6671	49.0	187811.71	677	0.00	2

Figure 8.35: First few rows of top5_features

3. Fit the **StandardScalar** function on the **X_train** data using the following code:

```
scaler = preprocessing.StandardScaler()\
                        .fit(X_train[top5_features])
```

4. Check the mean and scaled values. Use the following code to show the mean values of the five columns:

```
scaler.mean_
```

You should get the following output:

```
array([3.89098824e+01, 1.00183902e+05, 6.49955882e+02,
7.61412119e+04, 1.52882353e+00])
```

5. Now check the scaled values:

```
scaler.scale_
```

You should get the following output:

```
array([1.03706201e+01, 5.74453373e+04, 9.64815072e+01,
6.24292333e+04, 5.80460085e-01])
```

The preceding output shows the scaled values of the five columns. You can notice that the mean values have reduced slightly, making the entire dataset a better scaled-down version of the entire dataset.

> **NOTE**
>
> You can read more about the preceding two functions at https://scikit-learn.
> org/stable/modules/generated/sklearn.preprocessing.StandardScaler.html.

6. Apply the **transform** function to the **X_train** data. This function performs standardization by centering and scaling the training data:

```
X_train_scalar=scaler.transform(X_train[top5_features])
```

7. Next, apply the **transform** function to the **X_test** data and check the output:

```
X_test_scalar=scaler.transform(X_test[top5_features])
X_train_scalar
```

You will get the following output on checking the scalar transform data:

```
array([[-0.95557279,  1.67415272, -0.61105889,  0.34278858, -0.91104202],
       [ 0.00868971,  1.11123166, -0.37267123, -1.21964035,  0.81172932],
       [-1.14842529, -0.3411353 , -1.94810268,  1.61418462, -0.91104202],
       ...,
       [-0.56986779, -0.72635385,  0.36322108, -1.21964035, -0.91104202],
       [-0.37701529, -1.47154105,  0.91254915, -1.21964035, -0.91104202],
       [-0.08773654, -0.55862971, -1.11892823, -0.16336821, -0.91104202]])
```

Figure 8.36: Scalar transformed data

As you can notice in the preceding output, the values have now been changed after standardization. It's also important to note here that just by seeing the values, no significant inference can be made after standardization. In the next section, you will go over another method of data preprocessing, scaling, where you will see the values getting scaled to a specific range.

SCALING

Scaling is another method for preprocessing your data. Scaling your data cause the features to lie between a certain minimum and maximum value, mostly between zero and one. As a result, the maximum absolute value of each feature is scaled.

It's important to point out here that **StandardScaler** focuses on scaling down the standard deviation of the dataset to 1, and that's why the effect on the mean is not significant. However, scaling focuses on bringing down the values directly to a given range – mostly from 0 to 1.

Scaling can be effective for the machine learning algorithms that use the Euclidean distance, such as **K-Nearest Neighbors** (**KNN**) or *k*-means clustering:

$$x^i(norm) = \frac{x^i - x_{min}}{x_{max} - x_{min}}$$

Figure 8.37: Equation for scaling data

Here, x^i is the input data, x_{min} is the minimum value of the feature, and x_{max} is the maximum value of the feature. In scikit-learn, you use **MinMaxScaler** or **MaxAbsScaler** for scaling the data. Let's quickly see how to implement this using scikit-learn:

1. Import the **preprocessing** library from scikit-learn. This has the **MinMaxScaler** utility's implementation:

   ```
   from sklearn import preprocessing
   ```

2. Similar to the usage of **StandardScaler**, you will fit the scaler on training attributes:

   ```
   scaler = preprocessing.MinMaxScaler().fit(X_train)
   ```

3. Once you have the scaler ready, you can use it to transform both the training and test datasets' attributes:

   ```
   X_train_scalar=scaler.transform(X_train)
   X_test_scalar=scaler.transform(X_test)
   ```

Now, you can use these same steps to scale the data in the bank churn prediction problem in the exercise that follows.

> **NOTE**
>
> You can read more about the **MinMaxScaler** and **MaxAbsScaler** at https://scikit-learn.org/stable/modules/generated/sklearn.preprocessing.MinMaxScaler.html and https://scikit-learn.org/stable/modules/generated/sklearn.preprocessing.MaxAbsScaler.html.

EXERCISE 8.05: SCALING DATA AFTER FEATURE SELECTION

In this exercise, your objective is to scale data after feature selection. You will use the same bank churn prediction data to perform scaling. Ensure that you continue using the same Jupyter notebook. You can refer to *Figure 8.35* to examine the top five features:

1. Fit the **min_max** scaler on the training data:

```
min_max = preprocessing.MinMaxScaler().fit(X_train[top5_features])
```

2. Check the minimum and scaled values:

```
min_max.min_
```

You will get the following mean values:

```
array([-2.43243243e-01, -5.79055300e-05, -7.00000000e-01,
        0.00000000e+00, -3.33333333e-01])
```

Notice that **MinMaxScaler** has forced the dataset to change the minimum value to 0. This is because, by default, **MinMaxScaler** scales down the values to a range of 0 to 1. As pointed out earlier, **StandardScaler** changes the standard deviation, whereas **MinMaxScaler** directly changes the values with the intent of changing the upper and lower bounds of the dataset.

3. Now check the scaled values:

```
min_max.scale_
```

You will get the following scaled values:

```
array([1.35135135e-02, 5.00047755e-06, 2.00000000e-03, 3.98568200e-
06, 3.33333333e-01])
```

4. Transform the train and test data using **min_max**:

```
X_train_min_max=min_max.transform(X_train[top5_features])
X_test_min_max=min_max.transform(X_test[top5_features])
```

In this exercise, you saw how to perform scaling using the scikit-learn module's **MinMaxScaler**. Next, you will learn about the third method of data preprocessing – normalization.

NORMALIZATION

In normalization, individual training samples are scaled to have a unit norm. (The norm of a vector is the size or length of the vector. Hence, each of the training samples' vector lengths will be scaled to 1.) This method is mostly used when you want to use a quadratic form such as the dot product or any kernel to quantify sample similarity. It is most effective in clustering and text classification.

You use either the L1 norm or the L2 norm for normalization. The L1 norm is used to find the sum of the "magnitudes" of vectors, that's why you have the "absolute" part there in the equation. The L2 norm, on the other hand, finds the sum of the squares of values and then takes the square root to calculate the norm of the vector.

In general, the L2 norm is preferred simply because it's much faster compared to the L1 norm because of the implementation:

L1 Norm:

$$\|x\|_1 = \sum_i |x_i|$$

L2 Norm:

$$\|x\|_2 = \sqrt{\sum_i |x_i|^2}$$

Figure 8.38: Normalization

x_i is the input training samples.

> **NOTE**
>
> In scikit-learn, you use the **Normalize** and **Normalizer** utility classes. The difference between the two normalizations is out of the scope of this chapter.

You can use the **Normalizer** class in scikit-learn as follows:

1. Import the **preprocessing** library from scikit-learn. This has the **Normalizer** utility's implementation:

```
from sklearn import preprocessing
```

2. Similar to the usage of **StandardScaler**, you will fit the **Normalizer** class on the training attributes:

```
normalize = preprocessing.Normalizer().fit(X_train)
```

3. Once you have the **Normalizer** ready, you can use it to transform both the training and test dataset attributes:

```
X_train_normalize=normalize.transform(X_train)
X_test_normalize=normalize.transform(X_test)
```

Now that you have covered the theory of normalization, let's use the utility functions available in scikit-learn to perform normalization in the next exercise.

EXERCISE 8.06: PERFORMING NORMALIZATION ON DATA

In this exercise, you are required to normalize data after feature selection. You will use the same bank churn prediction data for normalizing. Continue using the same Jupyter notebook as the one used in the preceding exercise:

1. Fit the **Normalizer()** on the training data:

```
normalize = preprocessing.Normalizer()\
                        .fit(X_train[top5_features])
```

2. Check the **normalize** function:

```
normalize
```

This will give you the following output:

```
Normalizer()
```

3. Transform the training and testing data using **normalize**:

```
X_train_normalize=normalize.transform(X_train[top5_features])
X_test_normalize=normalize.transform(X_test[top5_features])
```

You can verify that the norm has now changed to **1** using the following code:

```
np.sqrt(np.sum(X_train_normalize**2, axis=1))
```

This gives the following output:

```
array([1., 1., 1., ..., 1., 1., 1.])
```

4. Similarly, you can also evaluate the norm of the normalized test dataset:

```
np.sqrt(np.sum(X_test_normalize**2, axis=1))
```

This gives the following output:

```
array([1., 1., 1., ..., 1., 1., 1.])
```

In the preceding exercise, you carried out data normalization using an L2-norm-based **Normalizer**. That completes the implementation of the three data preprocessing techniques. It's also important to note here that you do not need to perform all three preprocessing techniques; any one of the three methods would suffice. While these methods are carried out before feeding the data to a model for training, you will next discuss the methods for evaluating the model once it has been trained. This will help in choosing the best model out of a given set of models.

MODEL EVALUATION

When you train your model, you usually split the data into training and testing datasets. This is to ensure that the model doesn't overfit. **Overfitting** refers to a phenomenon where a model performs very well on the training data but fails to give good results on testing data, or in other words, the model fails to generalize.

In scikit-learn, you have a function known as **train_test_split** that splits the data into training and testing sets randomly.

When evaluating your model, you start by changing the parameters to improve the accuracy as per your test data. There is a high chance of leaking some of the information from the testing set into your training set if you optimize your parameters using only the testing set data. To avoid this, you can split data into three parts—training, testing, and validation sets. However, the disadvantage of this technique is that you will be further reducing your training dataset.

The solution is to use **cross-validation**. In this process, you do not need a separate validation dataset; instead, you split your dataset into training and testing data. However, the training data is split into k smaller sets using a technique called k-fold cross-validation, which can be explained using the following figure:

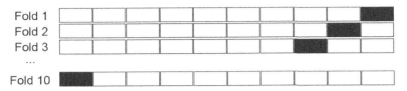

Figure 8.39: K-fold cross-validation

The algorithm is as follows. Assume **k=10**; that is, you will have 10 folds, as shown in the preceding figure:

1. The entire training data is divided into k folds, in this case, it's 10. In the preceding figure, you can see all the 10 folds, and each fold having 10 separations of the dataset.

2. The model is trained on *k-1* portions (white blocks highlighted in the preceding figure, with the black blocks signifying the untrained portion). In this case, you will be training the model on 9 different portions in each fold. You can notice that the black blocks are at different positions in each of the 10 folds, thus signifying that different portions are being trained in each fold.

3. Once the model is trained, the classifier is evaluated on the remaining 1 portion (black blocks highlighted in the preceding figure).

    Steps 2 and *3* are repeated **k** times. This is why you have 10 folds in the preceding figure.

4. Once the classifier has carried out the evaluation, an overall average score is taken.

This method doesn't work well if you have a **class imbalance**, and therefore you use a method known as **stratified K fold**.

> ### NOTE
>
> In many classification problems, you will find that classes are not equally distributed. One class may be highly represented, that is, 90%, while another class may consist of only 10% of the samples. For example, when dealing with a dataset containing information about the products purchased on an e-commerce website to predict whether a purchase will be returned or not, the percentage of returned orders will be significantly smaller than the non-returned ones. We will cover how to deal with imbalanced datasets in the next chapter.

You use stratified k-fold to deal with datasets where there is a class imbalance. In datasets where there is a class imbalance, during splitting, care must be taken to maintain class proportions. In the case of stratified k-fold, it maintains the ratio of classes in each portion.

In order to implement stratified k-fold cross-validation, use the following steps:

1. Import **StratifiedKFold** from the scikit-learn module:

    ```
    from sklearn.model_selection import StratifiedKFold
    ```

2. Create a **StratifiedKFold** instance. You can choose the value of the number of splits you want to make (*k*) and set a random state to make the results reproducible:

    ```
    skf = StratifiedKFold(n_splits=10, random_state=1)
    ```

3. Next, use the instance created in *step 2* to split the **X** and **y** values:

    ```
    skf.split(X, y)
    ```

Now that we have discussed the details of cross-validation, stratified k-fold cross-validation, and its implementation, let's apply it to the bank churn prediction dataset in the next exercise.

EXERCISE 8.07: STRATIFIED K-FOLD

In this exercise, you will fit the stratified k-fold function of scikit-learn to the bank churn prediction data and use the logistic regression classifier from the previous exercise to fit our k-fold data. Along with that, you will also implement the scikit-learn k-fold cross-validation scorer function:

> **NOTE**
>
> Please continue using the same notebook as the one used for the preceding exercise.

1. Import **StratifiedKFold** from **sklearn**:

```
from sklearn.model_selection import StratifiedKFold
```

2. Fit the classifier on the training and testing data with **n_splits=10**:

```
skf = StratifiedKFold(n_splits=10)\
    .split(X_train[top5_features].values,y_train.values)
```

3. Calculate the k-cross fold validation score:

```
results=[]
for i, (train,test) in enumerate(skf):
    clf.fit(X_train[top5_features].values[train],\
            y_train.values[train])
    fit_result=clf.score(X_train[top5_features].values[test],\
                    y_train.values[test])
    results.append(fit_result)
    print('k-fold: %2d, Class Ratio: %s, Accuracy: %.4f'\
            % (i,np.bincount(y_train.values[train]),fit_result))
```

You will get the following result:

```
k-fold:  0, Class Ratio: [6092 1558], Accuracy: 0.7894
k-fold:  1, Class Ratio: [6092 1558], Accuracy: 0.7918
k-fold:  2, Class Ratio: [6092 1558], Accuracy: 0.7882
k-fold:  3, Class Ratio: [6092 1558], Accuracy: 0.7929
k-fold:  4, Class Ratio: [6092 1558], Accuracy: 0.7882
k-fold:  5, Class Ratio: [6092 1558], Accuracy: 0.7988
k-fold:  6, Class Ratio: [6092 1558], Accuracy: 0.7824
k-fold:  7, Class Ratio: [6092 1558], Accuracy: 0.7894
k-fold:  8, Class Ratio: [6092 1558], Accuracy: 0.7800
k-fold:  9, Class Ratio: [6093 1557], Accuracy: 0.7941
```

Figure 8.40: Calculate the k-cross fold validation score

You can see that the class ratio has stayed constant across all the k-folds.

4. Find the accuracy:

```
print('accuracy for CV is:%.3f' % np.mean(results))
```

You will get an output showing an accuracy close to **0.790**.

5. Import the scikit-learn **cross_val_score** function:

```
from sklearn.model_selection import cross_val_score
```

6. Fit the classifier and print the accuracy:

```
results_cross_val_score=cross_val_score\
                    (estimator=clf,\
                     X=X_train[top5_features].values,\
                     y=y_train.values,cv=10,n_jobs=1)
print('accuracy for CV is:%.3f '\
      % np.mean(results_cross_val_score))
```

You will get an output showing the accuracy as **0.790**. Even though both the accuracies are the same, it is still recommended to use stratified k-fold validation when there is a class imbalance.

In this exercise, you implemented k-fold cross-validation using two methods, one where you used a **for** loop and another where you used the **cross_val_score** function of **sklearn**. You used logistic regression as your base classifier present in the **clf** variable from *Exercise 7.08, Building a Logistic Regression Model*, in *Chapter 7, Supervised Learning: Predicting Customer Churn*. From the cross-validation, your logistic regression gave an accuracy of around 79% overall.

In this section, we covered an important aspect of model evaluation. You can use the same concept to make your models better by tweaking the hyperparameters that define the model. In the next section, you will go over this concept, which is also referred to as fine-tuning.

FINE-TUNING OF THE MODEL

In the case of a machine learning model, there are two types of parameter tuning that can be performed:

- The first one includes the parameters that the model uses to learn from itself, such as the *coefficients* in the case of linear regression or the *margin* in the case of SVM.

- The second one includes parameters that must be optimized separately. These are known as **hyperparameters**, for example, the *alpha* value in the case of lasso linear regression or the *number of leaf nodes* in the case of decision trees. In the case of a machine learning model, there can be several hypermeters and hence it becomes difficult for someone to tune the model by adjusting each of the hyperparameters manually. Consider a scenario where you have built a decision tree for predicting whether a given product will be returned by a customer or not. However, while building the model, you used the default values of the hyperparameters. You notice that you are obtaining a mediocre accuracy of 75%. While you can move on to the next classifier, for example, a random forest, it's important to first make sure that you have got the best result you could using the same class of classifier (a decision tree in this case). This is because there is a limit to the different categories of classifiers you can build, and if you keep on going for default values, you won't always come up with the best results. Optimizing the model performance by changing the hyperparameters helps in getting the best results from the classifier you are working on and thus gives you a better sample space of models to choose the best model from.

There are two methods for performing hypermeter search operations in scikit-learn, which are described as follows:

- **Grid search**: Grid search uses a brute-force exhaustive search to permute all combinations of hyperparameters, which are provided to it as a list of values.

- **Randomized grid search**: Randomized grid search is a faster alternative to grid search, which can be very slow due to the use of brute force. In this method, parameters are randomly chosen from a distribution that the user provides. Additionally, the user can provide a sampling iteration specified by **n_iter**, which is used as a computational budget.

In the cases of both grid search and randomized grid search, the implementation using scikit-learn stays more or less the same:

1. Import **GridSearchCV** and **RandomizedSearchCV** from the scikit-learn module:

```
from sklearn.model_selection import GridSearchCV, RandomizedSearchCV
```

2. Specify the hyperparameters you want to run the search on:

```
parameters = [ {'kernel': ['linear'], 'C':[0.1, 1, 10]}, \
               {'kernel': ['rbf'], 'gamma':[0.5, 1, 2], \
                'C':[0.1, 1, 10]}]
```

3. Create instances of **GridSearchCV** and **RandomizedSearchCV**, specifying the estimator (classifier) to use and the list of hyperparameters. You can also choose to specify the method of cross-validation you want to use, for example with imbalanced data, you can go for **StratifiedKFold** cross-validation:

```
clf = GridSearchCV(svm.SVC(), parameters)
clf_random = RandomizedSearchCV(svm.SVC(), parameters)
```

4. Next, fit the preceding instances of grid search and randomized grid search on the training dataset:

```
clf.fit(X_train,y_train)
clf_random.fit(X_train,y_train)
```

5. You can then obtain the best score and the list of best hyperparameters, shown as follows:

```
print(clf.best_score_, clf_random.best_score_)
print(clf.best_params_, clf_random.best_params_)
```

In this section, we discussed the concept of fine-tuning a model using grid search and randomized grid search. You also saw how to implement both methods using the scikit-learn module. Now it's time to use these skills to fine-tune an SVM model on the bank churn prediction data you have been working on.

EXERCISE 8.08: FINE-TUNING A MODEL

In this exercise, you will implement a grid search to find out the best parameters for an SVM on the bank churn prediction data. You will continue using the same notebook as in the preceding exercise:

1. Import **SVM**, **GridSearchCV**, and **StratifiedKfold**:

```
from sklearn import svm
from sklearn.model_selection import GridSearchCV
from sklearn.model_selection import StratifiedKFold
```

2. Specify the parameters for the grid search as follows:

```
parameters = [{'kernel': ['linear'], 'C':[0.1, 1]}, \
              {'kernel': ['rbf'], 'C':[0.1, 1]}]
```

3. Fit the grid search with **StratifiedKFold**, setting the parameter as **n_splits = 3**.

> **NOTE**
>
> Due to the large number of combinations of the parameters mentioned above, the model fitting can take up to 2 hours.

```
clf = GridSearchCV(svm.SVC(), parameters, \
                   cv = StratifiedKFold(n_splits = 3),\
                   verbose=4,n_jobs=-1)
clf.fit(X_train[top5_features], y_train)
```

The preceding step gives the following output:

```
GridSearchCV(cv=StratifiedKFold(n_splits=3, random_state=None, shuffle=False),
             error_score=nan,
             estimator=SVC(C=1.0, break_ties=False, cache_size=200,
                           class_weight=None, coef0=0.0,
                           decision_function_shape='ovr', degree=3,
                           gamma='scale', kernel='rbf', max_iter=-1,
                           probability=False, random_state=None, shrinking=Tru
e,
                           tol=0.001, verbose=False),
             iid='deprecated', n_jobs=-1,
             param_grid=[{'C': [0.1, 1], 'kernel': ['linear']},
                         {'C': [0.1, 1], 'kernel': ['rbf']}],
             pre_dispatch='2*n_jobs', refit=True, return_train_score=False,
             scoring=None, verbose=4)
```

Figure 8.41: Fitting the model

4. Print the best score and the best parameters:

```
print('best score train:', clf.best_score_)
print('best parameters train: ', clf.best_params_)
```

You will get the following output:

```
best score train: 0.7963529355398448
best parameters train:  {'C': 0.1, 'kernel': 'rbf'}
```

Figure 8.42: The best score and parameters obtained from the grid search

> **NOTE**
>
> Grid search takes a lot of time to find out the optimum parameters, and hence, the search parameters given should be wisely chosen.

From this exercise, you can conclude that the best parameters chosen by the grid search were **C:0.1**, **Gamma:0.5**, and **kernel:rbf**

From the exercise, you saw how model tuning helps to achieve higher accuracy. Firstly, you implemented data preprocessing, which is the first step to improve the accuracy of a model. Later, you learned how cross-validation and grid search enable you to further tune the machine learning model and improve the accuracy. Now it's time for you to use these skills to fine-tune and optimize the random forest model you trained in *Activity 8.01, Implementing Different Classification Algorithms*.

ACTIVITY 8.02: TUNING AND OPTIMIZING THE MODEL

The models you built in the previous activity produced good results, especially the random forest model, which produced an accuracy score of more than 80%. You now need to improve the accuracy of the random forest model and generalize it. Tuning the model using different preprocessing steps, cross-validation, and grid search will improve the accuracy of the model. You will be using the same Jupyter notebook as the one used in the preceding activity. Follow these steps:

1. Store five out of seven features, that is, **Avg_Calls_Weekdays**, **Current_Bill_Amt**, **Avg_Calls**, **Account_Age**, and **Avg_Days_Delinquent**, in a variable called **top5_features**. Store the other two features, **Percent_Increase_MOM** and **Complaint_Code**, in a variable called **top2_features**. These features have values in the range of −1 to 7, whereas the other five features have values in the range of 0 to 374457. Hence, you can leave these features and standardize the remaining five features.

2. Use **StandardScalar** to standardize the five features.

3. Create a variable called **X_train_scalar_combined**, and combine the standardized five features with the two features (**Percent_Increase_MOM** and **Complaint_Code**) that were not standardized.

4. Apply the same scalar standardization to the test data (**X_test_scalar_combined**).

5. Fit the random forest model.

6. Score the random forest model. You should get a value close to **0.81**.

7. Import the library for grid search and use the following parameters:

```
parameters = [ {'min_samples_split': [9,10], \
                'n_estimators':[100,150,160]
                'max_depth': [5,7]}]
```

8. Use grid search cross-validation with stratified k-fold to find out the best parameters. Use **StratifiedKFold(n_splits = 3)** and **RandomForestClassifier()**.

9. Print the best score and the best parameters. You should get the following values:

```
best score train: 0.8033092269326684
best parameters train:  {'max_depth': 7, 'min_samples_split': 10, 'n_estimators': 150}
```

Figure 8.43: Best score and best parameters

10. Score the model using the test data. You should get a score close to **0.824**.

Combining the results of the accuracy score obtained in *Activity 8.01, Implementing Different Classification Algorithms* and *Activity 8.02, Tuning and Optimizing the Model,* here are the results for the random forest implementations:

Algorithm	Accuracy
Random Forest (Default)	0.810
Random Forest (Pre-Processing)	0.811
Random Forest (Grid Search and CV)	0.824

Figure 8.44: Comparing the accuracy of the random forest using different methods

You can conclude that data preprocessing and model-tuning methods can greatly improve model accuracy.

> **NOTE**
>
> The solution for this activity can be found on page 563.

In the preceding sections, you have been using accuracy as the primary evaluation metric, however, there are several other performance metrics. The choice of correct evaluation metric (performance metric) is a very important decision one needs to make. Let's go over the various performance metrics you can use in the next section.

PERFORMANCE METRICS

In the case of classification algorithms, we use a confusion matrix, which gives us the performance of the learning algorithm. It is a square matrix that counts the number of **True Positive (TP)**, **True Negative (TN)**, **False Positive (FP)**, and **False Negative (FN)** outcomes:

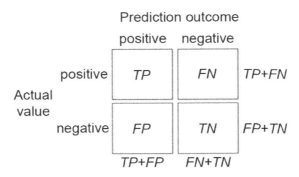

Figure 8.45: Confusion matrix

For the sake of simplicity, let's use 1 as the positive class and 0 as a negative class, then:

TP: The number of cases that were observed and predicted as 1.

FN: The number of cases that were observed as 1 but predicted as 0.

FP: The number of cases that were observed as 0 but predicted as 1.

TN: The number of cases that were observed as 0 and predicted as 0.

Consider the same case study of predicting whether a product will be returned or not. In that case, the preceding metrics can be understood using the following table:

Problem Statement: Given a product purchased by a customer, predict whether it will be returned or not.		**Predicted Result (Item returned or not)**	
		Item returned	Item not returned
Actual Result (Item returned or not)	Item returned	TP	FN
	Item not returned	FP	TN

Figure 8.46: Understanding the metrics

PRECISION

Precision is the ability of a classifier to not label a sample that is negative as positive. The precision for an algorithm is calculated using the following formula:

$$precision = \frac{t_p}{t_p + f_p}$$

Figure 8.47: Precision

This is useful in the case of email spam detection. In this scenario, you do not want any important emails to be detected as spam. In other words, you want to keep FPs as low as possible, even if it means recognizing some spam mails as not spam. In scenarios like these, precision is the recommended evaluation metric to use.

Similar to precision, there is another evaluation metric that is commonly used when you want to reduce FNs as much as possible. Let's go over this evaluation metric in the next section.

RECALL

Recall refers to the ability of a classifier to correctly identify all the positive samples, that is, out of the total pool of positive findings ($t_p + f_n$), how many were correctly identified. This is also known as the **True Positive Rate** (**TPR**) or **sensitivity** and is given by the following formula:

$$Recall = \frac{t_p}{t_p + f_n}$$

Figure 8.48: Recall

This is useful in scenarios where, for example, you want to detect whether a customer will churn or not. In that scenario, you can use the recall score, since your main objective is to detect all the customers who will churn so that you can give them some exciting offers to make sure they stay with your company. Even if the classifier predicts a customer that was not going to leave the company as "churn," the customer will just get an offer for free, which is not a huge loss.

F1 SCORE

This is the harmonic mean of precision and recall. It is given by the following formula:

$$F1 = \frac{precision * Recall}{precision + Recall}$$

Figure 8.49: F1 score

F1 score can be useful when you want to have an optimal blend of precision and recall. For example, referring to the case study of predicting whether an item will be returned or not, imagine the company decides to offer some discount to make sure that an item is not returned (which would mean extra logistics expenses). If you mistakenly predict an item as prone to being returned, the company will have to give a discount even when it was not required, thereby causing a loss to the company. On the other hand, if you mistakenly predict an item as *not to be returned*, the company will have to suffer the logistics expenses, again causing a loss. In situations like this, the F1 score can come to the rescue as it takes into account both precision and recall.

You will also use the **classification_report** utility function present in the scikit-learn library. This report shows a tabular representation of precision, recall, accuracy, and F1 score and helps in summarizing the performance of the classifier. To implement it, follow these steps:

1. Import **classification_report** from scikit-learn's **metrics** module:

   ```
   from sklearn.metrics import classification_report
   ```

2. Next, you can print the classification report by passing the parameters shown as follows:

   ```
   print(classification_report(y_test, y_pred, \
                       target_names=target_names))
   ```

   Here, **y_test** refers to the actual target values, **y_pred** refers to the predicted values, and **target_names** refers to the class names, for example, **Churn** and **No Churn**.

Now that you have gone through the three commonly used evaluation metrics, let's evaluate these metrics for the random forest model trained on the bank churn prediction dataset.

EXERCISE 8.09: EVALUATING THE PERFORMANCE METRICS FOR A MODEL

In this exercise, you will calculate the F1 score and the accuracy of our random forest model for the bank churn prediction dataset. Continue using the same notebook as the one used in the preceding exercise:

1. Import **RandomForestClassifier**, **metrics**, **classification_report**, **confusion matrix**, and **accuracy_score**:

```
from sklearn.ensemble import RandomForestClassifier
from sklearn.metrics import classification_report,confusion_
matrix,accuracy_score
from sklearn import metrics
```

2. Fit the random forest classifier using the following code over the training data:

```
clf_random = RandomForestClassifier(n_estimators=20, \
                                    max_depth=None,\
                                    min_samples_split=7, \
                                    random_state=0)
clf_random.fit(X_train[top5_features],y_train)
```

This code will give the following output on execution:

```
RandomForestClassifier(min_samples_split=7, n_estimators=20, random_
state=0)
```

> **NOTE**
>
> The output may slightly vary on your system.

3. Predict on the test data the classifier:

```
y_pred=clf_random.predict(X_test[top5_features])
```

4. Print the classification report:

```
target_names = ['No Churn', 'Churn']
print(classification_report(y_test, y_pred, \
                            target_names=target_names))
```

Your output will look as follows:

```
              precision    recall  f1-score   support

 No Churn          0.86      0.94      0.90      1194
    Churn          0.65      0.40      0.49       306

 accuracy                             0.83      1500
macro avg          0.75      0.67      0.70      1500
weighted avg       0.82      0.83      0.82      1500
```

Figure 8.50: Classification report

5. Fit the confusion matrix and save it into a pandas DataFrame named **cm_df**:

```
cm = confusion_matrix(y_test, y_pred)
cm_df = pd.DataFrame(cm,\
                index = ['No Churn','Churn'],\
                columns = ['No Churn','Churn'])
```

6. Plot the confusion matrix using the following code:

```
plt.figure(figsize=(8,6))
sns.heatmap(cm_df, annot=True,fmt='g',cmap='Greys_r')
plt.title('Random Forest \nAccuracy:{0:.3f}'\
          .format(accuracy_score(y_test, y_pred)))
plt.ylabel('True Values')
plt.xlabel('Predicted Values')
plt.show()
```

> **NOTE**
>
> The value **Greys_r** (emboldened) is used to generate graphs in grayscale. You can also refer to the following document to get the code for the colored plot and the colored output: http://packt.link/NOjgT.

You should get the following output:

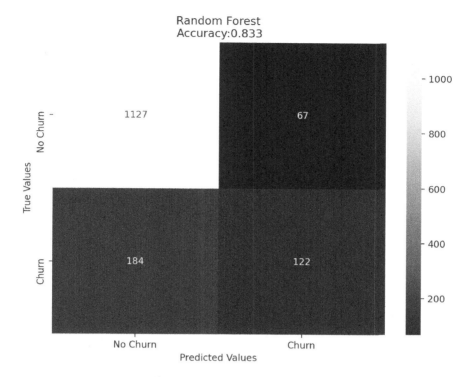

Figure 8.51: Confusion matrix

From this exercise, you can conclude that the random forest model has an overall F1 score of **0.82** (refer to the classification report). However, the F1 score of the customers who have churned is less than 50%. This is due to highly imbalanced data, as a result of which the model fails to generalize. You will learn how to make the model more robust and improve the F1 score for imbalanced data in the next chapter.

ROC CURVE

The **Receiver Operating Characteristic (ROC)** curve is a graphical method used to inspect the performance of binary classification models by shifting the decision threshold of the classifier. It is plotted based on the **TPR** (or recall) and the **False Positivity Rate (FPR)**. You saw what the TPR is in the last section. The FPR is given by the following equation:

$$FPR = \frac{f_p}{f_p + t_n}$$

Figure 8.52: The FPR (1−specificity)

This is equivalent to *1−specificity*.

Specificity is defined as **−ve Recall**.

Negative Recall is the ability of a classifier to correctly find all the negative samples, that is, out of the total pool of negatives (**t**$_n$ + **f**$_p$), how many were correctly identified as negative. It is represented by the following equation:

$$-ve\ Recall = \frac{t_n}{t_n + f_p}$$

Figure 8.53: −ve Recall

The following diagram illustrates how an ROC curve is plotted:

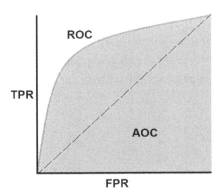

Figure 8.54: ROC curve

The diagonal of the ROC curve represents random guessing. Classifiers that lie below the diagonal are considered to perform worse than random guessing. A perfect classifier would have its ROC curve in the top left corner, having a TPR of **1** and an FPR of **0**.

Now that we have discussed some new evaluation metrics, let's use them in the bank churn prediction dataset for plotting the ROC curve and getting the area under the ROC curve in the next exercise.

EXERCISE 8.10: PLOTTING THE ROC CURVE

In this exercise, you will plot the ROC curve for the random forest model from the previous exercise on the bank churn prediction data. Continue with the same Jupyter notebook as the one used in the preceding exercise:

1. Import `roc_curve,auc`:

```
from sklearn.metrics import roc_curve,auc
```

2. Calculate the TPR, FPR, and threshold using the following code:

```
fpr, tpr, thresholds = roc_curve(y_test, y_pred, pos_label=1)
roc_auc = metrics.auc(fpr, tpr)
```

3. Plot the ROC curve using the following code:

```
plt.figure()
plt.title('Receiver Operating Characteristic')
plt.plot(fpr, tpr, label='%s AUC = %0.2f' % \
        ('Random Forest', roc_auc, color = 'gray'))
plt.plot([0, 1], [0, 1],'k--')
plt.xlim([0.0, 1.0])
plt.ylim([0.0, 1.05])
plt.ylabel('Sensitivity(True Positive Rate)')
plt.xlabel('1-Specificity(False Positive Rate)')
plt.title('Receiver Operating Characteristic')
plt.legend(loc="lower right")
plt.show()
```

> **NOTE**
>
> The **gray** value for the **color** attribute is used to generate the graph in grayscale. You can use values such as **red**, **r**, and so on as values for the **color** parameter to get the colored graphs. You can also refer to the following document to get the code for the colored plot and the colored output: http://packt.link/NOjgT.

Your plot should appear as follows:

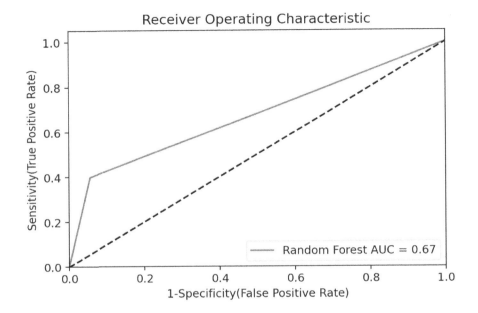

Figure 8.55: ROC curve

From our exercise, it can be concluded that the model has an area under the curve of **0.67**. Even though the F1 score of the model was calculated to be 0.82, from our classification report, the AUC (Area Under Curve) score is much less. The FPR is closer to 0, however, the TPR is closer to 0.4. The AUC curve and the overall F1 score can be greatly improved by preprocessing the data and fine-tuning the model using techniques that you implemented in the previous exercise.

In *Activity 8.02, Tuning and Optimizing the Model*, you saw how using fine-tuning techniques greatly improved your model accuracy. In the final activity for this chapter, you will have to find out the performance of the random forest model and compare the ROC curves of all the models.

ACTIVITY 8.03: COMPARISON OF THE MODELS

In the previous activity, you improved the accuracy score of the random forest model score to 0.82. However, you were not using the correct performance metrics. In this activity, you will have to find out the F1 score of the random forest model trained in the previous activities and also compare the ROC curve of different machine learning models created in *Activity 8.01, Implementing Different Classification Algorithms*.

Ensure that you use the same Jupyter notebook as the one used in the preceding activity. Follow these steps:

1. Import the required libraries.

2. Fit the random forest classifier with the parameters obtained from grid search in the preceding activity. Use the **clf_random_grid** variable.

3. Predict on the standardized scalar test data, **X_test_scalar_combined**.

4. Fit the classification report. You should get the following output:

	precision	recall	f1-score	support
No Churn	0.85	0.80	0.82	364
Churn	0.80	0.85	0.82	343
accuracy			0.82	707
macro avg	0.82	0.82	0.82	707
weighted avg	0.82	0.82	0.82	707

Figure 8.56: Classification report

5. Plot the confusion matrix. Your output should be as follows:

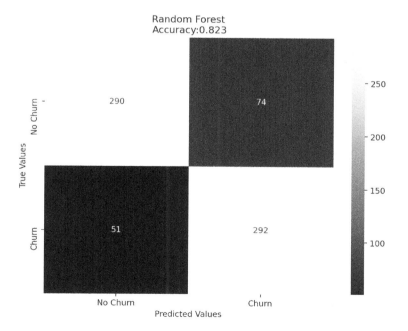

Figure 8.57: Confusion matrix

6. Import the library for the AUC and ROC curve.

7. Use the classifiers that were created in *Activity 8.01, Implementing Different Classification Algorithms*, that is, **clf_logistic**, **clf_svm**, **clf_decision**, and **clf_random_grid**. Create a dictionary of all these models.

8. Plot the ROC curve. The following **for** loop can be used as a hint:

```
for m in models:
    model = m['model']
    ------ FIT THE MODEL
    ------ PREDICT
    ------ FIND THE FPR, TPR AND THRESHOLD
    roc_auc =FIND THE AUC
    plt.plot(fpr, tpr, label='%s AUC = %0.2f' \
            % (m['label'], roc_auc))
plt.plot([0, 1], [0, 1],'r--')
plt.xlim([0.0, 1.0])
plt.ylim([0.0, 1.05])
plt.ylabel('Sensitivity(True Positive Rate)')
plt.xlabel('1-Specificity(False Positive Rate)')
plt.title('Receiver Operating Characteristic')
plt.legend(loc="lower right")
plt.show()
```

You plot should look as follows:

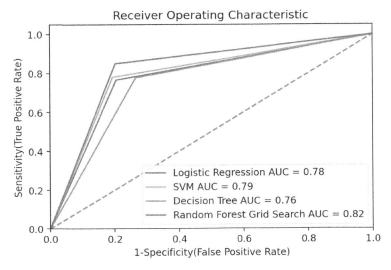

Figure 8.58: ROC curve

> **NOTE**
>
> The solution for this activity can be found on page 566.

SUMMARY

In this chapter, you learned how to perform classification using some of the most commonly used algorithms. After discovering how tree-based models work, you were able to calculate information gain, Gini values, and entropy. You applied these concepts to train decision tree and random forest models on two datasets.

Later in the chapter, you explored why the preprocessing of data using techniques such as standardization is necessary. You implemented various fine-tuning techniques for optimizing a machine learning model. Next, you identified the right performance metrics for your classification problems and visualized performance summaries using a confusion matrix. You also explored other evaluation metrics including precision, recall, F1 score, ROC curve, and the area under the curve.

You implemented these techniques on case studies such as the telecom dataset and customer churn prediction and discovered how similar approaches can be followed in predicting whether a customer will buy a product or not during a sales season.

In the next chapter, you will learn about multi-classification problems and how to tackle imbalanced data.

9

MULTICLASS CLASSIFICATION ALGORITHMS

OVERVIEW

In this chapter, you will learn how to identify and implement the algorithms that will help you solve multiclass classification problems in marketing analytics. You will be going through the different types of classifiers and implementing them using the scikit-learn library in Python. Next, you will learn to interpret the micro- and macro-performance metrics that are used to evaluate the performance of a classifier in multiclass problems. Moreover, you will be learning about different sampling techniques to solve the problem of imbalanced data. By the end of this chapter, you will be able to apply different kinds of algorithms and evaluation metrics to solve multiclass classification problems.

INTRODUCTION

The online shopping company you worked with in the previous chapter is busy planning a new feature. Currently, whenever customers search for a product on their website or their app, they are shown the desired product along with options to buy the same product from different sellers. For example, if a customer is looking for a washing machine, they'll get options to buy the product from seller A, seller B, seller C, and so on. Now, the company wants to predict which seller a specific user would be more inclined to buy the product from. They'll then make the most preferred seller a part of their "Verified Seller" program, thus showing that seller as the first option to users. This, in turn, will help the company increase the chances that the product will be bought by the user, consequently leading to an increase in the company's profits. The company is first targeting washing machines for this task, and they have shortlisted four suppliers to solve this problem.

By instinct, you might be inclined to use what you learned about in previous chapters. After all, by now, you should have quite a few techniques in your marketing analyst toolbox. Recall how, as you have worked through this book, you have learned about common classification algorithms such as logistic regression, **support vector machine** (**SVM**), decision tree, and random forest. You also learned about the advantages and disadvantages of each of these algorithms. You implemented these algorithms using the most popular machine learning API, **scikit-learn**. Later, you fine-tuned, optimized, and evaluated different machine learning models. However, much to your dismay, none of these techniques will help you solve this problem.

Remember that while talking about binary classification algorithms, we discussed a problem statement where you had to predict whether a product bought during the sales season will be returned or not. For such problems, binary classifications work quite well as there are two classes (*product returned* and *product not returned*). But what about cases where there are more than two classes?

In the scenario you just saw, you have four possible correct answers (the four sellers) for every input data. It's in cases like these that binary classification algorithms suffer. For these types of problems, you cannot use techniques such as logistic regression. Such problems are referred to as **multiclass classification problems**.

In this chapter, you will start by exploring multiclass classification. Then, you will deep dive into the intuition behind multiclass classification problems and see how to tackle class-imbalanced data. Finally, you will create a multiclass classification classifier. A dataset is considered **class-imbalanced** if a specific class has more samples compared to other classes.

You will primarily be using a dataset obtained from a UK-based online store for training models to give customer segment-focused discounts rather than a general discount.

Let's first start with getting a deeper understanding of multiclass classification and its categories.

UNDERSTANDING MULTICLASS CLASSIFICATION

The classification algorithms that you have seen so far were mostly binary classifiers, where the target variable can have only two categorical values or classes. However, there can be scenarios where you have more than two classes to classify samples into. For instance, given data on customer transactions, the marketing team may be tasked with identifying the credit card most suitable for a customer, such as cashback, air miles, gas station, or shopping. In scenarios such as these, where you have more than two classes, a slightly different approach is required compared to binary classification.

Multiclass classification problems can broadly be divided into the following three categories:

- **Multiclass classification**: Multiclass classification problems involve classifying instances or samples into one class out of multiple classes (more than two). Each sample is assigned only one label and cannot be assigned more than one label at a time. For example, a product can be bought from only one seller.

- **Multilabel classification**: In the case of multilabel classification, each sample is assigned a set of target labels. For example, given some movie that you want to advertise, there can be multiple genres it can be categorized into – horror, comedy, thriller, and more.

- **Multioutput regression**: In the case of multioutput regression, each sample is assigned several target variables with different properties. For instance, given a specific product, you might be asked to predict the number of purchases, the number of returns, the percentage discount applied to each purchase, and more.

In this chapter, you will be focusing only on the first category – multiclass classification – since that's the most common problem statement you will encounter as a marketing analyst. The other two categories are out of the scope of this book. Let's start by understanding what the classifiers that can be used in multiclass classification are and how to implement them using the scikit-learn library in Python.

CLASSIFIERS IN MULTICLASS CLASSIFICATION

Let's consider two problem statements:

- An online trading company wants to provide additional benefits to its customers. The marketing analytics team has divided the customers into five categories based on when the last time they logged in to the platform was.

- The same trading company wants to build a recommendation system for mutual funds. This will recommend their users a mutual fund based on the risk they are willing to take, the amount they are planning to invest, and some other features. The number of mutual funds is well above 100.

Before you jump into more detail about the differences between these two problem statements, let's first understand the two common ways of approaching multiclass classification.

Multiclass classification can be implemented by scikit-learn in the following two ways:

One-versus-all (one-versus-rest) classifier: Here, one classifier is fit against one class. For each of the classifiers, the class is then fit against all the other classes, producing a real-valued decision confidence score, instead of class labels. From the decision confidence score, the maximum value is picked up to get the final class label. The advantage of one-versus-all is its interpretability and efficiency. The following figure illustrates how this classifier works, where there is one classifier for each class to predict whether the data point will lie in the specific class or any of the left-out classes. Therefore, instead of just one classifier, you have three classifiers (for the three classes):

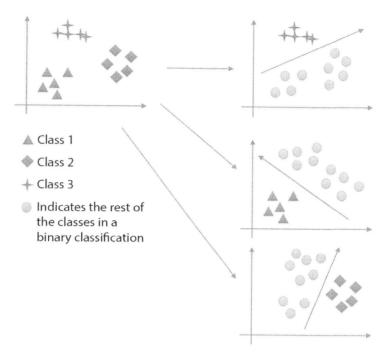

Figure 9.1: Diagram of the working of a one-versus-all classifier

A one-versus-all classifier can be implemented using the scikit-learn module by performing the following steps:

1. First, define the classifier type. All the classifiers that will be created for the one-versus-all classifier approach will only be of this type. For example, if you were to use SVM for the multiclassification problem, all the classifiers would be SVM classifiers. To create a logistic regression model, you can import the **LogisticRegression** model from scikit-learn as follows:

```
from sklearn.linear_model import LogisticRegression
```

2. You can then create the one-versus-all classifier by importing **OneVsRestClassifier** from scikit-learn and using it on the base model. Here, the base model is **LogisticRegression**:

```
from sklearn.multiclass import OneVsRestClassifier
ovr = OneVsRestClassifier(LogisticRegression())
```

3. Like the other models discussed in previous chapters, you can now fit the model created in the previous step on the training data using the following code:

```
ovr.fit(X_train,y_train)
```

4. You can use the one-versus-all classifier for prediction as well, as shown in the following code, using the **predict** function, as you have seen before in binary classification problems:

```
ovr.predict(X)
```

One-versus-one classifier: This constructs one classifier per pair of classes. The intuitive idea is to develop a binary classifier for each possible pair of classes, derive the decision boundary between these two classes, and build an ensemble. During prediction, the label is assigned by majority voting and in the event of a tie, the class with the highest aggregate classification confidence is selected. Majority voting, as a quick reminder, is the concept of taking the most frequent class output by each decision tree or each classifier.

The total number of classifiers that are generated using the one-versus-one technique is **N* (N-1) /2**, where **N** is the number of classes.

The implementation of the one-versus-one classifier using the scikit-learn module follows the same steps as the one-versus-all classifier. The only difference is that this time, you will need to import **OneVsOneClassifier** from scikit-learn and use it on the base model:

```
from sklearn.linear_model import LogisticRegression
from sklearn.multiclass import OneVsOneClassifier
ovo = OneVsOneClassifier(LogisticRegression())
ovo.fit(X_train,y_train)
ovo.predict(X)
```

Now that you have a good understanding of one-versus-one and one-versus-all classifiers, let's go back to the two cases about the online trading company. Both the cases discussed earlier fall under the category of multiclass classification; however, there is a huge variation in the number of classes (in the first case, you will have 5 classes, whereas, in the second one, you will have 100 classes). This difference is extremely important because if you were to train a separate classifier for each class (one-versus-one), you would end up with around 5,000 classifiers in the second case (**100*99/2 = 4,950** classes), which would make it computationally expensive.

However, if you were to go with the one-versus-all approach, you would end up with highly class-imbalanced data for each classifier (each classifier would have data equivalent to 1 class in one set and 99 classes in the other set), which would end up reducing the classifier performance. The conclusion is that each of the two methods discussed has its advantages and disadvantages, and you need to be very clear about when to use a specific technique.

Now that you have a good idea about the two kinds of classifiers used in multiclass classification and how to use them with the scikit-learn module in Python, it's time to put these skills to the test on a dataset obtained from a UK-based online store and compare the one-versus-one and one-versus-all techniques.

EXERCISE 9.01: IMPLEMENTING A MULTICLASS CLASSIFICATION ALGORITHM ON A DATASET

Consider the `Segmentation.csv` dataset. This dataset contains the transactions of customers for a UK-based online store from 2010 to 2011. `Segmentation.csv` contains several features describing customer transactions as well as the customers' relations with the store. You will read about these features in detail shortly.

> **NOTE**
>
> You can find `Segmentation.csv` at the following link:
> https://packt.link/U9Jht.

The manager of this store has reached out to you to help increase their sales by properly segmenting the customers into different categories, for example, loyal customer, potential customer, fence sitter, and more. The store will use this knowledge to give segment-specific discounts to their customers, which would help in increasing their sales and shifting more customers to the loyal customer category.

Since there are more than two classes, the given problem falls under the category of multiclass classification. You will have access to the following features of the dataset:

- **Frequency**: The number of purchases made by the customer.

- **Recency**: How recently the customer bought from the online retailer (in days).

- **MonetaryValue**: The total amount spent by the customer between 2010 and 2011.

- **Tenure**: How long the customer has been associated with the retailer (in days).

- **Segment**: Which segment the customer belongs to; that is, are they a loyal customer or a potential customer? With the help of segment details, marketing campaigns can be targeted effectively.

Given the segment details of the customer, you need to classify which segment a sample customer belongs to. You need to implement a multiclass classification algorithm to classify the customers into the three different classes using **OneVsRestClassifier** and **OneVsOneClassifier**. For both the classifiers, you will be using **LinearSVC** as the base classifier.

Perform the following steps to achieve the goal of this exercise:

1. Import **OneVsRestClassifier**, **OneVsOneClassifier**, and **LinearSVC** and create a new pandas DataFrame named **segmentation**. Also, import the **numpy** module for any computations that you will be doing on the DataFrame. Read the **Segmentation.csv** file into it:

```
import pandas as pd
import numpy as np
from sklearn.multiclass import OneVsRestClassifier,\
                                OneVsOneClassifier
from sklearn.svm import LinearSVC
segmentation = pd.read_csv('Segmentation.csv')
```

> **NOTE**
>
> Make sure you change the path (highlighted) to the CSV file based on its location on your system. If you're running the Jupyter notebook from the same directory where the CSV file is stored, you can run the preceding code without any modification.

2. Load all the features and the target to variables **X** and **y**, respectively. You will also have to drop **CustomerID** since it is going to be different for each customer and won't add any value to the model. Also, you will have to remove the **Segment** column, which is the target variable, from the features variable (**X**):

```
# Putting feature variable to X
X = segmentation.drop(['CustomerID','Segment'],axis=1)
# Putting response variable to y
y = segmentation['Segment']
```

3. Fit and predict using the one-versus-all classifier. Use the following code:

```
OneVsRestClassifier(LinearSVC(random_state=0)).fit(X, y)\
                                               .predict(X)
```

You will receive the following array as output:

```
array(['Fence Sitter', 'Potential', 'Fence Sitter', ..., 'Potential',
       'Potential', 'Potential'], dtype='<U12')
```

Figure 9.2: Output of the one-versus-all classifier

From the preceding output, you can see that our one-versus-all classifier has classified all the samples into different categories, which is also the expected behavior.

4. Fit and predict using the one-versus-one classifier. Use the following code:

```
OneVsOneClassifier(LinearSVC(random_state=0)).fit(X, y)\
                                             .predict(X)
```

You will receive the following array as output:

```
array(['Fence Sitter', 'Potential', 'Fence Sitter', ..., 'Potential',
       'Potential', 'Potential'], dtype=object)
```

Figure 9.3: Output of the one-versus-one classifier

From the preceding output, you will observe that both the classifiers give the same results. The difference between both, however, is the computation time, as discussed earlier.

In this exercise, you saw how easily you can create a one-versus-one or one-versus-all classifier with a base classifier such as **LinearSVC**, fit it on the training dataset (in this case, both the training and testing dataset were the same), and predict it on the training dataset.

So far, we have only discussed how to train the two kinds of classifiers, and you saw that one-versus-one and one-versus-all classifiers primarily differ in the computation time they use for training and prediction steps; however, computation time varies based on the system configuration and the number of ongoing processes. This makes it an unreliable performance metric.

In the next section, you will see how you can use the same metrics you have used for binary classification (F1 score, recall, precision, and more) for multiclass classification problems.

PERFORMANCE METRICS

The performance metrics in the case of multiclass classification would be the same as what you used for binary classification in the previous chapter, that is, **precision**, **recall**, and **F1 score**, obtained using a confusion matrix.

In the case of a multiclass classification problem, you average out the metrics to find the micro-average or macro-average of precision, recall, and F1 score in a k-class system, where **k** is the number of classes. Averaging is useful in the case of multiclass classification since you have multiple class labels. This is because each classifier is going to give one class as the prediction; however, in the end, you are just looking for one class. In such cases, an aggregation such as averaging helps in getting the final output.

The macro-average computes the metrics such as precision (**PRE**), recall (**Recall**), or F1 score (**F1**) of each class independently and takes the average (all the classes are treated equally):

$$PRE_{macro} = \frac{PRE_1 + PRE_2 + \cdots + PRE_k}{k}$$

$$Recall_{macro} = \frac{Recall_1 + Recall_2 + \cdots + Recall_k}{k}$$

$$F1_{macro} = 2x\frac{PRE_{macro}}{Recall_{macro}}$$

Figure 9.4: The macro-average of performance metrics

The micro-average sums the contributions of all classes to compute the average. If you suspect your dataset to be not balanced (one class having a higher presence than the other), then use the micro-average. The micro-average for precision, recall, and F1 metrics is calculated by summing up the individual **true positives (TPs)**, **false positives (FPs)**, and **false negatives (FNs)** as follows:

$$PRE_{micro} = \frac{TP_1 + TP_2 + \cdots + TP_k}{TP_1 + TP_2 + \cdots + TP_k + FP_1 + FP_2 + \cdots + FP_k}$$

$$Recall_{micro} = \frac{TP_1 + TP_2 + \cdots + TP_k}{TP_1 + TP_2 + \cdots + TP_k + FN_1 + FN_2 + \cdots + FN_k}$$

$$F1_{micro} = 2 \times \frac{PRE_{micro}}{Recall_{micro}}$$

Figure 9.5: The micro-average of performance metrics

Scikit-learn provides two very useful functions for evaluating the micro- and macro-averages of performance metrics. The first is **classification_report**, which you have seen in the previous chapter. The other is the **precision_recall_fscore_support** function, which allows the user to find out the precision, recall, F1 score, and more all at once. Let's see how to use this second function:

1. Import the **precision_recall_fscore_support** function from **sklearn**:

```
from sklearn.metrics import precision_recall_fscore_support
```

2. You can find the micro-average performance metrics using the following code:

```
precision_recall_fscore_support(y, y_pred, average='micro')
```

Here, **y** is the ground-truth class and **y_pred** is the predicted class.

3. Similarly, to find the macro-average performance metrics, you can use the function using the following code:

```
precision_recall_fscore_support(y, y_pred, average='macro')
```

Now that you understand the objective and reliable performance metrics, it is time to put them to use in the next exercise.

EXERCISE 9.02: EVALUATING PERFORMANCE USING MULTICLASS PERFORMANCE METRICS

In this exercise, you will continue with the same case study as in *Exercise 9.01, Implementing a Multiclass Classification Algorithm on a Dataset*. This time, you will train a decision tree classifier and evaluate the model using the micro- and macro-averages of the performance metrics discussed in the previous section. For evaluating the model performance, divide (with stratification) the dataset using an **80 : 20** ratio (**train : test**) and set **random_state** to **123**. You should be able to achieve a classification report like the following (a variation of up to 5% from the values we got is acceptable):

	precision	recall	f1-score	support
Fence Sitter	1.00	1.00	1.00	206
Loyal	0.99	1.00	0.99	86
Potential	1.00	0.99	1.00	318
accuracy			1.00	610
macro avg	0.99	1.00	0.99	610
weighted avg	1.00	1.00	1.00	610

Figure 9.6: Expected classification report

Perform the following steps to achieve the goal of this exercise:

1. Import **numpy, DecisionTreeClassifier, train_test_split, precision_recall_fscore_support, classification_report, confusion_matrix**, and **accuracy_score**:

```
import numpy as np
import pandas as pd
# Importing decision tree classifier from sklearn library
from sklearn.tree import DecisionTreeClassifier
from sklearn.model_selection import train_test_split
"""
Importing classification report and confusion matrix from sklearn
metrics
"""
from sklearn.metrics import classification_report, \
                            confusion_matrix, \
                            accuracy_score
from sklearn.metrics import precision_recall_fscore_support
```

2. Load the **Segmentation.csv** dataset into a variable called **segmentation**:

```
segmentation = pd.read_csv('Segmentation.csv')
```

> **NOTE**
>
> Make sure you change the path (highlighted) to the CSV file based on its location on your system. If you're running the Jupyter notebook from the same directory where the CSV file is stored, you can run the preceding code without any modification.

3. Check the first five rows of the DataFrame using the **head()** function:

```
segmentation.head()
```

You should get the following output:

	CustomerID	Recency	Tenure	Frequency	MonetaryValue	Segment
0	12346	326	326	2	0.00	Fence Sitter
1	12349	19	19	73	1757.55	Potential
2	12350	310	310	17	334.40	Fence Sitter
3	12353	204	204	4	89.00	Fence Sitter
4	12354	232	232	58	1079.40	Fence Sitter

Figure 9.7: The first five rows of the DataFrame

As discussed in the previous exercise, the preceding columns have the following meanings:

Recency is how recently the customer bought from the online retailer (in days).

Tenure is the duration of how long the customer has been associated with the retailer (in days).

Frequency is the number of purchases made by the customer.

MonetaryValue is the total amount spent by the customer between 2010 and 2011.

Segment is which segment the customer belongs to; that is, are they a loyal customer or a potential customer?

4. Print the summary of the DataFrame using the `info()` command and check whether there are any missing values:

```
segmentation.info()
```

You should get the following output:

```
<class 'pandas.core.frame.DataFrame'>
RangeIndex: 3046 entries, 0 to 3045
Data columns (total 6 columns):
 #   Column         Non-Null Count   Dtype
---  ------         --------------   -----
 0   CustomerID     3046 non-null    int64
 1   Recency        3046 non-null    int64
 2   Tenure         3046 non-null    int64
 3   Frequency      3046 non-null    int64
 4   MonetaryValue  3046 non-null    float64
 5   Segment        3046 non-null    object
dtypes: float64(1), int64(4), object(1)
memory usage: 142.9+ KB
```

Figure 9.8: Summary of the segmentation DataFrame

From the preceding figure, you can see that there are **3046** rows with no null values.

5. Use the `value_counts()` function to find the number of customers in each segment:

```
segmentation['Segment'].value_counts()
```

You should get the following output:

```
Potential       1587
Fence Sitter    1030
Loyal            429
Name: Segment, dtype: int64
```

Figure 9.9: Number of customers in each segment

From the preceding figure, you can infer that the number of potential customers is higher than the number of loyal customers.

6. Split the data into training and testing sets and store it in the **X_train**, **X_test**, **y_train**, and **y_test** variables, as follows:

```
# Putting feature variable to X
X = segmentation.drop(['CustomerID','Segment'],axis=1)
# Putting response variable to y
y = segmentation['Segment']
X_train, X_test, y_train, y_test = train_test_split\
                                    (X,y,test_size=0.20, \
                                    random_state=123, \
                                    stratify=y)
```

7. Store the **DecisionTreeClassifier** model in the **model** variable and fit the classifier to the training set. Store the fitted model in the **clf** variable:

```
model = DecisionTreeClassifier()
clf = model.fit(X_train,y_train)
```

8. Use the **predict** function of the classifier to predict on the test data and store the results in **y_pred**:

```
y_pred=clf.predict(X_test)
```

9. Fit the macro-averaging and the micro-averaging using the **precision_recall_fscore_support** function. The **precision_recall_fscore_support** function can directly calculate the metrics for the micro-average and macro-average, as follows:

```
precision_recall_fscore_support(y_test, y_pred, average='macro')
precision_recall_fscore_support(y_test, y_pred, average='micro')
```

You will get values more or less similar to the following as outputs for the macro-average and micro- average, respectively: **0.993, 0.996, 0.994, None** and **0.995, 0. 995, 0.995, None**. These values represent the precision, recall, F1 score, and support metrics, respectively (a variation of 5% is acceptable).

10. You can also calculate more detailed metrics statistics using the **classification_report** function. Generate the classification report using the **y_test** and **y_pred** variables:

```
print(classification_report(y_test, y_pred))
```

You should get the following output:

```
                  precision    recall   f1-score    support

 Fence Sitter        1.00        1.00       1.00         206
        Loyal        0.99        1.00       0.99          86
    Potential        1.00        0.99       1.00         318

     accuracy                               1.00         610
    macro avg        0.99        1.00       0.99         610
 weighted avg        1.00        1.00       1.00         610
```

Figure 9.10: Output of the classification_report function

From the preceding classification report, you can see that when using micro-averaging, since each of the classes is equally weighted, you get similar scores for precision, recall, and F1, whereas macro-averaging gives weightage to the most frequent class labels, resulting in different scores.

Now that we have discussed some examples about how to train one-versus-one and one-versus-all classifiers and evaluated their performance using micro- and macro-averages of performance metrics, it's time to use these concepts in the next activity, where you will be helping the marketing team of a major retail company to predict the most effective communication channel for different products.

ACTIVITY 9.01: PERFORMING MULTICLASS CLASSIFICATION AND EVALUATING PERFORMANCE

You have been provided with data on the annual spend amount of each of the 20,000 customers of a major retail company. The marketing team of the company used different channels to sell their goods and has segregated customers based on the purchases made using different channels, which are as follows:

- **0**: Retail

- **1**: Roadshow

- **2**: Social media

- **3**: Television

As a marketing analyst, you are tasked with building a machine learning model that will be able to predict the most effective channel that can be used to target a customer based on the annual spend on the following seven products (features) sold by the company: fresh produce, milk, groceries, frozen products, detergent, paper, and delicatessen.

To complete this task, you will have to train a random forest classifier and evaluate it using a confusion matrix and classification report. Perform the following steps to complete this activity:

1. Import the required libraries. You will need the **pandas**, **numpy**, **sklearn**, **matplotlib**, and **seaborn** libraries in this activity.

2. Load the marketing data into a DataFrame named **data** and look at the first five rows of the DataFrame. It should appear as follows:

	Fresh	Milk	Grocery	Frozen	Detergents_Paper	Delicassen	Channel
0	6623.613537	5513.093240	6019.057354	5669.568008	5898.660607	5179.234947	2
1	5642.542497	5829.866565	3960.339943	4270.020548	3498.818262	4327.423268	2
2	5292.078175	6634.370556	4444.335138	4888.286021	3265.391352	4887.560190	2
3	5595.227928	4754.860698	2977.856511	3462.490957	3609.264559	4268.641413	0
4	5126.693267	6009.649079	3811.569943	4744.115976	3829.516831	5097.491872	2

Figure 9.11: The first five rows of the data DataFrame

> **NOTE**
>
> You can find **MarketingData.csv** at the following link: https://packt.link/ou76r.

3. Check the shape and the missing values and show a summary report of the data.

    The shape should be **(20000,7)**, and there should be no null values in the data. The summary of the data should be as follows:

	Fresh	Milk	Grocery	Frozen	Detergents_Paper	Delicassen	Channel
count	20000.000000	20000.000000	20000.000000	20000.000000	20000.000000	20000.000000	20000.000000
mean	5853.350191	5267.873868	4873.362341	4899.477763	4786.331781	5613.672184	1.499350
std	1128.370297	1177.563192	1265.579790	1220.923393	1154.682284	1343.743103	1.118464
min	1.000000	1.000000	1.000000	1.000000	1.000000	1.000000	0.000000
25%	5155.249455	4438.167387	3983.317183	4071.997222	3877.943500	4705.582182	0.000000
50%	5988.720207	5337.741327	4828.100401	5048.099489	4857.070488	5425.888761	1.000000
75%	6573.895741	6081.755179	5784.992859	5684.876863	5602.146034	6574.281056	3.000000
max	10000.000000	10000.000000	10000.000000	10000.000000	10000.000000	10000.000000	3.000000

Figure 9.12: Summary of the data

4. Check the target variable, **Channel**, for the number of transactions for each of the channels. You should get the following output:

```
0    5007
3    5002
1    5001
2    4990
Name: Channel, dtype: int64
```

Figure 9.13: The number of transactions for each channel

5. Split the data into training and testing sets using the ratio **80:20** (**train:test**).

6. Fit a random forest classifier and store the model in a **clf_random** variable. Set the number of estimators to **20**, the maximum depth to **None**, and the number of samples to **7** and use **random_state=0**.

7. Predict on the test data and store the predictions in **y_pred**.

8. Find the micro- and macro-average reports using the **precision_recall_fscore_support** function.

9. Print the classification report. It should look as follows:

```
              precision    recall  f1-score   support

      Retail       0.90      0.90      0.90      1002
    RoadShow       0.87      0.85      0.86      1000
 SocialMedia       0.93      0.92      0.92       998
  Television       0.87      0.89      0.88      1000

    accuracy                           0.89      4000
   macro avg       0.89      0.89      0.89      4000
weighted avg       0.89      0.89      0.89      4000
```

Figure 9.14: Classification report for the random forest classifier

10. Plot the confusion matrix. It should appear as follows:

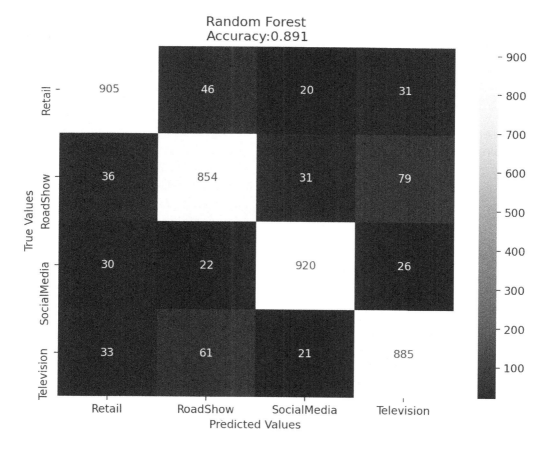

Figure 9.15: Confusion matrix for the random forest classifier

> **NOTE**
>
> The solution for this activity can be found on page 571.

Consider a scenario where the company was using the most used communication channel as the first choice for each product. In this case, not only would the company miss the correct audience for a specific product, but in some cases, it could also end up increasing the publicity cost. By coming up with a machine learning model, you can now come up with a product-specific choice rather than a global choice. This is an excellent example of how machine learning can be useful in marketing case studies.

So far, you have focused primarily on datasets where all the classes had a similar number of data points. For example, in this activity, each class had around 5,000 data points.

In the next section, you will see how to deal with datasets where one or more classes have either a very low or very high number of data points as compared to the rest of the classes.

CLASS-IMBALANCED DATA

Consider the scenario we discussed at the beginning of the chapter about the online shopping company. Imagine that out of the four shortlisted sellers, one is a very well-known company. In such a situation, there is a high chance of this company getting most of the orders as compared to the rest of the three sellers. If the online shopping company decided to divert all the customers to this seller, for a large number of customers, it would actually end up matching their preference. This is a classic scenario of class imbalance since one class is dominating the rest of the classes in terms of data points. Class imbalance is also seen in fraud detection, anti-money laundering, spam detection, cancer detection, and many other situations.

Before you go into the details about how to deal with class imbalance, let's first see how it can pose a big problem in a marketing analyst's work in the following exercise.

EXERCISE 9.03: PERFORMING CLASSIFICATION ON IMBALANCED DATA

For this exercise, you will be working with an online store company to help classify their customers based on their annual income, specifically, whether it exceeds 50,000 USD or not. The dataset used for this purpose is the Adult Census dataset from UCI.

> **NOTE**
>
> Dataset source: *Ronny Kohavi and Barry Becker (1996). UCI Machine Learning Repository [https://archive.ics.uci.edu/ml/datasets/adult]. Data Mining and Visualization. Silicon Graphics.*

> **NOTE**
>
> You can find **adult.csv** at the following link: https://packt.link/paedp.

However, there is a big issue with the dataset. Around 74% of the dataset has people earning less than 50,000 USD; hence, it is a highly imbalanced dataset. In this exercise, you will observe how imbalanced data affects the performance of a model, and why it is so important to modify your process while working on an imbalanced dataset. You will also have to drop the missing values that are stored in the dataset as **?** before you start using it for the model training step:

1. Import **pandas**, **RandomForestClassifier**, **train_test_split**, **classification_report**, **confusion_matrix**, **accuracy_score**, **metrics**, **seaborn**, and **svm** using the following code:

```
import pandas as pd
import numpy as np
from sklearn.ensemble import RandomForestClassifier
from sklearn.model_selection import train_test_split
from sklearn.metrics import classification_report,\
                            confusion_matrix,\
                            accuracy_score
from sklearn import metrics
import matplotlib.pyplot as plt
import seaborn as sns
```

2. Create a DataFrame named **data** and load **adult.csv** into it:

```
data = pd.read_csv('adult.csv')
```

> **NOTE**
>
> Make sure you change the path (highlighted) to the CSV file based on its location on your system. If you're running the Jupyter notebook from the same directory where the CSV file is stored, you can run the preceding code without any modification.

3. Check the first five rows of the **data** DataFrame using the following code:

```
data.head()
```

You should get the following output:

	age	workclass	fnlwgt	education	educational-num	marital-status	occupation	relationship	race
0	25	Private	226802	11th	7	Never-married	Machine-op-inspct	Own-child	Black
1	38	Private	89814	HS-grad	9	Married-civ-spouse	Farming-fishing	Husband	White
2	28	Local-gov	336951	Assoc-acdm	12	Married-civ-spouse	Protective-serv	Husband	White
3	44	Private	160323	Some-college	10	Married-civ-spouse	Machine-op-inspct	Husband	Black
4	18	?	103497	Some-college	10	Never-married	?	Own-child	White

Figure 9.16: First five rows of the Adult Census dataset

> **NOTE**
>
> The preceding image does not contain all the columns of the DataFrame. The image is used for demonstration purposes only.

4. As you can see from the output of *Step 3*, the dataset has some values filled with **?**. Replace them with **np.nan**:

```
data.replace('?',np.nan,inplace=True)
```

5. Drop the rows that contains null values:

```
data.dropna(inplace=True)
```

6. Check the number of people earning less than or equal to 50,000 USD and more than 50,000 USD using the following code:

```
data['income'].value_counts()
```

The number of people earning more than 50,000 USD will be **11208** and the number of people earning less than or equal to 50,000 USD will be **34014**.

7. You can see in the **data.head()** output that there are a lot of categorical values in the DataFrame. To perform classification, you need to convert the categorical values (**workclass**, **education**, **marital-status**, **occupation**, **relationship**, **race**, **gender**, **native country**, and **income**) into numerical values. You can use a label encoder for this conversion. Label encoders convert categorical values into numerical values:

```
#Encoding the Categorical values to Numericals using LabelEncoder
from sklearn.preprocessing import LabelEncoder

Labelenc_workclass = LabelEncoder()
data['workclass'] = Labelenc_workclass\
                    .fit_transform(data['workclass'])

Labelenc_education = LabelEncoder()
data['education'] = Labelenc_education\
                    .fit_transform(data['education'])

Labelenc_marital_status = LabelEncoder()
data['marital-status'] = Labelenc_marital_status\
                         .fit_transform(data['marital-status'])

Labelenc_occupation = LabelEncoder()
data['occupation'] = Labelenc_occupation\
                     .fit_transform(data['occupation'])

Labelenc_relationship = LabelEncoder()
```

```
data['relationship'] = Labelenc_relationship\
                        .fit_transform(data['relationship'])


Labelenc_race = LabelEncoder()
data['race'] = Labelenc_race\
                .fit_transform(data['race'])


Labelenc_gender = LabelEncoder()
data['gender'] = Labelenc_gender\
                    .fit_transform(data['gender'])


Labelenc_native_country = LabelEncoder()
data['native-country'] = Labelenc_native_country\
                            .fit_transform(data['native-country'])


Labelenc_income = LabelEncoder()
data['income'] = Labelenc_income\
                    .fit_transform(data['income'])
```

Please note that less than or equal to 50,000 is encoded as **0** and greater than 50,000 is encoded as **1** when you use the label encoder on the **income** column. This has been done since you are going to predict the income class at the end, and a machine learning model will always predict a number as an output rather than the class directly. Once you have the number **0** or **1** as the predicted class, you will have to decode it back to the corresponding income class (less than or equal to 50,000 and greater than 50K, respectively).

8. Look at the encoded DataFrame using the following command:

```
data.head()
```

You should get output like the following:

	age	workclass	fnlwgt	education	educational-num	marital-status	occupation	relationship	race	gender	capital-gain	capital-loss	hours-per-week	native-country	income
0	25	2	226802	1	7	4	6	3	2	1	0	0	40	38	0
1	38	2	89814	11	9	2	4	0	4	1	0	0	50	38	0
2	28	1	336951	7	12	2	10	0	4	1	0	0	40	38	1
3	44	2	160323	15	10	2	6	0	2	1	7688	0	40	38	1
5	34	2	198693	0	6	4	7	1	4	1	0	0	30	38	0

Figure 9.17: First five rows of the DataFrame

9. Put all the independent variables in the variable **X** and the dependent variable in **y**:

```
# Putting feature variable to X
X = data.drop(['income'],axis=1)
# Putting response variable to y
y = data['income']
```

10. Split the data into training and testing sets, as shown here:

```
X_train, X_test, y_train, y_test = train_test_split\
                                  (X,y,\
                                   test_size=0.20, \
                                   random_state=123)
```

11. Now, fit a random forest classifier using the following code and save the model to a **clf_random** variable:

```
clf_random = RandomForestClassifier(random_state=0)
clf_random.fit(X_train,y_train)
```

You should get the following output:

```
RandomForestClassifier(random_state=0)
```

12. Predict on the test data and save the predictions to the **y_pred** variable:

```
y_pred=clf_random.predict(X_test)
```

13. Generate the classification report using the following code:

```
print(classification_report(y_test, y_pred))
```

Your output will appear as follows:

	precision	recall	f1-score	support
0	0.88	0.93	0.91	6808
1	0.74	0.63	0.68	2237
accuracy			0.85	9045
macro avg	0.81	0.78	0.79	9045
weighted avg	0.85	0.85	0.85	9045

Figure 9.18: Output of the classification_report function

You can infer that the model was able to classify **class 0** (less than or equal to 50,000) with 88% precision whereas **class 1** (greater than 50,000) had a precision of 74%.

class 1 (greater than 50,000) has a lower score in terms of both precision and recall. This can be attributed to the fact that the dataset was highly imbalanced, and this has led to the poor performance of the model.

14. Finally, plot the confusion matrix:

```
cm = confusion_matrix(y_test, y_pred)

cm_df = pd.DataFrame(cm, \
                     index = ['<=50K', '>50K'], \
                     columns = ['<=50K', '>50K'])
plt.figure(figsize=(8,6))
sns.heatmap(cm_df, annot=True,fmt='g',cmap='Greys_r')
plt.title('Random Forest \nAccuracy:{0:.3f}'\
          .format(accuracy_score(y_test, y_pred)))
plt.ylabel('True Values')
plt.xlabel('Predicted Values')
plt.show()
```

> **NOTE**
>
> The value **Greys_r** (emboldened) is used to generate graphs in grayscale. You can also refer to the following document to get the code for the colored plot and the colored output: http://packt.link/NOjgT.

Your output should appear as follows:

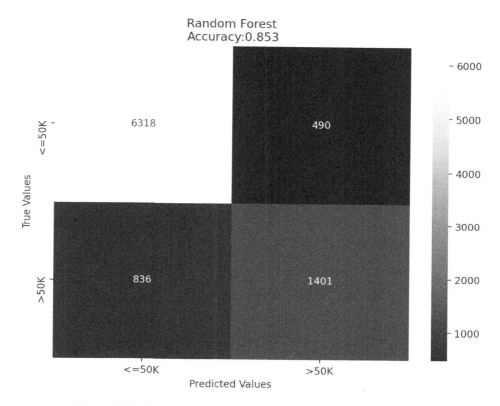

Figure 9.19: Confusion matrix for the random forest classifier

From the preceding confusion matrix, you can say that the model classified **836** people as earning less than or equal to 50,000 USD; however, they were actually earning more than 50,000 USD. Similarly, the model classified **490** people as earning more than 50,000 USD when they were actually earning less than or equal to 50,000 USD.

In real-world cases, you always get a problem statement like the one you have seen in this exercise. It is always the analyst's job to determine an imbalance in the dataset and decide on the approach accordingly. A company, in general, would never say that their dataset is imbalanced and that is why they are getting poor results. That's why you need to analyze the dataset carefully using EDA before directly jumping into the model training step.

It's therefore clear that class imbalance influenced the machine learning model to be more biased toward the majority class (people earning less than or equal to 50,000 USD). This is because the machine learning algorithm learns by implicitly optimizing predictions depending on the most abundant class in the dataset to minimize the cost function during training. As a result, the classifier failed to correctly predict the minority class (people earning more than 50,000 USD).

Now that you have a good understanding of the impact of class imbalance on the performance of a model, it's time to learn how to deal with a class-imbalanced dataset.

DEALING WITH CLASS-IMBALANCED DATA

One way of dealing with an imbalanced dataset is to assign a penalty to every wrong prediction on the minority class. This can be done using the **class_weight** parameter available in scikit-learn, which assigns a penalty for every wrong prediction of the minority class. As an example, let's see how to use this **class_weight** parameter in **RandomForestClassifier**:

```
clf_random = RandomForestClassifier(n_estimators=20, \
                                    max_depth=None, \
                                    min_samples_split=7, \
                                    random_state=0, \
                                    class_weight='balanced')
```

class_weight='balanced' ensures that the penalty for each wrong prediction is adjusted based on the distribution of the class. For example, for a majority class, smaller modifications would be done to the weights since you would encounter samples for the majority class more often as compared to the minority class.

There are other strategies to deal with imbalanced data as well. Some of them are as follows:

- **Random undersampling**: In the case of random undersampling, the majority class samples are randomly eliminated to maintain class balance. The advantage of using this method is that it reduces the number of training samples, and hence the training time decreases; however, it may lead to underfitted models.

- **Random oversampling**: In the case of random oversampling, the minority class samples are replicated randomly to represent a higher representation of the minority class in the training sample. The advantage of using this method is that there is no information loss; however, it may lead to overfitting of the data.

- **Synthetic Minority Oversampling Technique** (**SMOTE**): This technique is used to mitigate the problems you faced in random oversampling. In this method, a subset of the minority class data is taken, and a similar replica of the data is created, which is added to the main datasets. The advantage of using this method is that it reduces overfitting the data and does not lead to any loss of information. However, it is not very effective for high-dimensional data.

The following table summarizes the effect of the three sampling techniques mentioned previously on the number of data points after sampling. Consider a sample dataset that has a clear case of class imbalance, since `Class 2` has five times as many samples as `Class 1`. After performing random undersampling, the number of samples in `Class 2` is reduced to the same as `Class 1`, whereas, in the case of random oversampling and SMOTE, the number of samples in `Class 1` is increased to match the number of samples in `Class 2`. The only difference is that in the case of random oversampling, the existing samples will be repeated to increase the number of samples in `Class 1`. This can lead to overfitting, as mentioned earlier. On the other side, in the case of SMOTE, new samples will be generated based on (but not exactly the same as) the already existing samples. Random undersampling ends up reducing the total data size, which can lead to information loss and underfitting:

Class	Number of data points in the original dataset	Number of data points after sampling		
		Random	Random oversampling	SMOTE
Class 1	1,000	1,000	5,000 (repetition of existing points)	5,000 (new points generated)
Class 2	5,000	1,000	5,000	5,000

Figure 9.20: Effect of sampling techniques on the number of data points

As you can see from the preceding table, out of the three sampling techniques, SMOTE is the most recommended one to use since it ensures that no data points are lost while also ensuring that the new data points generated are not repetitions (which can lead to overfitting). To use SMOTE, please perform the following steps:

1. Import the **SMOTE** function from the **imblearn** module:

```
from imblearn.over_sampling import SMOTE
```

2. Next, to generate the resampled dataset with a larger number of samples, use the following code:

```
X_resampled, y_resampled = SMOTE().fit_resample(X_train,y_train)
```

This resampled dataset can then be used to train models.

Now that you have gone over various sampling techniques and how to implement SMOTE using the **imblearn** module, let's apply these concepts to the adult census dataset you used in *Exercise 9.03, Performing Classification on Imbalanced Data*.

EXERCISE 9.04: FIXING THE IMBALANCE OF A DATASET USING SMOTE

In *Exercise 9.03, Performing Classification on Imbalanced Data*, you noticed that your model was not able to generalize because of imbalanced data and your precision and recall scores were low. In this exercise, you will first resample your dataset using the SMOTE technique to obtain a balanced dataset. Then, you will use the same balanced dataset to fit a random forest classifier (which was initialized in the previous exercise).

By the end of the exercise, you should be able to see an improvement in model performance for the annual income of more than 50,000 USD class. This should happen since by using SMOTE technique, the number of samples in the minority class (greater than 50,000) would increase, which would fix the issue of overfitting that you saw in the previous exercise. This in turn should increase the number of correctly classified samples for this class (greater than 50,000). You will be able to see this information with the help of the confusion matrix.

The detailed steps to follow for completing this exercise are as follows:

> **NOTE**
>
> Use the same Jupyter notebook as the one used for the preceding exercise. You can download the notebook for *Exercise 9.03*, *Performing Classification on Imbalanced Data*, from https://packt.link/828oK.

1. First, import the **imblearn** library and the **SMOTE** function, which you will be using exclusively in this exercise:

```
import imblearn
from imblearn.over_sampling import SMOTE
```

2. Enter the following code to use **SMOTE** for sampling **X_train** and **y_train** data to build your classifier:

```
X_resampled, y_resampled = SMOTE().fit_resample(X_train,y_train)
```

3. Fit the random forest classifier on the sampled data using the following code:

```
clf_random.fit(X_resampled,y_resampled)
```

4. Predict on the test data:

```
y_pred=clf_random.predict(X_test)
```

5. Generate the classification report, as follows:

```
print(classification_report(y_test, y_pred))
```

Your output will be as follows:

```
              precision    recall  f1-score   support

           0       0.90      0.89      0.89      6808
           1       0.68      0.68      0.68      2237

    accuracy                           0.84      9045
   macro avg       0.79      0.79      0.79      9045
weighted avg       0.84      0.84      0.84      9045
```

Figure 9.21: Output of the classification_report function

One thing you will immediately see is a small drop in all the evaluation metrics as compared to the classification report output obtained in the previous exercise. While this can be daunting at first glance, it actually shows the true model performance. The same performance can now be expected if this model is used in a real-world scenario, unlike the model trained in the previous exercise, which was overfitting on one class. An overfitting model would be biased toward the majority class, which can have a strong negative effect in a real-world use case.

6. Plot the confusion matrix using the following code:

```
cm = confusion_matrix(y_test, y_pred)

cm_df = pd.DataFrame(cm, \
                     index = ['<=50K', '>50K'], \
                     columns = ['<=50K', '>50K'])
plt.figure(figsize=(8,6))
sns.heatmap(cm_df, annot=True, fmt='g', cmap='Greys_r')
plt.title('Random Forest \nAccuracy:{0:.3f}'\
          .format(accuracy_score(y_test, y_pred)))
plt.ylabel('True Values')
plt.xlabel('Predicted Values')
plt.show()
```

> **NOTE**
>
> The value **Greys_r** (emboldened) is used to generate graphs in grayscale. You can also refer to the following document to get the code for the colored plot and the colored output: http://packt.link/NOjgT.

It will appear as follows:

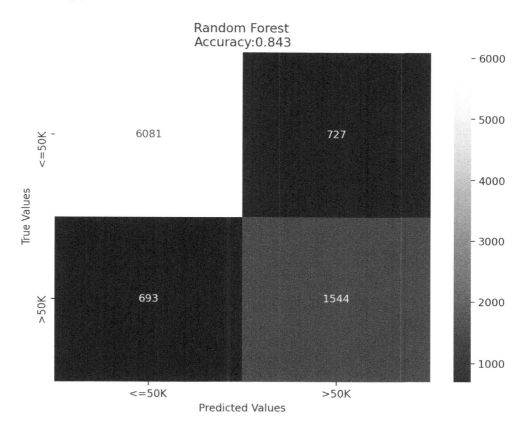

Figure 9.22: Confusion matrix

In *Figure 9.19*, you saw that without using class imbalance, your classifier was able to identify only **1401** people who were earning more than 50,000 USD, whereas by using sampling techniques (**SMOTE**), the classifier identified **1528** people who were earning more than 50,000 USD.

You have now learned the details of the SMOTE technique and how to use it to generate a balanced dataset from an imbalanced dataset. In the exercise, you also saw how to use this resampled (balanced) dataset to train a random forest classifier to achieve an improvement in model performance on the, earlier, minor class.

In the next activity, you will be utilizing all these techniques on a marketing campaign of a Portuguese banking institution.

ACTIVITY 9.02: DEALING WITH IMBALANCED DATA USING SCIKIT-LEARN

A lot of times, banks organize marketing campaigns to inform people about their deposit plans and increase their subscribers of these plans. These campaigns typically involve telephone calls to a large number of people, and based on their dataset, they are then approached one by one to get them on board with their deposit plan.

In this activity, you will be working on a similar scenario where you will have a dataset collected from a marketing campaign from a Portuguese bank.

> **NOTE**
>
> Dataset source: *[Moro et al., 2014] S. Moro, P. Cortez and P. Rita. A Data-Driven Approach to Predict the Success of Bank Telemarketing. Decision Support Systems, Elsevier, 62:22-31, June 2014.*

Similar to most campaigns, the same client was approached more than once to check whether they would be interested in a bank term deposit or not. The dataset contains some customer information (such as age, job, and so on) and campaign-related information (such as contact or communication type, day, month, and duration of the contact).

For the next marketing campaign, your company wants to use this data and only contact potential customers who will subscribe to the term deposit, thereby reducing the effort needed to contact those customers who are not interested. For this, you need to create a model that will be able to predict whether customers will subscribe to the term deposit (variable **y**).

> **NOTE**
>
> You can download the dataset from https://packt.link/TrTiQ.

To complete this activity, please follow the steps given here:

1. Import all the necessary libraries. You will primarily be working with the **sklearn**, **numpy**, **pandas**, **matplotlib**, and **seaborn** modules.

2. Read the dataset into a pandas DataFrame named **bank** and look at the first five rows of the data. Your output should be as follows:

	age	job	marital	education	default	balance	housing	loan	contact	day	month	duration	campaign	pdays	previous	poutcome	y
0	30	unemployed	married	primary	no	1787	no	no	cellular	19	oct	79	1	-1	0	unknown	no
1	33	services	married	secondary	no	4789	yes	yes	cellular	11	may	220	1	339	4	failure	no
2	35	management	single	tertiary	no	1350	yes	no	cellular	16	apr	185	1	330	1	failure	no
3	30	management	married	tertiary	no	1476	yes	yes	unknown	3	jun	199	4	-1	0	unknown	no
4	59	blue-collar	married	secondary	no	0	yes	no	unknown	5	may	226	1	-1	0	unknown	no

Figure 9.23: The first few rows of bank data

3. Rename the **y** column **Target**. This will add readability to the dataset.

4. Replace the **no** values with **0** and **yes** with **1**. This will help in converting the string-based classes to numerical classes, which would make further processing easier.

5. Check the shape and missing values in the data. The shape should be **(4334,17)** and there should be no missing values.

6. Use the **describe** function to check the continuous and categorical values. You should get the following output for continuous variables:

	age	balance	day	duration	campaign	pdays	previous	Target
count	4334.000000	4334.000000	4334.000000	4334.000000	4334.000000	4334.000000	4334.000000	4334.000000
mean	40.991924	1410.637517	15.913936	264.544301	2.806876	39.670974	0.544070	0.115828
std	10.505378	3010.612091	8.216673	260.642141	3.129682	99.934062	1.702219	0.320056
min	19.000000	-3313.000000	1.000000	4.000000	1.000000	-1.000000	0.000000	0.000000
25%	33.000000	67.000000	9.000000	104.000000	1.000000	-1.000000	0.000000	0.000000
50%	39.000000	440.000000	16.000000	186.000000	2.000000	-1.000000	0.000000	0.000000
75%	48.000000	1464.000000	21.000000	329.000000	3.000000	-1.000000	0.000000	0.000000
max	87.000000	71188.000000	31.000000	3025.000000	50.000000	871.000000	25.000000	1.000000

Figure 9.24: Output for continuous variables

HINT

While using the **describe()** function, specify **include=['O']** as an argument to get a summary of the categorical variables.

You will get the following output for categorical variables:

	job	marital	education	default	housing	loan	contact	month	poutcome
count	4334	4334	4334	4334	4334	4334	4334	4334	4334
unique	12	3	3	2	2	2	3	12	4
top	management	married	secondary	no	yes	no	cellular	may	unknown
freq	942	2680	2306	4261	2476	3650	2801	1339	3555

Figure 9.25: Output for categorical variables

7. Check the count of the class labels present in the target variable. You should get the following output:

```
0    3832
1     502
Name: Target, dtype: int64
```

Figure 9.26: Count of class labels

8. Use the **cat.codes** function to encode the **job, marital, default, housing, loan, contact**, and **poutcome** columns. Since **education** and **month** are ordinal columns, convert them as follows:

a) Replace **primary education** with **0**, **secondary education** with **1**, and **tertiary education** with **2**.

b) Replace the months **January** to **December** with their corresponding month number, **1** to **12**.

9. Check the first five rows of the bank data after the conversion. You will get the following output:

	age	job	marital	education	default	balance	housing	loan	contact	day	month	duration	campaign	pdays	previous	poutcome	Target
0	30	10	1	0	10	1787	1	0	0	19	10	79	1	-1	0	3	0
1	33	7	1	1	7	4789	1	1	0	11	5	220	1	339	4	0	0
2	35	4	2	2	4	1350	2	0	0	16	4	185	1	330	1	0	0
3	30	4	1	2	4	1476	1	1	2	3	6	199	4	-1	0	3	0
4	59	1	1	1	1	0	1	0	2	5	5	226	1	-1	0	3	0

Figure 9.27: The first few rows of bank data after conversion

10. Split the data into training and testing sets using the **train_test_split** function. Use a ratio of **85:15 (train:test)** for splitting the dataset.

11. Check the number of items in each class in **y_train** and **y_test** using the
value_counts method. You should get the following output for the number of
entries in each class in **y_train**:

```
0    3256
1     427
Name: Target, dtype: int64
```

Figure 9.28: Number of entries in each class in y_train

You should get the following output for the number of entries in each class
in **y_test**:

```
0    576
1     75
Name: Target, dtype: int64
```

Figure 9.29: Number of entries in each class in y_test

12. Use the **standard_scalar** function to scale the **X_train** and **X_test** data.
Assign it to the **X_train_sc** and **X_test_sc** variables.

13. Call the random forest classifier with the **n_estimators=20**,
max_depth=None, **min_samples_split=7**, and
random_state=0 parameters.

14. Fit the random forest model on the training dataset.

15. Predict on the test data using the random forest model.

16. Use the predictions and the ground-truth classes for test data to get the
classification report. You should get the following output:

```
              precision    recall  f1-score   support

          No       0.92      0.98      0.95       576
         Yes       0.67      0.32      0.43        75

    accuracy                           0.90       651
   macro avg       0.79      0.65      0.69       651
weighted avg       0.89      0.90      0.89       651
```

Figure 9.30: Classification report

17. Get the confusion matrix for the trained random forest model. You should get the output similar to the following (a variation of up to 5% is acceptable):

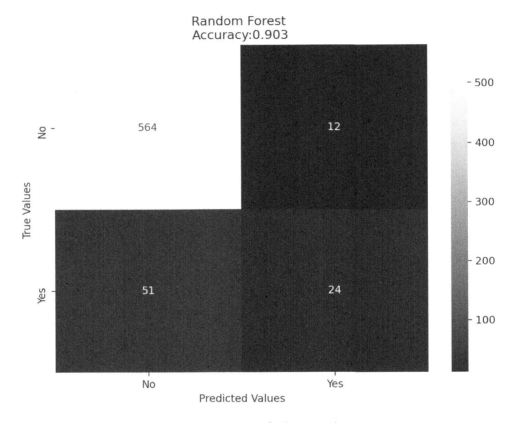

Figure 9.31: Confusion matrix

18. Use the **smote()** function on **x_train** and **y_train** to convert the imbalanced dataset into a balanced dataset. Assign it to the **x_resampled** and **y_resampled** variables, respectively.

19. Use **standard_scalar** to fit on **x_resampled** and **x_test**. Assign it to the **X_train_sc_resampled** and **X_test_sc** variables.

20. Fit the random forest classifier on **X_train_sc_resampled** and **y_resampled**.

21. Predict on **X_test_sc** and use the predictions and ground-truth classes to generate the classification report. It should look as follows (variation of up to 5% is acceptable):

```
              precision    recall  f1-score   support

          No       0.95      0.91      0.93       576
         Yes       0.46      0.60      0.52        75

    accuracy                           0.87       651
   macro avg       0.70      0.75      0.73       651
weighted avg       0.89      0.87      0.88       651
```

Figure 9.32: Classification report of the random forest classifier

22. Plot the confusion matrix for the new trained random forest model. It should appear as follows (a variation of up to 5% is acceptable):

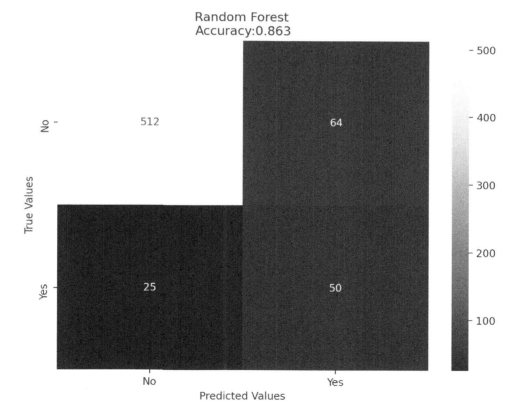

Figure 9.33: Confusion matrix of the random forest classifier

> Note
>
> The solution for this activity can be found on page 578.

SUMMARY

In this chapter, you started off by understanding the importance of multiclass classification problems and the different categories of these problems. You learned about one-versus-one and one-versus-all classifiers and how to implement them using the scikit-learn module in Python. Next, you went through various micro- and macro-averages of performance metrics and used them to understand the impact of class imbalance on the model performance. You also learned about various sampling techniques, especially SMOTE, and implemented them using the **imblearn** library in Python. At the end of the chapter, you used an imbalanced marketing campaign dataset to perform dataset exploration, data transformation, model training, performance evaluation, and dataset balancing using SMOTE.

This book started with the basics of data science and slowly covered the entire end-to-end data science pipeline for a marketing analyst. While working on a problem statement, depending on the need, you will have to use most (if not all) of these techniques to obtain important and useful information from the dataset. If there is one thing you should take away from this entire book, it is that the more time and energy you spend on understanding your data, the better your final results will be. It is the data that holds the highest importance and not the model.

APPENDIX

CHAPTER 1: DATA PREPARATION AND CLEANING

ACTIVITY 1.01: ADDRESSING DATA SPILLING

Solution:

1. Import the **pandas** and **copy** libraries using the following commands:

```
import pandas as pd
import copy
```

2. Create a new DataFrame, **sales**, and use the **read_csv** function to read the **sales.csv** file into it:

```
sales = pd.read_csv("sales.csv")
```

> **NOTE**
>
> Make sure you change the path (emboldened) to the CSV file based on its location on your system. If you're running the Jupyter notebook from the same directory where the CSV file is stored, you can run the preceding code without any modification.

3. Now, examine whether your data is properly loaded by checking the first five rows in the DataFrame. Do this using the **head()** command:

```
sales.head()
```

You should get the following output:

	Year	Product	line	Product.1	type	Product.2	Order	method	type.1	Retailer	country	Revenue
0	2004	Camping	Equipment	Cooking	Gear	TrailChef	Water	Bag	Telephone	United	States	315044.33
1	2004	Camping	Equipment	Cooking	Gear	TrailChef	Water	Bag	Telephone	Canada	NaN	14313.48
2	2004	Camping	Equipment	Cooking	Gear	TrailChef	Water	Bag	Telephone	Mexico	NaN	156644.47
3	2004	Camping	Equipment	Cooking	Gear	TrailChef	Water	Bag	Telephone	Brazil	NaN	59191.72
4	2004	Camping	Equipment	Cooking	Gear	TrailChef	Water	Bag	Telephone	Japan	NaN	7029.33

Figure 1.60: First five rows of the DataFrame

4. Look at the data types of **sales** using the following command:

```
sales.dtypes
```

You should get the following output:

```
Year            int64
Product         object
line            object
Product.1       object
type            object
Product.2       object
Order           object
method          object
type.1          object
Retailer        object
country         object
Revenue         float64
dtype: object
```

Figure 1.61: Looking at the data type of columns of sales.csv

You can see that apart from the **Year** and **Revenue** columns, other columns are of the object type.

5. Now, get some more information about the columns with the following command:

```
sales.info()
```

You should get the following output:

```
<class 'pandas.core.frame.DataFrame'>
RangeIndex: 100 entries, 0 to 99
Data columns (total 12 columns):
 #   Column     Non-Null Count   Dtype
---  ------     --------------   -----
 0   Year       100 non-null     int64
 1   Product    100 non-null     object
 2   line       100 non-null     object
 3   Product.1  100 non-null     object
 4   type       100 non-null     object
 5   Product.2  100 non-null     object
 6   Order      100 non-null     object
 7   method     100 non-null     object
 8   type.1     100 non-null     object
 9   Retailer   100 non-null     object
 10  country    9 non-null       object
 11  Revenue    100 non-null     float64
dtypes: float64(1), int64(1), object(10)
memory usage: 9.5+ KB
```

Figure 1.62: Looking at the information of the sales DataFrame

From the preceding screenshot, you can see that the **country** column has a lot of null values.

Revisiting the output of *Step 3*, you can see that the **Year** and **Revenue** columns seem to be of the correct data types:

	Year	Product	line	Product.1	type	Product.2	Order	method	type.1	Retailer	country	Revenue
0	2004	Camping	Equipment	Cooking	Gear	TrailChef	Water	Bag	Telephone	United	States	315044.33
1	2004	Camping	Equipment	Cooking	Gear	TrailChef	Water	Bag	Telephone	Canada	NaN	14313.48
2	2004	Camping	Equipment	Cooking	Gear	TrailChef	Water	Bag	Telephone	Mexico	NaN	156644.47
3	2004	Camping	Equipment	Cooking	Gear	TrailChef	Water	Bag	Telephone	Brazil	NaN	59191.72
4	2004	Camping	Equipment	Cooking	Gear	TrailChef	Water	Bag	Telephone	Japan	NaN	7029.33

Figure 1.63: First five rows of the sales DataFrame

6. Now, look at the **Product** and **Line** columns. As per the information from the product team, these two columns should have been represented as one. To do this, create a new column, **Product line**, by concatenating the **Product** and **Line** columns. Once the column is created, you can drop the old columns:

> **NOTE**
>
> Two or more columns in a Dataframe can be concatenated with the help of a **+** symbol provided the columns that your concatenating are of **object** type.

```
sales['Product line'] = sales['Product']+' '+sales['line']
sales = sales.drop(['Product', 'line'], axis = 1)
sales.head()
```

The DataFrame should now look as follows, where you can see the new column, **Product line**:

	Year	Product.1	type	Product.2	Order	method	type.1	Retailer	country	Revenue	Product line
0	2004	Cooking	Gear	TrailChef	Water	Bag	Telephone	United	States	315044.33	Camping Equipment
1	2004	Cooking	Gear	TrailChef	Water	Bag	Telephone	Canada	NaN	14313.48	Camping Equipment
2	2004	Cooking	Gear	TrailChef	Water	Bag	Telephone	Mexico	NaN	156644.47	Camping Equipment
3	2004	Cooking	Gear	TrailChef	Water	Bag	Telephone	Brazil	NaN	59191.72	Camping Equipment
4	2004	Cooking	Gear	TrailChef	Water	Bag	Telephone	Japan	NaN	7029.33	Camping Equipment

Figure 1.64: Concatenating two columns

7. Now, look at the values present in **Product.1** and **type** columns with the help of the **groupby** command:

```
sales.groupby(['Product.1','type'])['Year'].count()
```

You should get the following output:

```
Product.1   type
Cooking     Gear     100
Name: Year, dtype: int64
```

Figure 1.65: Output of the groupby operation

You can see that there is only one product type, **Cooking Gear**.

8. Similar to *Step 7*, combine the **Product.1** and **type** columns into a new column, **Product Type**:

```
sales['Product type'] = sales['Product.1']+' '+sales['type']
sales = sales.drop(['Product.1', 'type'], axis = 1)
sales.head()
```

The DataFrame should now look as follows, where you can see the new column, **Product type**:

	Year	Product.2	Order	method	type.1	Retailer	country	Revenue	Product line	Product type
0	2004	TrailChef	Water	Bag	Telephone	United	States	315044.33	Camping Equipment	Cooking Gear
1	2004	TrailChef	Water	Bag	Telephone	Canada	NaN	14313.48	Camping Equipment	Cooking Gear
2	2004	TrailChef	Water	Bag	Telephone	Mexico	NaN	156644.47	Camping Equipment	Cooking Gear
3	2004	TrailChef	Water	Bag	Telephone	Brazil	NaN	59191.72	Camping Equipment	Cooking Gear
4	2004	TrailChef	Water	Bag	Telephone	Japan	NaN	7029.33	Camping Equipment	Cooking Gear

Figure 1.66: Concatenating two columns

9. Move on to the next set of columns – **Product.2**, **Order**, and **method**. As per the information available, the name of the product is **TrailChef Water Bag**. You can get the product name by combining all three columns into a new column, **Product**:

```
sales['Product']=sales['Product.2']+' '+sales['Order']\
                +' '+sales['method']
sales = sales.drop(['Product.2', 'Order','method'], axis = 1)
sales.head()
```

The DataFrame should now look as follows, where you can see the new column, **Product**:

	Year	type.1	Retailer	country	Revenue	Product line	Product type	Product
0	2004	Telephone	United	States	315044.33	Camping Equipment	Cooking Gear	TrailChef Water Bag
1	2004	Telephone	Canada	NaN	14313.48	Camping Equipment	Cooking Gear	TrailChef Water Bag
2	2004	Telephone	Mexico	NaN	156644.47	Camping Equipment	Cooking Gear	TrailChef Water Bag
3	2004	Telephone	Brazil	NaN	59191.72	Camping Equipment	Cooking Gear	TrailChef Water Bag
4	2004	Telephone	Japan	NaN	7029.33	Camping Equipment	Cooking Gear	TrailChef Water Bag

Figure 1.67: Concatenating three columns to a new column

10. Now, look at the **type.1** column. Remember that you dropped the **order** and **method** columns in the previous step (which presumably refers to the **Order method** column). In this step, try to see whether the data in the **type.1** column contains the information you wanted from the dropped columns:

```
sales.groupby('type.1')['Year'].count()
```

You should get the following output:

```
type.1
Mail          16
Special       21
Telephone     21
Web           21
visit         21
Name: Year, dtype: int64
```

Figure 1.68: Output of the groupby operation

From the preceding screenshot, you can see that the values are the different order methods. So, rename the **type.1** column to **Order method**:

```
sales=sales.rename(columns = {'type.1':'Order method'})
```

Examine the result using the **head()** function:

```
sales.head()
```

The DataFrame should now look as follows:

	Year	Order method	Retailer	country	Revenue	Product line	Product type	Product
0	2004	Telephone	United	States	315044.33	Camping Equipment	Cooking Gear	TrailChef Water Bag
1	2004	Telephone	Canada	NaN	14313.48	Camping Equipment	Cooking Gear	TrailChef Water Bag
2	2004	Telephone	Mexico	NaN	156644.47	Camping Equipment	Cooking Gear	TrailChef Water Bag
3	2004	Telephone	Brazil	NaN	59191.72	Camping Equipment	Cooking Gear	TrailChef Water Bag
4	2004	Telephone	Japan	NaN	7029.33	Camping Equipment	Cooking Gear	TrailChef Water Bag

Figure 1.69: Renaming the column

11. You are now left with the columns **Retailer** and **country**. From the preceding screenshot, you can see that **Retailer** and **country** can be combined into one column as they represent country names, but you first have to handle the **NaN** values in the **country** column. You will fix this by filling the **Nan** values. Use the following code:

```
sales=sales.fillna('')
```

You have filled **NaN** with a blank value so that you can combine the **Retailer** and **country** columns. Now, combine the columns in a new column, **Retailer country**, with the following code:

```
sales['Retailer country']=sales['Retailer']+' '+sales['country']
sales = sales.drop(['Retailer', 'country'], axis = 1)
sales.head()
```

The DataFrame should now look as follows:

	Year	Order method	Revenue	Product line	Product type	Product	Retailer country
0	2004	Telephone	315044.33	Camping Equipment	Cooking Gear	TrailChef Water Bag	United States
1	2004	Telephone	14313.48	Camping Equipment	Cooking Gear	TrailChef Water Bag	Canada
2	2004	Telephone	156644.47	Camping Equipment	Cooking Gear	TrailChef Water Bag	Mexico
3	2004	Telephone	59191.72	Camping Equipment	Cooking Gear	TrailChef Water Bag	Brazil
4	2004	Telephone	7029.33	Camping Equipment	Cooking Gear	TrailChef Water Bag	Japan

Figure 1.70: A cleaned DataFrame

You can see that the DataFrame is now clean and has the right values in its column. This DataFrame can now be used to perform further analysis.

CHAPTER 2: DATA EXPLORATION AND VISUALIZATION

ACTIVITY 2.01: ANALYZING ADVERTISEMENTS

Solution:

Perform the following steps to complete this activity:

1. Import **pandas** and **seaborn** using the following code:

```
import pandas as pd
import seaborn as sns
import matplotlib.pyplot as plt
sns.set()
```

2. Load the **Advertising.csv** file into a DataFrame called **ads** and examine if your data is properly loaded by checking the first few values in the DataFrame by using the **head()** command:

```
ads = pd.read_csv("Advertising.csv", index_col = 'Date')
ads.head()
```

The output should be as follows:

	Products	Web	Newspaper	Radio	TV
Date					
01/01/2018	Mobile	230100	69200	37800	22100
01/02/2018	Mobile	44500	45100	39300	10400
01/03/2018	Mobile	17200	69300	45900	9300
01/04/2018	Mobile	151500	58500	41300	18500
01/05/2018	Mobile	180800	58400	10800	12900

Figure 2.65: First five rows of the DataFrame ads

3. Look at the memory usage and other internal information about the DataFrame using the following command:

```
ads.info
```

This gives the following output:

```
<class 'pandas.core.frame.DataFrame'>
Index: 200 entries, 01/01/2018 to 07/06/2019
Data columns (total 5 columns):
 #   Column      Non-Null Count   Dtype
---  ------      --------------   -----
 0   Products    200 non-null     object
 1   Web         200 non-null     int64
 2   Newspaper   200 non-null     int64
 3   Radio       200 non-null     int64
 4   TV          200 non-null     int64
dtypes: int64(4), object(1)
memory usage: 9.4+ KB
```

Figure 2.66: The result of ads.info()

From the preceding figure, you can see that you have five columns with 200 data points in each and no missing values.

4. Use **describe()** function to view basic statistical details of the numerical columns:

```
ads.describe()
```

This gives the following output:

	Web	Newspaper	Radio	TV
count	200.000000	200.000000	200.000000	200.000000
mean	147042.500000	30554.000000	23264.000000	14022.500000
std	85854.236315	21778.620839	14846.809176	5217.456566
min	700.000000	300.000000	0.000000	1600.000000
25%	74375.000000	12750.000000	9975.000000	10375.000000
50%	149750.000000	25750.000000	22900.000000	12900.000000
75%	218825.000000	45100.000000	36525.000000	17400.000000
max	296400.000000	114000.000000	49600.000000	27000.000000

Figure 2.67: The result of ads.describe()

From the preceding figure, you can see that mean of the views on the web is around 147,042. The minimum number of views that happened in a day is 0 which corresponds to that of Radio and the maximum being 296400 which corresponds to that of Web. This clearly shows that campaigns via the web have higher viewership than that of traditional mediums like newspaper, radio, and TV

5. To check how many unique categories are there in the **Products** column, use the **unique** function as follows:

```
ads['Products'].unique()
```

You should get the following output:

```
array(['Mobile', 'Electronics', 'Laptops'], dtype=object)
```

You can see that you have three different categories i.e., **Mobile**, **Electronics**, and **Laptops** in the **Products** column.

6. Now, check how many data points are present in each category of the **Products** column with the help of the **value_counts** function.

```
ads['Products'].value_counts()
```

You should get the following output:

```
Mobile          129
Electronics      53
Laptops          18
Name: Products, dtype: int64
```

Figure 2.68: Number of data points are present in each category of the Products column

From the preceding output, you can infer that the **Mobile** category has more data points when compared with Electronics and Laptops which implies that we have run more ad campaigns for Mobiles than for Electronics or Laptops.

7. To find out total views across different **Product** categories, use the **groupby** function and aggregate it across the different mediums of the campaign.

```
ads.groupby('Products')[['Web','Newspaper','Radio','TV']]\
    .sum()
```

You should get the following output:

Products	Web	Newspaper	Radio	TV
Electronics	7734400	1500100	1161200	698300
Laptops	2711700	379200	374000	257800
Mobile	18962400	4231500	3117600	1848400

Figure 2.69: total views across different Product categories

For all the products, the highest views are through the Web. With this data point, we can recommend that the business concentrate more on the Web as it is giving us a good viewership, but this data alone cannot help us in making a decision as we need to look at other parameters like Conversion ratio to determine the campaign effectiveness.

8. To find out which Products have a higher viewership on TV, plot a bar chart between Products and TV.

```
ads.groupby('Products').sum().plot(kind = 'bar', \
                                y = 'TV',color='gray')
```

NOTE

In *Steps 8*, and *9*, the value **gray** for the attribute **color** (emboldened) is used to generate graphs in grayscale. You can use other colors like **darkgreen**, **maroon**, etc. as values of **color** parameter to get the colored graphs. You can also refer to the following document to get the code for the colored plot and the colored output: http://packt.link/NOjgT.

The output should look like the following:

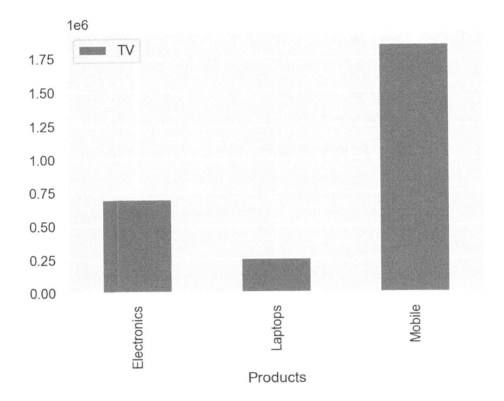

Figure 2.70: Bar Chart between Products and TV

You can observe that the mobile category has the highest viewership on TV followed by Electronics.

9. To find out which products have the lowest viewership on the web, plot a bar chart between **Products** and **Web** using the following command:

```
ads.groupby('Products').sum().plot(kind = 'bar', \
                                   y = 'Web',color='gray')
```

You should get the following output:

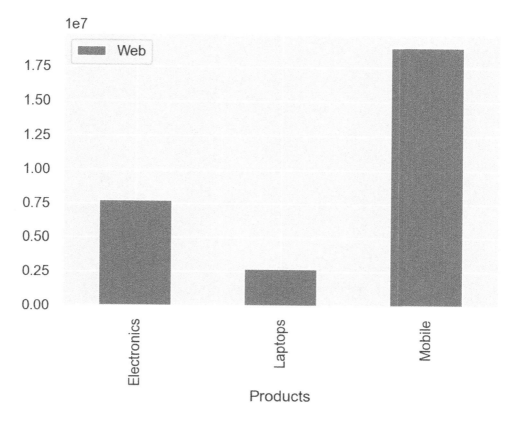

Figure 2.71: Bar chart across products and web

You can see that the **Laptops** category has the lowest viewership on the Web.

10. Understand the relationships between the various columns in the DataFrame with the help of a pair plot. Use the following command:

```
sns.pairplot(ads, hue='Products', palette='gray')
```

> **NOTE**
>
> The value **gray** for the attribute **palette** (emboldened) is used to generate graphs in grayscale. You can use other colors like **darkgreen**, **maroon**, etc. as values of **color** parameter to get the colored graphs. You can also refer to the following document to get the code for the colored plot and the colored output: http://packt.link/NOjgT.

This should give the following output:

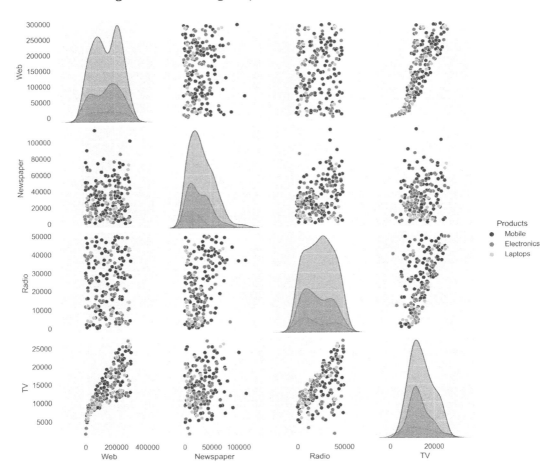

Figure 2.72: Output of pairplot of the ads feature

You can derive the following insights from the data: Look at the charts in your pair plot you can see that **TV** and **Radio** have a positive correlation along with **TV** and **Web**. The correlation between **TV** and **Newspaper** is random; that is, you can't determine whether there is a positive correlation or a negative correlation.

The answers to the questions can be summarized in the following table:

Question	Observation
What are the unique values present in the Products column?	Mobile, Electronics, and Laptops
How many data points belong to each category in the Products column?	Mobile 129 Electronics 53 Laptops 18
Which product has the highest viewership on TV?	Mobiles
Which Product has the lowest viewership on the Web?	Laptop

Figure 2.73: Summary of the derived insights

CHAPTER 3: UNSUPERVISED LEARNING AND CUSTOMER SEGMENTATION

ACTIVITY 3.01: BANK CUSTOMER SEGMENTATION FOR LOAN CAMPAIGN

Solution:

1. Import the necessary libraries for data processing, visualization, and clustering using the following code:

```
import numpy as np, pandas as pd
import matplotlib.pyplot as plt, seaborn as sns
from sklearn.preprocessing import StandardScaler
from sklearn.cluster import KMeans
```

2. Load the data into a **pandas** DataFrame and display the top five rows:

```
bank0 = pd.read_csv("Bank_Personal_Loan_Modelling-1.csv")
bank0.head()
```

> **NOTE**
>
> Make sure you change the path (highlighted) to the CSV file based on its location on your system. If you're running the Jupyter notebook from the same directory where the CSV file is stored, you can run the preceding code without any modification.

The first five rows get displayed as follows:

	ID	Age	Experience	Income	ZIP Code	Family	CCAvg	Education	Mortgage	Personal Loan	Securities Account	CD Account	Online	CreditCard
0	1	25	1	49	91107	4	1.6	1	0	0	1	0	0	0
1	2	45	19	34	90089	3	1.5	1	0	0	1	0	0	0
2	3	39	15	11	94720	1	1.0	1	0	0	0	0	0	0
3	4	35	9	100	94112	1	2.7	2	0	0	0	0	0	0
4	5	35	8	45	91330	4	1.0	2	0	0	0	0	0	1

Figure 3.31: First five rows of the dataset

You can see that you have data about customer demographics such as **Age**, **Experience**, **Family**, and **Education**. You also have data about the finances and services made use of by customers. The income of the customers should be particularly interesting for our exercise.

3. Use the **info** method to get more information about the column types and missing values:

```
bank0.info()
```

This results in the following information about the data:

```
<class 'pandas.core.frame.DataFrame'>
RangeIndex: 5000 entries, 0 to 4999
Data columns (total 14 columns):
 #   Column              Non-Null Count  Dtype
---  ------              --------------  -----
 0   ID                  5000 non-null   int64
 1   Age                 5000 non-null   int64
 2   Experience          5000 non-null   int64
 3   Income              5000 non-null   int64
 4   ZIP Code            5000 non-null   int64
 5   Family              5000 non-null   int64
 6   CCAvg               5000 non-null   float64
 7   Education           5000 non-null   int64
 8   Mortgage            5000 non-null   int64
 9   Personal Loan       5000 non-null   int64
 10  Securities Account  5000 non-null   int64
 11  CD Account          5000 non-null   int64
 12  Online              5000 non-null   int64
 13  CreditCard          5000 non-null   int64
dtypes: float64(1), int64(13)
memory usage: 547.0 KB
```

Figure 3.32: Output of the info method

You can see that there are no null values in the dataset to handle.

4. Perform standard scaling on the **Income** and **CCAvg** columns to create new columns, **Income_scaled** and **CCAvg_scaled**. You will be using these two variables for customer segmentation. Get a descriptive summary of the processed columns to verify that the scaling has been applied correctly:

```
scaler = StandardScaler()
bank0[['Income_scaled', 'CCAvg_scaled']] = scaler.fit_transform\
                                            (bank0[['Income', \
                                             'CCAvg']])
bank0[['Income_scaled', 'CCAvg_scaled']].describe()
```

You should get the following output:

	Income_scaled	CCAvg_scaled
count	5.000000e+03	5.000000e+03
mean	1.939449e-16	-2.078338e-17
std	1.000100e+00	1.000100e+00
min	-1.428969e+00	-1.108987e+00
25%	-7.554825e-01	-7.084116e-01
50%	-2.123482e-01	-2.506106e-01
75%	5.263146e-01	3.216407e-01
max	3.263712e+00	4.613525e+00

Figure 3.33: Descriptive summary of the processed columns

5. Perform **k-means** clustering, specifying **3** clusters using **Income** and **CCAvg** as the features. Specify **random_state** as **42**. Create a new column, **Cluster**, containing the predicted cluster from the model:

```
model = KMeans(n_clusters=3, random_state=42)

cluster_cols = ['Income_scaled', 'CCAvg_scaled']
model.fit(bank0[cluster_cols])

bank0['Cluster'] = model.predict(bank0[cluster_cols])
```

6. Visualize the clusters by using different markers and colors for the clusters on a scatter plot between **Income** and **CCAvg**:

```
markers = ['x', '.', '_']

plt.figure(figsize=[8,5])
for clust in range(3):
    temp = bank0[bank0.Cluster == clust]
    plt.scatter(temp.Income, temp.CCAvg, \
                marker=markers[clust], \
                color='gray',\
                label="Cluster "+str(clust) )

plt.xlabel('Income')
plt.ylabel('CCAvg')
plt.legend()
plt.show()
```

> **NOTE**
>
> The **gray** value for the **color** attribute is used to generate graphs in grayscale. You can use other colors such as **darkgreen**, **maroon**, and so on as values of **color** parameters to get the colored graphs. You can also refer to the following document to get the code for the colored plot and the colored output: http://packt.link/NOjgT.

You should get the following output:

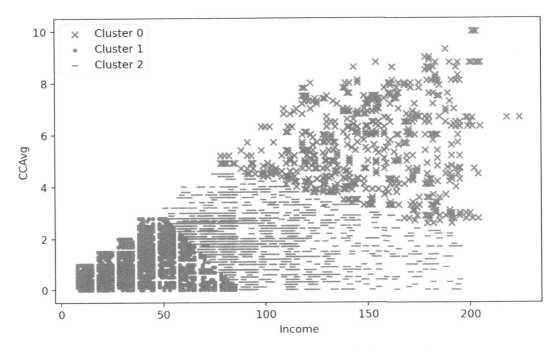

Figure 3.34: Visualizing the clusters using different markers

NOTE

The shapes and colors of the segments you get may vary slightly from the preceding figure. This is because of some additional randomness in the process, introduced by the random cluster center initialization that is done by the k-means algorithm. The cluster number assigned to each group may also differ. Unfortunately, the randomness remains even after setting the random seed and we can't control it. Nevertheless, while the assigned shapes may differ, the characteristics of the resulting clusters will not differ.

7. Print the average values of **Income** and **CCAvg** for the three clusters:

```
bank0.groupby('Cluster')[['Income', 'CCAvg']].mean()
```

You should see the following table:

Cluster	Income	CCAvg
0	150.390282	5.540345
1	39.135072	0.982417
2	96.142777	2.025165

Figure 3.35: Average values of Income and CCAvg for the three clusters

You can see that both **Income** and **CCAvg** vary significantly by the clusters.

8. Perform a visual comparison of the clusters using the standardized values for **Income** and **CCAvg**:

```
bank0.groupby('Cluster')[['Income_scaled', 'CCAvg_scaled']]\
                    .mean().plot\
                    .bar(color=['gray','black'])
plt.show()
```

NOTE

The **gray** and **black** values for the **color** attribute are used to generate graphs in grayscale. You can use other colors such as **darkgreen**, **maroon**, and so on as values of the **color** parameter to get the colored graphs. You can also refer to the following document to get the code for the colored plot and the colored output: http://packt.link/NOjgT.

The output should be as follows:

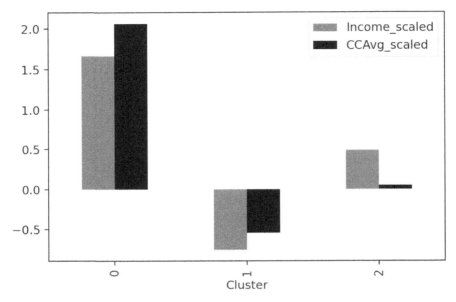

Figure 3.36: Visual comparison of the clusters using the standardized
values for Income and CCAvg

In *Figure 3.36*, you can see the average values of the features against each cluster
on a "standardized" scale. Notice how **Cluster 0** is closer to the average (**0** on
the standard scale) for both **Income** and **CCAvg. Cluster 2** is much higher
on both these variables, while **Cluster 1** has lower-than-average values for
both variables.

> **NOTE**
>
> The cluster numbers you observe may differ from the ones in the preceding
> image. This is again due to the additional randomness introduced by the
> k-means algorithm. Nevertheless, while the assigned cluster number may
> differ, the characteristics of the resulting clusters will not differ.

9. To understand the clusters better using other relevant features, print the
   average values against the clusters for the **Age**, **Mortgage**, **Family**,
   CreditCard, **Online**, and **Personal Loan** features and check which cluster
   has the highest propensity for taking a personal loan.

The average values against the clusters can be found by a simple **groupby** and **mean** calculation using the following code:

```
sel_cols = ['Income', 'CCAvg', 'Age', 'Mortgage', 'Family', \
            'CreditCard', 'Online', 'Personal Loan']

bank0.groupby('Cluster')[sel_cols].mean()
```

The summary should be as follows:

Cluster	Income	CCAvg	Age	Mortgage	Family	CreditCard	Online	Personal Loan
0	150.390282	5.540345	43.924765	89.537618	2.017241	0.285266	0.605016	0.413793
1	39.135072	0.982417	45.797197	42.231218	2.513429	0.294667	0.592448	0.000000
2	96.142777	2.025165	45.184049	65.185165	2.363636	0.296152	0.600112	0.120468

Figure 3.37: Summary of the average values against the clusters

The clusters have vastly different propensities for taking up a personal loan. **Cluster 2** has the highest by far – about 42% – while **Cluster 1** has 0 chance of taking a loan. We can see that the clusters discovered here correlate well with and can be used for marketing campaigns around personal loans.

10. Based on your understanding of the clusters, assign descriptive labels for the clusters.

Key differentiating features for the clusters are **Income, CCAvg**, and **Mortgage**.

Some basic labels for these clusters could be the following:

Cluster 0: Average Joes (medium income, medium spend)

Cluster 1: Low spend potential (low income, low spend)

Cluster 2: High rollers (high income, high spend)

ACTIVITY 3.02: BANK CUSTOMER SEGMENTATION WITH MULTIPLE FEATURES

Solution:

1. Create a copy of the dataset named **bank_scaled** (created in *Activity 3.01, Bank Customer Segmentation for Loan Campaign*) and perform standard scaling of the **Income**, **CCAvg**, **Age**, **Experience**, and **Mortgage** columns on it using the following code:

```
bank_scaled = bank0.copy()

cluster_cols = ['Income', 'CCAvg', 'Age', 'Experience', \
                'Mortgage']

bank_scaled[cluster_cols] = scaler.fit_transform\
                                (bank_scaled[cluster_cols])
```

2. Get a descriptive summary of the processed columns to verify that the scaling has been applied correctly:

```
bank_scaled[cluster_cols].describe()
```

The summary should be as follows:

	Income	CCAvg	Age	Experience	Mortgage
count	5.000000e+03	5.000000e+03	5.000000e+03	5.000000e+03	5.000000e+03
mean	1.939449e-16	-2.078338e-17	2.478018e-17	-1.693312e-16	2.810197e-16
std	1.000100e+00	1.000100e+00	1.000100e+00	1.000100e+00	1.000100e+00
min	-1.428969e+00	-1.108987e+00	-1.948906e+00	-2.014911e+00	-5.555239e-01
25%	-7.554825e-01	-7.084116e-01	-9.019702e-01	-8.812043e-01	-5.555239e-01
50%	-2.123482e-01	-2.506106e-01	-2.952359e-02	-9.121982e-03	-5.555239e-01
75%	5.263146e-01	3.216407e-01	8.429230e-01	8.629604e-01	4.375576e-01
max	3.263712e+00	4.613525e+00	1.889859e+00	1.996667e+00	5.688108e+00

Figure 3.38: Descriptive summary of the processed columns

The mean values are all practically **0** and the standard deviation is **1**, confirming that the standardization was done correctly.

3. Perform k-means clustering specifying **3** clusters using the scaled features. Specify **random_state** as **42**. Assign the clusters to the **Cluster** column:

```
model = KMeans(n_clusters=3, random_state=42)
model.fit(bank_scaled[cluster_cols])

bank_scaled['Cluster'] = model.predict(bank_scaled[cluster_cols])
```

4. Using **PCA** on the scaled columns, create two new columns, **pc1** and **pc2**, containing the data for PC1 and PC2 respectively:

```
from sklearn import decomposition


pca = decomposition.PCA(n_components=2)
pca_res = pca.fit_transform(bank_scaled[cluster_cols])


bank_scaled['pc1'] = pca_res[:,0]
bank_scaled['pc2'] = pca_res[:,1]
```

5. Visualize the clusters by using different markers and colors for the clusters on a scatter plot between **pc1** and **pc2**:

```
markers = ['x', '.', '_']
plt.figure(figsize=[10,12])
for clust in range(3):
    temp = bank_scaled[bank_scaled.Cluster == clust]
    plt.scatter(temp.pc1, temp.pc2, marker=markers[clust], \
                label="Cluster "+str(clust), \
                color='gray')

plt.xlabel('PC1')
plt.ylabel('PC2')
plt.legend()
plt.show()
```

> **NOTE**
>
> The **gray** value for the **color** attribute is used to generate graphs in grayscale. You can use other colors such as **darkgreen**, **maroon**, and so on as values of **color** parameters to get the colored graphs. You can also refer to the following document to get the code for the colored plot and the colored output: http://packt.link/NOjgT.

The plot should appear as follows:

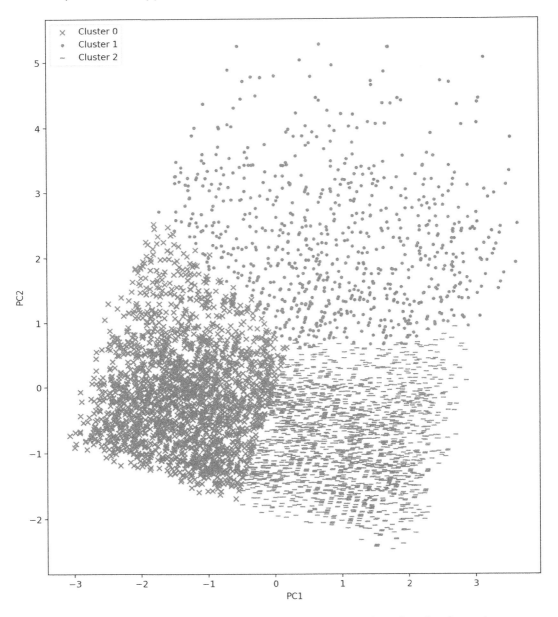

Figure 3.39: A plot of the data reduced to two dimensions denoting the three clusters

In the preceding figure, we can see the three clusters that the machine learning algorithm identified. We can see that in this case, the clusters are not very clearly naturally separated, as is the case in many real-world situations.

> **NOTE**
>
> The shapes and colors of the segments you get may vary slightly from the preceding figure. This is because of some additional randomness in the process, introduced by the random cluster center initialization that is done by the k-means algorithm. The cluster number assigned to each group may also differ. Unfortunately, the randomness remains even after setting the random seed and we can't control it. Nevertheless, while the assigned shapes may differ, the characteristics of the resulting clusters will not differ.

6. Print the average values of the original features used for clustering against the three clusters and check which features are the most differentiated for the clusters.

    We first create a new column, **Cluster**, in **bank0**, the dataset containing the variables on the original scale. We then calculate the mean for each clustering by using **groupby** as in the following code:

    ```
    bank0['Cluster'] = bank_scaled.Cluster
    bank0.groupby('Cluster')[cluster_cols].mean()
    ```

    You will get the following output:

Cluster	Income	CCAvg	Age	Experience	Mortgage
0	58.941774	1.367514	55.536044	30.233826	45.134935
1	147.650185	4.856403	43.672435	18.644005	116.279357
2	60.124322	1.382121	35.116428	9.873705	44.771584

Figure 3.40: Mean values for each cluster

We see that it is only **Age** and **Experience** that are different across the three clusters. All other features have similar values for two of the three clusters.

7. To understand the clusters better using other relevant features, print the average values against the clusters for the **Age, Mortgage, Family, CreditCard, Online,** and **Personal Loan** features and check which cluster has the highest propensity for taking a personal loan:

```
sel_cols = ['Income', 'CCAvg', 'Age', 'Experience', \
            'Mortgage', 'Family', 'CreditCard', 'Online', \
            'Personal Loan']

bank0.groupby('Cluster')[sel_cols].mean()
```

The mean values for different clusters are obtained as follows:

	Income	CCAvg	Age	Experience	Mortgage	Family	CreditCard	Online	Personal Loan
Cluster									
0	58.941774	1.367514	55.536044	30.233826	45.134935	2.397874	0.300370	0.604898	0.039741
1	147.650185	4.856403	43.672435	18.644005	116.279357	2.002472	0.299135	0.613103	0.398022
2	60.124322	1.382121	35.116428	9.873705	44.771584	2.552047	0.285150	0.581648	0.035520

Figure 3.41: Mean values for each cluster using other relevant features

We can clearly see that **Cluster 0** has the highest propensity for taking a personal loan. **Clusters 1** and **2** have a very similar propensity. It looks like we have identified a high potential segment.

8. Based on your understanding of the clusters, assign descriptive labels to the clusters.

We note that the key differentiating features for the clusters are **Age** and **CCAvg. Income**, **CCAvg**, and **Mortgage** follow similar patterns for the clusters.

Some basic labels for these clusters could be as follows:

Cluster 0: Middle-aged spenders (high income, high spend)

Cluster 1: Low-spending old-timers (low spend, high age, average income)

Cluster 2: Young low spenders (low spend, low age, average income)

In this activity, you helped Therabank identify high-potential segments from its existing customer base that may respond well to marketing campaigns. You achieved this by performing machine learning-based customer segmentation and included various customer variables in the model. Because you were dealing with a high number of dimensions, you employed PCA to visualize the clusters.

On examining the clusters, it was clear that **Cluster** 0 has the highest propensity for taking a personal loan. **Clusters** 1 and 2 have a similar propensity. You have found a great target segment in **Cluster** 0. A reasonable expectation here is that the type of customers that responded positively earlier to the campaign will respond positively in the next campaign as well. The segments can now be used effectively by the marketing team and help in creating a significant business impact.

CHAPTER 4: EVALUATING AND CHOOSING THE BEST SEGMENTATION APPROACH

ACTIVITY 4.01: OPTIMIZING A LUXURY CLOTHING BRAND'S MARKETING CAMPAIGN USING CLUSTERING

Solution:

1. Import the libraries required for DataFrame handling and plotting (**pandas**, **numpy**, **matplotlib**). Read in the data from the file **'Clothing_Customers.csv'** into a DataFrame and print the top 5 rows to understand it better.

```
import numpy as np, pandas as pd
import matplotlib.pyplot as plt, seaborn as sns

data0 = pd.read_csv('Clothing_Customers.csv')
data0.head()
```

> **NOTE**
>
> Make sure you place the CSV file in the same directory from where you are running the Jupyter Notebook. If not, make sure you change the path (emboldened) to match the one where you have stored the file.

The result should be the table below:

	income	age	days_since_purchase	annual_spend
0	37453	48	504	4441
1	50775	50	566	4239
2	71047	41	326	5834
3	52239	52	259	5456
4	112343	27	279	1749

Figure 4.24: Top 5 records of the data

The data contains the customers' income, age, days since their last purchase, and their annual spending. All these will be used to perform segmentation.

2. Standardize all the columns in the data. Use all four columns for the segmentation.

```
cluster_cols = data0.columns
data_scaled = data0.copy()

from sklearn.preprocessing import StandardScaler
scaler = StandardScaler()

data_scaled[cluster_cols] = scaler.fit_transform\
                            (data0[cluster_cols])
```

3. Visualize the data to get a good understanding of it. Since you are dealing with four dimensions, use **PCA** to reduce to two dimensions before plotting.

```
from sklearn import decomposition

pca = decomposition.PCA(n_components=2)
pca_res = pca.fit_transform(data_scaled[cluster_cols])

data_scaled['pc1'] = pca_res[:,0]
data_scaled['pc2'] = pca_res[:,1]

plt.figure(figsize=[8,5])
plt.scatter(data_scaled.pc1, data_scaled.pc2, color='gray')
plt.xlabel("PC1")
plt.ylabel("PC2")
plt.show()
```

The resulting plot should be as follows:

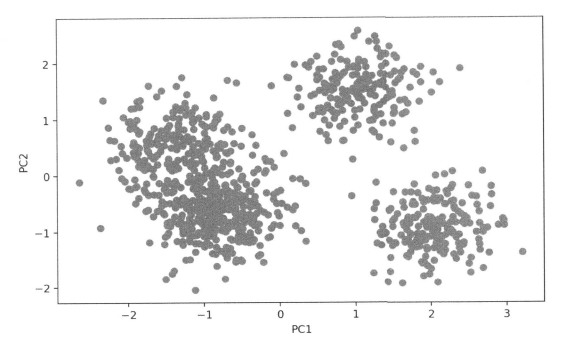

Figure 4.25: Scatterplot of the dimensionality reduced data

4. Visualize clustering for two through seven clusters:

```
from sklearn.cluster import KMeans

markers = ['x', '*', '.', '|', '_', '1', '2']

plt.figure(figsize=[15,10])
for n in range(2,8):
    model = KMeans(n_clusters=n, random_state=42)
    data_scaled['Cluster']= model.fit_predict\
                        (data_scaled[cluster_cols])

    plt.subplot(2,3, n-1)
    for clust in range(n):
        temp = data_scaled[data_scaled.Cluster == clust]
        plt.scatter(temp.pc1, temp.pc2, \
                marker=markers[clust], \
                label="Cluster "+str(clust), \
```

```
                    color='gray')
        plt.xlabel("PC1")
        plt.ylabel("PC2")
        plt.legend()
        plt.title("N clusters: "+str(n))

plt.show()
```

> **NOTE**
>
> The value **gray** for the attribute **color** (emboldened) in *Steps 3*, *4*, and *5* is used to generate graphs in grayscale. You can use other colors like **darkgreen**, **maroon**, etc. as values of **color** parameter to get the colored graphs. You can also refer to the following document to get the code for the colored plot and the colored output: http://packt.link/NOjgT.

This should result in the following plot.

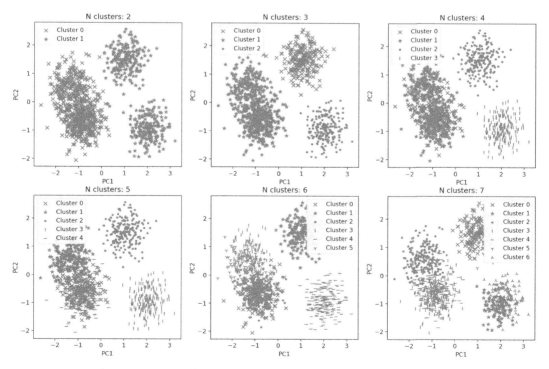

Figure 4.26: Resulting clusters for different number of clusters

From visual inspection, **3** seems to be the right number of clusters. Beyond **3**, the clusters overlap heavily.

5. Choosing clusters using `elbow` method - create a plot of the sum of squared errors and look for an elbow. Vary the number of clusters from **2** to **11**.

```python
inertia_scores = []

for K in range(2,11):
    inertia = KMeans(n_clusters=K, random_state=42)\
            .fit(data_scaled).inertia_
    inertia_scores.append(inertia)

plt.figure(figsize=[7,5])
plt.plot(range(2,11), inertia_scores, color='gray')
plt.xlabel("Number of clusters: K")
plt.ylabel('SSE/Inertia')
plt.show()
```

You should get the plot as below –

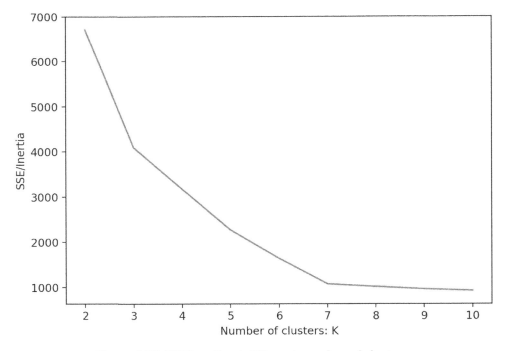

Figure 4.27: SSE/Inertia at different number of clusters

Notice that the elbow is at $K = 5$. The **elbow** method suggests using that five is the optimal number of clusters.

6.   Let us assess if the methods agree on the number of clusters.

The elbow method suggests five clusters being optimal while the visual inspection method suggests **3**. Recall that dimensionality-reduced data employing **PCA** loses some information in the **dimensionality reduction process**. The visual inspection method, therefore, is not completely reliable. Also, consider the number of customers the business can act on.

With this understanding, we decide that –

Even though visual inspection suggests **3**, it is not an optimal number of clusters. Looking at the **SSE** plot in *Figure 4.27*, we have significant gains in going beyond **3** clusters.

The elbow method suggests **5** clusters as optimal, which is not too many for the business to act upon. Unless the business has a hard constraint that they can use only up to **4** clusters, we choose **5** as the optimal number of clusters.

In this activity, you thoroughly approached customer segmentation, tried out different clustering techniques, and evaluated the clusters using statistical measures while employing the train-test approach to ensure greater reliability and stability of the clusters. You employed the silhouette score to not only identify the right number of clusters for the techniques, but also for a final comparison of the models on the test set. In this way, you utilized machine learning techniques to optimize the approach to customer segmentation and thus were able to come up with optimized customer segments. These customer segments will help the beverage company to optimize its campaigns and create a significant business impact.

ACTIVITY 4.02: EVALUATING CLUSTERING ON CUSTOMER DATA

Solution:

1. Import the necessary libraries for data handling, clustering and visualization. Import data from **customer_offers.csv** into a pandas DataFrame. Print the top five rows of the DataFrame.

```
import pandas as pd
from sklearn import cluster
from sklearn import metrics
import matplotlib.pyplot as plt
%matplotlib inline
df = pd.read_csv('customer_offers.csv')
df.head()
```

> **NOTE**
>
> Make sure you place the CSV file in the same directory from where you are running the Jupyter Notebook. If not, make sure you change the path (emboldened) to match the one where you have stored the file.

The first five rows get printed as:

	1	2	3	4	5	6	7	8	9	10	...	23	24	25	26	27	28	29	30	31	32
0	0	0	0	0	0	0	0	0	0	0	...	0	0	0	0	0	0	1	1	0	0
1	0	0	0	0	0	0	0	0	1	0	...	0	0	0	0	1	0	0	0	0	0
2	0	0	0	0	0	0	0	0	0	0	...	0	1	0	1	0	0	0	0	0	0
3	0	0	0	0	0	0	1	0	0	0	...	0	0	0	0	0	0	0	1	0	0
4	0	0	0	0	0	0	1	0	0	1	...	0	0	0	0	0	0	0	0	1	0

5 rows × 32 columns

Figure 4.28: First 5 records of the customer_offers data

The **32** columns correspond to the **32** initiatives in the past year. Each row represents a customer. We see that the values are **0** or **1**, indicators to whether the customer responded to the campaign, with **1** representing a response.

2. Divide the dataset into train and test sets by using **train_test_split** method from scikit-learn. Specify **random_state** as **100** for consistency.

```
from sklearn import model_selection


X_train, X_test = model_selection.train_test_split\
                  (df, random_state = 100)
```

3. Perform k-means on the data. Identify the optimal number of clusters by using the silhouette score approach on the train data by plotting the score for a different number of clusters, varying from **2** through **10**.

```
krange = list(range(2,11))
avg_silhouettes = []

for n in krange:
    model = cluster.KMeans(n_clusters=n, random_state=100)
    model.fit(X_train)
    cluster_assignments = model.predict(X_train)

    silhouette_avg = metrics.silhouette_score(X_train, \
                                        cluster_assignments)
    avg_silhouettes.append(silhouette_avg)

plt.plot(krange, avg_silhouettes, color='gray')
plt.xlabel(«Number of clusters»)
plt.ylabel(«Average Silhouette Score»)
plt.show()
```

> **NOTE**
>
> The value **gray** for the attribute **color** (emboldened) is used to generate graphs in grayscale. You can use other colors like **darkgreen**, **maroon**, etc. as values of **color** parameter to get the colored graphs. You can also refer to the following document to get the code for the colored plot and the colored output: http://packt.link/NOjgT.

You should obtain the following plot.

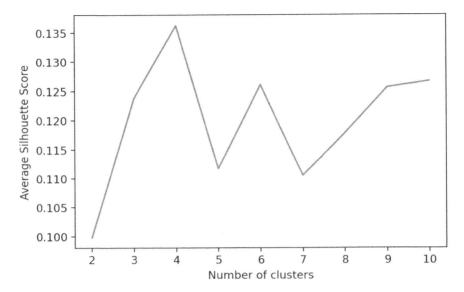

Figure 4.29: Silhouette scores for different number of clusters

From the plot for the Silhouette scores, you will observe that the maximum silhouette score is obtained at **k=4** and is around **0.135**.

4. Perform **K-Means clustering** using **k** found in the previous step. Print out the silhouette score on the test set:

```
model = cluster.KMeans(n_clusters=3, random_state=100)
model.fit(X_train)

km_labels = model.predict(X_test)
km_silhouette = metrics.silhouette_score(X_test, km_labels)

print('k-means silhouette score: ' + str(km_silhouette))
```

The resulting silhouette score should be around **0.103**. This is slightly lower than the train score of **0.135**. Note that the result does not generalize very well on the test data.

> **NOTE**
>
> You may find that the silhouette score you get may vary slightly from the result we got, despite setting the random seed. This is owing to the randomness in the cluster center initialization done by KMeans, which, unfortunately, we can't control. Nevertheless, while the value may differ slightly, the takeaways and learning would not change.

5. Perform mean-shift clustering on the data, using **estimate_bandwidth** method with a quantile value of **0.1** to estimate the bandwidth. Print out the silhouette score from the model on the test set.

```
bandwidth = cluster.estimate_bandwidth(X_train, quantile=0.1)

ms = cluster.MeanShift(bandwidth=bandwidth, bin_seeding=True)
ms.fit(X_train)

ms_labels = ms.predict(X_test)

ms_silhouette = metrics.silhouette_score(X_test, ms_labels)
print('mean-shift silhouette score: ' + str(ms_silhouette))
```

The resulting silhouette score should be around **0.073**. Note already that this is significantly lower than the score for the k-means technique.

6. Perform **k-modes** on the data. Identify the optimal number of clusters by using the silhouette score approach on the train data by plotting the score for a different number of clusters, varying from **3** through **10**.

```
from kmodes.kmodes import KModes

krange = list(range(3,11))
avg_silhouettes = []

for n in krange:
    km = KModes(n_clusters=n, random_state=100)
    km.fit(X_train)

    kmode_labels = km.predict(X_train)
    kmode_silhouette = metrics.silhouette_score\
                    (X_train, kmode_labels)
    avg_silhouettes.append(kmode_silhouette)

plt.plot(krange, avg_silhouettes, color='gray')
plt.xlabel("Number of clusters")
plt.ylabel("Average Silhouette Score")
plt.show()
```

NOTE

The value **gray** for the attribute **color** (emboldened) is used to generate graphs in grayscale. You can use other colors like **darkgreen**, **maroon**, etc. as values of **color** parameter to get the colored graphs. You can also refer to the following document to get the code for colored plot and the colored output: http://packt.link/NOjgT.

The silhouette score plot is as below:

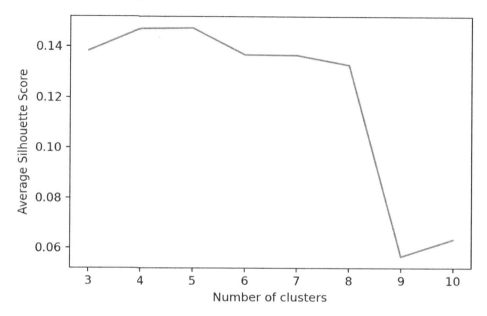

Figure 4.30: Silhouette scores for different K for K-modes

The silhouette score is practically the same for **4** and **5** clusters. We prefer **K=4** as we get the same silhouette score with a lower number of clusters.

7. Using **K** found in the previous step, perform K-modes on the data. Print out the silhouette score on the test set:

```
km = KModes(n_clusters=4, random_state=100)
km.fit(X_train)

kmode_labels = km.predict(X_test)
kmode_silhouette = metrics.silhouette_score\
                    (X_test, kmode_labels)

print('k-mode silhouette score: ' + str(kmode_silhouette))
```

The silhouette score for the test set is around **0.118**. Note that this is the highest value of all three approaches.

8. Compare the silhouette scores from the three techniques –

The silhouette score on the test set is the true evaluation of the clusters.

The k-means approach gave a score of **0.103**, which was a significant reduction from **0.135** on the train set.

The mean-shift approach gave a score of about **0.07**.

The k-modes technique gave a score of about **0.118**.

The clusters from k-mode are the most stable and generalize well. The final number of clusters we use is **4**. This number is not too low or high, as we discussed earlier, and is a convenient number for the business to work with. Now that we identified that there are 4 different types of customers, the segments can be used to optimize future campaigns for the beverage company.

CHAPTER 5: PREDICTING CUSTOMER REVENUE USING LINEAR REGRESSION

ACTIVITY 5.01: EXAMINING THE RELATIONSHIP BETWEEN STORE LOCATION AND REVENUE

Solution:

1. Import the **pandas**, **pyplot** from **matplotlib**, and **seaborn** libraries. Read the data into a DataFrame called **df** and print the top five records using the following code:

```
import pandas as pd
import matplotlib.pyplot as plt, seaborn as sns
df = pd.read_csv('location_rev.csv')
df.head()
```

> **NOTE**
>
> Make sure you change the path (highlighted) to the CSV file based on its location on your system. If you're running the Jupyter notebook from the same directory where the CSV file is stored, you can run the preceding code without any modification.

The data should appear as follows:

revenue	num_competitors	median_income	num_loyalty_members	population_density	location_age
42247.80	3.0	30527.57	1407.0	3302.0	12.0
38628.37	3.0	30185.49	1025.0	4422.0	11.0
39715.16	1.0	32182.24	1498.0	3260.0	12.0
35593.30	5.0	29728.65	2340.0	4325.0	10.0
35128.18	4.0	30691.17	847.0	3774.0	11.0

Figure 5.35: The first five rows of the location revenue data

You see that, as described earlier, you have the revenue of the store, its age, along with various fields about the location of the store. From the top five records, you get a sense of the order of the values for the different columns. You notice that the revenue values are in the order of tens of thousands, and so is the median income. Likewise, you note the scale and some sample values of the columns.

2. Create a scatter plot between **median_income** and the **revenue** of the store using the **plot** method:

```
df.plot.scatter("median_income", 'revenue', \
                figsize=[5,5], color='gray')
plt.show()
```

> **NOTE**
>
> The value **gray** for the attribute **color** is used to generate graphs in grayscale. You can use other colors such as **darkgreen**, **maroon**, and so on as values of the **color** parameter to get colored graphs. You can also refer to the following document to get the code for the colored plot and the colored output: http://packt.link/NOjgT.

The output should look as follows:

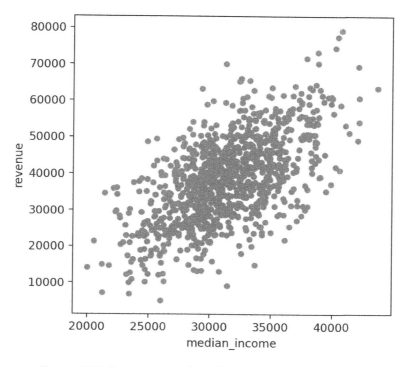

Figure 5.36: Scatter plot of median_income and revenue

There seems to be a decent association between the two variables. Let us examine the other associations in the data.

3. Use seaborn's **pairplot** function to visualize the data and its relationships:

```
sns.set_palette('Greys_r')
sns.pairplot(df)
plt.show()
```

> **NOTE**
>
> The value **Greys_r** (emboldened) is used to generate graphs in grayscale. You can also refer to the following document to get the code for the colored plot and the colored output: http://packt.link/NOjgT.

The plots should appear as shown here:

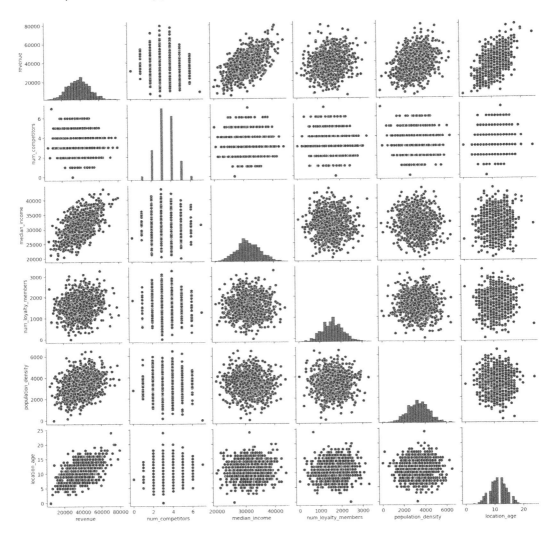

Figure 5.37: The seaborn pairplot of the entire dataset

The pairplot produces scatter plots for all possible combinations of variables. Notice that there are only a few cases where there is any decent association between any pairs of variables. The strongest relations seem to be between `revenue` and `location_age`, and `revenue` and `median_income`.

4. Using the **y_vars** parameter, plot the row for associations with the **revenue** variable:

```
sns.pairplot(df, x_vars=df.columns, y_vars="revenue")
plt.show()
```

You should get the following plot:

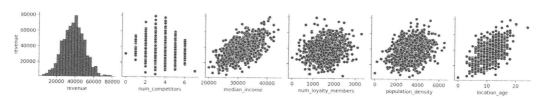

Figure 5.38: Associations with revenue

From this view focused on revenue, you see that revenue has decent associations with the **location_age** and **median_income** variables. A numeric value will help identify which of them is stronger.

5. Finally, use correlations to investigate the relationship between the different variables and location revenue:

```
df.corr()
```

You should get the following table as output:

	revenue	num_competitors	median_income	num_loyalty_members	population_density	location_age
revenue	1.000000	-0.156685	0.601888	0.173432	0.311653	0.552773
num_competitors	-0.156685	1.000000	-0.018398	-0.027283	0.035768	0.053796
median_income	0.601888	-0.018398	1.000000	0.011891	-0.041697	0.045621
num_loyalty_members	0.173432	-0.027283	0.011891	1.000000	-0.028611	0.036016
population_density	0.311653	0.035768	-0.041697	-0.028611	1.000000	-0.009977
location_age	0.552773	0.053796	0.045621	0.036016	-0.009977	1.000000

Figure 5.39: The correlations between each variable
and each other variable in the dataset

As you can see from the preceding figure, the highest correlation of revenue is with **median_income**. Looking at the magnitudes and signs, you can assess whether the results make business sense. The more competitors in the area, the lower the revenue of that location. Also, you can observe that the median income, loyalty members, and population density are all positively related. A location's age is also positively correlated with revenue, indicating that the longer a location is open, the better known it is, and the more customers it attracts (or perhaps, only locations that do well last a long time).

ACTIVITY 5.02: PREDICTING STORE REVENUE USING LINEAR REGRESSION

Solution:

1. Import the **numpy, pandas, pyplot** from **matplotlib**, and **seaborn** libraries. Read the data into a pandas DataFrame named **df** and use the **head** method to print the first five records:

```
import numpy as np, pandas as pd
import matplotlib.pyplot as plt, seaborn as sns

df = pd.read_csv('location_rev.csv')
df.head()
```

> **NOTE**
>
> Make sure you change the path (highlighted) to the CSV file based on its location on your system. If you're running the Jupyter notebook from the same directory where the CSV file is stored, you can run the preceding code without any modification.

You should get the following output:

	revenue	num_competitors	median_income	num_loyalty_members	population_density	location_age
0	42247.80	3.0	30527.57	1407.0	3302.0	12.0
1	38628.37	3.0	30185.49	1025.0	4422.0	11.0
2	39715.16	1.0	32182.24	1498.0	3260.0	12.0
3	35593.30	5.0	29728.65	2340.0	4325.0	10.0
4	35128.18	4.0	30691.17	847.0	3774.0	11.0

Figure 5.40: First five records of the store data

You see that as described and as you saw earlier, you have the revenue of the store and its age, along with various fields about the location of the store.

2. Create a variable, **X**, with the predictors (everything except **revenue**) in it, and store the outcome (**revenue**) in a separate variable, **y**:

```
X = df[['num_competitors',\
        'median_income',\
        'num_loyalty_members',\
        'population_density',\
        'location_age']]
y = df['revenue']
```

3. Split the data into training and test sets. Use **random_state = 100** (an arbitrary choice, to ensure consistent results):

```
from sklearn.model_selection import train_test_split
X_train, X_test, y_train, y_test = train_test_split\
                            (X, y, random_state = 100)
```

4. Create a linear regression model and fit it on the training data:

```
from sklearn.linear_model import LinearRegression

model = LinearRegression()
model.fit(X_train,y_train)
```

5. Print out the model coefficients using the following code:

```
model.coef_
```

The coefficients should be as follows:

```
array([-2.14765128e+03,  1.71903196e+00,  3.50665069e+00,
4.31777912e+00,  2.06703103e+03])
```

6. Print out the model intercept using the following code:

```
model.intercept_
```

You should get a value around **-51068.6**.

7. Produce a prediction for a location that has **3** competitors; a median income of **30,000**; **1,200** loyalty members; a population density of **2,000**; and a location age of **10**:

```
single_location = pd.DataFrame({'num_competitors': [3],\
                                'median_income': [30000],\
                                'num_loyalty_members': [1200],\
                                'population_density': [2000],\
                                'location_age': [10]})

model.predict(single_location)
```

The prediction should be around **27573**.

8. Plot the model predictions versus the true values on the test data:

```
plt.scatter(model.predict(X_test),y_test)
plt.xlabel('Model Predictions')
plt.ylabel('True Value')
plt.plot([0, 100000], [0, 100000], 'k-', color = 'gray')
plt.show()
```

> **NOTE**
>
> The value **gray** for the attribute **color** is used to generate graphs in grayscale. You can use other colors such as **darkgreen**, **maroon**, and so on as values of the **color** parameter to get colored graphs. You can also refer to the following document to get the code for the colored plot and the colored output: http://packt.link/NOjgT.

The result should be like the following:

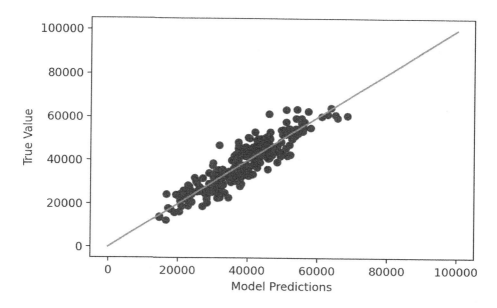

Figure 5.41: True values versus predictions

From the plot, it is evident that there is a very strong association between the predicted and actual values. This tells us that the model is doing a good job at predicting the revenue values for the stores. A correlation value will quantify this association.

9. Calculate the correlation between the model predictions and the true values of the test data using the following code:

```
np.corrcoef(model.predict(X_test), y_test)
```

The correlation should be around **0.91**. Taken together, this confirms that your model is working very well on the test data as well and, therefore, can be used reliably on newer, unseen data.

In this activity, you have used linear regression to effectively create a model to predict the revenue for a store based on its age and information about its location. The model performed extremely well on unseen test data. Using the understanding from the model, the company can predict revenue for any store. Also, more importantly, this understanding can help the company best place upcoming stores to maximize the revenue from these stores. You have now seen how easy-to-implement models such as linear regression can help solve business problems.

CHAPTER 6: MORE TOOLS AND TECHNIQUES FOR EVALUATING REGRESSION MODELS

ACTIVITY 6.01: FINDING IMPORTANT VARIABLES FOR PREDICTING RESPONSES TO A MARKETING OFFER

Solution:

Perform the following steps to achieve the aim of this activity:

1. Import **pandas**, read in the data from **offer_responses.csv**, and use the **head** function to view the first five rows of the data:

```
import pandas as pd

df = pd.read_csv('offer_responses.csv')
df.head()
```

> **NOTE**
>
> Make sure you change the path (emboldened) to the CSV file based on its location on your system. If you're running the Jupyter notebook from the same directory where the CSV file is stored, you can run the preceding code without any modifications.

You should get the following output:

	responses	offer_discount	offer_quality	offer_reach
0	4151.0	26.0	10.257680	31344.0
1	3397.0	35.0	15.194380	24016.0
2	3274.0	21.0	13.971468	28832.0
3	3426.0	27.0	6.054338	26747.0
4	5745.0	42.0	16.801365	46968.0

Figure 6.22: The first five rows of the offer_responses data

2. Extract the target variable (**y**) and the predictor variable (**X**) from the data:

```
X = df[['offer_quality',\
        'offer_discount',\
        'offer_reach'\]]

y = df['responses']
```

3. Import **train_test_split** from **sklearn** and use it to split the data into training and test sets, using responses as the **y** variable and all others as the predictor (**X**) variables. Use **random_state=10** for **train_test_split**:

```
from sklearn.model_selection import train_test_split

X_train, X_test, y_train, y_test = train_test_split\
                        (X, y, random_state = 10)
```

4. Import **LinearRegression** and **mean_squared_error** from **sklearn**. Fit the model to the training data (using all the predictors), get predictions from the model on the test data, and print out the calculated RMSE on the test data:

```
from sklearn.linear_model import LinearRegression
from sklearn.metrics import mean_squared_error

model = LinearRegression()
model.fit(X_train,y_train)

predictions = model.predict(X_test)

print('RMSE with all variables: ' + \
        str(mean_squared_error(predictions, y_test)**0.5))
```

You will get an output similar to the following:

```
RMSE with all variables: 966.2461828577945
```

5. Create **X_train2** and **X_test2** by dropping the **offer_quality** column from **X_train** and **X_test**. Train and evaluate the RMSE of the model using **X_train2** and **X_test2**:

```
X_train2 = X_train.drop('offer_quality',axis=1)
X_test2 = X_test.drop('offer_quality',axis=1)

model = LinearRegression()
model.fit(X_train2,y_train)

predictions = model.predict(X_test2)

print('RMSE without offer quality: ' + \
        str(mean_squared_error(predictions, y_test)**0.5))
```

You will get the following output:

```
RMSE without offer quality: 965.5346123758474
```

As you can see, by dropping the **offer_quality** column, the RMSE went down, which shows the model was able to give more accurate predictions. This shows an improvement in the model performance and robustness, which is a positive sign.

6. Repeat the instructions given in *step 5*, but this time dropping the **offer_discount** column instead of the **offer_quality** column:

```
X_train3 = X_train.drop('offer_discount',axis=1)
X_test3 = X_test.drop('offer_discount',axis=1)

model = LinearRegression()
model.fit(X_train3,y_train)

predictions = model.predict(X_test3)

print('RMSE without offer discount: ' + \
        str(mean_squared_error(predictions, y_test)**0.5))
```

You will get the following output:

```
RMSE without offer discount: 1231.6766556327284
```

7. Perform the same sequence of steps, but this time dropping the **offer_reach** column:

```
X_train4 = X_train.drop('offer_reach',axis=1)
X_test4 = X_test.drop('offer_reach',axis=1)

model = LinearRegression()
model.fit(X_train4,y_train)

predictions = model.predict(X_test4)

print('RMSE without offer reach: ' + \
    str(mean_squared_error(predictions, y_test)**0.5))
```

You will get the following output:

```
RMSE without offer reach: 1185.8456831644114
```

Let's summarize the RMSE values we have obtained so far:

Variables	RMSE Values
With all variables	966.2461828577945
Without offer_quality	965.5346123758474
Without offer_discount	1231.6766556327284
Without offer_reach	1185.8456831644114

Figure 6.23: Summary of the RMSE values

You should notice that the RMSE went up when the **offer_reach** column, or the **offer_discount** column, was removed from the model but remained about the same when the **offer_quality** column was removed. The change in RMSE values is directly related to the importance of the feature being removed.

For example, if the RMSE goes down, this means that the predictions made by the model were more accurate. This further means that the new model is a more accurate model than the original one. Similarly, if removing a feature results in the RMSE increasing, this means that the predictions have become further apart from the original values, which means that the feature was important and should not have been removed.

This suggests that the **offer_quality** column is not contributing to the accuracy of the model and could be safely removed to simplify the model.

ACTIVITY 6.02: USING RFE TO CHOOSE FEATURES FOR PREDICTING CUSTOMER SPEND

Solution:

Perform the following steps to achieve the aim of this activity:

1. Import **pandas**, use it to read the data in **customer_spend.csv**, and use the **head** function to view the first five rows of data:

```
import pandas as pd

df = pd.read_csv('customer_spend.csv')
df.head()
```

> **NOTE**
>
> Make sure you change the path (emboldened) to the CSV file based on its location on your system. If you're running the Jupyter notebook from the same directory where the CSV file is stored, you can run the preceding code without any modifications.

You should get the following output:

	cur_year_spend	prev_year_spend	days_since_last_purchase	days_since_first_purchase
0	5536.46	1681.26	7	61
1	871.41	1366.74	12	34
2	2046.74	1419.38	10	81
3	4662.70	1561.21	12	32
4	3539.46	1397.60	17	72

Figure 6.24: The first five rows of customer_spend.csv

> **NOTE**
>
> The preceding image does not contain all the columns of the DataFrame. The image is used for demonstration purposes only.

2. Extract the target variable (**y**) and the predictor variable (**X**) from the data:

```
cols = df.columns[1:]
X = df[cols]

y = df['cur_year_spend']
```

3. Use **train_test_split** from **sklearn** to split the data into training and test sets, with **random_state=100** and **cur_year_spend** as the **y** variable:

```
from sklearn.model_selection import train_test_split

X_train, X_test, y_train, y_test = train_test_split\
                                    (X, y, random_state = 100)
```

4. Import **RFE** from **sklearn** and use **LinearRegression** as the estimator. Use **n_features_to_select = 3**, since we only want the top three features:

```
from sklearn.feature_selection import RFE
rfe = RFE(estimator=LinearRegression(), n_features_to_select=3)
```

5. Next, fit RFE (created in the previous step) on the training dataset:

```
rfe.fit(X_train,y_train)
```

You will be able to see the following output:

```
RFE(estimator=LinearRegression(copy_X=True, fit_intercept=True,
n_jobs=None, normalize=False), n_features_to_select=3, step=1,
verbose=0)
```

> **NOTE**
>
> The output may vary from system to system.

6. Print the columns that were selected by RFE, along with their rank:

```
for featureNum in range(X_train.shape[1]):
  # If feature was selected
  if rfe.support_[featureNum] == True:
    # Print feature name and rank
    print("Feature: {}, Rank: {}"\
          .format(X_train.columns[featureNum],\
                  rfe.ranking_[featureNum]))
```

The output obtained for this code is given here:

```
Feature: days_since_first_purchase, Rank: 1
Feature: total_transactions, Rank: 1
Feature: engagement_score, Rank: 1
```

Notice that only three features were selected by RFE and all of those features were given a rank **1**, meaning that RFE considered all three features to be equally important.

7. Using the information from the preceding step, create a reduced dataset having just the columns selected by RFE:

```
X_train_reduced = X_train[X_train.columns[rfe.support_]]
X_test_reduced = X_test[X_train.columns[rfe.support_]]
```

8. Next, use the reduced training dataset to fit a new linear regression model:

```
rfe_model = LinearRegression()
rfe_model.fit(X_train_reduced,y_train)
```

You will get the following output:

```
LinearRegression(copy_X=True, fit_intercept=True, n_jobs=None,
normalize=False)
```

> **NOTE**
>
> The output may vary from system to system.

9. Import **mean_squared_error** from **sklearn** and use it to calculate the RMSE of the linear regression model on the test data:

```
from sklearn.metrics import mean_squared_error

rfe_predictions = rfe_model.predict(X_test_reduced)
print(mean_squared_error(rfe_predictions, y_test)**0.5)
```

The output should be **1075.9083016269915**.

ACTIVITY 6.03: BUILDING THE BEST REGRESSION MODEL FOR CUSTOMER SPEND BASED ON DEMOGRAPHIC DATA

Solution:

Perform the following steps to achieve the aim of the activity:

1. Import **pandas**, read the data in **spend_age_income_ed.csv** into a DataFrame, and use the **head** function to view the first five rows of the data:

```
import pandas as pd

df = pd.read_csv('spend_age_income_ed.csv')
df.head()
```

> **NOTE**
>
> Make sure you change the path (emboldened) to the CSV file based on its location on your system. If you're running the Jupyter notebook from the same directory where the CSV file is stored, you can run the preceding code without any modifications.

You should get the following output:

	spend	age	income	years_of_education
0	3304.0	36.0	45125.0	12
1	3709.0	43.0	41695.0	10
2	3305.0	47.0	39253.0	17
3	2170.0	33.0	32384.0	13
4	2113.0	30.0	33182.0	10

Figure 6.25: The first five rows of the spend_age_income_ed data

2. Extract the target variable (**y**) and the predictor variable (**X**) from the data:

```
X = df[['age','income','years_of_education']]
y = df['spend']
```

3. Perform a train-test split, with **random_state=10**:

```
from sklearn.model_selection import train_test_split

X_train, X_test, y_train, y_test = train_test_split\
                                    (X, y, random_state = 10)
```

4. Fit a linear regression model to the training data:

```
from sklearn.linear_model import LinearRegression

model = LinearRegression()
model.fit(X_train,y_train)
```

You will get the following output:

```
LinearRegression(copy_X=True, fit_intercept=True, n_jobs=None,
normalize=False)
```

> **NOTE**
>
> The output may vary from system to system.

5. Fit two regression tree models to the data, one with **max_depth=2** and one with **max_depth=5**:

```
from sklearn.tree import DecisionTreeRegressor

max2_tree_model = DecisionTreeRegressor(max_depth=2)
max2_tree_model.fit(X_train,y_train)

max5_tree_model = DecisionTreeRegressor(max_depth=5)
max5_tree_model.fit(X_train,y_train)
```

You will get the following output:

```
DecisionTreeRegressor(ccp_alpha=0.0, criterion='mse', max_depth=5,
                      max_features=None, max_leaf_nodes=None,
                      min_impurity_decrease=0.0, min_impurity_
split=None,
                      min_samples_leaf=1, min_samples_split=2,
                      min_weight_fraction_leaf=0.0,
presort='deprecated',
                      random_state=None, splitter='best')
```

NOTE

The output may vary from system to system.

6. Fit two random forest models to the data, one with **max_depth=2**, one with **max_depth=5**, using **random_state=10** for both:

```
from sklearn.ensemble import RandomForestRegressor

max2_forest_model = RandomForestRegressor(max_depth=2, \
                                          random_state=10)
max2_forest_model.fit(X_train,y_train)

max5_forest_model = RandomForestRegressor(max_depth=5, \
                                          random_state=10)
max5_forest_model.fit(X_train,y_train)
```

You will get the following output:

```
RandomForestRegressor(bootstrap=True, criterion='mse', max_depth=5,
          max_features='auto', max_leaf_nodes=None,
          min_impurity_decrease=0.0, min_impurity_split=None,
          min_samples_leaf=1, min_samples_split=2,
          min_weight_fraction_leaf=0.0, n_estimators=10, n_jobs=1,
          oob_score=False, random_state=10, verbose=0,
          warm_start=False)
```

NOTE

The output may vary from system to system.

7. Calculate and print out the RMSE on the test data for all five models:

```
from sklearn.metrics import mean_squared_error

linear_predictions = model.predict(X_test)
print('Linear model RMSE: ' + \
      str(mean_squared_error(linear_predictions, y_test)**0.5))

max2_tree_predictions = max2_tree_model.predict(X_test)
print('Tree with max depth of 2 RMSE: ' + \
      str(mean_squared_error(max2_tree_predictions, y_test)**0.5))

max5_tree_predictions = max5_tree_model.predict(X_test)
print('Tree with max depth of 5 RMSE: ' + \
      str(mean_squared_error(max5_tree_predictions, y_test)**0.5))

max2_forest_predictions = max2_forest_model.predict(X_test)
print('Random Forest with max depth of 2 RMSE: ' + \
      str(mean_squared_error(max2_forest_predictions, \
                             y_test)**0.5))

max5_forest_predictions = max5_forest_model.predict(X_test)
print('Random Forest with max depth of 5 RMSE: ' + \
      str(mean_squared_error(max5_forest_predictions, \
                             y_test)**0.5))
```

You will get the following output after running the preceding code:

```
Linear model RMSE: 348.19771532747865
Tree with max depth of 2 RMSE: 268.51069264082935
Tree with max depth of 5 RMSE: 125.53257106419696
Random Forest with max depth of 2 RMSE: 266.45844988320863
Random Forest with max depth of 5 RMSE: 115.2014058797442
```

You can see that, with this particular problem, a random forest with a maximum depth of **5** does best out of the models we tried since it has the least RMSE among the five regression models. This is similar to what we observed in the previous exercise. This further shows the power of tree-based models over linear regression models in the case of non-linear data.

In general, it's good to try a few different types of models and values for parameters (for example, maximum depth) to ensure that you get the model that captures the relationships in the data well.

CHAPTER 7: SUPERVISED LEARNING: PREDICTING CUSTOMER CHURN

ACTIVITY 7.01: PERFORMING THE OSE TECHNIQUE FROM OSEMN

Solution:

1. Import the necessary libraries:

```
# Removes Warnings
import warnings
warnings.filterwarnings('ignore')
#import the necessary packages
import pandas as pd
import numpy as np
import matplotlib.pyplot as plt
import seaborn as sns
```

2. Download the dataset from https://packt.link/80blQ and save it as **Telco_Churn_Data.csv**. Make sure to run the notebook from the same folder as the dataset.

3. Create a DataFrame called **data** and read the dataset using pandas' **read.csv** method. Look at the first few rows of the DataFrame:

```
data= pd.read_csv(r'Telco_Churn_Data.csv')
data.head(5)
```

> **NOTE**
>
> Make sure you change the path (emboldened in the preceding code snippet) to the CSV file based on its location on your system. If you're running the Jupyter notebook from the same directory where the CSV file is stored, you can run the preceding code without any modification.

The code will give the following output:

	Target Churn	Target Code	Current Bill Amt	Avg Calls	Avg Calls Weekdays	Account Age	Percent Increase MOM	Acct Plan Subtype	Complaint Code	Avg Days Delinquent	Current TechSupComplaints
0	No Churn	0	14210	17950.000000	30297.0000	24	-0.334193	Gold	Billing Problem	6.2	0
1	Churn	1	14407	0.000000	0.0000	28	0.000000	Silver	Moving	1.0	0
2	Churn	1	12712	204.666667	10393.6667	23	0.000000	Gold	Billing Problem	17.6	0
3	No Churn	0	13807	15490.333300	41256.3333	39	0.148986	Silver	Billing Problem	0.0	0
4	No Churn	0	3805	5075.000000	12333.3333	23	-0.686047	Gold	Billing Problem	3.8	0

Figure 7.61: First five rows of Telco_Churn_Data.csv

> **NOTE**
>
> The preceding image does not contain all the columns of the DataFrame. The image is for demonstration purposes only.

4. Check the length and shape of the data:

```
len(data)
data.shape
```

The length should be **4708** and the shape should be (**4708, 15**).

5. Check for any missing values present in the dataset using the following command:

```
data.isnull().values.any()
```

This will return **True**, implying that missing values are present.

6. Use the **info** method to check the missing values in each of the columns:

```
data.info()
```

This gives the following output:

```
<class 'pandas.core.frame.DataFrame'>
RangeIndex: 4708 entries, 0 to 4707
Data columns (total 15 columns):
 #   Column                      Non-Null Count   Dtype
---  ------                      --------------   -----
 0   Target Churn                4708 non-null    object
 1   Target Code                 4708 non-null    int64
 2   Current Bill Amt            4708 non-null    int64
 3   Avg Calls                   4708 non-null    float64
 4   Avg Calls Weekdays          4708 non-null    float64
 5   Account Age                 4708 non-null    int64
 6   Percent Increase MOM        4708 non-null    float64
 7   Acct Plan Subtype           4708 non-null    object
 8   Complaint Code              4701 non-null    object
 9   Avg Days Delinquent         4708 non-null    float64
 10  Current TechSupComplaints   4708 non-null    int64
 11  Current Days OpenWorkOrders 4708 non-null    float64
 12  Equipment Age               4708 non-null    int64
 13  Condition of Current Handset 4264 non-null   float64
 14  Avg Hours WorkOrderOpenned  4708 non-null    float64
dtypes: float64(7), int64(5), object(3)
memory usage: 551.8+ KB
```

Figure 7.62: Output of data.info

You can see that only two columns, **Condition of Current Handset** and **Complaint Code**, have missing values.

7. Convert all the spaces in column names to _; for example, rename **Target Code** to **Target_Code**:

```
data.columns=data.columns.str.replace(' ','_')
```

8. Next, fix the typo in the **Avg_Hours_WorkOrderOpenned** column by first creating a new column with the correct spelling (**Avg_Hours_WorkOrderOpened**) and then dropping the original column.

```
# Fix typo in Avg_Hours_WorkOrderOpenned column
data['Avg_Hours_WorkOrderOpened'] = \
data['Avg_Hours_WorkOrderOpenned']
# Let's drop the older column (with typo)
data.drop(["Avg_Hours_WorkOrderOpenned"],axis=1,inplace=True)
```

9. Next, get a list of all the columns in the dataset:

```
data.columns
```

You should get the following output:

```
Index(['Target_Churn', 'Target_Code', 'Current_Bill_Amt', 'Avg_Calls',
       'Avg_Calls_Weekdays', 'Account_Age', 'Percent_Increase_MOM',
       'Acct_Plan_Subtype', 'Complaint_Code', 'Avg_Days_Delinquent',
       'Current_TechSupComplaints', 'Current_Days_OpenWorkOrders',
       'Equipment_Age', 'Condition_of_Current_Handset',
       'Avg_Hours_WorkOrderOpened'],
      dtype='object')
```

Figure 7.63: The columns in the dataset

Notice that all the column names with spaces have now been modified and the typo in the **Avg_Hours_WorkOrderOpenned** column has been fixed, just like we wanted.

10. Check the descriptive statistics of the data using the following command:

```
data.describe()
```

The code will give the following output:

	Target_Code	Current_Bill_Amt	Avg_Calls	Avg_Calls_Weekdays	Account_Age
count	4708.000000	4708.000000	4708.000000	4708.000000	4708.000000
mean	0.485769	19828.815845	9269.690314	38127.994973	26.079652
std	0.499851	17204.510108	10437.339850	39172.244943	7.149933
min	0.000000	-690.000000	0.000000	0.000000	15.000000
25%	0.000000	12288.000000	2602.250002	13031.250025	20.000000
50%	0.000000	15254.000000	6396.333330	26765.833350	25.000000
75%	1.000000	22799.000000	12250.499975	50061.416675	32.000000
max	1.000000	325127.000000	181786.000000	374457.667000	40.000000

Figure 7.64: Output of the describe function

NOTE

The preceding image does not contain all the columns of the DataFrame. The image is for demonstration purposes only.

11. Check the descriptive statistics of the categorical variables:

```
data.describe(include='object')
```

This code will generate the following output. Notice that the frequency of **No Churn** is around half of the total count, meaning that there is no significant class imbalance problem in the dataset:

	Target_Churn	Acct_Plan_Subtype	Complaint_Code
count	4708	4708	4701
unique	2	2	6
top	No Churn	Silver	Billing Problem
freq	2421	3914	2908

Figure 7.65: Output of describe function

12. Change the data type of the **Target_Code**, **Condition_of_Current_Handset**, and **Current_TechSupComplaints** columns from continuous to the categorical object type. This has been done in order to convert them to categorical features since they have only distinct values:

```
data['Target_Code']=data.Target_Code.astype('object')
data['Condition_of_Current_Handset']=\
data.Condition_of_Current_Handset.astype('object')
data['Current_TechSupComplaints']=\
data.Current_TechSupComplaints.astype('object')
data['Target_Code']=data.Target_Code.astype('int64')
data.describe(include='object')
```

This gives the following output:

	Target_Churn	Acct_Plan_Subtype	Complaint_Code	Current_TechSupComplaints	Condition_of_Current_Handset
count	4708	4708	4701	4708	4264.0
unique	2	2	6	11	3.0
top	No Churn	Silver	Billing Problem	0	1.0
freq	2421	3914	2908	3589	4186.0

Figure 7.66: Output of the describe function for the categorical variables

13. Check the percentage of missing values and then impute the values of both **Complaint_Code** and **Condition_of_Current_Handset** with the most frequently occurring values:

```
round(data.isnull().sum()/len(data)*100,2)
```

You should get the following output. Note that there are around 9.43% missing values in the **Condition_of_Current_Handset** column. On the other hand, the **Complaint_Code** column has just 0.15% missing values:

```
Target_Churn                    0.00
Target_Code                     0.00
Current_Bill_Amt                0.00
Avg_Calls                       0.00
Avg_Calls_Weekdays              0.00
Account_Age                     0.00
Percent_Increase_MOM            0.00
Acct_Plan_Subtype               0.00
Complaint_Code                  0.15
Avg_Days_Delinquent             0.00
Current_TechSupComplaints       0.00
Current_Days_OpenWorkOrders     0.00
Equipment_Age                   0.00
Condition_of_Current_Handset    9.43
Avg_Hours_WorkOrderOpened       0.00
dtype: float64
```

Figure 7.67: Checking the percentages of missing values in the columns

14. Now that we know the percentage of missing values in the columns, we can impute these missing values by replacing them with the most commonly occurring values in the respective columns. First, find the frequency of the distinct values in the two columns that have missing values:

```
data.Complaint_Code.value_counts()
```

You should get the following output. As you can see, the most commonly occurring value in this column is **Billing Problem**:

```
Billing Problem          2908
Call Quality             1070
Moving                    511
Check Account             195
Inaccurate Sales Inf       13
Pricing                     4
Name: Complaint_Code, dtype: int64
```

Figure 7.68: Checking for missing values in the Complaint_Code column

15. Next, find the frequency of values in the **Condition_of_Current_Handset** column:

```
data.Condition_of_Current_Handset.value_counts()
```

You should get the following output. Note that **1.0** occurs most frequently in the column:

```
1.0     4186
2.0       74
3.0        4
Name: Condition_of_Current_Handset, dtype: int64
```

Figure 7.69: Checking for missing values in the Condition_of_Current_Handset column

16. Now that you know the most frequently occurring values for the two columns, replace the missing values with these values using the following code:

```
data['Complaint_Code']=data['Complaint_Code']\
                    .fillna(value='Billing Problem')
data['Condition_of_Current_Handset']=\
data['Condition_of_Current_Handset'].fillna(value=1)
data['Condition_of_Current_Handset']=\
data.Condition_of_Current_Handset.astype('object')
```

17. Perform data exploration initially by exploring the customer **Target_Churn** variable. Start by finding the frequency of the distinct values in the column:

```
data['Target_Churn'].value_counts(0)
```

This will give the following output.

```
No Churn      2421
Churn         2287
Name: Target_Churn, dtype: int64
```

Figure 7.70: Frequency of the distinct values in the column

Note that the values have a similar frequency, showing an absence of a class imbalance in the dataset.

18. Find the frequency in terms of percentages, which is a much better way of presenting and analyzing the values:

```
data['Target_Churn'].value_counts(1)*100
```

This will give the following output:

```
No Churn      51.42311
Churn         48.57689
Name: Target_Churn, dtype: float64
```

Figure 7.71: Percentage of the frequency of the distinct values in the column

Again, you can see that the values have roughly the same percentage of occurrence.

19. Finally, compare the data for churned customers versus those who haven't churned by grouping the data by the **Target_Churn** column as follows:

```
summary_churn = data.groupby('Target_Churn')
summary_churn.mean()
```

This will give the following output. This helps in understanding which columns have major variations in **Churn** and **No Churn** values. For example, **Avg_Hours_WorkOrderOpened** has a similar value for both cases. On the other hand, **Avg_Days_Delinquent** is higher for **Churn**. These inferences can help a marketing analyst to come up with certain hypothesis statements about the behavior of a given customer:

	Target_Code	Current_Bill_Amt	Avg_Calls	Avg_Calls_Weekdays	Account_Age
Target_Churn					
Churn	1.0	20182.709226	9348.878298	37524.030899	25.418452
No Churn	0.0	19494.510120	9194.885309	38698.530221	26.704254

Figure 7.72: Comparison of the data for churned customers
and those who haven't churned

NOTE

The preceding image does not contain all the columns of the DataFrame. The image is for demonstration purposes only.

20. Find the correlation among different variables:

```
corr = data.corr()
plt.figure(figsize=(15,8))
sns.heatmap(corr, \
            xticklabels=corr.columns.values, \
            yticklabels=corr.columns.values,annot=True,\
            cmap='Greys_r')
corr
```

NOTE

The **Grey_r** value for the **cmap** attribute is used to generate the graph in grayscale. You can remove this attribute to get the colored graph. The code would then look like the following:

```
sns.heatmap(corr, \
            xticklabels=corr.columns.values,\
            yticklabels=corr.columns.values,\
            annot=True)
```

You can also refer to the following document to get the code for the colored plot and colored output: http://packt.link/NOjgT.

This gives the following result:

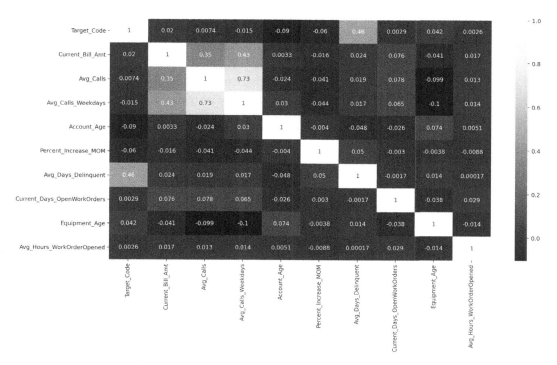

Figure 7.73: Correlation among different variables

From the plot, you will observe that **Avg_Calls_Weekdays** and **Avg_Calls** are highly correlated, as they both represent the same thing – average calls. **Current_Bill_Amt** seems to be correlated with both variables, which is as expected, since the more calls you make, the higher your bill will be.

21. Next, perform univariate and bivariate analyses. Here's the univariate analysis:

```
f, axes = plt.subplots(ncols=3, figsize=(15, 6))
sns.distplot(data.Avg_Calls_Weekdays, kde=True, \
             color="gray", \
             ax=axes[0]).set_title('Avg_Calls_Weekdays')
axes[0].set_ylabel('No of Customers')
sns.distplot(data.Avg_Calls, kde=True, color="gray", \
             ax=axes[1]).set_title('Avg_Calls')
axes[1].set_ylabel('No of Customers')
sns.distplot(data.Current_Bill_Amt, kde=True, color="gray", \
             ax=axes[2]).set_title('Current_Bill_Amt')
axes[2].set_ylabel('No of Customers')
```

> **NOTE**
>
> The **gray** value for the **color** attribute is used to generate the graphs in grayscale. You can use other colors, such as **darkgreen**, **maroon**, and so on, as values of the **color** parameter to get the colored graphs. You can also refer to the following document to get the code for the colored plot and the colored output: http://packt.link/NOjgT.

You should get the following output. Please ignore any warnings:

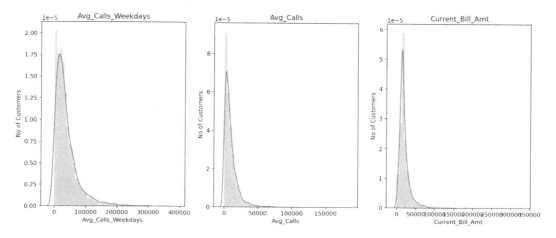

Figure 7.74: Univariate analysis

22. Now, perform the bivariate analysis.

The code for the plot of **Complaint_Code** versus **Target_Churn** is as follows:

```
plt.figure(figsize=(17,10))
p=sns.countplot(y="Complaint_Code", hue='Target_Churn', \
                data=data, palette="Greys_r")
legend = p.get_legend()
legend_txt = legend.texts
legend_txt[0].set_text("No Churn")
legend_txt[1].set_text("Churn")
p.set_title('Customer Complaint Code Distribution')
```

You should get an output like the following:

> **NOTE**
>
> The **Greys_r** value of the **palette** attribute is used to generate the graphs in grayscale. You can use **palette="Set2"** to get colored bar charts. You can also refer to the following document to get the code for the colored plots and the colored output: http://packt.link/NOjgT.

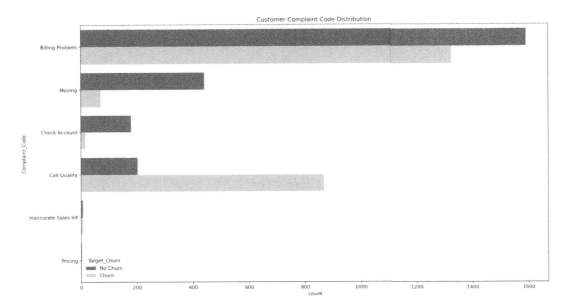

Figure 7.75: Bivariate analysis

From this plot, you'll observe that call quality and billing problems are the two main reasons for customer churn.

The code for the plot of **Acct_Plan_Subtype** versus **Target_Churn** is as follows:

```
plt.figure(figsize=(15,4))
p=sns.countplot(y="Acct_Plan_Subtype", hue='Target_Churn', \
                data=data,palette="Greys_r")
legend = p.get_legend()
legend_txt = legend.texts
legend_txt[0].set_text("No Churn")
legend_txt[1].set_text("Churn")
p.set_title('Customer Acct_Plan_Subtype Distribution')
```

You should get the following result:

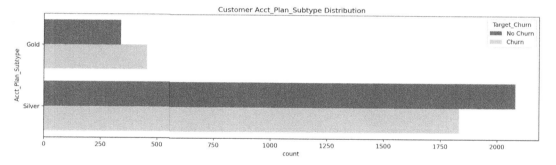

Figure 7.76: Plot of Acct_Plan_Subtype versus Target_Churn

From the preceding plot, we can infer that a larger percentage of customers from the Gold plan have churned. This can be an indicator that the Gold plan needs to be reviewed to understand why the customers are churning at a higher rate with that plan.

The code for the plot of **Current_TechSupComplaints** versus **Target_Churn** is as follows:

```
plt.figure(figsize=(15,4))
p=sns.countplot(y="Current_TechSupComplaints", hue='Target_Churn', \
                data=data,palette="Greys_r")
legend = p.get_legend()
legend_txt = legend.texts
legend_txt[0].set_text("No Churn")
legend_txt[1].set_text("Churn")
p.set_title('Customer Current_TechSupComplaints Distribution')
```

You should get the following result:

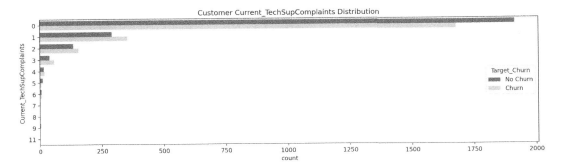

Figure 7.77: Plot of Current_TechSupComplaints versus Target_Churn

From the preceding plot, as expected, we can see that the **No Churn** count is highest for zero tech complaints. Moreover, for all non-zero tech complaints, the number of churned customers is higher than non-churned customers.

The code for the plot of **Avg_Days_Delinquent** versus **Target_Code** is as follows:

```
plt.figure(figsize=(15,4))
ax=sns.kdeplot(data.loc[(data['Target_Code'] == 0), \
                        'Avg_Days_Delinquent'] , \
            color=sns.color_palette("Greys_r")[0],\
            shade=True,label='no churn',\
            linestyle='--')
ax=sns.kdeplot(data.loc[(data['Target_Code'] == 1),\
                        'Avg_Days_Delinquent'] , \
            color=sns.color_palette("Greys_r")[1],\
            shade=True, label='churn')
ax.set(xlabel='Average No of Days Deliquent/Defaulted \
        from paying', ylabel='Frequency')
plt.title('Average No of Days Deliquent/Defaulted from \
          paying - churn vs no churn')
plt.legend()
```

> **NOTE**
>
> The **Greys_r** value is used to generate the graphs in grayscale. You can set the attribute value to **Set2** to get colored plots. You can also refer to the following document to get the code for the colored plots and the colored output: http://packt.link/NOjgT.

You should get the following output:

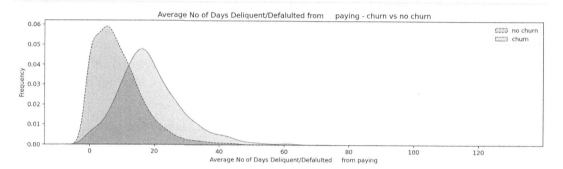

Figure 7.78: Plot of Avg_Days_Delinquent versus Target_Code

From this plot, you'll observe that if the average number of days delinquent is more than 16 days, customers start to churn.

The code for the plot of **Account_Age** versus **Target_Code** is as follows:

```
plt.figure(figsize=(15,4))
ax=sns.kdeplot(data.loc[(data['Target_Code'] == 0), \
                  'Account_Age'], \
            color=sns.color_palette("Greys_r")[0], \
            shade=True,label='no churn',\
            linestyle='--')
ax=sns.kdeplot(data.loc[(data['Target_Code'] == 1), \
                  'Account_Age'], \
            color=sns.color_palette("Greys_r")[1] ,\
            shade=True, label='churn')
ax.set(xlabel='Account_Age', ylabel='Frequency')
plt.title('Account_Age - churn vs no churn')
plt.legend()
```

You should get the following output:

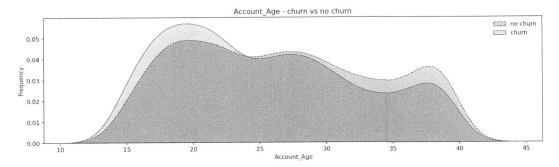

Figure 7.79: Plot of Account_Age versus Target_Code

From this plot, you'll observe that during the initial 15-20 days of opening an account, the amount of customer churn increases; however, after 20 days, the churn rate declines.

The code for the plot of **Percent_Increase_MOM** versus **Target_Code** is as follows:

```
plt.figure(figsize=(15,4))
ax=sns.kdeplot(data.loc[(data['Target_Code'] == 0), \
                    'Percent_Increase_MOM'], \
           color=sns.color_palette("Greys_r")[0], \
           shade=True, label='no churn',\
           linestyle='--')
ax=sns.kdeplot(data.loc[(data['Target_Code'] == 1), \
                    'Percent_Increase_MOM'], \
           color=sns.color_palette("Greys_r")[1], \
           shade=True, label='churn')
ax.set(xlabel='Percent_Increase_MOM', ylabel='Frequency')
plt.title('Percent_Increase_MOM- churn vs no churn')
plt.legend()
```

You should get the following output:

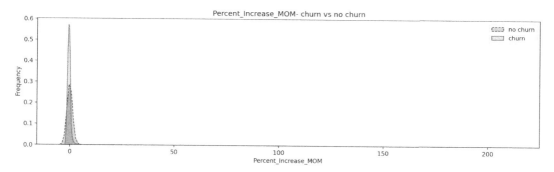

Figure 7.80: Plot of Percent_Increase_MOM versus Target_Code

From this plot, you can see that customers who have a **Percent_Increase_MOM** value within a range of 0% to 10% are more likely to churn.

So far, we have discussed how to perform EDA using graphical techniques. We went over various graphs that can be used for univariate, bivariate, and multivariate analyses and how to draw various conclusions from those graphs. However, we are yet to start training a model for fitting the data. We will see how to do that in the next section of the chapter.

ACTIVITY 7.02: PERFORMING THE MN TECHNIQUE FROM OSEMN

Solution:

1. Import the **RandomForestClassifier**, **train_test_split**, and **numpy** libraries:

```
from sklearn.ensemble import RandomForestClassifier
from sklearn.model_selection import train_test_split
import numpy as np
```

2. Encode the columns to convert the continuous columns into categorical columns and then show the top five rows of the dataset:

```
data["Acct_Plan_Subtype"] = data["Acct_Plan_Subtype"]\
                        .astype('category').cat.codes
data[«Complaint_Code»] = data[«Complaint_Code»]\
                        .astype('category').cat.codes
data[[«Acct_Plan_Subtype»,»Complaint_Code»]].head()
```

The preceding code will generate the following output:

	Acct_Plan_Subtype	Complaint_Code
0	0	0
1	1	4
2	0	0
3	1	0
4	0	0

Figure 7.81: Viewing the first five columns of the DataFrame after converting the continuous columns into categorical columns

3. Split the data into training and testing sets:

```
target = 'Target_Code'
X = data.drop(['Target_Code','Target_Churn'], axis=1)
y = data[target]
X_train, X_test, y_train, y_test = train_test_split\
                            (X, y, test_size=0.15, \
                            random_state=123, stratify=y)
```

4. Perform feature selection using the random forest classifier. To carry this out, first fit a random forest classifier on the dataset, and then obtain the feature importance. Plot the feature importance with the help of a bar graph:

```
forest=RandomForestClassifier(n_estimators=500,random_state=1)
forest.fit(X_train,y_train)

importances=forest.feature_importances_
features = data.drop(['Target_Code','Target_Churn'],axis=1)\
                .columns
indices = np.argsort(importances)[::-1]
plt.figure(figsize=(15,4))
plt.title(«Feature importances using Random Forest»)
plt.bar(range(X_train.shape[1]), importances[indices],\
        color='gray', align='center')
plt.xticks(range(X_train.shape[1]), features[indices], \
            rotation='vertical', fontsize=15)
plt.xlim([-1, X_train.shape[1]])
plt.show()
```

> **NOTE**
>
> The **gray** value for the **color** attribute is used to generate the graph in grayscale. You can use values such as **red**, **r**, and so on as values for the **color** parameter to get the colored graphs. You can also refer to the following document to get the code for the colored plot and the colored output: http://packt.link/NOjgT.

The preceding code will give the following bar graph:

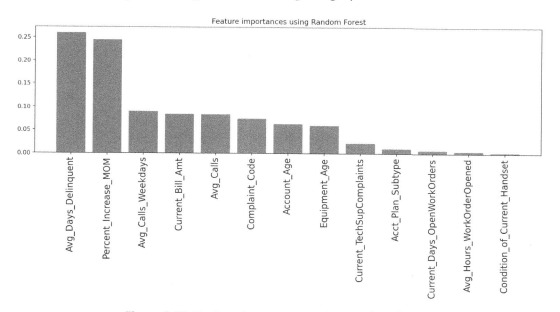

Figure 7.82: Feature importance using random forest

5. Import the **statsmodels** library and use it to fit a logistic regression model on the top seven features (based on the feature importance calculated in the previous step):

```
import statsmodels.api as sm
top7_features = ['Avg_Days_Delinquent','Percent_Increase_MOM',\
                 'Avg_Calls_Weekdays','Current_Bill_Amt',\
                 'Avg_Calls','Complaint_Code','Account_Age']
logReg = sm.Logit(y_train, X_train[top7_features])
logistic_regression = logReg.fit()
```

6. Find out the parameters of the logistic regression model:

```
logistic_regression.summary
logistic_regression.params
```

The code will generate the following output. Note that **Avg_Days_Delinquent** has the highest coefficient showing that it's going to have the maximum effect on the target variable:

```
Avg_Days_Delinquent       1.109226e-01
Percent_Increase_MOM     -3.922044e-01
Avg_Calls_Weekdays       -3.315366e-06
Current_Bill_Amt         -2.385475e-07
Avg_Calls                -1.817086e-06
Complaint_Code           -2.083688e-01
Account_Age              -4.794911e-02
dtype: float64
```

Figure 7.83: Parameters of the logistic regression model

7. Create a function to compute the target value for a given customer's attributes. The function will find the sum of products of each attribute/variable and its corresponding coefficient:

```
coef = logistic_regression.params

def y (coef, Avg_Days_Delinquent, Percent_Increase_MOM, \
       Avg_Calls_Weekdays, Current_Bill_Amt, Avg_Calls, \
       Complaint_Code, Account_Age): return coef[0]\
                                     *Avg_Days_Delinquent\
                                     +coef[1]\
                                     *Percent_Increase_MOM\
                                     +coef[2]\
                                     *Avg_Calls_Weekdays\
                                     +coef[3]\
                                     *Current_Bill_Amt\
                                     +coef[4]\
                                     *Avg_Calls\
                                     +coef[5]\
                                     *Complaint_Code\
                                     +coef[6]\
                                     *Account_Age
```

8. Input the given attributes of the customer to the function to obtain the output. Note that we are using the sigmoid calculation in order to obtain the probability:

Avg_Days_Delinquent: 40

Percent_Increase_MOM: 5

Avg_Calls_Weekdays: 39000

Current_Bill_Amt: 12000

Avg_Calls: 9000

Complaint_Code: 0

Account_Age: 17

Use the following code:

```
import numpy as np
y1 = y(coef, 40, 5, 39000,12000,9000,0,17)
p = np.exp(y1) / (1+np.exp(y1))
p
```

The preceding code will give the probability of the given customer churning as **0.8193916658925812** or **81.94%**.

In this activity, we first trained a random forest classifier to compute the feature importance. Based on the feature importance, the top seven features were chosen to fit a logistic regression model that was then used to predict the churning probability for a given customer. In real-life scenarios, the steps in the OSEMN pipeline will stay the same as well.

CHAPTER 8: FINE-TUNING CLASSIFICATION ALGORITHMS

ACTIVITY 8.01: IMPLEMENTING DIFFERENT CLASSIFICATION ALGORITHMS

Solution:

1. Import the logistic regression library:

```
from sklearn.linear_model import LogisticRegression
```

2. Fit the model:

```
clf_logistic = LogisticRegression(random_state=0,solver='lbfgs')\
                .fit(X_train[top7_features], y_train)
clf_logistic
```

The preceding code will give the following output:

```
LogisticRegression(random_state=0)
```

3. Score the model:

```
clf_logistic.score(X_test[top7_features], y_test)
```

You will get the following output: **0.7454031117397454**.

This shows that the logistic regression model is getting an accuracy of 74.5%, which is a mediocre accuracy but serves as a good estimate of the minimum accuracy you can expect.

4. Import the **svm** library:

```
from sklearn import svm
```

5. Scale the training and testing data as follows:

```
from sklearn.preprocessing import MinMaxScaler
scaling = MinMaxScaler(feature_range=(-1,1))\
          .fit(X_train[top7_features])
X_train_svm = scaling.transform(X_train[top7_features])
X_test_svm = scaling.transform(X_test[top7_features])
```

6. Fit the model:

```
clf_svm=svm.SVC(kernel='linear', C=1)
clf_svm.fit(X_train_svm,y_train)
```

The preceding code will give the following output.

```
SVC(C=1, kernel='linear')
```

7. Score the model:

```
clf_svm.score(X_test_svm, y_test)
```

This will give the following output: **0.76 37906647807637**.

This shows that the SVM classifier is performing better than the logistic regression model, which is expected.

8. Import the decision tree library:

```
from sklearn import tree
```

9. Fit the model:

```
clf_decision = tree.DecisionTreeClassifier()
clf_decision.fit(X_train[top7_features],y_train)
```

The preceding code will give the following output:

```
DecisionTreeClassifier()
```

> **NOTE**
>
> The output may slightly vary on your system.

10. Score the model:

```
clf_decision.score(X_test[top7_features], y_test)
```

This gives an output of approximately **0.751060820367751**. While this accuracy is better than the logistic regression model, it falls short of the SVM classifier accuracy. This is an important thing to note – a more powerful model will not always guarantee better performance. Therefore it is better to try out different classifiers and then choose the best one.

11. Import the random forest library:

```
from sklearn.ensemble import RandomForestClassifier
```

12. Fit the model:

```
clf_random = RandomForestClassifier(n_estimators=20, \
                                    max_depth=None, \
                                    min_samples_split=7, \
                                    random_state=0)
clf_random.fit(X_train[top7_features], y_train)
```

The preceding code will give the following output:

```
RandomForestClassifier(min_samples_split=7, n_estimators=20, random_
state=0)
```

> **NOTE**
>
> The output may slightly vary on your system.

13. Score the model:

```
clf_random.score(X_test[top7_features], y_test)
```

The preceding code will give an accuracy of **0.8104667609618105**, which is far better than the accuracies obtained using other classifiers.

From the results, you can conclude that the random forest has outperformed the rest of the algorithms, with logistic regression having the lowest accuracy. In a latter section of the chapter, you will learn why accuracy is not the correct way to find a model's performance.

ACTIVITY 8.02: TUNING AND OPTIMIZING THE MODEL

Solution:

1. Store five out of seven features, that is,
   Avg_Calls_Weekdays, **Current_Bill_Amt**, **Avg_Calls**, **Account_Age**,
   and **Avg_Days_Delinquent**, in a variable called **top5_features**. Store
   the other two features, **Percent_Increase_MOM** and **Complaint_Code**, in
   a variable called **top2_features**:

```
from sklearn import preprocessing
## Features to transform
top5_features=['Avg_Calls_Weekdays', 'Current_Bill_Amt', \
               'Avg_Calls', 'Account_Age','Avg_Days_Delinquent']
## Features Left
top2_features=['Percent_Increase_MOM','Complaint_Code']
```

2. Use **StandardScalar** to standardize the five features:

```
scaler = preprocessing.StandardScaler()\
                       .fit(X_train[top5_features])
X_train_scalar=pd.DataFrame\
              (scaler.transform(X_train[top5_features]),\
               columns = X_train[top5_features].columns)
X_test_scalar=pd.DataFrame\
              (scaler.transform(X_test[top5_features]),\
               columns = X_test[top5_features].columns)
```

3. Create a variable called **X_train_scalar_combined**, combine the
   standardized five features with the two features (**Percent_Increase_MOM**
   and **Complaint_Code**) that were not standardized:

```
X_train_scalar_combined=pd.concat([X_train_scalar, \
                                   X_train[top2_features]\
                                   .reset_index(drop=True)], \
                                   axis=1, sort=False)
```

4. Apply the same scalar standardization to the test data
   (**X_test_scalar_combined**):

```
X_test_scalar_combined=pd.concat([X_test_scalar, \
                                  X_test[top2_features]\
                                  .reset_index(drop=True)], \
                                  axis=1, sort=False)
```

5. Fit the random forest model:

```
clf_random.fit(X_train_scalar_combined, y_train)
```

This will give the following output:

```
RandomForestClassifier(min_samples_split=7, n_estimators=20, random_
state=0)
```

6. Score the random forest model:

```
clf_random.score(X_test_scalar_combined, y_test)
```

This will give an accuracy of **0.8118811881188119**. This is an improvement on the accuracy you had obtained in *Activity 8.01, Implementing Different Classification Algorithms*.

> **NOTE**
>
> Please note that there can be small variation in the outputs obtained. For example, the metrics like accuracy can vary around 5 to 10%. Similarly, the output for fitting a model can be much shorter than the one presented in the book. These variations are acceptable and can happen because of several reasons, including the difference in the version of libraries you are using, the operating system you are running the code on and so on.

7. Import the library for grid search and use the given parameters:

```
from sklearn.model_selection import GridSearchCV
from sklearn.model_selection import StratifiedKFold
parameters = [{'min_samples_split': [9,10], \
              'n_estimators':[100,150,160],\
              'max_depth': [5,7]}]
```

8. Use grid search cross-validation with stratified k-fold to find out the best parameters:

```
clf_random_grid = GridSearchCV(RandomForestClassifier(), \
                               parameters, cv = StratifiedKFold\
                                            (n_splits = 3))
clf_random_grid.fit(X_train_scalar_combined, y_train)
```

The preceding code will give the following output:

```
GridSearchCV(cv=StratifiedKFold(n_splits=3, random_state=None, shuffle=False),
          estimator=RandomForestClassifier(),
          param_grid=[{'max_depth': [5, 7], 'min_samples_split': [9, 10],
                    'n_estimators': [100, 150, 160]}])
```

Figure 8.59: Finding the best parameters

> **NOTE**
>
> The output may slightly vary on your system.

9. Print the best score and best parameters:

```
print('best score train:', clf_random_grid.best_score_)
print('best parameters train: ', clf_random_grid.best_params_)
```

This will give the following score and parameter list:

```
best score train: 0.800047650593308
best parameters train:  {'max_depth': 7, 'min_samples_split': 9,
'n_estimators': 160}
```

Figure 8.60: Printing the best score and best parameters

10. Score the model using the test data:

```
clf_random_grid.score(X_test_scalar_combined, y_test)
```

You will obtain a score of about **0.82826025459688826**, which is even higher than what you got with grid search. This is primarily because using randomized grid search, you were able to search for the best values for a larger number of hyperparameters by checking random values rather than every single value, which would have taken a large amount of time and resources.

ACTIVITY 8.03: COMPARISON OF THE MODELS

Solution:

1. Import the required libraries:

```
from sklearn.metrics import classification_report, \
                            confusion_matrix,accuracy_score
from sklearn import metrics
```

2. Fit the random forest classifier with the parameters obtained from grid search:

```
clf_random_grid = RandomForestClassifier(n_estimators=100, \
                                         max_depth=7,\
                                         min_samples_split=10, \
                                         random_state=0)
clf_random_grid.fit(X_train_scalar_combined, y_train)
```

The preceding code will give the following output on execution:

```
RandomForestClassifier(max_depth=7, min_samples_split=10, random_
state=0)
```

> **NOTE**
>
> The output may slightly vary on your system.

3. Predict on the standardized scalar test data, **X_test_scalar_combined**:

```
y_pred=clf_random_grid.predict(X_test_scalar_combined)
```

4. Fit the classification report:

```
target_names = ['No Churn', 'Churn']
print(classification_report(y_test, y_pred, \
                            target_names=target_names))
```

The preceding code will generate the following classification report:

	precision	recall	f1-score	support
No Churn	0.85	0.80	0.82	364
Churn	0.80	0.85	0.82	343
accuracy			0.82	707
macro avg	0.82	0.82	0.82	707
weighted avg	0.82	0.82	0.82	707

Figure 8.61: Fitting the classification report

5. Plot the confusion matrix:

```
cm = confusion_matrix(y_test, y_pred)
cm_df = pd.DataFrame(cm,\
                index = ['No Churn','Churn'], \
                columns = ['No Churn','Churn'])
plt.figure(figsize=(8,6))
sns.heatmap(cm_df, annot=True,fmt='g',cmap='Greys_r')
plt.title('Random Forest \nAccuracy:{0:.3f}'\
            .format(accuracy_score(y_test, y_pred)))
plt.ylabel('True Values')
plt.xlabel('Predicted Values')
plt.show()
```

> **NOTE**
>
> The value **Greys_r** (emboldened) is used to generate graphs in grayscale. You can also refer to the following document to get the code for the colored plot and the colored output: http://packt.link/NOjgT.

The preceding code will plot the following confusion matrix. You can also try manually calculating the precision and recall values using the following diagram and compare it with the values obtained in the previous step:

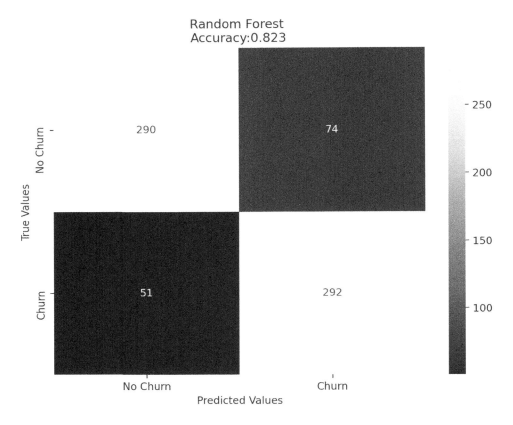

Figure 8.62: Confusion matrix

6. Import the libraries for **auc** and **roc_curve**:

```
from sklearn.metrics import roc_curve,auc
```

7. Use the classifiers that were created in *Activity 8.02, Tuning and Optimizing the Model*, that is, **clf_logistic**, **clf_svm**, **clf_decision**, and **clf_random_grid**. Create a dictionary of all these models:

```
models = [
{
    'label': 'Logistic Regression',
    'model': clf_logistic,
},
{
    'label': 'SVM',
    'model': clf_svm,
},
{
    'label': 'Decision Tree',
    'model': clf_decision,
},
{
    'label': 'Random Forest Grid Search',
    'model': clf_random_grid,
}
]
```

8. Plot the ROC curve:

```
for m in models:
    model = m['model']
    model.fit(X_train_scalar_combined, y_train)
    y_pred=model.predict(X_test_scalar_combined)
    fpr, tpr, thresholds = roc_curve(y_test, y_pred, pos_label=1)
    roc_auc = metrics.auc(fpr, tpr)
    plt.plot(fpr, tpr, label='%s AUC = %0.2f' \
             % (m['label'], roc_auc))
plt.plot([0, 1], [0, 1],'r--')
plt.xlim([0.0, 1.0])
plt.ylim([0.0, 1.05])
plt.ylabel('Sensitivity(True Positive Rate)')
plt.xlabel('1-Specificity(False Positive Rate)')
plt.title('Receiver Operating Characteristic')
plt.legend(loc="lower right")
plt.show()
```

The preceding code will generate the following ROC curve. Recall that the more a curve lies toward the top-left corner, the higher the performance of the model. Based on this, we can conclude that the random forest (grid search) is the best model out of the four models we have discussed so far in this particular case:

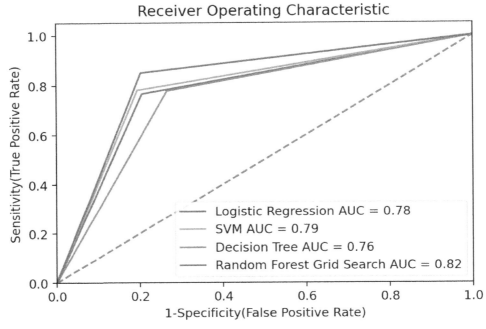

Figure 8.63: ROC curve

Comparing the AUC results of the different algorithms (logistic regression: **0.78**; SVM: **0.79**, decision tree: **0.77**, and random forest: **0.82**), we can conclude that random forest is the best performing model with an AUC score of **0.82** and can be chosen for the marketing team to predict customer churn.

CHAPTER 9: MULTICLASS CLASSIFICATION ALGORITHMS

ACTIVITY 9.01: PERFORMING MULTICLASS CLASSIFICATION AND EVALUATING PERFORMANCE

Solution:

1. Import the required libraries:

```
import pandas as pd
import numpy as np
from sklearn.ensemble import RandomForestClassifier
from sklearn.model_selection import train_test_split
from sklearn.metrics import classification_report,\
                            confusion_matrix,\
                            accuracy_score
from sklearn import metrics
from sklearn.metrics import precision_recall_fscore_support
import matplotlib.pyplot as plt
import seaborn as sns
```

2. Load the marketing data into a DataFrame named **data** and look at the first five rows of the DataFrame using the following code:

```
data= pd.read_csv('MarketingData.csv')
data.head()
```

> **NOTE**
>
> Make sure you change the path (highlighted) to the CSV file based on its location on your system. If you're running the Jupyter notebook from the same directory where the CSV file is stored, you can run the preceding code without any modification.

This will give the following output:

	Fresh	Milk	Grocery	Frozen	Detergents_Paper	Delicassen	Channel
0	6623.613537	5513.093240	6019.057354	5669.568008	5898.660607	5179.234947	2
1	5642.542497	5829.866565	3960.339943	4270.020548	3498.818262	4327.423268	2
2	5292.078175	6634.370556	4444.335138	4888.286021	3265.391352	4887.560190	2
3	5595.227928	4754.860698	2977.856511	3462.490957	3609.264559	4268.641413	0
4	5126.693267	6009.649079	3811.569943	4744.115976	3829.516831	5097.491872	2

Figure 9.34: The first five rows of the data DataFrame

3. To check the shape of the dataset, use the **shape** attribute as shown in the following code:

```
data.shape
```

This will give the output as **(20000, 7)**, which means that there are 20,000 data points and 7 features.

4. Next, to check whether there are any missing values in the data, use the following code:

```
data.isnull().values.any()
```

This gives the output as **False**, which means that there are no missing values in the dataset.

5. Similarly, check the summary of the data using the **describe()** method:

```
data.describe()
```

The summary of the data should be as follows. Note that the minimum value for each feature, except **Channel**, is **1**, whereas the maximum value for all features (except **Channel**) is **10000**:

	Fresh	Milk	Grocery	Frozen	Detergents_Paper	Delicassen	Channel
count	20000.000000	20000.000000	20000.000000	20000.000000	20000.000000	20000.000000	20000.000000
mean	5853.350191	5267.873868	4873.362341	4899.477763	4786.331781	5613.672184	1.499350
std	1128.370297	1177.563192	1265.579790	1220.923393	1154.682284	1343.743103	1.118464
min	1.000000	1.000000	1.000000	1.000000	1.000000	1.000000	0.000000
25%	5155.249455	4438.167387	3983.317183	4071.997222	3877.943500	4705.582182	0.000000
50%	5988.720207	5337.741327	4828.100401	5048.099489	4857.070488	5425.888761	1.000000
75%	6573.895741	6081.755179	5784.992859	5684.876863	5602.146034	6574.281056	3.000000
max	10000.000000	10000.000000	10000.000000	10000.000000	10000.000000	10000.000000	3.000000

Figure 9.35: Summary of the data

6. You can find out the number of transactions made for each channel using the **value_counts()** function as follows:

```
data['Channel'].value_counts()
```

You should get the following output:

```
0    5007
3    5002
1    5001
2    4990
Name: Channel, dtype: int64
```

Figure 9.36: The number of transactions for each channel

You can see that each channel has around 5,000 transactions.

7. Since you have to predict the channel for a given data point, you will have to set the target column as **Channel** and separate **X** and **y** data from the dataset:

```
target = 'Channel'
X = data.drop(['Channel'],axis=1)
y=data[target]
```

8. Split the data into training and testing sets using the **train_test_split** function. Set **random_state** to **123** to ensure that the results are reproducible:

```
X_train, X_test, y_train, y_test = train_test_split\
                                    (X.values,y,\
                                     test_size=0.20, \
                                     random_state=123, \
                                     stratify=y)
```

9. Enter the following command to create a random forest classifier using the parameters provided in the problem statement:

```
clf_random = RandomForestClassifier(n_estimators=20, \
                                    max_depth=None, \
                                    min_samples_split=7, \
                                    random_state=0)
```

10. Next, fit the model on the training dataset using the following code:

```
clf_random.fit(X_train,y_train)
```

This will give the following output, showing the parameters that were used to initialize the classifier:

```
RandomForestClassifier(min_samples_split=7, n_estimators=20, random_state=0)
```

11. Use the trained model to get the predictions for the test data (**X_test**):

```
y_pred=clf_random.predict(X_test)
```

12. Now that you have the predicted classes, use the
precision_recall_fscore_support function to find the macro-average
of the performance metrics:

```
precision_recall_fscore_support(y_test, y_pred, average='macro')
```

This will give the following output:

```
(0.8910950272506314, 0.8910093250373001, 0.891010381018051, None)
```

This means that the macro-average of precision, recall, and F1 score is
around **0.89**.

13. Similarly, find the micro-average report using the
precision_recall_fscore_support function:

```
precision_recall_fscore_support(y_test, y_pred, average='micro')
```

This will give the following output:

```
(0.891, 0.891, 0.891, None)
```

Similar to the macro-averages, you can see that the micro-average of precision,
recall, and F1 score is **0.891**.

14. You can get the micro- and macro-averages of the performance metrics using
the classification report as well. Enter the following code:

```
target_names = ["Retail","RoadShow","SocialMedia","Television"]
print(classification_report(y_test, y_pred,\
                    target_names=target_names))
```

The output should look as follows.

	precision	recall	f1-score	support
Retail	0.90	0.90	0.90	1002
RoadShow	0.87	0.85	0.86	1000
SocialMedia	0.93	0.92	0.92	998
Television	0.87	0.89	0.88	1000
accuracy			0.89	4000
macro avg	0.89	0.89	0.89	4000
weighted avg	0.89	0.89	0.89	4000

Figure 9.37: Classification report for the random forest classifier

You can see that you have obtained the same values for the micro- and macro-averages of the performance metrics as you got in the previous two steps.

15. You can also use the confusion matrix to get an idea about the predicted class and the ground-truth class. This will help in relating the performance of the classifier to the accuracy:

```
cm = confusion_matrix(y_test, y_pred)
```

16. Once you have the confusion matrix, plot it using the following code:

```
cm_df = pd.DataFrame(cm,\
                     index = target_names, \
                     columns = target_names)
plt.figure(figsize=(8,6))
sns.heatmap(cm_df, annot=True,fmt='g',cmap='Greys_r')
plt.title('Random Forest \nAccuracy:{0:.3f}'\
          .format(accuracy_score(y_test, y_pred)))
plt.ylabel('True Values')
plt.xlabel('Predicted Values')
plt.show()
```

> **NOTE**
>
> The value **Greys_r** (emboldened) is used to generate graphs in grayscale. You can also refer to the following document to get the code for the colored plot and the colored output: http://packt.link/NOjgT.

It should appear as follows. You can see that many predictions match the true class, which shows the high accuracy of the classifier:

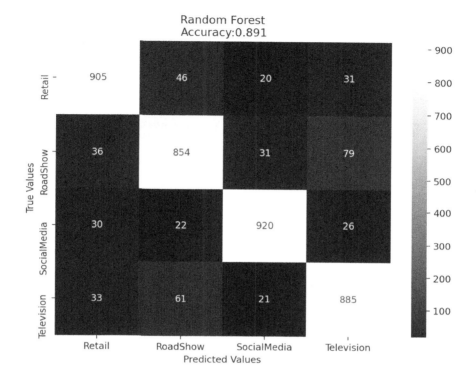

Figure 9.38: Confusion matrix for the random forest classifier

In this activity, you used the concepts discussed so far to train a random forest classifier to solve a multiclass classification problem. You should have also seen that the performance metric values obtained using the **classification_report** and **precision_recall_fscore_support** functions were the same. Moreover, the confusion matrix showed that the model was able to accurately predict the classes for most of the test data points. From a marketing analytics perspective, you have now trained a model that can be used to predict the best communication channel for a given product.

ACTIVITY 9.02: DEALING WITH IMBALANCED DATA USING SCIKIT-LEARN

Solution:

1. Import all the necessary libraries:

```
# Removes Warnings
import warnings
warnings.filterwarnings('ignore')
from sklearn.metrics import classification_report,\
                            confusion_matrix,\
                            accuracy_score
import numpy as np
import pandas as pd
import matplotlib.pyplot as plt
import seaborn as sns
from sklearn.ensemble import RandomForestClassifier
from sklearn.model_selection import train_test_split
from imblearn.over_sampling import SMOTE
from sklearn.preprocessing import StandardScaler
```

2. Read the dataset into a pandas DataFrame named **bank** using pandas' **read_csv** function and look at the first few rows of the data using the **head()** method. The dataset has values separated by a semicolon, instead of the commonly used comma. That's why you will have to provide **sep=';'** while reading the dataset:

```
bank = pd.read_csv('bank.csv', sep = ';')
bank.head()
```

> **NOTE**
>
> Make sure you change the path (highlighted) to the CSV file based on its location on your system. If you're running the Jupyter notebook from the same directory where the CSV file is stored, you can run the preceding code without any modification.

Your output should be as follows:

	age	job	marital	education	default	balance	housing	loan	contact	day	month	duration	campaign	pdays	previous	poutcome	y
0	30	unemployed	married	primary	no	1787	no	no	cellular	19	oct	79	1	-1	0	unknown	no
1	33	services	married	secondary	no	4789	yes	yes	cellular	11	may	220	1	339	4	failure	no
2	35	management	single	tertiary	no	1350	yes	no	cellular	16	apr	185	1	330	1	failure	no
3	30	management	married	tertiary	no	1476	yes	yes	unknown	3	jun	199	4	-1	0	unknown	no
4	59	blue-collar	married	secondary	no	0	yes	no	unknown	5	may	226	1	-1	0	unknown	no

Figure 9.39: The first few rows of bank data

3. Rename the **y** column **Target** using the **rename()** method:

```
bank = bank.rename(columns={'y': 'Target'})
```

4. Replace the **no** values with **0** and **yes** with **1** in the **Target** column created in the preceding step:

```
bank['Target']=bank['Target'].replace({'no': 0, 'yes': 1})
```

5. Now check the shape of the dataset using the **shape** attribute of the DataFrame:

```
bank.shape
```

This gives the output **(4334,17)**. This means that there are **4334** samples and **17** features in the dataset.

6. Next, to check the missing values in the dataset, use the **isnull()** method:

```
bank.isnull().values.any()
```

This gives the output **False**, which means that there are no missing values in the dataset.

7. Now, use the **describe** function to check the statistics of the continuous values:

```
bank.describe()
```

You should get the following output:

	age	balance	day	duration	campaign	pdays	previous	Target
count	4334.000000	4334.000000	4334.000000	4334.000000	4334.000000	4334.000000	4334.000000	4334.000000
mean	40.991924	1410.637517	15.913936	264.544301	2.806876	39.670974	0.544070	0.115828
std	10.505378	3010.612091	8.216673	260.642141	3.129682	99.934062	1.702219	0.320056
min	19.000000	-3313.000000	1.000000	4.000000	1.000000	-1.000000	0.000000	0.000000
25%	33.000000	67.000000	9.000000	104.000000	1.000000	-1.000000	0.000000	0.000000
50%	39.000000	440.000000	16.000000	186.000000	2.000000	-1.000000	0.000000	0.000000
75%	48.000000	1464.000000	21.000000	329.000000	3.000000	-1.000000	0.000000	0.000000
max	87.000000	71188.000000	31.000000	3025.000000	50.000000	871.000000	25.000000	1.000000

Figure 9.40: Output for continuous variables

Notice that there is high variation in the minimum, maximum, mean, and standard deviation values in the features. This can result in one feature dominating other features. To fix this, you will need to scale these features. But, before you do that, check the statistics of the categorical values too. This will help in scaling all the features (continuous and categorical) at the same time.

8. Use the **describe** function to check the categorical values by passing the **include = ['O']** argument to the function:

```
bank.describe(include=['O'])
```

You should get the following output:

	job	marital	education	default	housing	loan	contact	month	poutcome
count	4334	4334	4334	4334	4334	4334	4334	4334	4334
unique	12	3	3	2	2	2	3	12	4
top	management	married	secondary	no	yes	no	cellular	may	unknown
freq	942	2680	2306	4261	2476	3650	2801	1339	3555

Figure 9.41: Output for categorical variables

You can see that the number of unique values in each feature ranges from **2** to **12**. In the next few steps, you will convert these categorical columns into numerical columns by replacing these categories with numbers. But before that, let's also have a look at the distribution of samples in the class labels. This will complete the statistical description of the dataset.

9. Check the count of the class labels present in the target variable using the **value_counts** function:

```
bank['Target'].value_counts(0)
```

You should get the following output:

```
0    3832
1     502
Name: Target, dtype: int64
```

Figure 9.42: Count of class labels

You can see that there is a huge difference in the number of samples for the **0** and **1** class labels, which means that this is an imbalanced dataset. However, before immediately trying to fix this issue, let's see the effect of using an imbalanced dataset on the model performance.

10. Use the **cat.codes** function to encode the **job**, **marital**, **default**, **housing**, **loan**, **contact**, and **poutcome** columns:

```
bank["job"] = bank["job"].astype('category').cat.codes
bank["marital"] = bank["marital"].astype('category').cat.codes
bank["default"] = bank["default"].astype('category').cat.codes
bank["housing"] = bank["housing"].astype('category').cat.codes
bank["loan"] = bank["loan"].astype('category').cat.codes
bank["contact"] = bank["contact"].astype('category').cat.codes
bank["poutcome"] = bank["poutcome"].astype('category').cat.codes
```

Since **education** and **month** are ordinal columns, convert them as follows:

```
bank['education'].replace({'primary': 0, 'secondary': 1,\
                           'tertiary':2}, inplace= True)

bank['month'].replace(['jan', 'feb', 'mar','apr','may','jun',\
                       'jul', 'aug', 'sep','oct','nov','dec'], \
                      [1,2,3,4,5,6,7,8,9,10,11,12], \
                      inplace = True)
```

11. Check the bank data after the conversion using the **head()** method:

```
bank.head()
```

You will get the following output:

	age	job	marital	education	default	balance	housing	loan	contact	day	month	duration	campaign	pdays	previous	poutcome	Target
0	30	10	1	0	10	1787	1	0	0	19	10	79	1	-1	0	3	0
1	33	7	1	1	7	4789	1	1	0	11	5	220	1	339	4	0	0
2	35	4	2	2	4	1350	2	0	0	16	4	185	1	330	1	0	0
3	30	4	1	2	4	1476	1	1	2	3	6	199	4	-1	0	3	0
4	59	1	1	1	1	0	1	0	2	5	5	226	1	-1	0	3	0

Figure 9.43: The first few rows of bank data after conversion

You can see that all the categorical columns have been converted into numerical columns, which will make it easier to process them in later steps.

12. Next, split the data into training and testing sets using **train_test_split**. Use the ratio of **85:15** for splitting the dataset. Thus, use the **test_size = 0.15** argument in the **train_test_split** function:

```
target = 'Target'
X = bank.drop(['Target'], axis=1)
y=bank[target]

X_train, X_test, y_train, y_test = train_test_split\
                                   (X,y,test_size=0.15, \
                                    random_state=123, \
                                    stratify=y)
```

13. Now check the number of samples in each of the two classes in the train and test sets using the **value_counts()** function. First, use the function on the train set:

```
y_train.value_counts()
```

You will get the following output.

```
0    3256
1     427
Name: Target, dtype: int64
```

Figure 9.44: Number of entries in each class in y_train

You can see the class imbalance in the training dataset as well. Verify this for the test set in the next step.

14. Use the **value_counts ()** function on the test column to get the number of entries in each class:

```
y_test.value_counts()
```

You will get the following output:

```
0       576
1        75
Name: Target, dtype: int64
```

Figure 9.45: Number of entries in each class in y_test

Like the training dataset, the class imbalance is also clearly present in the test set.

15. Now, as mentioned earlier, scale the training and test set features to remove any effect of different orders of magnitude of mean, minimum, maximum, and standard deviation for these features. This will be done using the **standard_scalar** function:

```
standard_scalar = StandardScaler()
X_train_sc = standard_scalar.fit_transform(X_train)
X_test_sc = standard_scalar.transform(X_test)
```

16. You are now ready to train a random forest classifier on the imbalanced dataset. First, create a random forest classifier using the following code:

```
clf_random = RandomForestClassifier(n_estimators=20, \
                            max_depth=None,\
                            min_samples_split=7, \
                            random_state=0)
```

17. Fit the random forest model created in the preceding step on the training dataset:

```
clf_random.fit(X_train_sc,y_train)
```

This will give the following output, showing the parameters that were passed while initializing the random forest classifier:

```
RandomForestClassifier(min_samples_split=7, n_estimators=20, random_
state=0)
```

18. Next, use the trained random forest classifier to obtain the predictions for the test dataset. These predictions will be used in the next step to obtain the classification report:

```
y_pred=clf_random.predict(X_test_sc)
```

19. Get the classification report using the **classification_report** function. Assign a **['No', 'Yes']** list to the **target_names** variable to add more readability to the classification report:

```
target_names = ['No', 'Yes']
print(classification_report(y_test, y_pred,\
                    target_names=target_names))
```

You should get an output like the following:

```
              precision    recall  f1-score   support

          No       0.92      0.98      0.95       576
         Yes       0.67      0.32      0.43        75

    accuracy                           0.90       651
   macro avg       0.79      0.65      0.69       651
weighted avg       0.89      0.90      0.89       651
```

Figure 9.46: Classification report

Notice the low precision, recall, and F1 scores for the **Yes** class. This shows the clear impact of an imbalanced dataset on the performance of the model.

You can also see the impact of class imbalance using the confusion matrix. Enter the following code:

```
cm = confusion_matrix(y_test, y_pred)

cm_df = pd.DataFrame(cm,\
                  index = ['No', 'Yes'], \
                  columns = ['No', 'Yes'])
plt.figure(figsize=(8,6))
sns.heatmap(cm_df, annot=True,fmt='g',cmap='Greys_r')
plt.title('Random Forest \nAccuracy:{0:.3f}'\
          .format(accuracy_score(y_test, y_pred)))
plt.ylabel('True Values')
plt.xlabel('Predicted Values')
plt.show()
```

> **NOTE**
>
> The value **Greys_r** (emboldened) is used to generate graphs in grayscale. You can also refer to the following document to get the code for the colored plot and the colored output: http://packt.link/NOjgT.

You will get the following confusion matrix, which shows that only 24 **Yes** values were correctly classified:

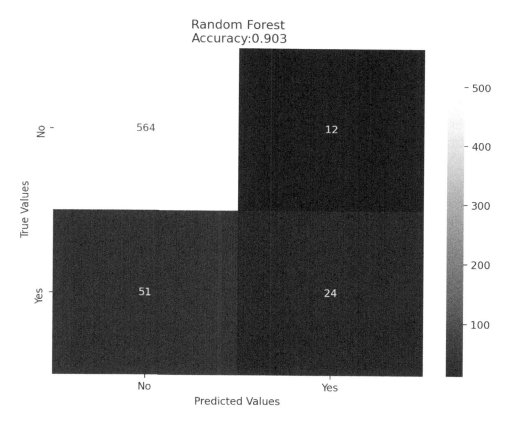

Figure 9.47: Confusion matrix

20. Use the **SMOTE ()** function on **x_train** and **y_train** to resample the dataset in order to remove the class imbalance from the training dataset. Assign it to the **x_resampled** and **y_resampled** variables, respectively:

```
X_resampled, y_resampled = SMOTE().fit_resample(X_train,y_train)
```

21. Similar to previous steps, use **standard_scalar** to scale the resampled dataset and the test set:

```
standard_scalar = StandardScaler()
X_train_sc_resampled = standard_scalar.fit_transform(X_resampled)
X_test_sc = standard_scalar.transform(X_test)
```

22. Fit the random forest classifier initialized earlier on **X_train_sc_resampled** and **y_resampled**:

```
clf_random.fit(X_train_sc_resampled,y_resampled)
```

This will give the following output, which again shows the parameters that were used to initialize the current random forest classifier:

```
RandomForestClassifier(min_samples_split=7, n_estimators=20, random_
state=0)
```

23. Similar to the previous steps, use the trained classifier to obtain predictions on the test set:

```
y_pred=clf_random.predict(X_test_sc)
```

The previously obtained predictions can now be used to generate the classification report. Enter the following code:

```
target_names = ['No', 'Yes']
print(classification_report(y_test, y_pred,\
                            target_names=target_names))
```

The output should look as follows:

	precision	recall	f1-score	support
No	0.95	0.91	0.93	576
Yes	0.46	0.60	0.52	75
accuracy			0.87	651
macro avg	0.70	0.75	0.73	651
weighted avg	0.89	0.87	0.88	651

Figure 9.48: Classification report of the random forest classifier

The main point to note in the preceding output is the increased values of the precision, recall, and F1 scores for the **Yes** class label, which shows the impact of balancing the dataset on the model performance.

24. Plot the confusion matrix using the following code:

```
cm = confusion_matrix(y_test, y_pred)

cm_df = pd.DataFrame(cm, \
                     index = ['No', 'Yes'], \
                     columns = ['No', 'Yes'])
plt.figure(figsize=(8,6))
sns.heatmap(cm_df, annot=True, fmt='g', cmap='Greys_r')
plt.title('Random Forest \nAccuracy:{0:.3f}'\
          .format(accuracy_score(y_test, y_pred)))
plt.ylabel('True Values')
plt.xlabel('Predicted Values')
plt.show()
```

> **NOTE**
>
> The value **Greys_r** (emboldened) is used to generate graphs in grayscale. You can also refer to the following document to get the code for the colored plot and the colored output: http://packt.link/NOjgT.

The output should appear as follows:

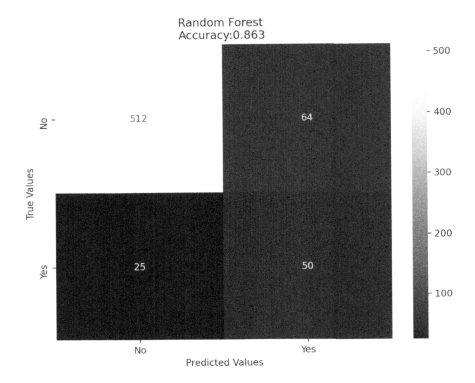

Figure 9.49: Confusion matrix of the random forest classifier

Notice that the number of correctly classified points in the **Yes** class has increased to **46**, which further shows the importance of balancing an imbalanced dataset. This also matches with what you had set out to do at the beginning of the activity – you first increased the number of sample points in the minority class using the SMOTE technique, then you used the revised dataset to train a machine learning model. This model showed comparatively lower performance; however, the performance was similar for both the classes, which was not the case last time. This was also seen by the improvement in the number of correctly classified points in the **Yes** class.

In this activity, you performed all the steps that are extremely important for a marketing analyst. You first explored the dataset and realized the need for scaling the features. Next, you transformed the categorical columns into numerical columns to make the processing easy. Once your dataset was ready to use, you trained a random forest classifier. The low performance for the minor class clearly showed the need for class balancing. After resampling the dataset using the SMOTE technique, you reduced the class imbalance and again trained a random forest classifier. The final model performance showed a significant increase for the minor class. All these steps are commonly used based on the dataset and the problem statement. This brings us to the end of the chapter and the book.

HEY!

Mirza Rahim Baig

Gururajan Govindan

Vishwesh Ravi Shrimali

We're Mirza Rahim Baig, Gururajan Govindan, and Vishwesh Ravi Shrimali, the authors of this book. We really hope you enjoyed reading our book and found it useful for learning data science.

It would really help us (and other potential readers!) if you could leave a review on Amazon sharing your thoughts on *Data Science for Marketing Analytics, Second Edition*.

Go to the link https://packt.link/r/1800560478.

OR

Scan the QR code to leave your review.

Your review will help us to understand what's worked well in this book and what could be improved upon for future editions, so it really is appreciated.

Best wishes,

Mirza Rahim Baig, Gururajan Govindan, and Vishwesh Ravi Shrimali

INDEX

X

xlabel: 105, 121, 140, 153, 171, 176, 185, 187, 189, 200, 206, 222-223, 258, 291-293, 295-297, 342-344, 422, 425, 428, 456, 462

xticks: 105, 357

Y

ylabel: 105, 140, 153, 171, 176, 185, 187, 189, 200, 206, 222-223, 258, 291-293, 295-297, 338-339, 342-344, 422, 425, 428, 456, 462

Z

z-score: 128

Made in the USA
Middletown, DE
28 August 2022

72498667R00356